Developments in Concurrency and Communication

EDITED BY

C. A. R. HOARE

Oxford University

Addison-Wesley Publishing Company
Reading, Massachusetts • Menlo Park, California • New York
Don Mills, Ontario • Wokingham, England • Amsterdam • Bonn
Sydney • Singapore • Tokyo • Madrid • San Juan

This book is in the University of Texas at Austin Year of Programming Series.

Library of Congress Cataloging-in-Publication Data

Developments in concurrency and communication / edited by C. A. R. Hoare
    p. cm. — (The UT year of programming series)
  Includes bibliographical references.
  ISBN 0–201–17232–1
  1. Parallel Processing (Electronic computers) I. Hoare, C. A. R.
(Charles Antony Richard), 1934– . II. Series.
QA76.58.D48   1990
004'.35—dc20   90–41294
                                        CIP

Reproduced by Addison-Wesley from camera-ready copy supplied by the U.T. Year of Programming office.

ABCDEFGHIJ–MA–943210

004.35
D489h

244245

The UT Year of Programming Series

Series editor: HAMILTON RICHARDS JR. The University of Texas at Austin

Developments in Concurrency and Communication
    Editor: C. A. R. HOARE Oxford University

Logical Foundations of Functional Programming
    Editor: GERARD HUET INRIA Rocquencourt

Research Topics in Functional Programming
    Editor: DAVID TURNER University of Kent

Formal Development of Programs and Proofs
    Editor: EDSGER W. DIJKSTRA The University of Texas at Austin

The UT Year of Programming Series

The design for the books was commissioned by the publisher, Addison-Wesley. The designer was Jean Hammond, and the design was transformed into a LATEX style specification by William H. Miner Jr. of TEX*niques* in Austin, Texas. The book was composed in LATEX, primarily by the UT Year of Programming staff —Suzanne Kain Rhoads, Ana M. Hernandez, and Hamilton Richards Jr.— using Macintosh[1] SE personal computers, but also by several authors who supplied their manuscripts as TEX[2] or LATEX source files. The Macintosh implementation of TEX —TEXTURES— is a product of Blue Sky Research of Portland, Oregon. Illustrations were redrawn for the book using Cricket Draw[3] and MacDraw II[4]. Draft versions of the manuscript were printed on an Apple[5] LaserWriter II NTX printer, and the final copy was produced on a Linotronic 100[6] by Publishing Experts of Austin.

The typeface in which the book is set is Lucida,[7] a product of Adobe Systems Incorporated, whose permission to use a beta version of the Lucida Math fonts is gratefully acknowledged; a few additional POSTSCRIPT characters were created using Fontographer.[8] Lucida was installed in LATEX and TEXTURES by Buff Miner and by David Mallis of Publishing Experts; the value of their dedication and expertise is beyond calculation.

The publisher's vital assistance and patient encouragement were personified by Peter S. Gordon (Publishing Partner for Computer Science), Helen M. Goldstein (Assistant Editor), Helen M. Wythe (Production Supervisor), Mona Zeftel (Electronic Production Consultant), and Stephanie Kaylin (Copy Editor).

---

1. Macintosh is a trademark of Apple Computer, Inc.
2. TEX is a trademark of the American Mathematical Society.
3. Cricket Draw is a trademark of Cricket Software, Inc.
4. MacDraw is a registered trademark of CLARIS Corporation.
5. Apple and LaserWriter are registered trademarks of Apple Computer, Inc.
6. Linotronic 100 is a trademark of Allied Corporation.
7. Lucida is a registered trademark of Bigelow & Holmes.
8. Fontographer is a registered trademark of Altsys Corporation.

Contents

*T*his volume is a product of the 1987 University of Texas Year of Programming ("YoP"), an initiative of UT-Austin's Department of Computer Sciences underwritten by grants from Lockheed/Austin, an anonymous donor, and —principally— the U. S. Office of Naval Research.[1]

The Year of Programming's general objectives were

> to advance the art and science of programming by bringing together leading computing scientists for discussions and collaboration, and

> to disseminate among leading practitioners the best of what is known— and being discovered—about the theory and practice of programming.

These objectives grew out of the original proposal's statement of purpose:

> Programming includes all aspects of creating an executable representation of a problem [solution]... from mathematical formulation to representation of an algorithm [for a] specific architecture.... The Year of

---

1. Under Contract N00014–86–K–0763.

> Programming will...address...the conversion of programming into a mathematical...discipline.

Almost from the outset, it was agreed that the Year of Programming would make its greatest contribution by steering away from topics and formats already well addressed by industrial concerns, government agencies, and the technical societies. Hence it was decided to leave such topics as programming psychology, sociology, and management to entities better qualified to deal with them, and to concentrate on those aspects of programming most amenable to scientific treatment.

As planning progressed, the YoP developed mainly into a series of Programming Institutes. Although each institute focused on a different sector of computing's scientific frontier, all proceeded from a conviction that good programming is the art and science of keeping things simple, and that the conversion of programming from a craft into a mathematical discipline requires an unorthodox type of mathematics in which the traditional distinction between "pure" and "applied" need not appear.

Each institute was organized by a scientific director recruited for his contributions to the art and science of programming or to the mathematics that it requires. Each director in turn enlisted a few colleagues —between four and a dozen or so— to assist him in discussing, refining, and presenting their school of thought. Over a period of one or two weeks, each institute team presented tutorials, research papers, and public lectures, and engaged in panel discussions and workshops. The institutes' audiences numbered from 30 to over 100, and converged on Austin from many parts of North America and Europe.

The selection criterion was wide enough to admit a broad variety of approaches, and many institute topics were considered. From a welter of conflicting schedules and commitments finally emerged six Programming Institutes, whose scientific directors and topics were as follows:

1. C. A. R. Hoare, Oxford University (visiting UT Austin for the academic year 1986–87). *Concurrent Programming*, 23 February–6 March.

2. David Gries, Cornell University. *Encapsulation, Modularization, and Reusability*, 1–10 April.

3. Gérard Huet, INRIA. *Logical Foundations of Functional Programming*, 8–12 June.

4. Michael J. C. Gordon, Cambridge University, and Warren A. Hunt Jr., University of Texas, Austin (codirectors). *Formal Specification and Verification of Hardware*, 8–17 July.

5. David A. Turner, University of Kent, Canterbury, U.K. *Declarative Programming*, 24–29 August.

6. Edsger W. Dijkstra, University of Texas, Austin. *Formal Development of Programs and Proofs*, 26–30 October.

The volume you hold in your hands is a product of the first Programming Institute. It is not a proceedings in the usual sense, for it is not a mere collection of materials brought to the Institute by its participants. Instead, it attempts to capture the essence of the institute as seen after the fact —and after some reflection— by its principal participants. Some of the articles do indeed closely resemble their authors' presentations in Austin; others were not presented at all, but are included here as indispensable background material. Still others represent work that was carried out either at the institute or as a result of it.

Whatever success YoP has achieved reflects primarily the caliber and dedication to excellence of the many computing scientists who contributed as scientific directors, lecturers, workshop participants, and authors. Enlisting such dedicated colleagues to serve as scientific directors was mainly the achievement of the YoP executive subcommittee's three leaders —James C. Browne, Edsger W. Dijkstra, and C. A. R. Hoare. Their task was greatly eased by the resources put at YoP's disposal by its sponsors, which made it possible for YoP to attract the very best scientific talent in the field; personifying the sponsors' support and encouragement were Charles Holland and Andre van Tilborg at the Office of Naval Research, and Stephen Sherman at Lockheed. Finally, the YoP Management Committee deserves great credit for its guidance, and for much sage advice and wise counsel, from YoP's earliest days.

Hamilton Richards Jr.

Preface

---

*T*hroughout the last half century, human intelligence has been subjected to a rapid series of challenges posed by the development of the stored-program digital computer. Exploitation of the expanding potential of the hardware has required the development of a new kind of intellectual ability, that of computer programming. It has given rise to a vast new market for a new kind of product —software— and a new industry to supply it. The associated needs for education, innovation, and research have given rise to a new academic discipline, and departments of computing science are now established in major universities throughout the world.

The development of the digital computer has coincided with (and contributed to) amazing advances in many other branches of science and engineering, with benefits that penetrate all aspects of technological society. These advances have been made possible by the discovery of fruitful links between mathematical theories and experimental verification, between academic research and industrial exploitation.

Establishment of a proper link between theory and practice has never been easy: Theorists and practitioners have always described their interdependence in terms that belittle the contributions of the other. In no field is this more noticeable than in computing science. Fortunately there is one clear example of a development in computing science recognized by many scientists who use computers in physics and engineering, although it dates back several generations of hardware development to the earliest days of the computer era. FORTRAN was designed originally in the 1950s.

Parallel processing is the most recent of the major challenges presented to the users of computers by the rapid evolution of computer hardware. The most advanced supercomputers incorporate increasing numbers of independent processors. At the humbler end of the scale of costs, the ubiquitous microprocessor can now be cheaply and efficiently connected into communicating networks of thousandfold power. Even further increases in power can be obtained by the design of highly replicated, application-specific VLSI. As always, the only barrier to the immediate exploitation of this power is the development of our skill in the design of algorithms and programs.

The introduction of concurrency into computer programs leads rapidly to a number of serious and novel problems, for example, interference, livelock, deadlock, and nondeterminacy. The most challenging of these is nondeterminacy, which magnifies all the other problems and seriously reduces the effectiveness of traditional methods of program development by trial and error. But the first and most immediate barrier to fuller exploitation of concurrency is the mental block that inhibits parallel thinking by programmers entrenched in a purely sequential culture. The block is less apparent in experienced designers of hardware, which naturally operates in parallel unless special measures are taken to enforce sequentiality.

Fortunately, problems summarized in the previous paragraphs have been studied intensively by advanced research in university departments of computing science, and solutions are now available to anyone prepared to make the necessary connections between theory and practice. The promotion of these links was the primary objective of the Year of Programming, of the Institute of Concurrent Programming, and of this collection of its proceedings.

The choice of speakers and topics for this institute was a personal one. I have had the good fortune to work on a theory of communication and concurrency which is relevant to the design and use of microprocessors communicating with each other by a form of synchronized input and output [2, 3]. Instances of successful transfer of theory to practice are sufficiently rare that I wished to share my good fortune with an international audience; I was able to recruit for this purpose an outstanding list of speakers. That is why this collection of papers centers on a specific approach to concurrency involving communication. There are of course many other approaches that have found successful application, or deserve it. An approach based on temporal logic was ably presented at the institute by Amir Pnueli; this contribution, however, will soon be readily accessible from other publications (e.g., [4]), and has been omitted from this volume.

The first chapter of this volume reports a major achievement of mathematical design methods for the development of correct systems implemented as asynchronous VLSI circuits. By following a discipline with a series of small design steps, it has been proved possible with moderate effort to produce a correct design of a complexity and efficiency that would never have been contemplated by use of purely informal methods.

The next three chapters report the experience of a silicon manufacturer that has chosen to base the design of a new distributed processing architecture upon a mathematical theory, namely, the theory of Communicating Sequential Processes (CSP). The product is the INMOS transputer and its low-level programming language occam[1]. The language is sufficiently abstract that it can be used equally for multiprogramming, for multiprocessing, and even for hardware design. The manufacturer is continuing to search for appropriate mathematical theories that will improve its design methods as well as its products. These achievements have been recently (1990) recognized in the U.K. by a Queen's Award for Technology.

The fifth chapter is a report on a long-standing project for the development of a novel computing architecture based on multiple processors, and of the software needed for its practical application.

The next three chapters explore further applications of the CSP paradigm in the design of communications protocols, including the current X.25 standard, and in the exploration of security and recoverability of computer systems.

Chapters 9 and 10 are an introduction to formal reasoning in CSP, the first using purely algebraic methods and the second using abstract specifications. Both of them are based on a simple trace model, but the methods generalize to the standard model of CSP.

The final chapter contributes a degree of welcome balance: It solves a problem of distributed detection of termination, which is not readily tractable by the paradigm of communicating sequential processes. It is an admirable introduction to UNITY (which is described more fully in [1]) and an admirable illustration of the power of its concepts.

The success of this Concurrent Programming Institute was due not only to those who have contributed to these proceedings, but also to many others who spoke or contributed to the discussion. In addition to his lectures on transaction-processing primitives, Jim Woodcock gave a prior tutorial on

---

1. Occam is a trademark of INMOS Limited.

Communicating Sequential Processes. Leslie Lamport, in addition to his scientific contributions, acted as codirector of the institute and moderator of the panel discussions. Other active contributors were Edsger W. Dijkstra, Mohamed Gouda, Ernst-Rudiger Olderog, Gordon Plotkin, Fred Schneider, Jan van de Snepscheut, Rob Strom, and Pierre Wolper. I am sorry that this volume cannot give the reader a full account of their many spoken contributions. The authors of the written contributions, however, have been able to take advantage of the exposure of their ideas to the participants at the institute— a significant indirect benefit.

Finally, it is a pleasure to acknowledge the generosity of the sponsors of the Year of Programming and the endowment of the Admiral B. R. Inman Centennial Chair in Computing Theory; also the support of Professors J. C. Browne and Edsger W. Dijkstra as fellow directors of the Year of Programming; and the organizational efforts of the Year of Programming staff —Ham Richards, Suzanne Kain Rhoads, and Ana M. Hernandez— which was put to its first and severest test by the rapid organization of this, the first of the institutes, and again by the final editing of these proceedings.

References

[1] Chandy, K. M. and Misra, J. *Parallel Program Design: A Foundation.* Addison-Wesley, Reading, Mass., 1988.

[2] Hoare, C. A. R. "Communicating sequential processes". *Communications of the ACM 17*, 10 (October 1974), pp. 549–557.

[3] Hoare, C. A. R. *Communicating Sequential Processes.* Prentice-Hall International, Hemel Hempstead, U.K., 1985.

[4] Manna, Z. and Pnueli, A. *The Temporal Logic of Reactive Systems.* Springer-Verlag, Berlin (to appear).

Programming in VLSI

From Communicating Processes

to Delay-Insensitive Circuits

1

Alain J. Martin

California Institute of Technology

> Delays have dangerous ends.
> —William Shakespeare

Introduction

With chip size reaching one million transistors, the complexity of VLSI algorithms —i.e., algorithms implemented as digital VLSI circuits— is approaching that of software algorithms— i.e., algorithms implemented as code for a stored-program computer. Yet design methods for VLSI algorithms lag far behind the potential of the technology.

Since a digital circuit is the implementation of a concurrent algorithm, we propose a concurrent programming approach to digital VLSI design. The circuit to be designed is first implemented as a concurrent program that fulfills the logical specification of the circuit. The program is then compiled —manually or automatically— into a circuit by applying semantic-preserving program transformations. Hence, the circuit obtained is correct by construction.

The main obstacle to such a method is finding an interface that provides a good separation of the physical and algorithmic concerns. Among the physical parameters of the implementation, *timing* is the most difficult to isolate from the logical design, because the timing properties of a circuit are essential not only to its real-time behavior, but also to its logical correctness if the usual synchronous techniques are used to implement sequencing.

For this reason, *delay-insensitive* techniques are particularly attractive for VLSI synthesis. A circuit is delay-insensitive when its correct operation is independent of any assumption on delays in operators and wires except that the delays be finite [17]. Such circuits do not use a clock signal or knowledge about delays.

Let us clarify a matter of definitions right away: The class of entirely delay-insensitive circuits is very limited. Different asynchronous techniques distinguish themselves in the choice of the compromises about delay-insensitivity.

Speed-independent techniques assume that delays in gates are arbitrary, but that there are no delays in wires. *Self-timed* techniques assume that a circuit can be decomposed into *equipotential* regions inside which wire delays are negligible [16]. In our method, certain local "forks" are introduced to distribute a variable as inputs of several operators. We assume that the differences in delays between the branches of the fork are shorter than the delays in the operators to which the fork is an input. We call such forks *isochronic* [6].

Although we initially chose delay-insensitive techniques for reasons of methodology, those techniques present other important advantages in terms of efficiency and robustness:

> The clock rate of a synchronous design has to be slowed to account for the worst-case clock skews in the circuit and for the slowest step in a sequence of actions. Since delay-insensitive circuits do not use clocks, they are potentially faster than their synchronous equivalents.

> Since the logical correctness of the circuits is independent of the values of the physical parameters, delay-insensitive circuits are very robust to variations of these parameters caused by scaling or fabrication, or by some nondeterministic behavior such as the metastability of arbiters. For instance, all the chips we have designed have been found to be functional in a range of voltage values (for the constant voltage level encoding the high logical value) from above 10V to below 1V.

> Delay-insensitive circuit design can be modular: A part of a circuit can be replaced by a logically equivalent one and safely incorporated into

the design without changes of interfaces.

Because an operator of a delay-insensitive circuit is "fired" only when its firing contributes to the next step of the computation, the power consumption of such a circuit can be much lower than that of its synchronous equivalent.

Since the correctness of the circuits is independent of propagation delays in wires and, thus, of the length of the wires, the layout of chips is facilitated.

The method indeed produces correct and efficient circuits. It has been applied, with both "hand" compilation and automatic compilation, to a series of difficult design problems such as distributed mutual exclusion, fair arbitration, routing automata, stacks, and serial multipliers. All fabricated chips have been found to be correct on "first silicon". Although our CMOS implementation of the basic operators has been overly cautious, and the electrical optimization techniques have been rather tame, the performance of the chips has been found at least equal to that of synchronous implementations. We have just completed the design of a general-purpose microprocessor, and its performances are very encouraging: In $1.6\mu m$ SCMOS, it runs at 18 million instructions per second. (See the conclusion, Section 23, for more detail.)

The main reason for the efficiency of the method is that, rather than going in one step from program to circuit, the designer applies a series of transformations to the original program. At each stage, powerful algebraic manipulations can be performed leading to important optimizations in terms of speed or area.

In the first part of this chapter, we present the "source code" notation, the "object code" notation, and a VLSI implementation of the production rules in CMOS technology. The source notation is inspired by C. A. R. Hoare's CSP [4]: A program is a set of concurrent processes communicating by input and output commands on channels. (A similar experience in the use of communicating processes for programming in VLSI is described in [13].) The object code notation, called *production rule set*, is one of the main innovations of the method and is an interesting notation for digital VLSI all by itself.

In the second part, we describe the four main steps of the compilation (process decomposition, handshaking expansion, production rule expansion, operator reduction), illustrating them with a number of examples. In particular, we present the different algebraic transformations that can be applied at different stages of the compilation and that give the method its flexibility and efficiency.

Part I: The Source Code and the Object Code

1 *The Program Notation*

For the sequential part of the notation, we use a subset of Edsger W. Dijkstra's guarded command language [3], with a slightly different syntax. We give only an informal definition of the constructs' semantics.

(i) $b\uparrow$ stands for $b :=$ **true**, $b\downarrow$ stands for $b :=$ **false**. Those assignments are called "simple assignments".

(ii) The execution of the *selection* command $[G_1 \rightarrow S_1 []\ \ldots [] \ G_n \rightarrow S_n]$, where G_1 through G_n are boolean expressions, and S_1 through S_n are program parts (G_i is called a "guard", and $G_i \rightarrow S_i$ a "guarded command"), amounts to the execution of an arbitrary S_i for which G_i holds. If $\neg(G_1 \vee \ldots \vee G_n)$ holds, the execution of the command is suspended until $(G_1 \vee \ldots \vee G_n)$ holds.

(iii) The execution of the *repetition* command $*[G_1 \rightarrow S_1 []\ \ldots [] \ G_n \rightarrow S_n]$, where G_1 through G_n are boolean expressions, and S_1 through S_n are program parts, amounts to repeatedly selecting an arbitrary S_i for which G_i holds and executing S_i. If $\neg(G_1 \vee \ldots \vee G_n)$ holds, the repetition terminates.

(iv) *Sequencing*: Besides the usual sequential composition operator '$x; y$', we introduce two other operators. For atomic actions x and y, 'x, y' stands for the execution of x and y in any order leading to termination. For noninterfering communication actions x and y, "$x \bullet y$" stands for the simultaneous execution of x and y. (We shall return to this definition when we discuss the implementation of communication in Section 19.)

(v) $[G]$, where G is a boolean expression, stands for $[G \rightarrow$ **skip**$]$ and thus for "wait until G holds". (Hence "$[G]; S$" and $[G \rightarrow S]$ are equivalent.)

(vi) $*[S]$ stands for $*[$**true** $\rightarrow S]$ and thus for "repeat S forever".

(vii) From (ii) and (iii), the operational description of the statement

$$*[[G_1 \rightarrow S_1 []\ \ldots [] \ G_n \rightarrow S_n]]$$

is "repeat forever: wait until some G_i holds; execute an S_i for which G_i holds".

(viii) Tail recursion is allowed, but not general recursion. Functions and procedures with a simple parameter mechanism are also used, but we will not discuss them here.

1.1 *Communicating Processes*

A concurrent computation is described as a set of processes composed by the usual concurrent composition operator ∥. The concurrent composition is *weakly fair*; i.e., if, in a given state of the computation, x is the next atomic action of one of the processes, then x will be executed after a possibly unbounded but finite number of atomic actions from other processes.

Processes communicate by communication actions on *ports*; they do not share variables.[1] A port of a process is paired with a port of another process to form a *channel*. When no messages are transmitted, communication on a port is reduced to synchronization signals. The name of the port is then sufficient to identify a communication action.

If two processes, $p1$ and $p2$, share a channel with port X in $p1$ and port Y in $p2$, at any time the number of completed X-actions in $p1$ equals the number of completed Y-actions in $p2$. In other words, the completion of the nth X-action "coincides" with the completion of the nth Y-action. If, for example, $p1$ reaches the nth X-action before $p2$ reaches the nth Y-action, the completion of X is suspended until $p2$ reaches Y. The X-action is then said to be *pending*. When, thereafter, $p2$ reaches Y, both X and Y are completed. The predicate "X is pending" is denoted as $\mathbf{q}X$. If, for an arbitrary command A, $\mathbf{c}A$ denotes the number of completed A-actions, the semantics of a pair (X, Y) of communication commands is expressed by the two axioms:

$$\mathbf{c}X = \mathbf{c}Y \tag{A1}$$

$$\neg\mathbf{q}X \vee \neg\mathbf{q}Y \tag{A2}$$

Surprisingly, it is possible (and even advantageous) to define communication actions as coincident and yet implement the actions in completely asynchronous ways.

1.2 *Probe*

Instead of the usual selection mechanism by which a set of pending communication actions can be selected for execution, we provide a general boolean command on ports, called the *probe*. The definition of the probe given in [5] states that in process $p1$, the probe command $\overline{X}$ has the same value as $\mathbf{q}Y$. For the time being, we use a weaker definition, namely:

$$\overline{X} \Rightarrow \mathbf{q}Y$$

$$\mathbf{q}Y \Rightarrow \diamond\overline{X},$$

---

1. We have made a restricted use of shared variables in the design of the microprocessor.

where $\diamond P$ means *P holds eventually*. (We will return to the first definition in the example on the implementation of a fair arbiter.)

1.3 *Communication*

Matching communication actions are also used to implement a form of distributed assignment statement, to "pass messages", as it is often said. In that case, the pair of commands is specified to consist of an input command and an output command by adjoining them to the symbols "?" and "!", respectively. For example, X? is an input command and X is therefore an input port, and Y! is and output command and Y is therefore and output port.

Axiom   Communication axiom

Let $X?u$ and $Y!v$ be matching, where u is a process variable and v is an expression of the same type as u. The communication implements the assignment $u := v$. In other words, if $v = V$ before the communication, then $u = V$ and $v = V$ after the communication.

1.4 *First Example: Port Selection*

Process *sel* repeatedly performs communication action X or communication action Y, whichever can be completed; *sel* is blocked if and only if neither X nor Y can be completed:

$$sel \equiv *[[\ \overline{X} \rightarrow\ X\ []\ \overline{Y} \rightarrow Y]]\ .$$

Obviously, process *sel* is not fair because of the nondeterministic choice of a guard when both guards are true. Negated probes make it possible to transform *sel* into a fair version, *fsel*:

$$fsel \quad \equiv \quad *[[\ \overline{X} \rightarrow X;\ [\overline{Y} \rightarrow Y\ []\ \neg\overline{Y} \rightarrow \mathbf{skip}]$$
$$[]\ \ \overline{Y} \rightarrow Y;\ [\overline{X} \rightarrow X\ []\ \neg\overline{X} \rightarrow \mathbf{skip}]$$
$$]]\ .$$

Negated probes are necessary for implementing fairness.

1.5 *Second Example: Lazy Stack*

We implement a stack S of size n, $n > 0$, as a string of n communicating processes defined as follows:

$$S = \begin{cases} h, & \text{if } n = 1, \\ (h\|T), & \text{if } n > 1, \end{cases}$$

where h, the head of the stack, is a process, and T, the tail of the stack, is a stack of size $n - 1$. Process h communicates with the environment of the stack by the communication actions $in?x$ and $out!x$, and with T by the communication actions $put!x$ and $get?x$. Hence, $h.put$ matches $T.in$, and $h.get$ matches $T.out$. (We assume that no attempt is ever made to add a portion to a full stack, or to remove a portion from an empty stack.)

Each stack element either is empty and behaves like program E, or is full and behaves like program F. The epithet "lazy" is attributed to this stack because no reshuffling of portions takes place after a portion has been removed from a full stack element.

$$E \equiv [\,\overline{in} \rightarrow in?x;\ F$$

$$[]\ \overline{out} \rightarrow get?x;\ out!x;\ E$$

$$]$$

$$F \equiv [\,\overline{out} \rightarrow out!x;\ E$$

$$[]\ \overline{in} \rightarrow put!x;\ in?x;\ F$$

$$].$$

The following alternative coding of the stack element process, due to Peter Hofstee, illustrates the advantages of the probe construct:

$$*[[\,\overline{in} \rightarrow in?x$$

$$[]\ \overline{out} \rightarrow get?x$$

$$];$$

$$[\,\overline{out} \rightarrow out!x$$

$$[]\ \overline{in} \rightarrow put!x$$

$$]]\,.$$

We assume that each stack element is initially empty.

2 *The Object Code: Production Rules*

Carrying the discrete model of computation down to the transistor level requires that the MOS transistor be idealized as an on/off switch. Unfortunately, the simple semantics of the switch ignore too many electrical phenomena

that play an important role in the functioning of the circuit. A crucial innovation of the method is that the transistor need not be viewed as a discrete
switch; voltages can change continuously from one stable level to the other
one, provided that the changes are monotonic.

The notation for the object code provides the weakest possible form of
control.structure and the smallest possible number of program constructs.
In fact, it contains exactly one construct, the *production rule* (PR), and one
control structure, the *production-rule set*.

We consider the production-rule notation to be the canonical representation of a digital circuit. This representation can be decomposed into several
equivalent networks of digital operators, depending on the set of building
blocks used, but the production-rule set represents the circuit independently
of fhe chosen implementation.

Definition   A PR is a construct of the form $G \mapsto S$, where S is either a
simple assignment or an unordered list "$s1, s2, s3, \ldots$" of simple assignments,
and G is a boolean expression called the guard of the PR.

Example

$$x \wedge y \mapsto z\uparrow$$

$$\neg x \mapsto u\uparrow, v\downarrow$$

The semantics of a PR are defined only if the PR is *stable*:

Definition   A PR $G \mapsto S$ is said to be stable in a given computation, if, at
any point of the computation, G either is **false** or remains invariantly **true**
until the completion of S.

Stability is not guaranteed by the implementation. It has to be enforced by
the compilation procedure.

Definition   An execution of the stable PR $G \mapsto S$ is an unbounded sequence of *firings*. A firing of $G \mapsto S$ with G **true** amounts to the execution of
S. A firing of $G \mapsto S$ with G **false** amounts to a **skip**.

Definition   A PR set is the concurrent composition of all PRs of the set.

2.1 *Operations on PR Sets*

The only composition operation on two PR sets is the set union.

Theorem

The implementation of two concurrent processes is the set union of the two PR sets implementing the processes and of the PR sets implementing the channels between the processes, if any.

The proof follows from the associativity of the concurrent composition operator.

The other operations on the PRs of a set are those allowed by the following properties:

> Multiple occurrences of the same PR are equivalent to one as a consequence of the idempotence of the concurrent composition.

> The two rules $G \mapsto S1$ and $G \mapsto S2$ are equivalent to the single rule $G \mapsto S1, S2$.

> The two rules $G1 \mapsto S$ and $G2 \mapsto S$ are equivalent to the single rule $G1 \vee G2 \mapsto S$.

2.2 *Noninterference*

We require that *complementary* PRs —i.e., PRs of the type $G1 \mapsto x\uparrow$ and $G2 \mapsto x\downarrow$— be *noninterfering*.

Definition   Two complementary PRs are noninterfering when $\neg G1 \vee \neg G2$ holds invariantly.

It can be proven that, under the stability of each PR and noninterference among complementary PRs, the concurrent execution of the PRs of a set is equivalent to the following sequential execution:

> *[select a PR with a true guard; fire the PR]*

where the selection is weakly fair (each PR is selected infinitely often). From now on, we ignore the firings of a PR with a **false** guard; a firing will mean a firing of a PR with a **true** guard.

Until we return to these issues, we shall assume that the stability and noninterference requirements are fulfilled.

3 *VLSI Implementation of PRs*

Stability and noninterference are the two properties that make the VLSI implementation of PRs (almost) straightforward. As an example, we describe how PRs can be implemented in CMOS technology.

3.1 *The CMOS Transistors*

A CMOS circuit is a network of "nodes" —variables— interconnected by transistors. Certain nodes are also connected to the input-output "pads", which provide the interface with the environment; we will ignore the pads in this presentation. Other nodes are directly connected to the *power* node, providing the constant high-voltage value —called *VDD*— that represents the logical constant **true** or 1. Yet other nodes are directly connected to the *ground* node —called *GND*— providing the constant low-voltage value that represents the logical constant **false** or 0.

A node takes the continuous range of voltage values between the high voltage and the low voltage. Above a certain voltage $v1$ the value is interpreted as 1. Below another voltage $v0$, the value is interpreted as 0. Thanks to the stability property, the precise values of $v1$ and $v0$, which vary from node to node, are irrelevant provided that $v0 < v1$ and the voltage changes are *monotonic*. (Strict monotonicity is not necessary and is actually impossible to achieve because of noise, but we will not enter into these details here.)

A CMOS transistor is of either *n*-type or *p*-type. A transistor relates three nodes in the following way. Let g, standing for "gate", and x and y be the three nodes. When g is **false** for an *n*-transistor, and **true** for a *p*-transistor, no current passes through the region between x and y, called the *channel*;[2] thus x and y are left unchanged.

When g is set to **true** for an *n*-transistor, or **false** for a *p*-transistor, the channel becomes conducting. In this case, either x and y have the same voltages and are left unchanged, or a current is established in the channel until x and y reach the same voltage. The common value reached by x and y depends on electrical properties of x and y that are determined by the physical sizes (capacitances) of the nodes implementing x and y and by their interactions with the rest of the circuit. (Differences in node capacitances may cause charges to flow through the channel of a transistor in a way that results in unintended values of the nodes. This phenomenon, called *charge sharing*, may make it quite difficult to predict the final voltage value reached by x and y.)

In order to define the net effect of a PR independently of the physical parameters of its implementation, we are going to restrict the use of transistors. (In particular, the restriction will eliminate most occurrences of charge sharing.)

We impose the condition that a transistor used in isolation connect only two variables of the circuit: the gate g and one of the other two nodes, say z.

---

2. This notion of channel is unrelated to the one we introduced for communication among processes.

The third node of the transistor is either the power or the ground. With this restriction, the behavior of a single *n*-transistor is

$$g \mapsto z\uparrow \quad \text{or} \quad g \mapsto z\downarrow.$$

The behavior of a single *p*-transistor is

$$\neg g \mapsto z\uparrow \quad \text{or} \quad \neg g \mapsto z\downarrow.$$

3.2 *Threshold Voltages*

The current in the channel of a transistor is a function of the so-called gate-to-source voltage, V_{gs}, defined as $V(g) - min(V(x), V(y))$ for an *n*-transistor and as $V(g) - max(V(x), V(y))$ for a *p*-transistor. In first approximation, the current is assumed to be zero when

$$V_{gs} \leq V_{tn}$$

for an *n*-transistor and

$$V_{gs} \geq V_{tp}$$

for a *p*-transistor. V_{tn} and V_{tp} are called the *threshold voltages*. (Typically, $V_{tn} \approx 1V$ and $V_{tp} \approx -1V$.)

Because of the existence of threshold voltages, if an *n*-transistor is used to implement $g \mapsto z\uparrow$, the final value of *z* is not a "strong" 1, since the channel will stop conducting as soon as the voltage of *z* is within V_{tn} of the gate voltage. And symmetrically, a *p*-transistor used to implement $\neg g \mapsto z\downarrow$ does not produce a "strong" zero as the final value of *z*. Since the voltage drops caused by the threshold voltages accumulate as we compose operators, it is important to produce strong signals in order to be able to compose an arbitrary number of operators. We shall therefore restrict our use of *n*-transistors to PRs of the form

$$g \mapsto z\downarrow \tag{1}$$

and *p*-transistors to production rules of the form

$$\neg g \mapsto z\uparrow. \tag{2}$$

With these restrictions, all implementations produce strong signals.

Threshold voltages are difficult to adjust in CMOS technology. Actually, they tend to become more variable as the feature size decreases. (They may also vary during the activity of the circuit because of some electrical interaction with the substrate, called *body effect*.) For constant node capacitance, variations in thresholds account for most of the discrepancies in propagation delays on a CMOS chip. In particular, these variations exclude the possibility that the ordering in space of a set of variables along a common wire be used to infer an ordering in time of a set of transitions of these variables.

3.3 *Switching Circuits*

Consider the canonical (stable) PR

$$b \mapsto z\!\downarrow, \tag{3}$$

where b is a boolean expression in terms of a set of variables. These variables are used as gates of transistors implementing a switching circuit s corresponding to b: s is a series-parallel switching circuit between the ground node and z. The switches are n-transistors whose gates are the variables of b, possibly negated. Furthermore, we have

$$b \equiv \textit{"there is a path from ground to z in s"}.$$

By the construction of s, if b holds and remains stable, z is eventually set to 0. (For this reason, s is called a *pull-down circuit*.) Hence, s is exactly the implementation of production rule (3).

Using a symmetrical argument, we can show that the same series-parallel circuit as s, but with the power node and z connected, and whose switches are p-transistors, implements the production rule

$$bneg \mapsto z\!\uparrow, \tag{4}$$

where $bneg$ is derived from b by negating all variables. (This circuit is called a *pull-up circuit*.)

4 *Operators*

Two PRs that set and reset the same variable, such as

$$b1 \;\; \mapsto \;\; z\!\uparrow$$
$$b2 \;\; \mapsto \;\; z\!\downarrow, \tag{5}$$

are implemented as one operator.

Let $s1$ be the pull-up circuit corresponding to $b1$, and let $s2$ be the pull-down circuit corresponding to $b2$. The two circuits are connected through the common node z (see Figure 1). Since noninterference has been enforced, $\neg b1 \vee \neg b2$ holds at any time. This guarantees the absence of a conducting path between power and ground when the operator is not firing. (A path may exist for a short time when the operator is firing.)

Definition   The operator implementing the two rules is called "combinational" if $b1 \lor b2$ holds at any time, and "state-holding" otherwise.

By definition, if (5) is combinational, there is always a conducting path between either *VDD* or *GND* and the output z. Hence, the value of the output is always a strong 0 or a strong 1, and therefore $s1$ and $s2$ are together a valid implementation of (5).

For example, PRs (1) and (2) together implement an inverter as represented in Figure 2. The circuit of Figure 3 implements the *nand*-operator defined by

Figure 1.   CMOS implementation of a combinational operator.

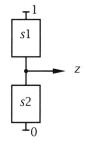

Figure 2.   A CMOS inverter.

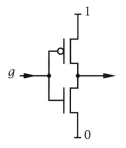

the PRs

$$a \wedge b \;\mapsto\; z\!\downarrow$$

$$\neg a \vee \neg b \;\mapsto\; z\!\uparrow.$$

If (5) is a state-holding operator, $\neg b1 \wedge \neg b2$ may hold in a certain state. In such a state, node z is isolated; there is no path between z and either *VDD* or *GND*. In MOS technology, an isolated node does not retain its value forever; eventually the charges leak away through the substrate and also through the transistors of the pull-up and pull-down circuits. If the PRs of the operator are fired frequently enough to prevent leakage, the implementation of Figure 1 can be used for a state-holding operator. Such an implementation is called *dynamic*.

Otherwise, it is necessary to add a storage element to the output node of a state-holding operator. Such an implementation is called *static*. In the sequel, we assume that only static implementations are used for state-holding operators.

(A standard CMOS implementation of such a storage element consists of two cross-coupled inverters (see Figure 4). This implementation inverts the value of z. The "weak" inverter, marked with a letter w on the figure, connects z to either *VDD* or *GND* through a high resistance, so as to maintain z at its intended voltage value [18].)

The implementation of a static state-holding operator is slightly more costly than that of a combinational operator because of the need for a storage device. Hence, given a pair of PRs that are not combinational, we may first try to modify the guards —under the invariance of the semantics— so as to make them combinational.

Figure 3.   CMOS implementation of a *nand*-gate.

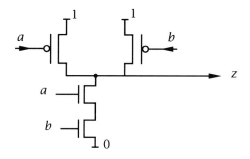

5 *The Standard Operators*

All operators of one or two inputs are used, and are therefore viewed as the standard operators.

5.1 *One-Input Operators*

The two operators with one input and one output are the *wire*:

$$x \underline{w} y \quad \equiv \quad x \;\longmapsto\; y{\uparrow}$$
$$\neg x \;\longmapsto\; y{\downarrow},$$

and the *inverter*:

$$\neg x \underline{w} y \quad \equiv \quad \neg x \;\longmapsto\; y{\uparrow}$$
$$x \;\longmapsto\; y{\downarrow}\,.$$

Most operators we use have more inputs than outputs. In general, however, the components we design have as many outputs as inputs. Hence, we need to reset the balance by introducing at least one operator, the *fork*, with more outputs than inputs. A fork with two outputs is defined as

$$x \underline{f}(y, z) \quad \equiv \quad x \;\longmapsto y{\uparrow}, z{\uparrow}$$
$$\neg x \;\longmapsto y{\downarrow}, z{\downarrow}\,.$$

Figure 4.   A static implementation of a state-holding operator.

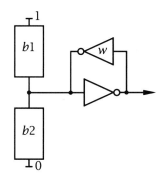

The wire and the fork are the only two operators that are implemented not as a pull-up/pull-down circuit —called a *restoring* circuit— but as a simple conducting interconnection between input and outputs.

5.2 *The Wire as a Renaming Operator*

Because the implementation of a wire is the same as that of a node, the wire behaves as a renaming operator when composed with another operator: The composition of an arbitrary operator O with output variable x with the wire $x \underline{w} y$ is equivalent to O in which x is renamed y. The composition of operator O with input variable x with the wire $y \underline{w} x$ is equivalent to O in which x is renamed y. (Observe that O can even be a wire.)

Unfortunately, the fork is not a renaming operator since the concurrent assignments to the different outputs of the fork are not completed simultaneously. In order to use a fork as a renaming operator, we will later have to make the timing assumption that such a fork is *isochronic*.

5.3 *Combinational Operators with Two Inputs*

We construct all functions B of two variables x and y such that

$$B \;\mapsto\; z\uparrow$$
$$\neg B \;\mapsto\; z\downarrow \;.$$

We get for B: $x \wedge y$, $x \vee y$, and $x = y$. We will not list the functions obtained by inverting inputs of B. (In the figures, a negated input or output is represented by a small circle on the corresponding line.) This gives the following set:

The *and*, with the infix notation $(x, y) \wedge z$, is defined as

$$x \wedge y \;\mapsto\; z\uparrow$$
$$\neg x \vee \neg y \;\mapsto\; z\downarrow \;.$$

The *or*, with the infix notation $(x, y) \underline{\vee} z$, is defined as

$$x \vee y \;\mapsto\; z\uparrow$$
$$\neg x \wedge \neg y \;\mapsto\; z\downarrow \;.$$

The *equality*, with the infix notation $(x, y)\, \underline{eq}\, z$, is defined as

$$x = y \;\mapsto\; z\uparrow$$
$$x \neq y \;\mapsto\; z\downarrow \;.$$

5.4 *State-Holding Operators with Two Inputs*

Next, we construct all different two-input-one-output operators of the form

$$b1 \;\mapsto\; z\!\uparrow$$
$$b2 \;\mapsto\; z\!\downarrow$$

such that $\neg b1 \lor \neg b2$ holds at any time, but $b1 \neq \neg b2$. We select for $b1$ either $x \land y$, or $x \lor y$, or $x = y$. For each choice of $b1$, we construct $b2$ as any of the effective strengthenings of $\neg b1$.

For $b1 \equiv (x \land y)$, we get for $b2$: $\neg x \land \neg y$, $\neg x \land y$, $\neg x$, and $x \neq y$. The first three choices of $b2$ lead to the following state-holding operators:

The *C-element*:

$$(x, y) \underline{C} z \;\equiv\; x \land y \;\mapsto\; z\!\uparrow$$
$$\neg x \land \neg y \;\mapsto\; z\!\downarrow\;.$$

(The C-element, introduced by David Muller, is described in [15].)

The *switch*:

$$(x, y) \underline{sw} z \;\equiv\; x \land y \;\mapsto\; z\!\uparrow$$
$$\neg x \land y \;\mapsto\; z\!\downarrow\;.$$

The *asymmetric C-element*:

$$(x, y) \underline{aC} z \;\equiv\; x \land y \;\mapsto\; z\!\uparrow$$
$$\neg x \;\mapsto\; z\!\downarrow\;.$$

For $b2 \equiv (x \neq y)$, we get the operator

$$x \land y \;\mapsto\; z\!\uparrow$$
$$x \neq y \;\mapsto\; z\!\downarrow\;.$$

If the stability condition is fulfilled, however, this operator is not state-holding. Because of the stability requirement, the state in which $\neg x \land \neg y$ holds —the "storage state"— can be reached only from states $x \land \neg y$ and $\neg x \land y$. In both states, $\neg z$ holds, and, therefore, $\neg z$ holds in the storage state. Hence, we can weaken the guard of the second PR as $(x \neq y) \lor (\neg x \land \neg y)$, i.e., $\neg x \lor \neg y$. Hence, the operator is equivalent to the *and*-operator $(x, y) \land z$.

For $b1 \equiv (x \lor y)$, no effective strengthening of $\neg b1$ is possible.

For $b1 \equiv (x = y)$, we get the operator:

$$x = y \quad \mapsto \quad z\uparrow$$
$$x \wedge \neg y \quad \mapsto \quad z\downarrow .$$

If the stability condition is fulfilled, however, this operator is not state-holding for the same reasons that the operator with $b1 \equiv x \wedge y$ and $b2 \equiv (x \neq y)$ is not.

5.5 *Flip-Flop*

The canonical form we choose for the *flip-flop* is

$$(x, y)\, \underline{ff}\, z \quad \equiv \quad x \quad \mapsto \quad z\uparrow$$
$$\neg y \quad \mapsto \quad z\downarrow ,$$

which requires the invariance of $\neg x \vee y$ to satisfy noninterference. Observe that the flip-flop $(x, y)\, \underline{ff}\, z$ can always be replaced with the C-element $(x, y)\, \underline{C}\, z$, but not vice versa.

6 *Multi-Input Operators*

Since there are already 164 different operators with three inputs and one output, we shall not pursue the systematic enumeration that we started with two-input operators. We use n-input *and, or, C-element*, whose definitions are straightforward.

We use a *multi-input flip-flop* defined as

$$(x_1, \ldots, x_k, y_1, \ldots, y_l)\, \underline{mff}\, z \quad \equiv \quad \bigvee i : x_i \quad \mapsto \quad z\uparrow$$
$$\bigvee i : \neg y_i \quad \mapsto \quad z\downarrow$$

where $(\forall i : \neg x_i) \vee (\forall i : y_i)$.

We also use the combinational *if*-operator —sometimes called *multiplexer*— defined as

$$(x, y, z)\, \underline{if}\, u \quad \equiv \quad (x \wedge y) \vee (\neg x \wedge z) \quad \mapsto \quad u\uparrow$$
$$(x \wedge \neg y) \vee (\neg x \wedge \neg z) \quad \mapsto \quad u\downarrow .$$

The most general and most often used operator is the *generalized C-element*, of which all other forms of C-elements are a special case. It implements a pair of PRs

$$B1 \;\mapsto\; x\uparrow$$

$$B2 \;\mapsto\; x\downarrow$$

in which $B1$ and $B2$ are arbitrary conjunctions of elementary terms. (As usual, the two guards have to be mutually exclusive.) For example,

$$a \wedge b \wedge \neg c \;\mapsto\; x\uparrow$$

$$\neg a \wedge d \;\mapsto\; x\downarrow$$

can be directly implemented with a generalized C-element. Observe that the limiting factor for the size of the guards is not the number of inputs, but the number of terms in a conjunction.

7 *Arbiter and Synchronizer*

So far, we have considered only PR sets in which all guards are stable and noninterfering. But we shall have to implement sets of guarded commands —selections or repetitions— in which the guards are *not* mutually exclusive, as in the probe-selection example. Therefore, we need at least one operator that provides a nondeterministic choice between two **true** guards.

7.1 *Arbiter*

The simplest selection between nonexclusive guards is of the form

$$*[[x \to \cdots$$
$$[\!] \; y \to \cdots$$
$$]],$$

where x and y are simple boolean variables, and the two guards are stable. In order to distinguish among the three basic states of the system —i.e., neither x nor y is selected, x is selected, or y is selected— we must introduce two outputs, say u and v, as follows:

$$*[[x \to u\uparrow; \;\cdots$$
$$[\!] \; y \to v\uparrow; \;\cdots$$
$$]].$$

Initially, $\neg u \wedge \neg v$ holds as coding of the state "no selection made". Hence, when the selection is considered completed, which is just a matter of definition, u and v should be set back to **false**. We get

$$*[[x \rightarrow u\uparrow; [\neg x]; u\downarrow$$

$$[\![y \rightarrow v\uparrow; [\neg y]; v\downarrow \qquad\qquad (6)$$

$$]\!] .$$

If $\neg u \wedge \neg v$ holds initially, $\neg u \vee \neg v$ holds at any time.

The preceding program is a description of the operator known as the "basic arbiter" or "mutual-exclusion element," denoted as (x, y) *arb* (u, v). Observe that the choice between the two guards is not fair.

7.2 *Synchronizer*

When negated probes are used, for instance to implement fairness, we have to implement selection commands with unstable guards. The synchronizer is the only operator that accepts nonstable guards. It is defined as

$$*[[b \wedge z \rightarrow u\uparrow; [\neg z]; u\downarrow$$

$$[\![\neg b \wedge z \rightarrow v\uparrow; [\neg z]; v\downarrow \qquad\qquad (7)$$

$$]\!] .$$

Variable b may change at any time from **false** to **true**, but both b and z remain **true** until u or v has changed. Hence, the guard $\neg b \wedge z$ is unstable, whereas the guard $b \wedge z$ is stable. As in the arbiter case, if $\neg u \wedge \neg v$ holds initially, $\neg u \vee \neg v$ holds at any time. (The synchronizer operator was introduced in [7].)

7.3 *Implementation and Metastability*

The PR sets for (6) and (7) necessarily contain unstable rules. The PR set for the "unstable arbiter" is

$$x \wedge \neg v \;\longmapsto\; u\uparrow$$

$$y \wedge \neg u \;\longmapsto\; v\uparrow$$

$$\neg x \vee v \;\longmapsto\; u\downarrow$$

$$\neg y \vee u \;\longmapsto\; v\downarrow .$$

The PR set for the "unstable synchronizer" is

$$b \wedge z \wedge \neg v \;\longmapsto\; u\uparrow$$
$$\neg b \wedge z \wedge \neg u \;\longmapsto\; v\uparrow$$
$$\neg z \vee v \;\longmapsto\; u\downarrow$$
$$\neg z \vee u \;\longmapsto\; v\downarrow \,.$$

The first two PRs of the arbiter are unstable and can fire concurrently. The same holds for the first two production rules of the synchronizer: Since b can change from **false** to **true** at any time, both guards may evaluate to **true**.

Let us analyze the PR set implementation of the arbiter. The synchronizer case is very similar. The state $x \wedge y \wedge (u = v)$ of the arbiter is called *metastable*. When started in the metastable state, with $\neg u \wedge \neg v$, the set of PRs specifying the arbiter may produce the following unbounded sequence of firings:

$$*[(u\uparrow, v\uparrow); (u\downarrow, v\downarrow)] \,.$$

In the implementation, nodes u and v may stabilize to a common intermediate voltage value for an unbounded period of time. Eventually, the inherent asymmetry of the physical realization (impurities, fabrication flaws, thermal noise, etc.) will force the system into one of the two stable states where $u \neq v$. But there is no upper bound on the time the metastable state will last, which means that it is impossible to include an arbitration device into a clocked system with absolute certainty that a timing failure cannot occur.

The spurious values of u and v produced during the metastable state must be eliminated since they violate the requirement $\neg u \vee \neg v$. Hence, we compose the "bare" arbiter with a "filter" taking u and v as input and producing uf and vf as "filtered outputs". The net effect of the filter is

$$uf, vf := (u \wedge \neg v), (v \wedge \neg u) \,.$$

(In the CMOS construction of the filter shown in Figure 5, we use the threshold voltages to our advantage: The channel of transistor $t1$ is conducting only when $(u \wedge \neg v)$ holds, and the channel of transistor $t2$ is conducting only when $(v \wedge \neg u)$ holds.)

In delay-insensitive design, the correct functioning of a circuit containing an arbiter or a synchronizer is independent of the duration of the metastable state; therefore, relatively simple implementations of arbiters and synchronizers can be used. In synchronous design, however, the implementations have to meet the additional constraint that the probability of the metastable state lasting longer than the clock period should be negligible.

8 *Sequencing and Stability*

In the second part of this chapter, we shall see how an arbitrary program in the source notation can be decomposed —by a transformation called *hand-shaking expansion*— into a collection of sequences of the type

$$S \equiv *[[w_0]; \ t_0; \ [w_1]; \ t_1; \ldots; \ [w_{n-1}]; \ t_{n-1}] \ .$$

The w_i, the *wait-conditions*, are boolean expressions, possibly identical to **true**, and the t_i are simple assignments. The extension to the case of multiple assignments between the wait-conditions is straightforward.

The next step of the compilation procedure —the *production-rule expansion*— (also to be explained in the second part) is the transformation of S into a semantically equivalent set of production rules. Let

$$P \equiv \{b_i \mapsto t_i | 0 \leq i < n\}$$

be such a set.

Notations and Definitions   For an arbitrary PR p, $p.g$ and $p.a$ denote the guard and the assignment of p, respectively. The predicate $R(a)$, the *result* of the simple assignment a, is defined as: $R(x \uparrow) = x$, and $R(x \downarrow) = \neg x$. An

---

Figure 5.   An implementation of the basic arbiter.

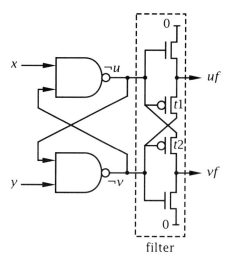

filter

execution of a PR that changes the value of the assigned variable is called *effective*; otherwise, it is called *vacuous*.

With these definitions, the stability of a PR can be reformulated as follows:

Stability   A PR p is stable in a computation if and only if $p.g$ can be falsified only in states where $R(p.a)$ holds.

The production-rule expansion algorithm compiles a handshaking expansion S into a set P of PRs, all of which are stable except those whose guards contain negated probes. Since, as we shall see, the guards of the PRs are obtained by strengthening the wait-conditions of S, the stability of the wait-conditions is necessary to satisfy the stability of the PRs.

A wait-condition w is stable if once w is **true**, it remains **true** at least until the completion of the following assignment. Unstable wait-conditions can be caused by negated probes only. These cases are dealt with separately by introducing synchronizers. (An example of how this is achieved is given in Section 22.)

8.1 *Sequencing*

The set P of PRs implements S when the following conditions are fulfilled:

1. *Guard strengthening:* The guards of the PRs of P are obtained by strengthening the wait conditions of S: $\forall i :: b_i \Rightarrow w_i$ and, in the initial state, $w_0 \Rightarrow b_0$.

2. *Sequential execution:* $(\mathbf{N}i :: b_i \wedge \neg R(t_i)) \leq 1$, i.e., at most one effective PR can be executed at a time.

3. *Program-order execution:* The order of execution of effective PRs of P is the order specified by S, called the *program order*, and no deadlock is introduced in the construction of P.

As we shall see in Part 2, it is not always possible to construct, for a given handshaking expansion, a PR set that satisfies the preceding three conditions. In certain cases, the handshaking expansion must be augmented with assignments to new variables, called *state variables*. This transformation, which is always possible, will be explained in Part 2.

8.2 *Acknowledgment*

Fulfilling the second and third conditions requires that for any two PRs p : $b \mapsto t$ and $p' : b' \mapsto t'$, such that p immediately precedes p' in the program order,

$$b' \Rightarrow R(t)$$

holds in the states where p' is effectively executed. We say that b' is the *acknowledgment* of t. Hence the following property:

Acknowledgment Property   For a PR set executed in program order, the guard of each PR is an acknowledgment of the immediately preceding assignment.

We shall see that the acknowledgment property is necessary but not sufficient to ensure program-order execution.

We use two kinds of acknowledgments, depending on the type of variable used in the assignment. But other forms of acknowledgments can be envisioned. If t assigns an internal variable, then the acknowledgment is implemented by strengthening b' as $b' \wedge R(t)$.

For example, if t is $x\uparrow$, the acknowledgment is $b' \wedge x$.

If t assigns an external variable, i.e., a variable that implements a communication command, another kind of acknowledgment, which we shall introduce later, can be used. For instance, if lo is an output variable used together with input variable li to implement a so-called active handshaking protocol, a possible acknowledgment of $lo\uparrow$ is li, since $li \Rightarrow lo$ at this point of the protocol.

8.3 *Implementation of Stability*

Consider a PR set P, which implements a given program S. We are going to show that the acknowledgment property, which is necessary to construct a P that implements S, is also sufficient to guarantee stability.

The execution of a PR p of P establishes a path between a constant node (either *VDD* or *GND*), and the node implementing the variable —say, x— assigned by p. Either $p.g$ holds forever after p, or the firing of another PR I, the *invalidating* PR of p, will establish $\neg p.g$, thereby cutting the path from the constant node to x.

Let $\tilde{p}$ be the complementary PR of p, i.e., the PR with the complementary assignment. If the PR set contains both p and $\tilde{p}$, then it also contains I because of the noninterference requirement between complementary PRs. And we have the order of execution:

$$p \preceq I \prec \tilde{p}.$$

In all the states between I and $\tilde{p}$, the original path to x is cut. In that case, we have to see to it that the assignment to x is completed before the path is cut. Hence the following requirement:

Completion requirement   Assignment $p.a$ is completed when a PR q is completed whose guard is an acknowledgment of $p.a$. The execution order of the PR set must satisfy

$$p \prec q \preceq I \,.$$

Since this requirement is already implied by the acknowledgment property, the construction of P automatically guarantees stability.

8.4 *Self-Invalidating PRs*

Definition   A PR p is *self-invalidating* when $R(p.a) \Rightarrow \neg p.g$.

For example, $\neg x \mapsto x{\uparrow}$ is self-invalidating.

Self-invalidating PRs are excluded by the completion requirement since it implies $I \neq p$.

For instance, the circuit consisting of an inverter with its output connected to its input is excluded by the completion requirement since it corresponds to the PR set:

$$\neg x \;\mapsto\; x{\uparrow}$$
$$x \;\mapsto\; x{\downarrow}$$

and the two PRs of the set are self-invalidating. However, the PR set

$$\neg x \;\mapsto\; y{\uparrow}$$
$$y \;\mapsto\; x{\uparrow}$$
$$x \;\mapsto\; y{\downarrow}$$
$$\neg y \;\mapsto\; x{\downarrow}$$

fulfills the completion requirement, although it is the same circuit as previously, since the only change is the addition of the wire $y \, w \, x$.

We eliminate such "disguised" self-invalidating PRs by adding the following requirement:

Restoring Acknowledgment Requirement   There is at least one restoring PR r satisfying $p \prec r \preceq I$, where r is restoring if it is not part of a wire or a fork.

With this extra requirement, all forms of self-invalidating PRs are eliminated.

It is remarkable that the acknowledgment requirement, which is necessary to enforce the sequential execution of a PR set, is also sufficient to satisfy stability. From now on, we can manipulate PRs as if the transitions were discrete. We have, however, made no simplifying assumption on the physical behavior of the system. The only physical requirement so far is that of monotonicity.

Another requirement on the implementation is that the rings of operators that constitute a circuit keep oscillating. It turns out that eliminating self-invalidating PRs enforces the condition that a ring contain at least three restoring operators, which is a necessary (and in practice also sufficient) condition for the ring to oscillate, thanks to the "gain" property of restoring gates. (See [14] for an explanation of gain.)

Part II: The Compilation Method

In this part, we describe how a program in the source notation is transformed into a semantically equivalent set of VLSI operators. Four major transformations are used, each of which plays an equally important role. In particular, one step of the compilation, the *handshaking expansion*, introduces an intermediate program representation, between communicating processes and PRs, that allows for important algebraic manipulations of the program: reshuffling, process factorization, and process quotient. We illustrate the method with a series of examples that covers practically all cases.

9 *Process Decomposition*

The first step of the compilation, called *process decomposition,* consists in replacing one process with several processes by application of the following rule:

Decomposition Rule   A process P containing an arbitrary program part S is semantically equivalent to two processes, $P1$ and $P2$, where $P1$ is derived from P by replacing S with a communication action, C, on a newly introduced channel (C, D) between $P1$ and $P2$, and $P2$ is the process $*[[D \rightarrow S; D]]$.

The structure of $P2$ will be used so frequently that we introduce an operator to denote it: the *call* operator. We denote it by (D/S), and we say that D *calls* (or *activates*) S.

Observe that process decomposition does not introduce concurrency. Although $P1$ and $P2$ are potentially concurrent, they are never active concurrently; $P2$ is activated from $P1$, much as a procedure or a coroutine would be. The newly created subprocesses may share variables, but, since the subprocesses are never active concurrently, there is no conflicting access to the shared variables. The subprocesses may also share channels; this will require a special implementation for such channels. Decomposition is applied for each construct of the language. For construct S, the corresponding process $P2$ can be simplified as follows:

If S is the selection $[B_1 \rightarrow S_1 [\!] B_2 \rightarrow S_2]$, $P2$ is simplified as

$$*[[\overline{D} \wedge B_1 \rightarrow S_1; D$$

$$[\!] \ \overline{D} \wedge B_2 \rightarrow S_2; D \tag{8}$$

$$]] \, .$$

If S is the repetition $*[B_1 \rightarrow S_1 [\!] B_2 \rightarrow S_2]$, $P2$ is simplified as

$$*[[\overline{D} \wedge B_1 \rightarrow S_1$$

$$[\!] \ \overline{D} \wedge B_2 \rightarrow S_2$$

$$[\!] \ \overline{D} \wedge \neg B_1 \wedge \neg B_2 \rightarrow D \tag{9}$$

$$]] \, .$$

The assignment $x := B$, where B is an arbitrary boolean expression, is implemented as the selection $[B \rightarrow x\!\uparrow [\!] \neg B \rightarrow x\!\downarrow]$, which gives for $P2$

$$*[[\overline{D} \wedge B \rightarrow x\!\uparrow; D$$

$$[\!] \ \overline{D} \wedge \neg B \rightarrow x\!\downarrow; D$$

$$]] \, .$$

The generalizations to the cases of an arbitrary number of guarded commands in selection and repetition are obvious. All assignments to the same variable are also grouped in the same process. Process decomposition is applied repeatedly until the right-hand side of each guarded command is a straight-line program.

Process decomposition makes it possible to reduce a process with an arbitrary control structure to a set of subprocesses of only two different types: either a (finite or infinite) sequence of communication actions, or a repetition of type (8) or (9).

10 *Handshaking Expansion*

The next step of the transformation, the *handshaking expansion,* replaces each communication action in a program with its implementation in terms of elementary actions, and each channel with a pair of wire operators. We shall first ignore the issue of message transmission and implement only the synchronization property of communication primitives.

Channel (X, Y) is implemented by the two wires $(xo \; \underline{w} \; yi)$ and $(yo \; \underline{w} \; xi)$. If X belongs to process $P1$ and Y to process $P2$, then xo and xi belong to $P1$, and yo and yi to $P2$. Initially, xo, xi, yo, and yi —which we will call the "handshaking variables of (X, Y)"— are **false**. Assume that the program has been proven to be deadlock-free and that we can identify a pair of matching actions X and Y in $P1$ and $P2$, respectively. We replace X and Y by the sequences U_x and U_y, respectively, where

$$U_x \;\; \equiv \;\; xo\uparrow; \; [xi]$$
$$U_y \;\; \equiv \;\; [yi]; \; yo\uparrow \; . \tag{10}$$

Also,

$$xo \;\; \mapsto \;\; yi\uparrow$$
$$\neg xo \;\; \mapsto \;\; yi\downarrow$$
$$yo \;\; \mapsto \;\; xi\uparrow$$
$$\neg yo \;\; \mapsto \;\; xi\downarrow \; , \tag{11}$$

by definition of the wires. By (10) and (11), any concurrent execution of $P1$ and $P2$ contains the following sequence of assignments:

$$xo\uparrow; \; yi\uparrow; \; yo\uparrow; \; xi\uparrow \; .$$

10.1 *Simultaneous Completion of Nonatomic Actions*

We introduce a definition of *completion* of a nonatomic action which makes it possible to use the notion of simultaneous completion of two nonatomic actions.

By definition, the execution of an atomic action is considered instantaneous, and thus the simultaneous completion of two atomic actions does not make sense. (Atomic actions are simple assignments $x \uparrow$ and $x \downarrow$, and evaluation of simple guards, i.e., guards containing one variable. A wait action of the form $[ai]$ is a nonatomic action that may be treated as the repetition $*[\neg ai \rightarrow skip]$.)

A nonatomic action is *initiated* when its first atomic action is executed. A nonatomic action is *terminated* when its last atomic action is executed.

For nonatomic actions, the notion of completion does not coincide with that of termination. A nonatomic action might be considered completed even if it has not terminated, i.e., even if some atomic actions that are part of the action have not been executed. The definition of suspension is derived from that of completion.

Definition   A nonatomic action X is completed when it is initiated and is guaranteed to terminate, i.e., when all possible continuations of the computation contain the complete sequence of atomic actions of X.

The preceding definition can be further explained as follows: Consider a prefix $t1$ of an arbitrary *trace* of a computation. (A trace is a sequence of atomic actions corresponding to a possible execution of the program.) The completion of X is identified with the point in the computation where $t1$ has been completed, if (1) X is initiated in $t1$, and (2) all possible sequences $t2$, such that $t1$ extended with $t2$ is a valid trace of the computation, contain the remaining atomic actions of X. *Hence the completions of two nonatomic actions coincide if their completion points coincide.*

(Observe that there may be several points in a trace that can act as completion point, which makes it easier to align the two completion points of two overlapping sequences so as to implement the bullet operator.)

Definition   Between initiation and completion, an action is *suspended.*

These definitions of completion and suspension are valid because they satisfy the three semantic properties of completion and suspension that are used in correctness arguments, namely:

1. $\{\mathbf{c}X = x\} \, X \, \{\mathbf{c}X = x + 1\}$,

2. $\mathbf{q}X \Rightarrow pre(X)$, where $pre(X)$ is any precondition of X in terms of the program variables and auxiliary program variables,

3. If X is completed, eventually X is terminated.

These definitions will be used to implement the bullet operator and the communication primitives as defined by axioms $A1$ and $A2$. Consider the interleaving of U_x and U_y. At the first semicolon, i.e., after $xo \uparrow$, U_x has been initiated, but it cannot be considered completed since the valid continuation that does not contain U_y does not contain the rest of U_x. At the second semicolon, both U_x and U_y have been initiated, and thus all continuations contain the rest of the interleaving of U_x and U_y. Hence, U_x and U_y are guaranteed to terminate when they are both initiated, i.e., they fulfill $A1$ and $A2$.

10.2 *Four-Phase Handshaking*

Unfortunately, when the communication implemented by U_x and U_y terminates, all handshaking variables are **true**. Hence, we cannot implement the next communication on channel (X, Y) with U_x and U_y. The complementary implementation, however, can be used for the next matching pair, that is:

$$D_x \equiv xo\downarrow; [\neg xi]$$

$$D_y \equiv [\neg yi]; yo\downarrow .$$

The solution consisting in alternating U_x and D_x as an implementation of X, and U_y and D_y as an implementation of Y, is called *two-phase handshaking*, or *two-cycle signaling*. Since it is in most cases impossible to determine syntactically which X- or Y-actions follow each other in an execution, the general two-phase handshaking implementations require testing the current value of the variables as follows:

$$xo := \neg xo; [xi = xo]$$

$$[yi \neq yo]; yo := \neg yo .$$

In general, we prefer to use a simpler solution, known as *four-phase handshaking*, or *four-cycle signaling*. In a four-phase handshaking protocol, X-actions are implemented as "$U_x; D_x$" and Y-actions as "$U_y; D_y$". Observe that the D-parts in X and Y introduce an extra communication between the two processes whose only purpose is to reset all variables to **false**.

Both protocols have the property that for a matching pair (X, Y) of actions, the implementation is not symmetrical in X and Y. One action is called *active* and the other one *passive*. The four-phase implementation, with X active and Y passive, is

$$X \equiv xo\uparrow; [xi]; xo\downarrow; [\neg xi] \tag{12}$$

$$Y \equiv [yi]; yo\uparrow; [\neg yi]; yo\downarrow . \tag{13}$$

(Later, we will introduce an alternative form of active implementation, called *lazy-active*.) Although four-phase handshaking contains twice as many actions as two-phase handshaking, the actions involved are simpler and are more amenable to the algebraic manipulations we shall introduce later. When operator delays dominate the communication costs, which is the case for communication inside a chip, four-phase handshaking will, in general, lead to more efficient solutions. When transmission delays dominate the communication costs, which is the case for communication between chips, two-phase handshaking is preferred.

10.3 *Probe*

A simple implementation of the probe $\overline{X}$ is xi, with X implemented as passive. (Given our definition of suspension, the proof that this implementation of the probe fulfills its definition is straightforward.)

A probed communication action $\overline{X} \to \ldots X$ is then implemented as

$$xi \to \ldots xo\!\uparrow;\ [\neg xi];\ xo\!\downarrow\ .$$

10.4 *Choice of Active versus Passive Implementation*

When no action of a matching pair is probed, the choice of which action should be active and which passive is arbitrary, but a choice has to be made. The choice can be important for the composition of identical circuits. A simple rule is that, for a given channel (X, Y), all actions on one port (called the *active port*) are active, and all actions on the other port (called the *passive port*) are passive. If $\overline{X}$ is used, all X-actions are passive— with the obvious restriction that $\overline{Y}$ cannot be used in the same program.

We shall see, however, that this criterion for choosing active and passive ports may conflict with another criterion related to the implementation of input and output commands.

10.5 *Properties of the Handshaking Protocol*

For a matching pair (X, Y) of actions implemented as (12) and (13), and the wires $(xo\ \underline{w}\ yi)$ and $(yo\ \underline{w}\ xi)$, the concurrent execution of X and Y causes the sequence of assignments

$$xo\!\uparrow;\ yi\!\uparrow;\ yo\!\uparrow;\ xi\!\uparrow;\ xo\!\downarrow;\ yi\!\downarrow;\ yo\!\downarrow;\ xi\!\downarrow,$$

called the *handshaking protocol*. The following properties of the handshaking protocol play an important role in the compilation method.

Property 1   For xo and xi used as in the active protocol of (12), xi is an acknowledgment of $xo\!\uparrow$ and $\neg xi$ is an acknowledgment of $xo\!\downarrow$. For yo and yi used as in the passive protocol of (13), $\neg yi$ is an acknowledgment of $yo\!\uparrow$ and yi is an acknowledgment of $yo\!\downarrow$.

Property 2   In (12) and (13), D_x and D_y are used only to reset all variables to **false**. Hence, provided that the cyclic order of the actions of (12) and (13) is maintained, the sequences D_x and D_y can be inserted at any place in the program of each of the processes without invalidating the semantics of the communication involved. This transformation, called *reshuffling*, may introduce a deadlock.

Property 3   The wait-actions of (12) and (13) are stable. Reshuffling maintains the stability.

Reshuffling, which is the source of significant optimizations, will be used extensively. It is therefore important to know when Property 2 can be applied without introducing deadlock.

There are two simple cases where the reshuffling of sequence "$U_x; D_x; S$" into sequence "$U_x; S; D_x$" does not introduce deadlock:

S contains no communication action, or

X is an internal channel introduced by process decomposition.

11 *Production-Rule Expansion*

Production-rule expansion is the transformation from a handshaking expansion to a set of PRs. It is the most crucial and most difficult step of the compilation since it requires the enforcement of sequencing by semantic means. It consists of three steps:

1. State assignment,

2. Guard strengthening,

3. Symmetrization.

We shall explain the algorithms for production-rule expansion with an example: the implementation of the simple process (L/R), where R is an active channel. This process is one of the basic building blocks for implementing sequencing. The handshaking expansion gives

$$* [[li]; \; ro\uparrow; \; [ri]; \; ro\downarrow; \; [\neg ri]; \; lo\uparrow; \; [\neg li]; \; lo\downarrow] . \tag{14}$$

We now consider the handshaking expansion as the specification of the implementation: Any implementation of the program has to satisfy the ordering defined by (14). The next step is to construct a production-rule set that satisfies this ordering. We start with the production-rule set that is syntactically derived from (14):

$$li \; \mapsto \; ro\uparrow$$
$$ri \; \mapsto \; ro\downarrow$$
$$\neg ri \; \mapsto \; lo\uparrow$$
$$\neg li \; \mapsto \; lo\downarrow .$$

(As a clue to the reader, PRs of a set are listed in program order.)

Since the program is deadlock-free, effective execution of the PRs in program order is always possible. Some other execution orders, however, may also be possible. The production-rule set satisfies the handshaking-expansion specification if, and only if, the only possible execution order is the program order. If execution orders other than the program order are possible for the production-rule set, the guards of some rules are strengthened so as to eliminate these execution orders.

In our example, program order is not the only execution order for the syntactic production-rule set: Since $\neg ri$ holds initially, the third PR can be executed first. This is also true for the fourth PR, but the execution of the fourth rule in the initial state is vacuous. Because all handshaking variables of R are back to **false** when R is completed, we cannot find a guard for the transition $lo\uparrow$ that holds only as a precondition of $lo\uparrow$ in (14). Hence, we cannot distinguish the state following R from the state preceding R, and thus the sequential execution condition introduced in Section 8 cannot be satisfied.

This is a general problem, since it arises for each unshuffled communication action. In order to fulfill the sequential-execution condition, we have to guarantee that each state of the handshaking expansion is unique, i.e., that there exists a predicate in terms of variables of the program that holds only in this state. The task of transforming the handshaking expansion so as to make each state unique is called *state assignment*.

11.1 *State Assignment with State Variables*

The first technique to define uniquely the state in which the transition $lo\uparrow$ is to take place consists in introducing a state variable, say x, initially **false**. Handshaking expansion (14) becomes

$$* [[li];\ ro\uparrow;\ [ri];\ x\uparrow;\ [x];\ ro\downarrow;\ [\neg ri];\ lo\uparrow;\ [\neg li];\ x\downarrow;\ [\neg x];\ lo\downarrow]. \qquad (15)$$

Observe that (15) is semantically equivalent to (14) since the two sequences of actions that are added to (14), namely, $x\uparrow;\ [x]$ and $x\downarrow;\ [\neg x]$, are equivalent to a **skip**. (The newly introduced variable x is used nowhere else.)

There are several places where the two assignments to the state variable can be introduced. In general, a good heuristic is to introduce those assignments at such places that the alternation between waits and assignments is maintained. There are other heuristics, however, that can play a role in the placement of the variables.

Once state variables have been introduced so as to distinguish any two states of the handshaking expansion, it is possible to strengthen the guards of the PRs to enforce program-order execution. The basic algorithm for guard strengthening can be found in [10]. We shall not describe it here. Applied to (15), it gives

$$\neg x \wedge li \;\mapsto\; ro\uparrow \tag{16}$$

$$ri \;\mapsto\; x\uparrow \tag{17}$$

$$x \;\mapsto\; ro\downarrow \tag{18}$$

$$x \wedge \neg ri \;\mapsto\; lo\uparrow \tag{19}$$

$$\neg li \;\mapsto\; x\downarrow \tag{20}$$

$$\neg x \;\mapsto\; lo\downarrow. \tag{21}$$

It is easy to check that the acknowledgment property is fulfilled and that the only possible execution order for the preceding production-rule set is the program order defined by (15).

12 *Operator Reduction*

The last step of the compilation, called *operator reduction*, groups together the PRs that assign the same variables. Those PRs are then identified with (and implemented as) an operator. The program is thus identified with a set of operators.

Since we have enforced the stability of each rule and noninterference be-tween any two complementary rules, we can implement any set of PRs di-rectly. (For reasons of efficiency, we must see to it that the guards do not contain too many variables in a conjunct, which would lead to too many transistors in series. Hence, the implementation of the set may also involve decomposing a PR into several PRs by introducing new internal variables.)

The direct implementation of the PR set (16) through (21) is straightfor-ward:

(16) and (18) correspond to the asymmetric C-element $(\neg x, li)$ $\underline{aC}\, ro$.

(19) and (21) correspond to the asymmetric C-element $(x, \neg ri)$ $\underline{aC}\, lo$.

(17) and (20) correspond to the flip-flop (ri, li) $\underline{ff}\, x$.

If the preceding operators are implemented as dynamic, this implemen-tation of process (L/R) is the simplest possible. If static implementations of the operators are required, another implementation might be considered with fewer state-holding elements since, as we have explained in the first part, static state-holding operators are slightly more difficult to realize than combinational operators.

A last transformation, called *symmetrization*, may be performed on the PR set to minimize the number of state-holding operators. Since symmetrization also introduces inefficiencies of its own, however, it should not be applied blindly.

13 *Symmetrization*

Symmetrization is performed on the two guards of PRs $b1 \mapsto z\uparrow$ and $b2 \mapsto z\downarrow$, when one of the two guards, say, $b1$, is already in the form $x \wedge \neg b2$. If we replace guard $b2$ with $\neg x \vee b2$, then the two guards are complements of each other, i.e., the operator is combinational. Of course, weakening guard $b2$ is a dangerous transformation since it may introduce a new state where the guard holds. We have to check that this does not occur by checking the following invariant:

Given the new rule $\neg x \vee b2 \mapsto z\downarrow$, $\neg z$ must hold in any state where $\neg x \wedge \neg b2$ holds, i.e., we have to check the invariant truth of

$$x \vee b2 \vee \neg z \; .$$

13.1 *Operator Reduction of the (L/R)-element*

The symmetrization of PRs (16) and (18), and of (19) and (21) of the (L/R)-element, gives

$$\neg x \wedge li \;\mapsto\; ro\uparrow \tag{16}$$

$$ri \;\mapsto\; x\uparrow \tag{17}$$

$$\neg li \vee x \;\mapsto\; ro\downarrow \tag{18}$$

$$x \wedge \neg ri \;\mapsto\; lo\uparrow \tag{19}$$

$$\neg li \;\mapsto\; x\downarrow \tag{20}$$

$$ri \vee \neg x \;\mapsto\; lo\downarrow \; . \tag{21}$$

(16) and (18) correspond to the *and*-operator $(\neg x, li) \wedge ro$.

(17) and (20) correspond to the flip-flop $(ri, li) \; \underline{f\!f} \, x$.

(19) and (21) correspond to the *and*-operator $(x, \neg ri) \triangle lo$.

(17) and (20) can also be implemented as the C-element $(li, ri) \; \underline{C}\, x$.

The resulting circuit is shown in Figure 6. (The dot identifies the input that is activated first.) This implementation of (L/R), either with a flip-flop or with a C-element, is called a *Q-element*. The Q-element implementing (L/R) as before is described by the infix notation $(li, lo) \; \underline{Q}\,(ri, ro)$.

14 *Isochronic Forks*

In the previous operator reduction, li is an input to the flip-flop (li, ri) $\underline{ff}x$ and to the *and*-operator $(li, \neg x) \wedge ro$. Formally, in order to compose the PRs together to form a circuit, we have to introduce the fork $li\underline{f}(l1, l2)$ and replace li by $l1$ as input of the *and*-operator, and by $l2$ as input of the flip-flop. We also have to introduce the forks $ri\underline{f}(r1, r2)$ and $x\underline{f}(x1, x2)$ for the same reason.

Let us analyze the effect of the first fork only. The PR set that includes the PRs of the fork is

$$li \;\longmapsto\; l1\!\uparrow, l2\!\uparrow \tag{16a}$$

$$\neg x \wedge l1 \;\longmapsto\; ro\!\uparrow \tag{16b}$$

$$ri \;\longmapsto\; x\!\uparrow \tag{17}$$

$$\neg l1 \vee x \;\longmapsto\; ro\!\downarrow \tag{18}$$

$$x \wedge \neg ri \;\longmapsto\; lo\!\uparrow \tag{19}$$

$$\neg li \;\longmapsto\; l1\!\downarrow, l2\!\downarrow \tag{20a}$$

$$\neg l2 \;\longmapsto\; x\!\downarrow \tag{20b}$$

$$ri \vee \neg x \;\longmapsto\; lo\!\downarrow \;. \tag{21}$$

Now we observe that transition $l1\!\uparrow$ of (16a) is acknowledged by the guard of (16b) but $l2\!\uparrow$ is not, and transition $l2\!\downarrow$ of (20a) is acknowledged by the guard of (20b) but $l1\!\downarrow$ is not. Hence, the assignments $l2\!\uparrow$ and $l1\!\downarrow$ do not fulfill the completion requirement and thus are not stable!

We solve this problem by making a simplifying assumption: We assume that the fork is *isochronic*. That is, the difference in delays between the two branches of the fork is shorter than the delays in the operators to which the

---

Figure 6. Implementation of (L/R) with a Q-element.

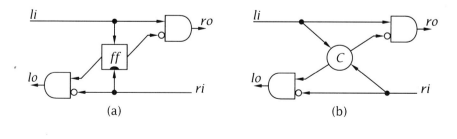

(a)   (b)

fork is an input. Hence, when a transition on one output is acknowledged and thus completed, the transition on the other output is also acknowledged and thus completed.

This is the only timing condition that must be fulfilled. In general, the constraint is easy to meet because it is one-sided. The isochronicity requirement is more difficult to meet, however, when a negated input introduces an inverter on a branch of the fork, since the transition delays of an inverter are of the same order of magnitude as the transition delays of other operators. We have proved that, for the implementation of each language construct, these inverters can always be eliminated from the isochronic forks by simple transformations.[3] (See [1, 2].)

In [11], we have proved that the class of entirely delay-insensitive circuits is very limited: Practically all circuits of interest fall outside the class. We believe that the notion of isochronic fork is the weakest compromise to delay-insensitivity sufficient to implement any circuit of interest.

Which forks have to be isochronic is easy to decide by a simple analysis of the PR sets. For instance, the fork $ri\ f(r1, r2)$ also has to be isochronic, but the fork $x\ f(x1, x2)$ does not. We shall ignore the issue of isochronic forks in the rest of this presentation.

15 *Reshuffled Implementations of (L/R)*

We illustrate the use of reshuffling by deriving two other implementations of (L/R). If L is an internal channel introduced for process decomposition, we can reshuffle the handshaking expansions of L and R without the risk of introducing deadlock. Let us return to handshaking expansion (14).

15.1 *First Reshuffling*

We postpone the second half of the handshaking expansion of R —i.e., the sequence $ro\downarrow; [\neg ri]$— until after $[\neg li]$. We get

$$*[[li];\ ro\uparrow;\ [ri];\ lo\uparrow;\ [\neg li];\ ro\downarrow;\ [\neg ri];\ lo\downarrow]\ .$$

---

3. These transformations have not been applied to the circuits presented here as examples, but they are always applied before the circuits are actually implemented.

The syntactic PR expansion we now derive is already "program-ordered":

$$li \;\mapsto\; ro\uparrow$$
$$ri \;\mapsto\; lo\uparrow$$
$$\neg li \;\mapsto\; ro\downarrow$$
$$\neg ri \;\mapsto\; lo\downarrow .$$

The first and third rules specify the wire $(li \underline{w} ro)$; the second and fourth rules specify the wire $(ri \underline{w} lo)$. Hence, the implementation reduces to two wires!

15.2 *Second Reshuffling: The D-element*

We now postpone the whole handshaking expansion of R until after $[\neg li]$. We get

$$*[[li]; \; lo\uparrow; \; [\neg li]; \; ro\uparrow; \; [ri]; \; ro\downarrow; \; [\neg ri]; \; lo\downarrow] .$$

We need to introduce a state variable, say x, as follows:

$$*[[li]; \; x\uparrow; \; [x]; \; lo\uparrow; \; [\neg li]; \; ro\uparrow; \; [ri]; \; x\downarrow; \; [\neg x]; \; ro\downarrow; \; [\neg ri]; \; lo\downarrow] .$$

The PR expansion gives

$$li \;\mapsto\; x\uparrow$$
$$(ri\vee)x \;\mapsto\; lo\uparrow$$
$$x \wedge \neg li \;\mapsto\; ro\uparrow$$
$$ri \;\mapsto\; x\downarrow$$
$$(li\vee)\neg x \;\mapsto\; ro\downarrow$$
$$\neg x \wedge \neg ri \;\mapsto\; lo\downarrow .$$

The terms between parentheses have been added for symmetrization. The operator reduction gives

$$(li, \neg ri) \quad \underline{ff} \quad x$$
$$(ri, x) \quad \underline{\vee} \quad lo$$
$$(x, \neg li) \quad \underline{\wedge} \quad ro .$$

The flip-flop can be replaced with the C-element $(li, \neg ri)\underline{C}x$. The circuit, shown in Figure 7, is called a D-element.

16 *Sequencing*

There are many ways to implement the sequencing of n arbitrary actions. We shall introduce the basic operators that are used in the most straightforward implementations.

16.1 *The Active-Active Buffer*

Consider the program $*[S_1; S_2]$, where S_1 and S_2 are two arbitrary program parts. Process decomposition of this program gives

$$*[L; R] \parallel (L'/S_1) \parallel (R'/S_2) .$$

Hence the basic sequencing operator is the process

$$B(L_a, R_a) \equiv *[L; R] ,$$

where both L and R are active. This process is called an *active-active buffer*. The handshaking expansion gives

$$* [lo\uparrow;\ [li];\ lo\downarrow; [\neg li];\ ro\uparrow;\ [ri];\ ro\downarrow;\ [\neg ri]] . \tag{22}$$

Since ri is **false** initially, we can rewrite (22) as

$$* [[\neg ri];\ lo\uparrow;\ [li];\ lo\downarrow; [\neg li];\ ro\uparrow;\ [ri];\ ro\downarrow] . \tag{23}$$

By comparing (23) with (14) —the handshaking expansion of the Q-element— we observe that $B(L_a, R_a) \equiv (\neg ri, ro)\ \underline{Q}(li, lo)$, which gives the implementation of Figure 8.

Figure 7.   The *D*-element.

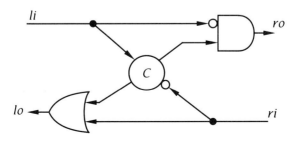

16.2 *The (L/A;R)-element*

In order to generalize the preceding construction to the case of an arbitrary number of actions, we must implement the generalization of the (L/R)-element. Sequence

$$* [S_1; S_2; \ldots; S_n] \tag{24}$$

can be decomposed into a number of shorter sequences by repeatedly applying process decomposition. There are as many ways to decompose (24) as there are binary trees of *n* leaves. But observe that, if $n > 2$, all decompositions will require at least one process of the form

$(L/A; R)$,

where *A* and *R* are active communication actions. (The semicolon binds more tightly than the process call.) We shall use two different reshufflings to implement this process. Again, these reshufflings maintain the semantics of the original program if the handshaking expansion of *L'* is not reshuffled. The first reshuffling is

*[[*li*]; *ao*↑; [*ai*]; *lo*↑; [¬*li*]; *ao*↓; [¬*ai*]; *R*; *lo*↓] .

We decompose it into two sequences by applying a process-factorization decomposition described in [10]:

(*[[*li*]; *ao*↑; [¬*li*]; *ao*↓]

‖ * [[*ai*]; *lo*↑; [¬*ai*]; *R*; *lo*↓]

) .

The first sequence is the wire (*li* $\underline{w}$ *ao*). The second sequence is the D-element $(ai, lo) \underline{D} (ri, ro)$.

Figure 8. Implementation of the active-active buffer with a *Q*-element.

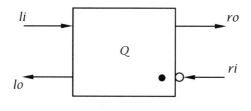

The second reshuffling is

$$*[[li]; A; ro\uparrow; [ri]; lo\uparrow; [\neg li]; ro\downarrow; [\neg ri]; lo\downarrow].$$

Again, we decompose it into two sequences by process factorization:

$$(*[[ri]; lo\uparrow; [\neg ri]; lo\downarrow]$$
$$\| * [[li]; A; ro\uparrow; [\neg li]; ro\downarrow]$$
$$).$$

The first sequence is the wire ($ri\,\underline{w}\,lo$). The second sequence is the Q-element (li, ro) $Q(ai, ao)$. Both implementations are shown in Figure 9.

Now the implementation of a sequence of n actions is straightforward. For instance, for $n = 4$, we have two "linear" decompositions of ($L/S_1; S_2; S_3; S_4$). The first one is

$$((L/S_1; L_1) \| (L_1/S_2; L_2) \| (L_2/S_3; S_4)).$$

The second one is

$$((L/L_2; S_4) \| (L_2/L_1; S_3) \| (L_1/S_1; S_2)).$$

These two decompositions lead to the linear implementations shown in Figure 10.

16.3 *The Passive-Active Buffer*

In order to compose one-place buffers in a linear chain, one channel must be active and the other one passive. We implement the buffer with L passive and R active. This version is denoted by $B(L_p, R_a)$. In order to take advantage of

Figure 9. Implementations of the ($L/A; R$)-element.

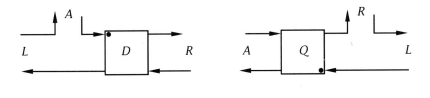

the active-active case, we decompose the buffer into two processes q and t:

$$q \equiv *[D';R]$$
$$t \equiv (D/L).$$

Process q is an active-active buffer. The compilation of t is straightforward. The handshaking expansion gives

$$*[[di]; [li]; lo\uparrow; [\neg li]; lo\downarrow; do\uparrow; [\neg di]; do\downarrow].$$

Since D is an internal channel, we can reshuffle the sequence $[\neg li]; lo\downarrow$ with respect to D without introducing deadlock. (Also observe that since $do\downarrow$ remains the last action of the sequence, we have not changed the order of L relative to R.) We get

$$*[[di]; [li]; lo\uparrow; do\uparrow; [\neg di]; [\neg li]; lo\downarrow; do\downarrow].$$

The PR expansion leading to the circuit of Figure 6 is

$$di \wedge li \; \mapsto \; lo\uparrow, do\uparrow$$
$$\neg di \wedge \neg li \; \mapsto \; lo\downarrow, do\downarrow.$$

Process t is used to connect the two ports of a channel when they are both active. It is called a "passive-passive adaptor". The complete circuit is shown in Figure 11.

The passive-active buffer can be compiled directly by introducing a state variable. The circuit obtained is slightly different. See [8].

Figure 10.   Implementations of $(L/S_1; S_2; S_3; S_4)$.

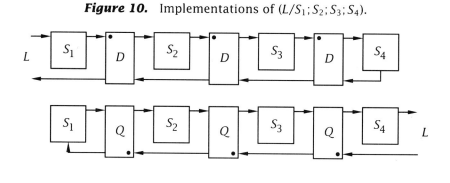

17 *Single-Variable Register*

Consider the following *register* process, which provides read and write access to a simple boolean variable, x:

$$*[[\overline{P} \rightarrow P?x$$

$$[\![\overline{Q} \rightarrow Q!x \tag{25}$$

$$]\!],$$

where $\neg\overline{P} \vee \neg\overline{Q}$ holds at any time.

The handshaking expansion of (25) uses the *double-rail* technique: The boolean value of x is encoded on two wires, one for the value **true** and one for the value **false**. Input channel P has two input wires, $pi1$ for receiving the value **true** and $pi2$ for receiving the value **false**, and one output wire, po. Output channel Q has two output wires, $qo1$ for sending the value **true** and $qo2$ for sending the value **false**, and one input wire, qi. Each guarded command of (25) is expanded to two guarded commands:

$$*[[pi1 \rightarrow x\uparrow; \ [x]; \ po\uparrow; \ [\neg pi1]; \ po\downarrow$$

$$[\![\ pi2 \rightarrow x\downarrow; \ [\neg x]; \ po\uparrow; \ [\neg pi2]; \ po\downarrow$$

$$[\![\ x \wedge qi \rightarrow qo1\uparrow; \ [\neg qi]; \ qo1\downarrow \tag{26}$$

$$[\![\ \neg x \wedge qi \rightarrow qo2\uparrow; \ [\neg qi]; \ qo2\downarrow$$

$$]\!] \ .$$

17.1 *Mutual Exclusion between Guarded Commands*

We are now faced with a new problem: enforcing mutual exclusion between the production-rule sets of different guarded commands. (This problem is

---

Figure 11. An implementation of the passive-active buffer.

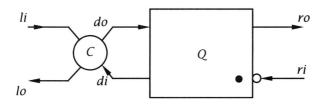

not concerned with making the *guards* of the different commands mutually exclusive. For the time being, we are considering only examples where the guards of the commands are already mutually exclusive.) Let us illustrate our problem with the compilation of the first two guarded commands. If we just concatenate the production-rule sets of these two commands, we get

$$pi1 \mapsto x\uparrow$$
$$pi1 \wedge x \mapsto po\uparrow$$
$$\neg pi1 \mapsto po\downarrow$$
$$pi2 \mapsto x\downarrow$$
$$pi2 \wedge \neg x \mapsto po\uparrow$$
$$\neg pi2 \mapsto po\downarrow .$$

We now observe, however, that the second and the sixth guarded commands are interfering (they set and reset the same variable *po*), and that, for reasons of symmetry, the same holds for the third and the fifth PRs.

Hence, the problem of ensuring mutual exclusion between PRs of different guarded commands is the same as enforcing program order between PRs of the same guarded command. We use the same technique, which consists in strengthening the guards of the production rules, if necessary, by introducing state variables to distinguish between the states corresponding to each true guard.

In the case at hand, we strengthen the guards of the third and the sixth rules as

$$x \wedge \neg pi1 \mapsto po\downarrow$$
$$\neg x \wedge \neg pi2 \mapsto po\downarrow .$$

The rest of the implementation is straightforward. The first and fourth PRs correspond to the flip-flop $(pi1, \neg pi2)$ *ff* x. The other PRs can be transformed into

$$(pi1 \wedge x) \vee (pi2 \wedge \neg x) \mapsto po\uparrow$$
$$(\neg pi1 \wedge \neg x) \vee (\neg pi2 \wedge x) \mapsto po\downarrow,$$

which is the definition of the *if*-operator $(pi1, pi2, x)$ *if po* .

The production-rule expansion of the last two guarded commands of (26) gives

$$x \wedge qi \;\mapsto\; qo1\uparrow$$
$$\neg x \vee \neg qi \;\mapsto\; qo1\downarrow$$
$$\neg x \wedge qi \;\mapsto\; qo2\uparrow$$
$$x \vee \neg qi \;\mapsto\; qo2\downarrow,$$

which corresponds to the two operators $(x, qi) \wedge qo1$ and $(\neg x, qi) \wedge qo2$. The circuit is represented in Figure 12.

In the next example, we shall refer to the implementation of the first two guarded commands of (26) as the *register* operator:

$$(pi1, pi2) \; \underline{reg} \,(po, x) \,.$$

We shall refer to the implementation of the last two guarded commands of (26) as the *read* operator:

$$(qi, x) \; \underline{read} \,(qo1, qo2) \,.$$

18 *Implementation of the Stack*

The implementation of the stack will be used to explain the general method for implementing communications that involve passing messages. The method relies on the time-honored "divide-and-conquer" principle: We first construct the so-called *control part* of the program, which is the original program where the messages have been removed from each communication action. We then

---

Figure 12.   Single boolean register.

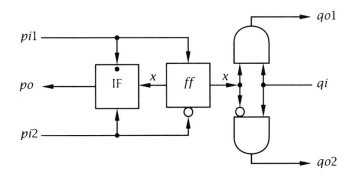

combine this control part with a *data path*, which is a program implementing the assignment parts of the communication actions. (See Figure 16 in Section 20.) The basic technique for combining control and data was introduced in [9].

18.1 *The Control Part of the Stack*

The control part of the stack consists of programs E and F, from which message communication has been removed. We assume that the stack is empty initially. We introduce the channel (t, t') so that F can be called from within E by process decomposition. We get

$$E \equiv *[[\overline{in} \rightarrow in;\ t$$
$$[\!] \ \overline{out} \rightarrow get;\ out$$
$$]\!]$$

$$F \equiv *[[\overline{t'} \wedge \overline{in} \rightarrow put;\ in$$
$$[\!] \ \overline{t'} \wedge \overline{out} \rightarrow out;\ t'$$
$$]\!] .$$

In the handshaking expansion, we let the choice of active and passive communications be dictated by the occurrence of the probes. (We will, however, return to this choice later.) We get

$$E \equiv *[[\neg ti \wedge ini \rightarrow ino\!\uparrow;\ [\neg ini];\ ino\!\downarrow;\ to\!\uparrow;\ [ti];\ to\!\downarrow$$
$$[\!] \ \neg ti \wedge outi \rightarrow geto\!\uparrow;\ [geti];\ geto\!\downarrow;\ [\neg geti];\ outo\!\uparrow;\ [\neg outi];\ outo\!\downarrow$$
$$]\!]$$

$$F \equiv *[[ti' \wedge ini \rightarrow puto\!\uparrow;\ [puti];\ puto\!\downarrow;\ [\neg puti];\ ino\!\uparrow;\ [\neg ini];\ ino\!\downarrow$$
$$[\!] \ ti' \wedge outi \rightarrow outo\!\uparrow;\ [\neg outi];\ outo\!\downarrow;\ to'\!\uparrow;\ [\neg ti'];\ to'\!\downarrow$$
$$]\!] .$$

Observe that, after handshaking expansion, the symmetry between E and F has been restored. The choice of whether ti or ti' should be negated in the guards determines whether E or F should be called initially, i.e., whether we start with an empty or a full stack element.

18.2 *Compilation of E*

The first guarded command, $E1$, is a standard passive-active buffer. The second guarded command, $E2$, is a standard Q-element. The implementation of E must combine the implementations of $E1$ and $E2$ in a way that enforces mutual exclusion between the execution of $E1$ and that of $E2$.

Since the execution of *in* and that of *out* are mutually exclusive, it suffices to guarantee that when *in* is completed in $E1$, $E2$ cannot start until t is completed. We introduce the variable z (initially **true**) in the handshaking expansion of $E1$, as indicated in Figure 13, and we strengthen the guard of $E2$ with z. We get

$$E1 \equiv z \wedge ini \rightarrow ino\uparrow;\ z\downarrow;\ [\neg z];\ [\neg ini];\ ino\downarrow;\ to\uparrow;\ [ti];\ to\downarrow;\ [\neg ti];\ z\uparrow,$$

$$E2 \equiv \neg ti \wedge outi \wedge z \rightarrow geto\uparrow;\ [geti];\ geto\downarrow;\ [\neg geti];\ outo\uparrow;\ [\neg outi];\ outo\downarrow.$$

Now $E2$ cannot start until $z\uparrow$ is completed, i.e., until $E1$ is completed. Since, by the structure of $E1$, $z \Rightarrow \neg ti$, we can simplify the guard of $E2$ to $outi \wedge z$. For symmetrization, we also weaken $\neg outi$ as $\neg outi \vee \neg z$. Hence, mutual exclusion is enforced by replacing input $outi$ with the *and*-operator $(outi, z) \wedge outi'$ in the Q-element implementation of $E2$. This gives the circuit of Figure 14 as an implementation of E.

18.3 *Compilation of F*

The compilation of $F1$ is identical to that of $E2$ with the appropriate change of variables. The compilation of $F2$, however, can be simplified by reshuffling. Since channel (t, t') is internal, we can reshuffle the handshaking sequence of

Figure 13. Implementation of the first g.c. of E with variable z.

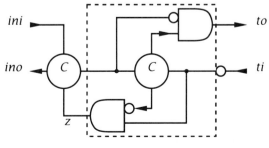

t' without deadlock. The handshaking expansion of $F2$ becomes

$$ti' \wedge outi \rightarrow outo\uparrow;\ to'\uparrow;\ [\neg ti' \wedge \neg outi];\ outo\downarrow;\ to'\downarrow,$$

which compiles immediately into the "forked" C-element $(ti', outi)\underline{C}(outo, to')$. The reshuffling guarantees that $F1$ cannot be started before $F2$ is completed.

The channels *in* and *out* are used in both E and F, so we must merge the local copies of *in* and the local copies of *out* in a standard way that we do not describe here. The resulting circuit for the control part of the stack element is shown in Figure 15.

19 *Implementation of the Data Path*

We now have to extend the implementation of the control part $S2$ so as to obtain an implementation of the whole program $S1$. We want to leave $S2$ unchanged by introducing a datapath process, P, such that the parallel composition of $S2$ and P implements $S1$.

Figure 14.   Implementation of E.

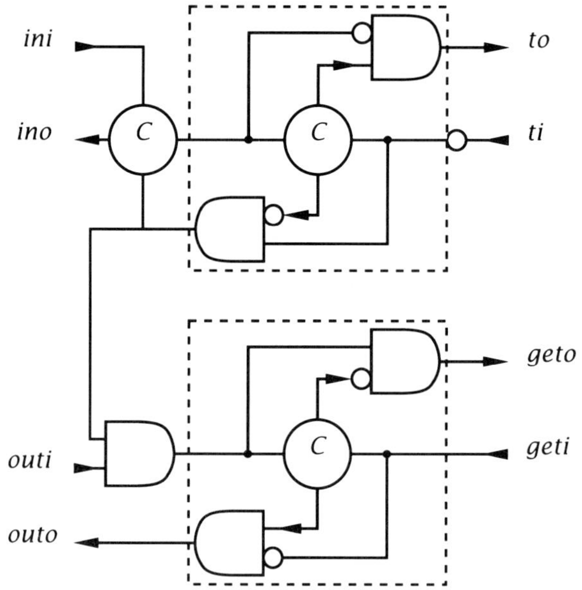

The channels *in, out, get, put* of *S2* are renamed *in', out', get', put'*. *P* communicates with *S2* via *in', out', get', put'* and with the environment via *in, out, get, put*. (See Figure 16.)

Let *C* be a channel of *S1*, and *C'* be the renamed channel of *S2* to which *C* corresponds. For (*S2 ∥ P*) to implement *S1*, each communication on *C* must coincide with a communication on *C'*; i.e., *P* must implement the so-called *channel interface* process

$$I_C \equiv \, *[C \bullet C'] \, .$$

Figure 15.   The control part of the stack element.

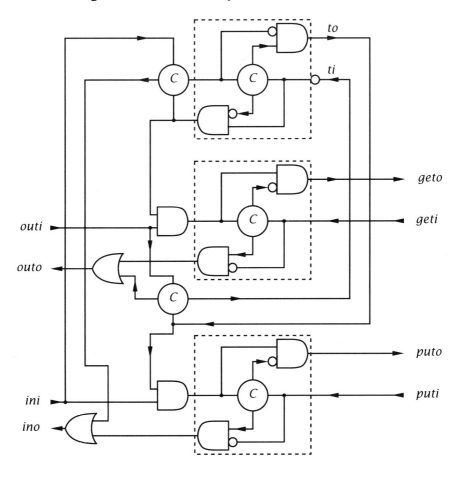

Hence, *P* has to implement the four channel interfaces:

* $[in' \bullet in?x]$

* $[out' \bullet out!x]$

* $[get' \bullet get?x]$

* $[put' \bullet put!x]$.

20 *Implementation of Channel Interfaces*

There are four types of channel interfaces, depending on whether the port is active or passive, and whether the communication is an input or an output.

20.1 *Input Actions on a Passive Port*

We want to implement the interface I_C for action $C?x$ on the passive port C. I_C communicates with $S2$ by the active port C', and with the environment by the passive port D. Furthermore, in the standard double-rail encoding technique, the two-wire implementation (ci, co) of C has to be interfaced to the three-wire input port D in which the two input wires, $di1$ and $di2$, are used to encode the two values of the incoming message. (See Figure 17.)

Figure 16.   Adding the data path.

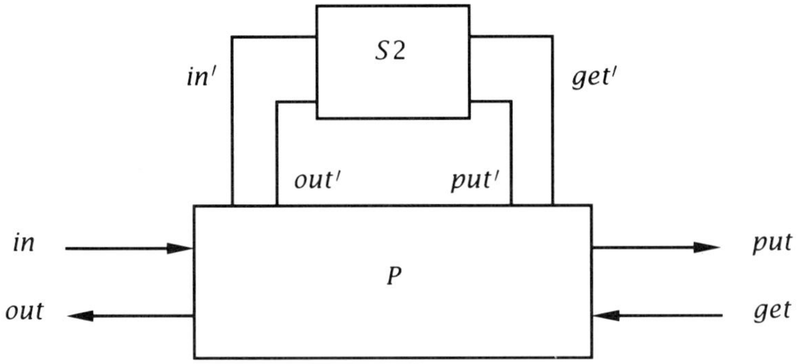

I_C has to implement an interleaving of the following three sequences:

$$S_C \equiv *[ci'\uparrow; [co']; ci'\downarrow; [\neg co']]$$

$$S_D \equiv *[[di1 \lor di2]; do\uparrow; [\neg di1 \land \neg di2]; do\downarrow]$$

$$S_X \equiv *[[di1 \rightarrow x\uparrow; [x] [] di2 \rightarrow x\downarrow; [\neg x]]] \,.$$

An implementation of $C' \bullet D$ interleaves sequences S_C and S_D as

$$* [[di1 \lor di2]; ci'\uparrow; [co']; do\uparrow; [\neg di1 \land \neg di2]; ci'\downarrow; [\neg co']; do\downarrow] \,. \tag{28}$$

In the interleaving of (28) and S_X, the assignment to x is inserted after $[co']$ so as to ensure that communication action C has been started when the assignment to x is performed:

$$*[[di1 \lor di2]; ci'\uparrow; [co' \land di1 \rightarrow x\uparrow; [x][] co' \land di2 \rightarrow x\downarrow; [\neg x]];$$
$$do\uparrow; [\neg di1 \land \neg di2]; ci'\downarrow; [\neg co']; do\downarrow] \,. \tag{29}$$

Next, we factor (29) as

$$* [[di1 \lor di2]; ci'\uparrow; [\neg di1 \land \neg di2]; ci'\downarrow] \tag{30}$$

and

$$*[[co' \land di1 \rightarrow x\uparrow; [x]; do\uparrow; [\neg co']; do\downarrow$$
$$[] co' \land di2 \rightarrow x\downarrow; [\neg x]; do\uparrow; [\neg co']; do\downarrow \tag{31}$$
$$]] \,.$$

Sequence (30) is realized by the operator $(di1, di2) \underline{\lor} ci'$. We factor (31) so as

---

Figure 17.   Channel interface for input port.

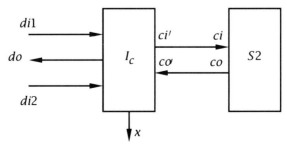

to isolate the register part:

$$(co', di1) \, \underline{aC} \, x1 \; \equiv \; *[[co' \wedge di1]; \; x1\uparrow; \; [\neg co']; \; x1\downarrow]$$

$$(co', di2) \, \underline{aC} \, x2 \; \equiv \; *[[co' \wedge di2]; \; x2\uparrow; \; [\neg co']; \; x2\downarrow]$$

$$(x1, x2) \, \underline{reg} \, (x, do) \; \equiv \; *[[x1 \rightarrow x\uparrow; \; [x]; \; do\uparrow; \; [\neg x1]; \; do\downarrow$$
$$\qquad [\!] \; x2 \rightarrow x\downarrow; \; [\neg x]; \; do\uparrow; \; [\neg x2]; \; do\downarrow$$
$$\qquad]] \, .$$

The implementation is shown in Figure 18.

20.2 *Input Actions on an Active Port*

For port C active, the communication variables of the interface I_C remain the same. But now the handshaking expansions of C' and D are different, since C' is passive and D is active. We get

$$S_C \; \equiv \; *[[co']; \; ci'\uparrow; \; [\neg co']; \; ci'\downarrow]$$
$$S_D \; \equiv \; *[do\uparrow; \; [di1 \vee di2]; \; do\downarrow; \; [\neg di1 \wedge \neg di2]]$$
$$S_X \; \equiv \; *[[di1 \rightarrow x\uparrow; \; [x] \; [\!] \; di2 \rightarrow x\downarrow; \; [\neg x]]] \, .$$

Figure 18.   Input actions on passive port.

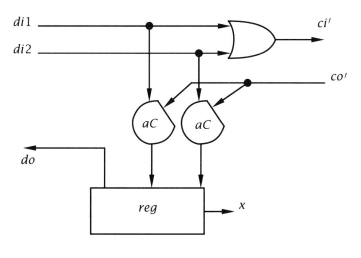

(Observe that S_X is not changed.) An interleaving of S_C and S_D that implements $C' \bullet D$ is the interleaving corresponding to two wires:

$$*[[co']; \ do\uparrow; \ [di1 \lor di2]; \ ci'\uparrow; \ [\neg co']; \ do\downarrow; \ [\neg di1 \land \neg di2]; \ ci'\downarrow] \ .$$

As to the implementation of the assignment to x, we now observe that, since C and D are active, there is no risk of the assignment to x being started before C is. The interleaving obtained is

$$*[[co']; \ do\uparrow; \quad [di1 \rightarrow x\uparrow \ [] \ di2 \rightarrow x\downarrow]; \tag{32}$$
$$ci'\uparrow; \ [\neg co']; \ do\downarrow; \ [\neg di1 \land \neg di2]; \ ci'\downarrow] \ ,$$

which can be factored into the wire

$$(co' \ \underline{w} \ do) \ \equiv \ *[[co']; \ do\uparrow; \ [\neg co']; \ do\downarrow]$$

and the register

$$(di1, di2) \ \underline{reg} \ (x, ci') \ \equiv \ *[[di1 \rightarrow x\uparrow; \ [x]; \ ci'\uparrow; \ [\neg di1]; \ ci'\downarrow$$
$$[] \ di2 \rightarrow x\downarrow; \ [\neg x]; \ ci'\uparrow; \ [\neg di2]; \ ci'\downarrow$$
$$]] \ .$$

The implementation of the interface is shown in Figure 19.

Figure 19.   Input actions on active port.

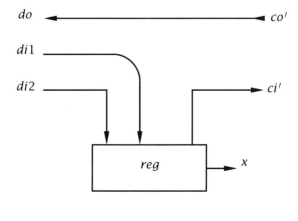

20.3 *Output Actions*

In the case of an output, like *out*!*x* or *put*!*x*, the implementation turns out to be the same for passive and active ports. Given the same nomenclature as in the input case, port D is now implemented with two output variables, $do1$ and $do2$, and one input variable, di. Port C' is not changed. The rest of the derivation is straightforward and is left as an exercise for the reader. It leads to a wire and a *read* operator, which we have introduced in the implementation of the register:

$$di \underline{w} cin \quad \equiv \quad *[[di]; \; ci'\!\uparrow; \; [\neg di]; \; ci'\!\downarrow]$$

$$(co', x) \; \underline{read} \, (do1, do2) \quad \equiv \quad *[[x \wedge co' \to do1\!\uparrow; \; [\neg co']; \; do1\!\downarrow$$

$$[] \; \neg x \wedge co' \to do2\!\uparrow; \; [\neg co']; \; do2\!\downarrow$$

$$]] \, .$$

The only difference between the active and the passive cases is that, in the active case, the *read* is activated first. In the passive case, the wire is activated first. The circuit is shown in Figure 20.

20.4 *Active Input and Passive Output*

A somewhat surprising result of this implementation of input and output commands is that, contrary to common belief, it is simpler to implement in-

Figure 20.   Output-action interface.

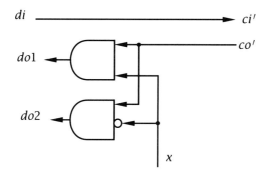

put commands with active ports than with passive ports. The gain is quite important: For *n* bits of data, the active implementation saves $2 \times n$ asymmetric C-elements and *n* or-gates. On the other hand, the implementation of output actions is the same for active and passive ports.

Therefore, we shall always implement input actions with active ports. When the input port is probed, like *in* in the stack example, we shall use a slightly more complicated implementation of the handshaking protocol that makes it possible to probe an active port.

20.5 *Lazy-Active Protocol*

Consider the active implementation of communication command *X*:

$xo\uparrow; [xi]; xo\downarrow; [\neg xi]$.

We introduce an alternative active protocol, called *lazy-active*:

$[\neg xi]; xo\uparrow; [xi]; xo\downarrow$.

The lazy-active protocol is derived from the active one by postponing wait action $[\neg xi]$ until the beginning of the next communication on *X*, and by adding a vacuous wait action $[\neg xi]$ at the beginning of the first communication *X*. Hence, the lazy-active protocol is a correct implementation.

Consider sequence $X; S$, where *S* is an arbitrary program part. With *X* lazy-active, half of the communication delays overlap with the execution of *S*. The gain is particularly important when data communication is involved, since half of the data-transmission delays and half of the "completion-tree" delays can overlap with the rest of the computation.

This important property of lazy-active protocols was discovered recently by Steve Burns. All input actions are now implemented as lazy-active. We have not done so in the stack, which is an older design.

21 *The Complete Circuit for the Stack*

The sharing of register *x* by ports *in* and *get* has to be implemented either by a multiplexer or by a multiport flip-flop. Since only two ports share the register, we choose to use a dual-port flip-flop. The complete datapath is shown in Figure 21.

The complete circuit obtained by composing the different parts together is shown in Figure 22. An important optimization has been added to the design. It concerns the implementation of the second guard of *E*:

$$\overline{out} \rightarrow get?x;\ out!x\,.$$

We observe that the value of *x* involved in the second action (*out!x*) is the same as the value of *x* involved in the first action (*get?x*). We can therefore encode the transmitted value in the handshaking expansion of the guarded command without having to use register *x*. We are tempted to make this optimization available to the programmer by allowing assignments to ports. We would then write

$$\overline{out} \rightarrow out!get\,.$$

The preceding modification leads to a significant simplification of the circuit since we can eliminate a D-element, and, *for each bit of the data path*, we can eliminate an IF-element and replace the multiport flip-flop with a simple flip-flop. The chip we have fabricated includes this modification, as well as the optimization that consists in making input port *in* active.

Figure 21.   The complete datapath.

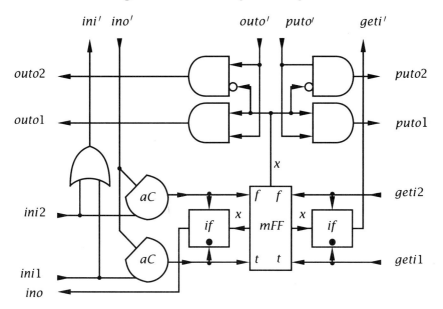

Figure 22.   The complete circuit for a one-bit stack element.

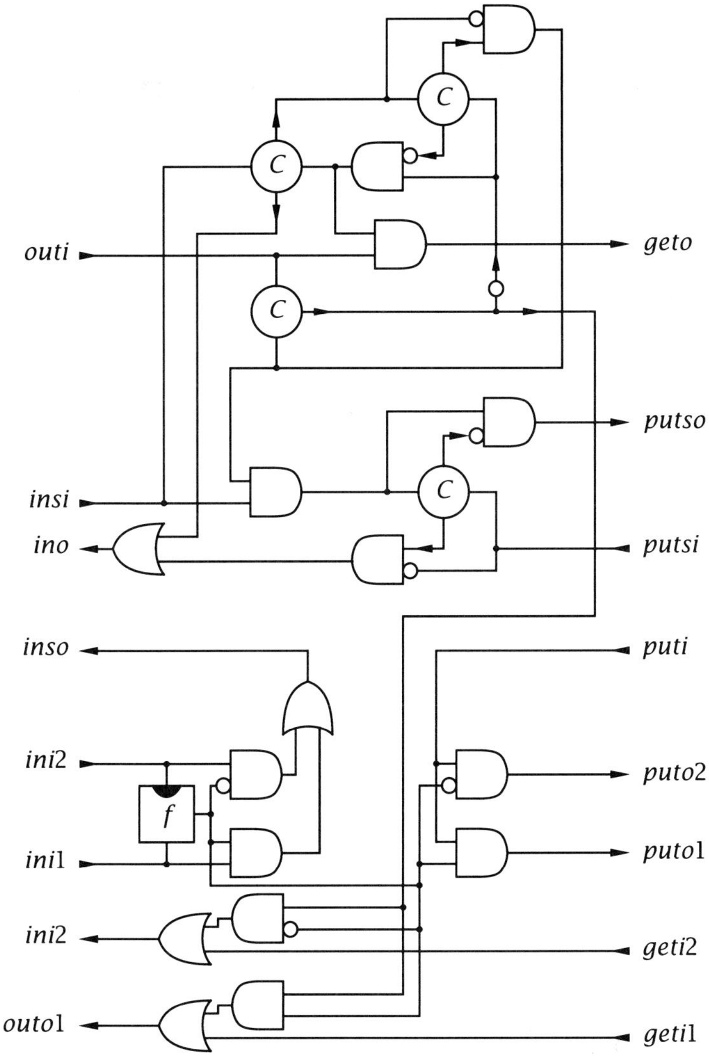

22 *A Delay-Insensitive Fair Arbiter*

This last example addresses the issues of arbitration between guards and unstable guards. We have already discussed the metastability property of arbiters. The realization of a delay-insensitive arbiter, however, raises another issue: fairness. An arbiter is *strongly fair* when a pending communication request is granted after a bounded number of other requests are granted. An arbiter is *weakly fair* when a request is granted after a finite but possibly unbounded number of other requests. Whether it is possible to construct a delay-insensitive fair arbiter has been, so far, an open question. It has been conjectured that delay-insensitive fair arbiters do not exist. In this example, we prove the existence of delay-insensitive fair arbiters by constructing one.

22.1 *A Fair-Arbiter Program*

The process *fsel* described in the first part defines a fair arbitration program between two unrelated inputs. We choose to implement the following simplified version of *fsel*:

$$* \, [[\overline{A} \rightarrow A[] \, \neg A \rightarrow \textbf{skip}]; [B \rightarrow B[] \, \neg B \rightarrow \textbf{skip}]] \, . \tag{33}$$

According to (33), when $\overline{A}$ holds, A will be completed after at most one B action, regardless of the current state of the computation. Hence, the arbiter is strongly fair towards requests A and B. Assume that A' is pending at a certain point of the computation. By definition of the probe, $\overline{A}$ is **true** eventually; i.e., a finite but unbounded number of B actions can be completed between the moment $\textbf{q}A'$ holds and the moment $\overline{A}$ holds. Hence, the arbiter is only *weakly* fair towards requests A' and B'.

Therefore, *with this definition of suspension of an action*, we can say that the arbiter is strongly fair towards requests that have reached the arbiter and weakly fair towards all requests. (We could redefine the suspension of a communication action X such that $\textbf{q}X$ holds only when the initiation of action X can be observed by the other process. With this definition of suspension, we have $\textbf{q}A' = \overline{A}$. The arbiter is then strongly fair towards all requests.)

22.2 *The Compilation*

Applying the process decomposition rule, we decompose (33) into three processes ($P1 \parallel P2 \parallel P3$). Channels (C, D) between $P1$ and $P2$, and (E, F) between

$P1$ and $P3$ are introduced:

$$P1 \equiv *[E; C]$$

$$P2 \equiv *[[\overline{D} \wedge \overline{B} \rightarrow B; D$$
$$[] \overline{D} \wedge \neg B \rightarrow D$$
$$]]$$

$$P3 \equiv *[[\overline{F} \wedge \overline{A} \rightarrow A; F$$
$$[] \overline{F} \wedge \neg A \rightarrow F$$
$$]] .$$

Ports D and F are implemented as passive; ports C and E are implemented as active. Hence $P1$ is the standard active-active buffer. The handshaking expansion of $P2$ gives

$$P2 \equiv *[[di \wedge bi \rightarrow bo\uparrow; [\neg bi]; bo\downarrow; do\uparrow; [\neg di]; do\downarrow$$
$$[] di \wedge \neg bi \rightarrow do\uparrow; [\neg di]; do\downarrow$$
$$]] .$$

Because bi can change from **false** to **true** asynchronously, the second guard of $P2$ is not stable; i.e., its value can change from **true** to **false** at any time. In order to make both guards of $P2$ stable, we introduce the synchronizer

$$sync \equiv *[[di \wedge bi \rightarrow u\uparrow; [\neg di]; u\downarrow$$
$$[] di \wedge \neg bi \rightarrow v\uparrow; [\neg di]; v\downarrow$$
$$]] .$$

Sync is the standard operator we have described in Part I. We now have to find a process, X, such that $(X\|sync) = P2$. Since *sync* is entirely defined, we would like to be able to perform the inverse operation of $\|$, or "process quotient", so as to compute X as $X = (P2 \div sync)$. A way to perform this quotient is to remove all actions of *sync* from $P2$, and then to check whether the result fulfills $(X\|sync) = P2$.

To perform the quotient as suggested, $P2$ should be extended to contain all actions of *sync*, so that the orders of actions are compatible in *sync* and in the extended version of $P2$. (This procedure is explained in [10].) The extension of *P2* gives

$$*[[\ di \wedge bi \rightarrow u\uparrow;\ [u];\ bo\uparrow;\ [\neg bi];\ bo\downarrow;\ do\uparrow;\ [\neg di];\ u\downarrow;\ [\neg u];\ do\downarrow$$

$$[\!]\ di \wedge \neg bi \rightarrow v\uparrow;\ [v];\ do\uparrow;\ [\neg di];\ v\downarrow;\ [\neg v];\ do\downarrow$$

$$]]\ .$$

We obtain for *X*

$$*[[u \rightarrow bo\uparrow;\ [\neg bi];\ bo\downarrow;\ do\uparrow;\ [\neg u];\ do\downarrow$$

$$[\!]\ v \rightarrow do\uparrow;\ [\neg v];\ do\downarrow$$

$$]]\ .$$

The compilation of the first guarded command is facilitated if transition $bo\downarrow$ is postponed until after $[\neg u]$. This transformation does not introduce deadlock since the completion of *D* does not depend on the completion of *B*. After this transformation, the PR expansion gives

$$
\begin{array}{rclcrcl}
u & \mapsto & bo\uparrow & \quad & \neg u & \mapsto & bo\downarrow \\
u \wedge \neg bi & \mapsto & do\uparrow & \quad & v & \mapsto & do\uparrow \\
bi \vee \neg u & \mapsto & do\downarrow & \quad & \neg v & \mapsto & do\downarrow\ .
\end{array}
$$

The operator reduction, which includes the introduction of auxiliary variables do' and do'', gives

$$
\begin{array}{rcl}
u & \underline{w} & bo \\
(u, \neg bi) & \underline{\wedge} & do' \\
v & \underline{w} & do'' \\
(do', do'') & \underline{\vee} & do\ .
\end{array}
$$

The circuit is shown in Figure 23. The implementation of *P3* is identical.

22.3 *The Circuit*

The final circuit, shown in Figure 24, is obtained by composing the two identical circuits implementing *P2* and *P3* with the circuit of *P1*. The reshuffled version of *P1*, consisting of a wire and an inverter, can also be used if it can be proved that the reshuffling does not introduce deadlock. The circuit shown in Figure 24 includes a minor optimization that eliminates the negated inputs that are also the output of a fork.

23 *Conclusion*

We have described a method for implementing a concurrent program (a set of communicating processes) as a network of digital operators that can be directly mapped into a delay-insensitive VLSI circuit. The circuit is derived from the program by applying a series of systematic, semantics-preserving transformations that we have compared to compiling. Hence, the circuits are correct by construction, and their logical correctness is independent of the

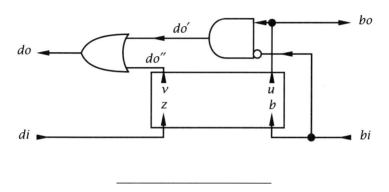

Figure 23. Implementation of *P2*.

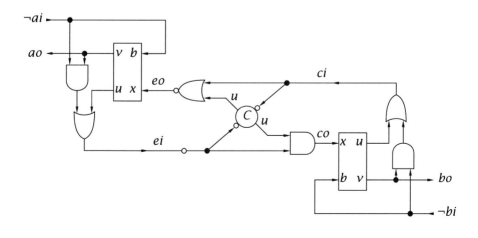

Figure 24. Implementation of the fair arbiter.

delays in operators and wires, with the exception of isochronic forks.

The examples cover most of the constructs of the language but not all of them: We have not shown how to implement an arbitrary set of guards. Therefore, we have not quite shown that *any* program in the language can be compiled. Such a proof has been given in [1] and [2], where the compilation of each construct is described as part of the basic algorithm for an automatic compiler. It is shown that any program in a subset of the language can be implemented as a delay-insensitive circuit using only a small set of basic elements: the two-input C-element, the two-input or-gate or two-input and-gate, the synchronizer, the inverter, and the isochronic fork.

There is no reason, however, for confining the designer to a minimal set of operators. On the contrary, since an advantage of VLSI is the possibility to create operators at no cost, introducing the special-purpose operator that exactly implements an arbitrary set of production rules often simplifies a circuit drastically.

In order to convince the VLSI community of the practicality of our method, it was essential to fabricate the circuits we had designed. Hence, all significant examples that we have used in our research —distributed mutual exclusion, queues, stacks, routing automata for a communication network, the $3X + 1$ engine— have been fabricated in SCMOS using the MOSIS foundry service. They have all be found to be correct on "first silicon". They are also very robust and —given the low level of circuit optimization applied— surprisingly fast. The $3x + 1$ engine, constructed by Tony Lee, is a special-purpose processor consisting of a state-machine and an 80-bit-wide datapath. It contains approximately 40,000 transistors and operates at over 8 MIPS (million instructions per second) in $2\mu m$ MOSIS SCMOS technology.

At the moment of writing, we have just completed the design of the first asynchronous general-purpose microprocessor [12]. It is a 16-bit RISC-like architecture with independent instruction and data memories. It has 16 registers, four buses, an ALU, and two adders. The size is about 20,000 transistors. Two versions have been fabricated: one in $2\mu m$ MOSIS SCMOS, and one in $1.6\mu m$ MOSIS SCMOS. (On the $2\mu m$ version, only 12 registers were implemented in order to fit the chip on an 84-pin $6600\mu m \times 4600\mu m$ package.)

The chips are entirely delay-insensitive, with the sole exception of the interface with the memories and, of course, the isochronic forks. In the absence of available memories with asynchronous interfaces, we have simulated the completion signal from the memories with an external —off-chip— delay. For testing purposes, the delay on the instruction memory interface is variable.

In spite of the presence of floating n-wells, the $2\mu m$ version runs at 12 MIPS. The $1.6\mu m$ version runs at 18 MIPS. (Those performance figures are based on measurements from sequences of ALU instructions without carry. They take no advantage of the overlap between ALU and memory instructions.) Those performances are quite encouraging given that the design is very conservative: no pass-transistors, static gates, dual-rail encoding of data, completion trees, etc.

Only 2 of the 12 2μm chips passed all tests, but 34 of the 50 1.6μm chips were found to be entirely functional.

We have tested the chips under a wide range of *VDD* voltage values. At room temperature, the 2μm version is functional in a voltage range from 7V down to 1V! It reaches 15 MIPS at 7V. We have also tested the chips cooled in liquid nitrogen. The 2μm version reaches 20 MIPS at 5V and 30 MIPS at 12V. The 1.6μm version reaches 30 MIPS at 5V. Of course, these measurements are made without adjusting any clocks (there are none), but simply by connecting the processor to a memory containing a test program and observing the rate of instruction execution. The power consumption is 145mW at 5V, and 6.7mW at 2V.

24 *Acknowledgments*

I am indebted to my students Steve Burns, Dražen Borković, Pieter Hazewindus, Tony Lee, Marcel van der Goot, José Tierno, and Kevin Van Horn for their contributions to the research and their comments on the manuscript. Acknowledgments are also due to Chuck Seitz, Jan van de Snepscheut, Martin Rem, and Huub Schols for numerous discussions on the topic.

References

[1] Burns, S. M. "Automated compilation of concurrent programs into self-timed circuits". Technical Report CS–TR–88–2, M.S. Thesis, Computer Science Department, California Institute of Technology, 1988.

[2] Burns, S. M. and Martin, A. J. "Syntax-directed translation of concurrent programs into self-timed circuits". *Proceedings of the Fifth MIT Conference on Advanced Research in VLSI*, J. Allen and F. Leighton, eds., pp. 35–40. MIT Press, Cambridge, Mass., 1988.

[3] Dijkstra, Edsger W. *A Discipline of Programming*. Prentice-Hall, Englewood Cliffs, N.J., 1976.

[4] Hoare, C. A. R. "Communicating sequential processes". *Communications of the ACM 21*, 8 (August 1978), pp. 666–677.

[5] Martin, A. J. "The probe: An addition to communication primitives". *Information Processing Letters 20* (1985), pp. 125–130.

[6] Martin, A. J. "Compiling communicating process into delay-insensitive VLSI circuits". *Distributed Computing 1*, 4 (1986).

[7] Martin, A. J. "A delay-insensitive fair arbiter". Technical Report 5193:TR:85, Computer Science Department, California Institute of Technology, 1985.

[8] Martin, A. J. "FIFO: An exercise in compiling programs into circuits". In *From HDL Description to Guaranteed Correct Circuit Design*, D. Borrione, ed. North-Holland, Amsterdam, 1986.

[9] Martin A. J. "A synthesis method for self-timed VLSI circuits". *ICCD 87: 1987 IEEE International Conference on Computer Design*, pp. 224–229. IEEE Computer Society Press, Los Alamitos, Calif., 1987.

[10] Martin, A. J. "Formal program transformations for VLSI circuit synthesis". In *Formal Development of Programs and Proofs*, E. W. Dijkstra, ed. Addison-Wesley, Reading, Mass., 1989.

[11] Martin, A. J. "The limitations to delay-insensitivity in asynchronous circuits". *Proceedings of the Sixth MIT Conference on Advanced Research in VLSI*, W. J. Dally, ed. MIT Press, Cambridge, Mass., 1990.

[12] Martin, A. J., Burns, S. M., Lee, T.K., Borkovic, D., and Hazewindus, P. J. "The design of an asynchronous microprocessor". *Decennial Caltech Conference on VLSI*, C. L. Seitz, ed., pp. 351–373. MIT Press, Cambridge, Mass., 1989.

[13] May, D. "Compiling occam into silicon". This volume (Chapter 3).

[14] Mead, C. and Conway, L. *Introduction to VLSI Systems*. Addison-Wesley, Reading, Mass., 1980.

[15] Miller, R. E. *Switching Theory*, Vol. 2. Wiley, New York, 1965.

[16] Seitz, C. L. "System timing." *Introduction to VLSI systems*. Chapter 7 of [14].

[17] Snepscheut, J. v. d. *Trace Theory and VLSI Design*. Lecture Notes in Computer Science, vol. 200. Springer-Verlag, Berlin, 1985.

[18] Weste, N. and Eshraghian, K. *Principles of CMOS VLSI Design*. Addison-Wesley, Reading, Mass., 1985.

Occam and the Transputer[1]

2

David May
INMOS, Ltd.

1 *Introduction*

The occam programming language [4] enables an application to be described as a collection of processes that operate concurrently and communicate through channels. In such a description, each occam process describes the behavior of one component of the implementation, and each channel describes a connection between components.

The design of occam allows the components and their connections to be implemented in many different ways. This allows the implementation technique to be chosen to suit available technology, to optimize performance, or to minimize cost.

A number of processes can be combined by occam's parallel construct, which allows them to be executed concurrently. Concurrent processes communicate through channels by performing inputs and outputs. Mutual exclu-

---

sion is provided by an alternative construct which allows input from any one of a set of channels.

2 *Architecture*

Many programming languages and algorithms depend on the existence of the uniformly accessible memory provided by a conventional computer. Within the computer, memory addressing is implemented by a global communication system such as a bus. The major disadvantage of such an approach is that speed of operation is reduced as system size increases. The reduction in speed arises both from the increased capacitance of the bus, which slows down every bus cycle, and from bus contention.

The aim of occam is to remove this difficulty by enabling arbitrarily large systems to be expressed in terms of localized processing and communication. The effective use of concurrency requires new algorithms designed to exploit this locality.

The main design objective of occam was therefore to provide a language that could be directly implemented by a network of processing elements, and could directly express concurrent algorithms. In many respects, occam is intended as an assembly language for such systems; there is a one-one relationship between occam processes and processing elements, and between occam channels and links between processing elements.

2.1 *Locality*

Almost every operation performed by a process involves access to a variable, and so it is desirable to provide each processing element with local memory in the same VLSI device.

The speed of communication between electronic devices is optimized by the use of one-directional signal wires, each connecting only two devices. This provides local communication between pairs of devices.

Occam can express the locality of processing, in that each process has local variables; it can express the locality of communication, in that each channel connects only two processes.

3 *Simulated and Real Concurrency*

Many concurrent languages have been designed to provide simulated concurrency. This is not surprising, since until recently it has not been economically feasible to build systems with a lot of real concurrency.

Because almost anything can be simulated by a sequential computer, there is no guarantee that a language designed to provide simulated concurrency will be relevant to the needs of systems with real concurrency. The choice of features in such languages has been motivated largely by the need to share one computer among many independent tasks. In contrast, the choice of features in occam has been motivated by the need to use many communicating computers to perform a single task.

An important objective in the design of occam was to use the same concurrent programming techniques both for a single computer and for a network of computers. In practice, this meant that the choice of features in occam was partly determined by the need for an efficient distributed implementation. Once this had been achieved, only simple modifications were needed to ensure an efficient implementation of concurrency on a single sequential computer. This approach to the design of occam perhaps explains some of the differences between occam and other "concurrent" languages.

4 *Occam*

Occam programs are built from three primitive processes:

v := e	assign expression **e** to variable **v**
c ! e	output expression **e** to channel **c**
c ? v	input variable **v** from channel **c**

The primitive processes are combined to form constructs:

SEQ	sequence
IF	conditional
WHILE	loop
PAR	parallel
ALT	alternative

A construct is itself a process, and may be used as a component of another construct.

Conventional sequential programs can be expressed with variables and assignments, combined in sequential and conditional constructs. The order of expression evaluation is unimportant, because there are no side effects and operators always yield a value.

Conventional iterative programs can be written using a while loop. The absence of explicit transfers of control in a modern programming language probably needs no justification; in occam it also removes the need to prohibit, or to define the effect of, transfer of control out of a parallel component or procedure.

Concurrent programs make use of channels —i.e., inputs and outputs—combined using parallel and alternative constructs.

The definition and use of occam procedures follows ALGOL-like scope rules, with channel, variable, and value parameters. The body of an occam procedure may be any process, sequential or parallel. To ensure that expression evaluation has no side effects and always terminates, occam does not include functions.

A very simple example of an occam program is the following buffer process:

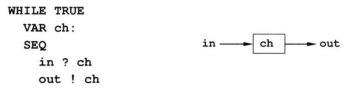

```
WHILE TRUE
    VAR ch:
    SEQ                          in ──────▶│ ch │─────▶ out
        in ? ch
        out ! ch
```

Indentation is used to indicate program structure. The buffer consists of an endless loop, first setting the variable **ch** to a value from the channel **in**, and then outputting the value of **ch** to the channel **out**. The variable **ch** is declared by **VAR ch**. The direct correspondence between the program text and the pictorial representation is important, because a picture of the processes (processors) and their connections is often a useful starting point in the design of a concurrent algorithm that can be implemented efficiently.

4.1 *The Parallel Construct*

The components of a parallel construct may not share access to variables, and communicate only through channels. Each channel provides one-way communication between two components; one component may only output to the channel and the other may only input from it. These rules are checked by the compiler.

The parallel construct specifies that the component processes are "executed together". This means that the primitive components may be interleaved in any order. More formally,

```
PAR                    SEQ
    SEQ          =         x := e
        x := e            PAR
        P                     P
    Q                     Q
```

so the initial assignments of two concurrent processes may be executed in sequence until both processes start with an input or output. If one process starts with an input on channel **c** and the other an output on the same channel **c**, communication takes place:

```
PAR                    SEQ
   SEQ        =           x := e
      c ! e                 PAR
      P                       P
   SEQ                        Q
      c ? x
      Q
```

The preceding rule states that communication can be thought of as a distributed assignment.

Two examples of the parallel construct follow:

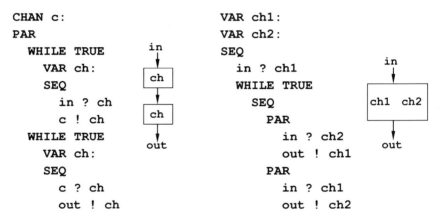

```
CHAN c:                   VAR ch1:
PAR                       VAR ch2:
   WHILE TRUE                 SEQ
      VAR ch:                    in ? ch1
      SEQ                        WHILE TRUE
         in ? ch                   SEQ
         c ! ch                       PAR
   WHILE TRUE                            in ? ch2
      VAR ch:                            out ! ch1
      SEQ                             PAR
         c ? ch                          in ? ch1
         out ! ch                        out ! ch2
```

The first consists of two concurrent versions of the previous example, joined by a channel to form a "double buffer". The second is perhaps a more conventional version. As "black boxes", each with an input and an output channel, the behavior of these two programs is identical; only their internals differ.

4.2 *Synchronized Communication*

Synchronized, zero-buffered communication greatly simplifies programming, and can be implemented efficiently. In fact, such communication corresponds directly to the conventions of self-timed signalling [7]. Zero-buffered communication eliminates the need for message buffers and queues. Synchronized communication prevents accidental loss of data arising from programming errors. In an unsynchronized scheme, failure to acknowledge data often results in a program that is sensitive to scheduling and timing effects.

Synchronized communication requires that one process must wait for the other. A process that requires processing to continue while communicating, however, can easily be written:

```
PAR
  c ! x
  P
```

4.3 *The Alternative Construct*

In occam programs, it is sometimes necessary for a process to input from any one of several other concurrent processes. This could have been provided by a channel "test", which is true if the channel is ready, false otherwise. This is unsatisfactory, however, because it requires a process to poll its inputs "busily"; in some (but by no means all) cases this is inefficient.

Consequently, occam includes an alternative construct similar to that of CSP [3]. As in CSP, each component of the alternative starts with a guard— an input, possibly accompanied by a boolean expression. From an implementation point of view, the alternative has the advantage that it can be implemented either "busily" by a channel test or by a "nonbusy" scheme. The alternative enjoys a number of useful semantic properties more fully discussed elsewhere [8, 9]; in particular, the formal relationship between parallel and alternative is shown by

```
                                ALT
                                  c ? x
                                    PAR
PAR                                   P
  SEQ                                 SEQ
    c ? x                               d ? y
    P            =                      Q
  SEQ                               d ? y
    d ? y                             PAR
    Q                                   Q
                                        SEQ
                                          c ? x
                                          P
```

This equivalence states that if two concurrent processes are both ready to input (communicate) on different channels, then either input (communication) may be performed first.

One feature of CSP omitted from occam is the automatic failure of a guard when the process connected to the other end of the channel terminates. Although this is a convenient programming feature, it complicates the channel communication protocol, introducing the need for further kinds of messages. In addition, it can be argued that many programs are clearer if termination is expressed explicitly.

A simple example of the alternative is the "stoppable" buffer program

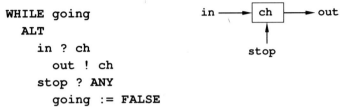

```
WHILE going
  ALT
    in ? ch
      out ! ch
    stop ? ANY
      going := FALSE
```

in which **stop ? ANY** inputs any value from the channel **stop**, and as a result causes the loop to terminate.

4.4 *Output Guards*

Output guards are a very convenient programming tool. In particular, they allow programs such as the following buffer process to be written in a natural way.

```
WHILE TRUE
  ALT
    count>0 & output ! buff [ outpointer ]
      SEQ
        outpointer := (outpointer + 1) REM max
        count := count - 1
    count<max & input ? buff [ inpointer ]
      SEQ
        inpointer := (inpointer + 1) REM max
        count := count + 1
```

It is very tempting to include output guards in a communicating-process language, and attempts have been made to include output guards in occam. The major difficulty is in the distributed implementation. In a program such as

```
PAR
  ALT
    c ! x1
    d ? x2
  ALT
    c ? y1
    d ! y2
```

what is expected to happen in the event that two identical processors both
enter their alternative at exactly the same time? Clearly some asymmetry
must be introduced; the easiest way to do this is to give each processor in
a system a unique number. Even so, the provision of output guards greatly
complicates the communication protocol. For this reason, output guards are
omitted from occam, and the preceding buffer must be written as follows:

```
PAR
  WHILE TRUE
    ALT
      count>0 & req ? ANY
        SEQ
          reply ! buff [ outpointer ]
          outpointer := (outpointer + 1) REM max
          count := count - 1
      count<max & input ? buff [ inpointer ]
        SEQ
          inpointer := (inpointer + 1) REM max
          count := count + 1
  WHILE TRUE
    SEQ
      req ! ANY
      reply ? ch
      output ! ch
```

It would be possible to use an occam implementation with only input
guards to write the communications kernel for a "higher-level" version of
occam with output guards. An example of an algorithm to implement output
guards in CSP is given in [2]; an example for occam is given in [1].

4.5 *Channels and Hierarchical Decomposition*

An important feature of occam is the ability to successively decompose a
process into concurrent component processes. This is the main reason for the
use of named communication channels in occam. Once a named channel is
established between two processes, neither process need have any knowledge
of the internal details of the other. Indeed, the internal structure of each
process can change during execution of the program.

The parallel construct, together with named channels, provides for decomposition of an application into a hierarchy of communicating processes,
enabling occam to be applied to large-scale applications. This technique can-

not be used in languages that use process (or "entry") names, rather than channels, for communication.

In specifying the behavior of a process, it is important that a specification of the protocol used on the channel exists; the best way to do this varies from program to program (or even from channel to channel!). For example, Backus-Naur Form is often suitable for describing the messages that pass between the individual processes of a linear pipeline of processes. On the other hand, for more complex interactions between processes, it is often useful to describe the interactions by an occam "program" in which all unnecessary features are omitted. This often enables the interactions between processes to be studied independently of the data values manipulated. For example:

```
SEQ
   request ?
   WHILE TRUE
     PAR
        reply !
        request ?
```

describes a process which inputs a request and then endlessly inputs a new request and outputs a reply, in either order. Such a process would be compatible, in some sense, with any of the following processes:

```
WHILE TRUE            SEQ                   SEQ
   SEQ                   request !             request !
      request !          WHILE TRUE            WHILE TRUE
      reply ?              SEQ                   PAR
                             request !              request !
                             reply ?                reply ?
```

More design aids are needed to assist in the specification and checking of channel protocols. The protocol declarations of the recently introduced occam2 language [5] are a step in this direction.

4.6 *Arrays and Replicators*

In common with most languages, occam includes arrays and "for" loops. In occam the conventional **FOR** loop is generalized and its semantics simplified. An occam "replicator" can be used with any of **SEQ**, **PAR**, **ALT**, and **IF**; its meaning is defined by:

```
X n = b FOR c      =        X
    P (n)                        P (b)
                                 P (b+1)
                                 . . .
                                 P (b+c-1)
```

where **X** is one of **SEQ**, **PAR**, **ALT**, and **IF**, **n** is a name, and **b** and **c** are expressions. This definition implicitly defines the "control variable" **n**, and prevents it from being changed by assignments within **P**.

The introduction of arrays of variables and channels does complicate the rules governing the correct use of channels and variables. Simple compile-time checks that are not too restrictive are as follows:

> No array changed by assignment (to one of its components) in any of the components of a parallel may be used in any other component.

> No two components of a parallel may select channels from the same array using variable subscripts.

> A component of a parallel that uses an array for both input and output may not select channels from the array using variable subscripts,

where a variable subscript is a subscript that cannot be evaluated by the compiler.

4.7 *Time*

The treatment of time in occam directly matches the behavior of a conventional alarm clock.

Time itself is represented in occam by values that cycle through all possible integer values. Of course, it would have been possible to represent time by a value large enough (say 64 bits) to remove the cyclic behaviour, but this would require the use of multiple-length arithmetic to maintain the clock and is probably not justified.

Using an alarm clock, it is possible at any time to observe the current time or to wait until the alarm goes off. Similarly, a process must be able to read the clock at any time or to wait until a particular time. If it were possible only to read the clock, a program could only wait until a particular time "busily". Like the alternative construct, the "wait-until-a-time" operation has the advantage that it can be implemented "busily" or "nonbusily".

A timer is declared in the same way as a channel or variable. This gives rise to a relativistic concept of time, with different timers being used in different parts of a program. A localized timer is much easier to implement than a global timer.

A timer is read by a special "input"

```
time ? v
```

which is always ready, and sets the variable **v** to the time. Similarly, the "input"

```
time ? AFTER t
```

waits until time **t**.

The use in occam of absolute times instead of delays simplifies the construction of programs such as

```
WHILE TRUE
  SEQ
    time ? AFTER t
    t := t + interval
    output ! bell
```

in which **n** rings of the bell will always take between **(n*interval)** and **n*(interval+1)** ticks. This would not be true of a program such as

```
WHILE TRUE
  SEQ
    DELAY interval
    output ! bell
```

because of the time taken to ring the bell.

It is not possible for an occam process to implement a timer. This would require a "timer output" such as

```
timer ! PLUS n
```

which advances the timer by **n** ticks. There is no obvious reason why this feature could not be included in occam. It would be particularly useful in constructing timers of different rates, or in writing a process to provide "simulated time".

4.8 *Types and Data Structures*

The occam described so far makes few assumptions about data types. Any data type could be used, provided that values of that type can be assigned, input, and output according to the rule

```
PAR
  c ! x      =      y := x
  c ? y
```

To preserve this rule, and to keep the implementation of communication simple, assignment does not make type conversions.

The initial version of occam provides untyped variables and one-dimensional arrays. No addressing operations are provided, because this would make it impossible for the compiler to check that no variables are shared between concurrent processes.

Occam has been extended to include data types. The simple variable is replaced with boolean, byte, and integer types, and multidimensional arrays are provided. Communication and assignment operate on variables of any data type, allowing arrays to be communicated and assigned.

A detailed description can be found in [5].

5 *The Transputer Implementation of Occam*

VLSI technology allows large numbers of identical devices to be manufactured cheaply. For this reason, it is attractive to implement an occam program using a number of identical components, each programmed with the appropriate occam process. A transputer [6] is such a component.

A transputer is a single VLSI device with memory, processor, and communications links for direct connection to other transputers. Concurrent systems can be constructed from a collection of transputers that operate concurrently and communicate through links.

The transputer can therefore be used as a building block for concurrent processing systems, with occam as the associated design formalism.

5.1 *Transputer Architecture*

An important property of VLSI technology is that communication between devices is very much slower than communication on the same device. In a computer, almost every operation that the processor performs involves the use of memory. A transputer therefore includes both processor and memory in the same integrated-circuit device.

In any system constructed from integrated-circuit devices, much of the physical bulk arises from connections between devices. The size of the package for an integrated circuit is determined more by the number of connection pins than by the size of the device itself. In addition, connections between devices provided by paths on a circuit board consume a considerable amount of space.

The speed of communication between electronic devices is optimized by the use of one-directional signal wires, each connecting two devices. If many devices are connected by a shared bus, electrical problems of driving the bus require that the speed be reduced. Also, additional control logic and wiring is required to control sharing of the bus.

To provide maximum speed with minimal wiring, the transputer uses point-to-point serial communication links, rather than buses, for direct connection to other transputers.

5.2 *The Transputer*

A transputer system consists of a number of interconnected transputers, each executing an occam process and communicating with other transputers. Because a process executed by a transputer may itself consist of a number of concurrent processes, the transputer has to support the occam programming model internally. Within a transputer, concurrent processing is implemented by sharing the processor time between the concurrent processes.

The most effective implementation of simple programs by a programmable computer is provided by a sequential processor. Consequently, the transputer processor is fairly conventional, except that additional hardware and microcode support the occam model of concurrent processing.

5.3 *Occam Implementation*

For run-time efficiency, the advantages of allocating processors and memory at compile time are clear. To allow the compiler to allocate memory, some implementation restrictions are imposed. Firstly, the number of components of an array, and the number of concurrent processes created by a parallel replicator, must be known at compile time. Secondly, no recursive procedures are allowed. The effect of these restrictions is that the compiler can establish the amount of space needed for the execution of each component of a parallel construct, making the construct's run-time overhead very small.

On the other hand, there is nothing in occam itself to prevent an implementation without these restrictions, and this would be fairly straightforward for a single computer with dynamic memory allocation.

5.4 *Sequential Processing*

The design of the transputer processor exploits the availability of fast on-chip memory by having only a small number of registers; six registers are used in the execution of a sequential process. The small number of registers, together with the simplicity of the instruction set, enables the processor to have relatively simple (and fast) datapaths and control logic.

The six registers are:

The workspace pointer, which points to an area of store where local variables are kept.

The instruction pointer, which points to the next instruction to be executed.

The operand register, which is used in the formation of instruction operands.

The A, B, and C registers, which form an evaluation stack and are the sources and destinations for most arithmetic and logical operations. Loading a value into the stack pushes B into C, and A into B, before loading A. Storing a value from A pops B into A and C into B.

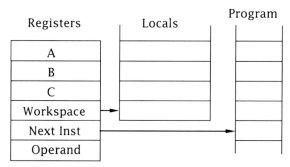

Expressions are evaluated on the evaluation stack, and instructions refer to the stack implicitly. For example, the "add" instruction adds the top two values in the stack and places the result on the top of the stack. Statistics gathered from a large number of programs show that three registers provide an effective balance between code compactness and implementation complexity.

No hardware mechanism is provided to detect that more than three values have been loaded onto the stack. It is easy for the compiler to introduce temporary workspace variables to ensure that this never happens.

5.5 *Support for Concurrency*

The processor provides efficient support for the occam model of concurrency and communication. It has a microcoded scheduler, which enables any number of concurrent processes to be executed together, sharing the processor time. This removes the need for a software kernel. The processor does not need to support the dynamic allocation of storage as the occam compiler is able to perform the allocation of space to concurrent processes.

At any time, a concurrent process may be

    Active: • Being executed

                 • On a list waiting to be executed

    Inactive: • Ready to input

                 • Ready to output

                 • Waiting until a specified time

The scheduler operates in such a way that inactive processes consume no processor time.

The active processes waiting to be executed are held on a list. This is a linked list of process workspaces implemented using two registers, one of which points to the first process on the list and the other to the last. In the illustration in Figure 1, S is executing and P, Q, and R are active, awaiting execution.

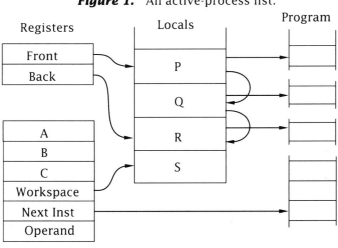

Figure 1. An active-process list.

A process is executed until it is unable to proceed because it is waiting to input or output, or waiting for the timer. Whenever a process is unable to proceed, its instruction pointer is saved in its workspace and the next process is taken from the list. Actual process-switch times are very small because little state needs to be saved; it is not necessary to save the evaluation stack on rescheduling.

The processor provides a number of special operations to support the process model. These include "start-process" and "end-process". When a parallel construct is executed, "start-process" instructions are used to create the necessary concurrent processes. A "start-process" instruction creates a new process by adding a new workspace to the end of the scheduling list, enabling the new concurrent process to be executed together with the ones already being executed.

Correct termination of a parallel construct is assured by use of the "end-process" instruction. This uses a workspace location as a counter of the components of the parallel construct that have yet to terminate. The counter is initialized to the number of components before the processes are started. Each component ends with an "end-process" instruction, which decrements and tests the counter. For all but the last component, the counter is nonzero and the component is descheduled. For the last component, the counter is zero and the component continues.

5.6 *Communications*

Communication between processes is achieved by means of channels. Occam communication is point-to-point, synchronized, and unbuffered. As a result, a channel needs no process queue, no message queue, and no message buffer.

A channel between two processes executing on the same transputer is implemented by a single word in memory; a channel between processes executing on different transputers is implemented by point-to-point links. The processor provides a number of operations to support message passing, the most important being "input-message" and "output-message".

A process performs an input or output by loading the evaluation stack with a pointer to a message, the address of a channel, and a count of the number of bytes to be transferred, and then executing an "input-message" or an "output-message" instruction.

The "input-message" and "output-message" instructions use the address of the channel to determine whether the channel is internal or external. This means that the same instruction sequence can be used for both internal and external channels, allowing a process to be written and compiled without knowledge of where its channels are connected.

As in the occam model, communication takes place when the inputting and outputting processes are both ready. Consequently, the process that becomes ready first must wait until the second one is also ready.

5.7 *Internal Channel Communication*

At any time, an internal channel (a single word in memory) holds either the identity of a process or the special value "empty". The channel is initialized to "empty" before it is used.

When a message is passed using the channel, the identity of the first process to become ready is stored in the channel, and the processor starts to execute the next process from the scheduling list. When the second process to use the channel becomes ready, the message is copied, the waiting process is added to the scheduling list, and the channel reset to its initial state. Which of the two processes becomes ready first does not matter.

In the following illustration, a process P is about to execute an output instruction on an "empty" channel C. The evaluation stack holds a pointer to a message, the address of channel C, and a count of the number of bytes in the message.

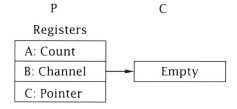

After executing the output instruction, channel C holds the address of P's workspace, and the address of the message to be transferred is stored in P's workspace. P is descheduled, and the processor starts to execute the next process from the scheduling list.

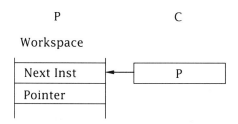

Channel C and process P remain in this state until a second process, Q, executes an output instruction on the channel.

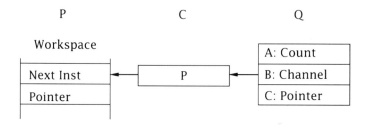

The message is copied, the waiting process P is added to the scheduling list, and channel C is reset to its initial "empty" state.

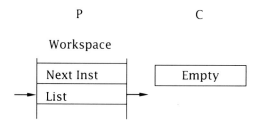

5.8 *External Channel Communication*

When a message is passed via an external channel, the processor delegates to an autonomous link interface the job of transferring the message and deschedules the process. When the message has been transferred, the link interface causes the processor to reschedule the waiting process. This allows the processor to continue the execution of other processes while the external message transfer is taking place.

    Each link interface uses three registers:

1. A pointer to a process workspace,

2. A pointer to a message, and

3. A count of bytes in the message.

    In the following illustration, processes P and Q, which are executed by different transputers, communicate using a channel C implemented by a link connecting two transputers. P outputs, and Q inputs.

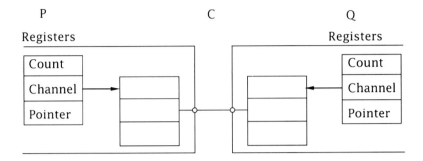

When P executes its output instruction, the registers in the link interface of the transputer executing P are initialized and P is descheduled. Similarly, when Q executes its input instruction, the registers in the link interface of the process executing Q are initialized and Q is descheduled.

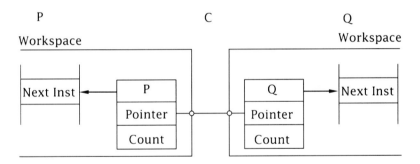

The message is now copied through the link, after which the workspaces of P and Q are returned to the corresponding scheduling lists. The protocol used on P and Q ensures that which of P and Q becomes ready first does not matter.

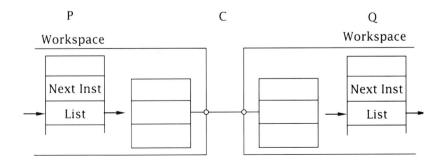

5.9 *Timer*

The transputer has a clock, which "ticks" every microsecond. The current value of the processor clock can be read by executing a "read-timer" instruction.

A process can arrange to perform a "timer-input", in which case it will become ready to execute after a specified time has been reached.

The timer-input instruction requires a time to be specified. If this time is in the "past" (i.e., *ClockReg* **AFTER** *SpecifiedTime*), then the instruction has no effect. If the time is in the "future" (i.e., *SpecifiedTime* **AFTER** *Clockreg* or *SpecifiedTime* = *ClockReg*), then the process is descheduled. When the specified time is reached, the process is scheduled again.

5.10 *Alternative*

The occam alternative construct enables a process to wait for input from any one of a number of channels, or until a specific time occurs. This requires special instructions, because the normal "input" instruction deschedules a process until a specific channel becomes ready, or until a specific time is reached. The instructions used are:

> enable channel
>
> enable timer
>
> disable channel
>
> disable timer
>
> alternative wait

The alternative is implemented by "enabling" the channel input or timer input specified in each of its components. The "alternative wait" is then used to deschedule the process if none of the channel or timer inputs is ready; the process will be rescheduled when any one of them becomes ready. The channel and timer inputs are then "disabled". The "disable" instructions are also designed to select the component of the alternative to be executed; the first component found to be ready is executed.

5.11 *Intertransputer Links*

To provide synchronized communication, each message must be acknowledged. Consequently, a link requires at least one signal wire in each direction.

A link between two transputers is implemented by connecting a link interface on one transputer to a link interface on the other transputer by two one-directional signal lines, along which data is transmitted serially.

The two signal wires of the link can be used to provide two occam channels, one in each direction. This requires a simple protocol. Each signal line carries data and control information.

The link protocol provides occam's synchronized communication. Each message is transmitted as a sequence of single-byte communications, requiring only the presence of a single-byte buffer in the receiving transputer to ensure that no information is lost. Each byte is transmitted as a start bit, a one bit, the eight data bits, and a stop bit. After transmitting a data byte, the sender waits until an acknowledgment is received; this consists of a start bit followed by a zero bit. The acknowledgment signifies both that a process was able to receive the acknowledged byte and that the receiving link is able to receive another byte. The sending link reschedules the sending process only after the acknowledgment for the final byte of the message has been received.

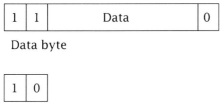

Data byte

Acknowledge message

Data bytes and acknowledgments are multiplexed down each signal line. An acknowledgment is transmitted as soon as reception of a data byte starts (if there is room to buffer another one). Consequently, transmission may be continuous, with no delays between data bytes.

6 *Summary*

The transputer demonstrates that the concurrent processing features of occam can be implemented by a processor that is small, simple, and fast. The time taken for a process to start and terminate is about 1.5 microseconds— an overhead small enough to allow processes consisting of only a few statements. An interprocess communication has a fixed overhead of about 1.5 microseconds and also requires time to transfer the message. Messages are transferred at up to 40 million bytes per second on-chip, and up to 1.8 million bytes per second through a link.

Experience with occam has shown that many applications decompose naturally into a large number of fairly simple processes. Once an application has been described in occam, a variety of implementations are possible. In particular, the use of occam together with the transputer enables the designer to exploit the peformance and economics of VLSI technology.

The transputer therefore has two important uses. First, it provides a new system "building block" which enables occam to be used as a design formalism. In this role, occam serves both as a system description language and as a programming language. Second, occam and the transputer can be used for prototyping highly concurrent systems in which the individual processes are ultimately intended to be implemented by dedicated hardware.

References

[1] Bornat, R. "A protocol for generalised occam". Department of Computer Science, Queen Mary College, London, 1984.

[2] Buckley, G. N. and Silberschatz, A. "An effective implementation for the generalized input-output construct of CSP". *Transactions on Programming Languages and Systems 5*, 2 (April 1983), p. 223–235.

[3] Hoare, C. A. R. "Communicating sequential processes". *Communications of the ACM 21*, 8 (August 1978), p. 666–677.

[4] INMOS, Ltd. *The occam Programming Manual*. Prentice-Hall International, Hemel Hempstead, U.K., 1984.

[5] INMOS, Ltd. *The occam2 Reference Manual*. Prentice-Hall International, Hemel Hempstead, U.K., 1988.

[6] INMOS, Ltd. *The Transputer Reference Manual*. Prentice-Hall International, Hemel Hempstead, U.K., 1988.

[7] Mead, C. A. and Conway, L. A. *Introduction to VLSI Systems*. Addison-Wesley, Reading, Mass., 1980 (Section 5).

[8] Roscoe, A. W. "Denotational semantics for occam". Presented at NSF/SERC Seminar on Concurrency, Carnegie-Mellon University, July 1984.

[9] Roscoe, A. W. and Hoare, C. A. R. "The laws of occam programming". Technical Monograph PRG–53, Oxford University Computing Laboratory, Programming Research Group, 1986.

Compiling Occam into Silicon[1]

3

David May

INMOS, Ltd.

---

1 Introduction

The occam language [2] allows a system to be decomposed hierarchically into a collection of concurrent processes communicating via channels. An occam program can be implemented by a single programmable microcomputer, or by a collection of programmable computers each executing an occam process. An occam process can also be implemented directly in hardware. This paper describes a compiler that translates occam programs into silicon layout.

---

2 *VLSI Design*

In designing a VLSI device, it is useful to have a behavioral description of what the device does, as well as a hardware description of the components of the device and how they are interconnected.

Hardware description languages are used in many computer-aided design systems. The hardware description of a device can be checked against the silicon layout supplied by the designer, and it can be used as input to simulators. The hardware description language used by INMOS allows libraries of standard checked modules to be assembled. All of these techniques combine to remove much of the risk from silicon design once the hardware description of a device has been constructed.

Behavioral description languages have been used to design sequential processors for many years. Because the process of interpreting instructions in a sequential computer is (nearly) sequential, such a processor's behavioral description can be written in a conventional sequential programming language. An advantage of using a programming language for this purpose is that the description of the device can be compiled into an efficient simulator of the device.

The behavior of VLSI devices with many interacting components can be expressed only in a language that can express parallelism and communication. Communicating-process languages are therefore beginning to be used to describe the behavior of such devices. For example, occam has been used extensively for this purpose in the design of the INMOS transputer.

Occam has several advantages as a behavioral description language. First, the concepts of concurrency and communication in occam correspond closely to the behavior of hardware devices. Second, as a programming language occam has a very efficient implementation, enabling fast execution of a system description as a simulation. Third, occam has a rich formal semantics [6] which facilitates program transformation and proof, and a simple interactive transformation system has been constructed. These techniques have been used to formally establish the correctness of an occam implementation of IEEE standard 754 floating-point arithmetic [1], a task that takes too long to be performed by experimental testing. The transformation system can also be used to optimize programs and can, for example, transform certain kinds of sequential programs into equivalent parallel programs, and conversely.

The problem of ensuring that the hardware description of a device indeed implements the behavioral description in occam is a significant one. One possible approach is to write a compiler to compile an occam program into a hardware description.

3 *Occam*

Occam programs are built from three primitive processes:

v := e   assign expression **e** to variable **v**
c ! e   output expression **e** to channel **c**
c ? v   input variable **v** from channel **c**

The primitive processes are combined to form constructs:

SEQ   sequence
IF   conditional
WHILE   loop

PAR   parallel
ALT   alternative

A construct is itself a process, and may be used as a component of another construct.

Conventional sequential programs can be expressed with variables and assignments, combined in sequential and conditional constructs. Conventional iterative programs can be written using a while loop.

Concurrent programs make use of channels, inputs, and outputs, which are combined using parallel and alternative constructs.

In hardware terms, it is useful to think of a variable as a storage register and a channel as a communication path with no storage.

Each occam channel provides a communication path between two concurrent processes. Communication is synchronized and takes place when both the inputting and the outputting processes are ready. The data to be output is then copied from the outputting process to the inputting process, and both processes continue.

An alternative process may be ready to input from any one of a number of channels. In this case, the input is taken from the channel that is first used for output by another process.

4 *Implementation of Occam*

The concepts of sequence and concurrency in occam are abstract and allow a wide variety of implementations. An occam process can be implemented:

1. By compilation into a program for execution by a general purpose computer such as a transputer,

2. With a fixed program held in ROM,

3. By compilation into a special-purpose computer, with just sufficient registers, ALU operations, memory, and microcode to implement the process, or

4. By compilation into "random" logic.

Similarly, the concept of communication is abstract and allows a channel to be implemented in various ways:

1. As store location(s) and a program,

2. As a microprogram instead of a program,

3. As a parallel path with handshaking signals,

4. As a (more) serial version of (3), the communicating processes breaking the data into several pieces, or

5. As a completely serial path.

Any of the preceding can be implemented using any clocking scheme, ranging from a globally synchronous system to a fully self-timed system. It should be possible to mix the implementation techniques within a system, though this requires a range of different channel implementations that operate as "adaptors" to provide communication between processes implemented in different ways.

Implementation of occam processes using programmable computers and transputers has been described elsewhere [4]. Implementation of processes using self-timed circuit elements is the subject of current research, e.g., [3]. This paper concentrates on the compilation of a process into a tailored datapath controlled by compiled microcode. A set of concurrent processes may be compiled into a corresponding set of such machines, with each communication channel implemented by a simple synchronous connection between two machines.

5 *The Abstract Micromachine*

Each process is compiled into a datapath controlled by horizontal microcode. The datapath contains a set of registers connected to an arithmetic logic unit by three buses called the **Xbus**, **Ybus**, and **Zbus**. Each cycle of the machine transfers the contents of two selected registers via the **Xbus** and **Ybus** to the arithmetic logic unit for use as operands, and transfers the result from the logic unit back to a selected register via the **Zbus**.

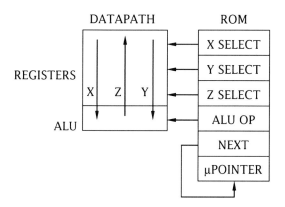

The selection of the registers and of the operation to be performed by the logic unit is determined by four components of a microinstruction held in the read-only memory (ROM). The registers in the datapath are designed so that a single microinstruction can use the same register both as an operand and as the result, but this is not essential (a compiler can easily allocate registers to avoid the need for it). The microinstruction ROM is addressed by a microinstruction-pointer register.

A further "next-address" component of each microinstruction gives the next value of the microinstruction register. The microinstruction pointer register is loaded from this field as each microinstruction is executed. If the process to be implemented consists only of a simple loop with no conditional behavior, the "next-address" field can be omitted and the microinstruction-pointer register can be replaced by an incrementer.

A number of other components of the microinstruction may be needed, depending on the program being compiled. These are described in Section 7.

6 *The Compiler Output*

The compiler makes extensive use of the module library used in the INMOS transputer itself. This library contains all of the hardware modules needed to construct ALUs and registers, together with special control logic for fast multiplication, division, shifts, etc. It also provides for microinstruction-pointer registers, control line drivers, and clock generators. The microcode ROM itself can be generated and optimized automatically from the textual form of the microinstructions. The output of the compiler is therefore:

1. A microprogram ready for input to the ROM generator,

2. An HDL (INMOS hardware-description language) description of the datap-ath, including the fewest registers and the simplest ALU that are sufficient to implement the process, and

3. An "array" file containing information about the physical placement of the modules comprising the datapath.

The output can be input to the INMOS CAD system, enabling logic and circuit simulations to be performed, allowing the layout to be inspected, and ultimately enabling masks to be produced. It is envisaged, however, that the design process would be interactive, and that having inspected the result of a compilation the designer would modify the occam specification (probably using correctness-preserving transformations) and try again.

7 *Variables, Expressions, Assignment, and SEQ*

Values of variables are held in registers, and expressions are evaluated by a sequence of microinstructions of the form described in Section 5.

Expressions also involve "literal" operands, which are compiled directly into "literal" components of microinstructions. It is only necessary to supply each microinstruction with a single literal operand, as any operation involv-ing two literal operands can be performed by the compiler.

The compilation of

```
WHILE TRUE
    P
```

where *P* is a sequence of assignments, therefore proceeds as follows:

1. Identify the number of registers needed. At any point in the program, a number *V* of variables is in scope; each must have a register allocated to it. Also, a number *T* of temporary registers may be needed to hold temporary values arising during the evaluation of complex expressions. The number of registers needed for *P* is the largest value taken by *V+T* in *P*. This is a conventional compiling technique.

2. Identify the operations needed in the arithmetic logic unit. This depends on the expression operators used in the program being compiled. If only bit operators are used, the carry path can be omitted, and it is worthwhile to include

the carry path (adder),

the shifter,

the multiply divide step control logic, and

the conditional logic

only if they are needed. The multiply- and divide-control logic require conditional selection of the next microinstruction to be executed, as described in Section 8.

3. Break all expressions and assignments into a sequence of operations of the form

$$Z := X \text{ op } Y$$

For example:

```
VAR a, b, result:
SEQ
  a := 10
  b := 20
  result := (a + b) - 5
```

generates microcode field definitions to control the registers, the "constants box", and the ALU, in addition to the "next" field. The following example is the definition of the register control field:

```
FIELD "Regfield" Microword[22, 23, 24, 25, 26, 27]
  XbusFromR0    = #B100000
  XbusFromR2    = #B010000
  YbusFromR1    = #B001000
  R0FromZbus    = #B000100
  R1FromZbus    = #B000010
  R2FromZbus    = #B000001;
```

Register **R0** is used for **a**, **R1** for **b**, and **R2** for **result**. **R0** and **R2** can supply data to the X bus, and R1 to the Y bus. All three registers can be loaded from the Z bus.

A microinstruction is constructed by combining values from each of a number of fields; for example,

```
LAB1:  XbusFromR0    YbusFromR1
       ZbusFromXbusPlusYbus   R2FromZbus   LAB2;
```

selects **R0** and **R1** as the sources for the **Xbus** and **Ybus**, respectively; selects the ALU operation as Plus (**ZbusFromXbusPlusYbus**); and selects **R2** as the destination for the result. **LAB2** indicates the next microinstruction to be executed.

The microcode for the preceding program is:

```
START: XbusFrom10    ZbusFromXbus
       R0FromZbus  LAB0;
LAB0:  XbusFrom20    ZbusFromXbus
       R1FromZbus  LAB1;
LAB1:  XbusFromR0    YbusFromR1
       ZbusFromXbusPlusYbus  R2FromZbus   LAB2;
LAB2:  XbusFromR2    YbusFrom5
       ZbusFromXbusMinusYbus R2FromZbus   END;
```

An example of the HDL generated is the following implementation of registers **a**, **b**, and **result**:

```
MODULE Registers (IN  Clocks[4:1], ROMoutputs[27:22],
                      Zbus[31:0],
                  OUT Xbus[31:0], Ybus[31:0])
   Xreg32 R0(IN  Clocks[4:1], ROMoutputs[22],
                 ROMoutputs[25], Zbus[31:0],
             OUT Xbus[31:0])
   Yreg32 R1(IN  Clocks[4:1], ROMoutputs[24],
                 ROMoutputs[26], Zbus[31:0],
             OUT Ybus[31:0])
   Xreg32 R2(IN  Clocks[4:1], ROMoutputs[23],
                 ROMoutputs[27], Zbus[31:0],
             OUT Xbus[31:0])
END REGISTERS
```

which defines the collection of the three registers and their control signals and bus connections. **XReg32** is itself the name of a module that defines a 32-bit register with outputs to the X bus; **YReg32** similarly defines a register with outputs to the Y bus.

8 *IF and WHILE*

The occam IF and WHILE constructs can both be implemented by allowing the address of the next microinstruction to be determined by a selected condition.

Conditional behavior is provided by arranging for the least significant bit of the microinstruction pointer to be loaded from a selected conditional input, the selection being made by a further microinstruction field connected to a multiplexor. To allow unconditional branching, one input from the multiplexor is derived from the least significant bit in the "next-address" field.

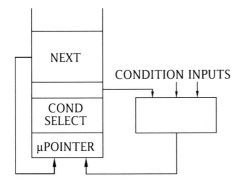

An example is the following process, which computes the greatest common divisor of two numbers:

```
VAR m, n, result:
SEQ
  m := 100
  n := 35
  WHILE (m <> n)
    IF
      (m > n)
        m := m - n
      (m < n)
        n := n - m
    TRUE
      SKIP
  result := m
```

This process generates the following microcode, and requires three registers for **m, n,** and **result**:

```
START: XbusFrom100   ZbusFromXbus
       R0FromZbus   LAB0;
LAB0:  XbusFrom35    ZbusFromXbus
       R1FromZbus   LBL0;
LBL0:  XbusFromR0   YbusFromR1    ZbusFromXbusMinusYbus
```

```
                (CondFromNotZbusEq0 -> LAB1, LBL1);
     LAB1:    XbusFromR1    YbusFromR0    ZbusFromXbusMinusYbus
                (CondFromZbusGr0 -> LBL2, LAB2);
     LAB2:    XbusFromR0    YbusFromR1    ZbusFromXbusMinusYbus
                R0FromZbus   LBL0;
     LBL2:    XbusFromR0    YbusFromR1    ZbusFromXbusMinusYbus
                (CondFromZbusGr0 -> LBL0, LAB3)
     LAB3:    XbusFromR1    YbusFromR0    ZbusFromXbusMinusYbus
                R1FromZbus   LBL0;
     LBL1:    XbusFromR0    ZbusFromXbus
                R2FromZbus   END;
```

9 *Arrays*

Arrays are implemented by including a random-access memory. Indexing operations are provided by constructing the bitwise OR of the base address and the subscript (the base being a literal and the subscript being held in a register), eliminating the need for address arithmetic and enabling a selected component of an array to be transferred to or from a register in a single cycle. The base address of each array in the process is chosen to make this possible, and unused rows are omitted from the memory array.

10 *Procedures*

Occam procedures can be implemented either by substitution of the procedure body before compilation or by a conventional closed procedure call.

Because no recursion is permitted, the maximum depth of calling is known to the compiler, which can compile a stack of microinstruction pointer registers of the appropriate depth.

Registers must be allocated for the variables at each level of procedure calling. A single register can be allocated to several procedures, however, provided that the procedures cannot be active at the same time.

Occam procedure calls cannot introduce *aliasing*; every name identifies a unique variable. This property of occam allows register variables to be passed as parameters without the need for forming register addresses; thereby eliminating the need for intricate (and slow) hardware to allow registers to be addressable by values held in other registers. Scalar value parameters can be passed by copying the value. Other scalar parameters can be passed by copying the value when the procedure is called and copying the result back when the procedure returns.

Array values passed as parameters are always held in random-access memory and so can always be implemented by passing their addresses.

11 *PAR*

The easiest way to implement concurrent processes is to use one processing element for each process; the present compiler does this.

12 *Channels and Communication*

Synchronization of input and output requires that the processor idles as the first process waits for the second. This is achieved by a microprogram polling loop.

It is clearly desirable to minimize the amount of hardware associated with each channel, as well as the number of connections needed to implement a channel.

For any process that includes channel communication, the compiler generates a shift register, two control signals *sync* and *shift*, and an input to the condition multiplexer *ready*.

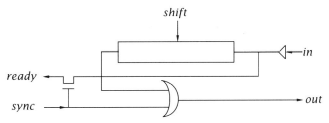

For each pair of communicating devices, two connections are used to form a link. Each link is connected to a device as shown; the only additional control signal needed for each link on a device is used to select which link is in use.

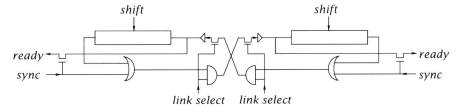

An input or output is performed by asserting the *sync* signal together with the appropriate *link-select* signal and polling the *ready* signal. When a ready signal is detected, this indicates that both devices are ready to communicate. At this point, the process at the other end of the link will also have detected a ready signal. Both devices now release their *sync* signals and clock their shift registers using the *shift* signals. With only the *link-select* signals asserted, the two shift registers at either end of the channel effectively form one long cyclic shift register, so the data in the two shift registers is exchanged. After the data has been exchanged, the *link-select* signals are released.

Clearly, this operation is completely symmetrical. Each link between two devices can be used for both input and output; it is not necessary for these to be performed concurrently because each device implements only one process.

An example of a simple process that inputs a value, adds 1, and outputs the result is:

```
CHAN c, d:
VAR x:
SEQ
  c ? x
  d ! (x + 1)
```

The microcode is as follows:

```
SETUP0:    YbusFrom32   ZbusFromYbus   T0FromZbus
           SelectCh0    SYNC
           (CondFromReady -> TRANSFER0, SETUP0) ;
TRANSFER0: XbusFromT0   YbusFrom1   ZbusFromXbusMinusYbus
           T0FromZbus
           SelectCh0    ShiftChan
           (CondFromNotZbusEq0 -> TRANSFER0, DONE0) ;
DONE0:     XbusFromChan ZbusFromXbus
           R0FromZbus   LAB0 ;
LAB0:      XbusFromR0   YbusFrom1   ZbusFromXbusPlusYbus
           ChanFromZbus    SETUP1 ;
SETUP1:    YbusFrom32   ZbusFromYbus   T0FromZbus
           SelectCh1    SYNC
           (CondFromReady -> TRANSFER1, SETUP1)
TRANSFER1: XbusFromT0   YbusFrom1   ZbusFromXbusMinusYbus
           T0FromZbus
           SelectCh1    ShiftChan
           (CondFromNotZbusEq0 -> TRANSFER1, END) ;
```

A temporary register (**T0**) is introduced to count the number of bits to be transferred to or from the channel register (**Chan**). The value of **x** is held in a further register (**R0**). The ALU is used to decrement the count register and test for zero at the same time that each bit is shifted through the link.

13 *ALT*

Alternative input requires that the inputting processor poll a number of channels in turn until one is found to be ready for input. The link implementation described in the preceding section can be used for this purpose; an example follows.

```
ALT
  in1 ? x
    count := count + 1
  in2 ? x
    count := count - 1
```

The microcode for polling the channels is:

```
LBL1:         SelectCh0   SYNC
              (CondFromReady -> TRANSFER1, LBL2)
TRANSFER1:    ...

LBL2:         SelectCh1   SYNC
              (CondFromReady -> TRANSFER2, LBL1)
TRANSFER2:    ...
```

244245

The microcode loop attempts to synchronize with each of the two links until it succeeds, in which case it continues with the input.

14 *Example: The Prime Farm*

Prime numbers can be generated concurrently using a "processor farm". The program given in [5] uses a controller that farms out successive numbers to an arbitrary number of primality testers. Each tester stores all of the primes up to the square root of the number to be tested; it uses these to test whether or not the number is prime, and responds to the controller accordingly.

Here we use an even simpler program. Each tester divides its new number by all numbers up to the square root of the new number. This removes the need for an array to store the prime numbers up to the square root.

This is entirely justified because we are trying to optimize the use of silicon area; *the area taken for one tester with memory can be better used for many testers without memory.* This is certainly true for generating primes up to 2^{32}.

```
PROC primetest(CHAN from.controller, to.controller)
  DEF isprime = 0, notprime = 1:
  VAR mextest, candidate, active:
  SEQ
     active := true
     WHILE TRUE
       SEQ
         from.controller ? maxtest; candidate
         IF
           maxtest = 0
             active := FALSE
           maxtest <> 0
             VAR nexttest:
             SEQ
               nexttest := 3
               WHILE ((candidate REM nexttest) <> 0) AND
                      (nexttest < maxtest)
                 nexttest := nexttest + 2
               IF
                 nexttest < maxtest
                   to.controller !  not.prime
                 TRUE
                   to.controller !  is.prime
```

The controller is about 1.5mm × 2.5mm in area; each tester is about 1.2mm × 2.3mm. The space occupied by a controller with 16 testers is about 50 sq mm, which fits easily on a single chip using a current manufacturing process. Such a chip would require very few external connections: a single link, clock and reset inputs, and power. There is a great deal of freedom in configuring the devices on the chip, because they communicate only by two-wire links. It seems likely that "process farms" are an effective way of organizing specialized VLSI systems.

15 *Example: Signal Processing*

The following example is a second-order filter that filters a stream of values. It would normally be used as a component in a pipeline in which each component filter has different parameters.

```
PROC Filter (Chan In, Out)
  VAR x, y, t1, t2, t3, z1, z2:
  SEQ
    z1 := 3
    z2 := 4
    WHILE TRUE
      SEQ
        in ? x
        t1 := x - (b2 * z2)
        t2 := a2 * z2
        z2 := t1 - (b1 * z1)
        t3 := t2 + (a1 * z1)
        out !  t3 + (a0 * z2)
        in ? x
        t1 := x - (b2 * z1)
        t2 := a2 * z1
        z2 := t1 - (b1 * z2)
        t3 := t2 + (a1 * z2)
        out !  t3 + (a0 * z1)
```

This requires nine registers and 43 microinstructions; each multiplication is implemented by a microsubroutine call. This performs one bit of the multiplication per microinstruction cycle. Multiplication speed could be improved (at the expense of area) by use of a parallel multiplier.

The filter occupies 3 sq mm, so a pipeline of 20 filters could be fitted on a single VLSI device.

16 *Example: A Simple Processor*

Our final example is a simple programmable processor with a (very) reduced instruction set. Despite its tiny instruction set, it provides all of the functions needed to implement a sequential occam process; in fact, it is very easy to compile an occam process into the instruction set of this processor. The processor has four input links, four output links, and 256 bytes of random-access memory.

```
PROC Processor(CHAN In0, In1, In2, In3,
               CHAN Out0, Out1, Out2, Out3)
  VAR Iptr, Wptr:
  VAR Areg, Breg:
  VAR Instruction, Function, Operand:
```

```
VAR Memory[256]:
SEQ
  Memory[0] := Boot
  Iptr := 0
  Operand := 0

  WHILE TRUE
    SEQ
      Instruction := Memory [ Iptr ]
      Iptr := Iptr + 1
      Function := Instruction /\ #F0
      Operand := (Instruction /\ #0F) \/ Operand

      IF
        Function=Prefix
          Operand := Operand << 4

        TRUE
          SEQ
            IF
              Function=Loadavar
                Areg := Memory[Wptr+Operand]

              Function=Loadbvar
                Breg := Memory[Wptr+Operand]

              Function=Loadalit
                Areg := Operabd

              Function=Loadblit
                Breg := Operand

              Function=Storeavar
                Memory[Wptr+Operand] := Areg

              Function=Loadaind
                Areg := Memory[Areg+Operand]

              Function=Storebind
                Memory[Areg+Operand] := Breg
```

```
Function=Jump
  Iptr := Iptr + Operand

Function=Jumpfalse
  IF
    Areg = 0
      Iptr := Iptr + Operand
    TRUE
      SKIP

Function=Equalalit
  Areg := Areg = Operand

Function=Addalit
  Areg := Areg + Operand

Function=Adjust
  Wptr := Wptr + Operand

Function=Call
  SEQ
    Areg := Iptr
    Iptr := Iptr + Operand

Function=Operate
  IF
    Operand=input
      IF
        Areg=0
          In0 ? Areg
        Areg=1
          In1 ? Areg
        Areg=2
          In2 ? Areg
        Areg=3
          In3 ? Areg

    Operand=output
      IF
        Areg=1
          Out0 !  Breg
```

```
            Areg=2
              Out1 !  Breg
            Areg=4
              Out2 !  Breg
            Areg=8
              Out3 !  Breg

  Operand=Alternative
    ALT
      ((Areg /\ 1) <> 0) & In0 ? Areg
        Iptr := Iptr + 0
      ((Areg /\ 2) <> 0) & In1 ? Areg
        Iptr := Iptr + 1
      ((Areg /\ 4) <> 0) & In2 ? Areg
        Iptr := Iptr + 2
      ((Areg /\ 8) <> 0) & In3 ? Areg
        Iptr := Iptr + 3

  Operand=Greater
    Areg := Areg > Breg

  Operand=Shiftleft
    Areg := Areg << Breg

  Operand=Shiftright
    Areg := Areg >> Breg

  Operand=Xorbits
    Areg := Areg >< Breg

  Operand=Andbits
    Areg := Areg /\ Breg

  Operand=Add
    Areg := Areg + Breg

  Operand=Subtract
    Areg := Areg - Breg

  Operand= Boot
    SEQ
```

```
                     In0 ? Wptr
                     Iptr := 0
                       WHILE Iptr < Wptr
                         SEQ
                            In0 ? Memory [ Iptr ]
                            Iptr := Iptr + 1
                     Iptr := 0
            Operand := 0
```

On reset, the processor waits for a program to be supplied via link 0. It then loads the program and executes it until a "boot" instruction is executed.

There is obviously considerable scope for better optimization in this case; in particular, it would be desirable to implement the instruction-decoding "IF" construct with a mechanism that replaces the microinstruction pointer register with a value held in a register.

The processor requires 11 registers and has 140 microinstructions. The whole device including the memory occupies about 6.25 sq mm; 10 such devices with their interconnections would take less area than a typical 32-bit microprocessor.

17 *Conclusions*

A communicating-process language such as occam can be used to design VLSI devices, and can be compiled into silicon layout. Some parts of the design process are still performed by hand (such as the final placement of the functional blocks), but this cannot introduce errors. It is therefore possible to design concurrent VLSI systems using occam, to establish that the design behaves as intended using the formal semantics of occam (or in simple cases by experimental testing of the occam program), and finally to compile the occam source into correct silicon layout.

In order to simplify the construction of the compiler, many issues have been ignored. For example, the synchronous communication system is appropriate only for local communication between devices sharing a common clock. This problem can be overcome by using a different link implementation for "long-distance" communication (for example, the link used in the transputer itself).

Expressing an application in a form that exploits silicon area efficiently involves careful consideration of the relative costs of memory, processing, and communication. Concurrent algorithms that perform "redundant" calculations can be faster *and consume less area* than sequential algorithms that store values. An important use of a silicon compiler is to aid in the evaluation of "'silicon algorithms".

References

[1] Barrett, G. "Formal methods applied to a floating-point number system". Technical Monograph PRG–58, Oxford University Computing Laboratory, Programming Research Group, 1987.

[2] INMOS, Ltd. *The occam Programming Manual.* Prentice-Hall International, Hemel Hempstead, U.K., 1984.

[3] Martin, A. J. "Compiling communicating processes into delay-insensitive VLSI circuits". *Distributed Computing 1*, 4 (1986).

[4] May, D. and Shepherd, R. "The transputer implementation of occam". *Communicating Process Architecture,* pp. 19–29. Prentice-Hall International, Hemel Hempstead, U.K., 1988.

[5] May, D. and Shepherd, R. "Communicating process computers". *Communicating Process Architecture,* pp. 31–44. Prentice-Hall International, Hemel Hempstead, U.K., 1988.

[6] Roscoe, A. W. and Hoare, C. A. R. "The laws of occam programming". Technical Monograph PRG–53, Oxford University Computing Laboratory, Programming Research Group, 1986.

Use of
Formal Methods
by a
Silicon Manufacturer[1]

4

David May
INMOS, Ltd.

1 Introduction

A VLSI semiconductor manufacturer faces the problem of specifying very complex devices— and of ensuring that the implementation of the specification is correct. Exhaustive testing of the device may be impossible because the number of cases to be considered is too large, or impractical because of the complexity of an adequate test environment. Yet VLSI devices are employed as components of high-volume products where the cost of correcting a fault is high— and in safety-critical environments where a fault may endanger human life. Indeed, to a semiconductor manufacturer, each design fault in a VLSI device normally incurs substantial cost and —worse still in such a competitive market— delays introduction of the product.

In an attempt to tackle these problems, INMOS has recently started to employ formal techniques of specification, transformation, and proof in the de-

---

1. This chapter, the copyright ©1989 of INMOS Limited, is published with the permission of INMOS Limited.

sign of microcomputer products. This chapter discusses the use of such techniques in the semiconductor industry and describes the process by which recent work at Oxford University on the formal semantics of occam[2] was employed by INMOS in the design of the recently announced T800 floating-point transputer [10].

2 *VLSI Design Techniques*

Current VLSI devices are far too large and complex to be designed by hand. For many years, computers have been used to maintain the design database and to allow simulation of the design. More recently, computers have been used to provide various forms of design checking.

For example, until recently circuit-connectivity checking was performed manually by comparing the circuit diagrams with a large-scale drawing of the silicon layout. These drawings became so large that designers had to crawl over them following the tracks with colored pencils! Even for a design with only 10,000 components, this task is very tedious, time-consuming, and error-prone. Automatic connectivity checking, which has become *essential* in VLSI design systems, ensures that the description of a device in a hardware description language (HDL), the circuit diagram, and the actual silicon layout all express the same connectivity. Similarly, automatic checking of silicon-design rules —such as ensuring the two metal tracks are not too close together— is now performed automatically.

In designing a VLSI device, it is important to have a behavioral description of what the device does and a hardware description of the components of the device and the way in which they are interconnected. Current design systems support design at the hardware description language level; they provide little or no support for behavioral description and verification.

2.1 *The INMOS CAD System*

The computer-aided design system developed by INMOS for hardware design has many features that enable designs to be made correct. The system runs interactively, and enables a designer to examine portions of the silicon design on a color display and to lay down new tracks. The system immediately checks for design-rule violations and prevents designs that contravene these rules. Hence, assuming that the design rules reflect the capabilities of the fabrication process, the actual chip should reflect the design made using the design system. The system supports multiuser access to the same design database, with record locking used to prevent two people from modifying

2. Occam is a trademark of INMOS Limited.

the same data.

The silicon design is specified in the INMOS hardware description language. This is a hierarchical language which allows the design to be specified in a top-down modular fashion. It allows modules such as register cells and latches to be defined in terms of silicon layout. More complex modules such as registers and ALUs can then be defined in terms of the simpler modules. The hardware description language is used to express the structure of the design, but not its behavior.

The silicon design is checked for electrical equivalence to this HDL specification. This guarantees that the finished chip is a correct implementation of the HDL specification.

2.2 *The Module Library*

The HDL is a hierachical module-based language. As designs are produced, a library of modules is generated. If the same HDL specification is required in another design, then the silicon design that already exists can be reused. This greatly reduces both design time and the probability of introducing errors, because module designs in the library have already been checked— and may even have been demonstrated in existing products.

The floating-point unit of the IMS T800 was designed as a separate microcoded processor. This enabled major parts of the logic of the IMS T414 to be reused. In addition to the main processor on the IMS T800 (which had only minor modifications from the IMS T414), the microcode-decode logic and much of the arithmetic-unit logic of the floating-point unit could be taken from the module library.

2.3 *Behavioral Description*

Behavioral description languages have been used to design sequential processors for many years. Because the process of interpreting instructions in a sequential computer is (nearly) sequential, a conventional sequential programming language can be used to write the behavioral description of a processor. VLSI devices, however, consist of many interacting components, and their behavior can therefore be expressed only in a language with concurrency and communication.

The obvious difficulty is that there is no way of checking automatically that the hardware description of a device actually implements the behavioral description. This problem is the subject of several current research projects. Examples include the proof of correctness of a simple microcoded processor [3] and the verification of the design of various low-level hardware modules

[8]. The tools that have been used in this work are LCF_LSM [4], VERITAS [9], and HOL [5].

This work has made significant progress by choosing design problems simple enough to be proved correct. A manufacturer of microprocessors, however, cannot simplify the problem in this way: To remain competitive in the world market it is necessary to design products of increasing function and performance. At present, the markets for a "proven" microprocessor are small and specialized, though this situation may change.

It may become possible to associate with each module in the library a set of axioms that defines its behavior. This would be used in a proof system to formally derive the behavior of compositions of modules. These techniques should give more knowledge of the behavior of a set of modules than simulation would, and may be more efficient in time and resources.

2.4 *Occam*

The occam language [11] allows a system to be decomposed hierarchically into a collection of concurrent processes communicating via channels. This allows the system to be used to represent the behavior of a VLSI device in a very natural way: The various top-level modules can be mapped onto individual processes, with their interfacing handled by channel communication. Thanks to occam's very efficient implementation, execution of such a behavioral description provides a fast simulation. Most important for the purposes of this paper, occam has rich formal semantics [12] which facilitate program transformation and proof.

Occam was designed by INMOS as a language for describing and programming concurrent systems. It is the programming language for the INMOS transputer products. Occam has also been used extensively within INMOS, however, as a behavioral description language. The development of the transputer architecture relied on an occam simulation in which the component parts of the transputer are represented as occam processes.

For the first transputer products, the implementation of this occam behavioral description in HDL was performed informally, and logic simulations were used (as far as possible) to check the correctness of the design.

3 *The First Proof*

Difficulties in the informal method of testing became apparent in several areas of design. Many of the algorithms used in computer arithmetic are intricate and cannot be tested exhaustively. Floating-point arithmetic is particularly intricate, and many computers have faulty implementations of basic arithmetic operations. Often these give rise to minor errors in rounding and are not noticed by users.

In the first 32–bit transputer, floating-point arithmetic was supported primarily by a software package written in occam. A few special instructions were added to the processor to speed up the package. Attempts were made to validate the package and the special instructions. The normal validation process for floating-point arithmetic is to execute a large number of test cases. In fact, the normal tests employ four different bit patterns, each of which is used in every mantissa bit position. For each mantissa value, all possible exponent values and both signs are used. In 32-bit arithmetic, this gives rise to about 50,000 values for each operand. There are five operations and four rounding modes, and it is therefore necessary to execute 50×10^9 floating-point operations; if each operation took one microsecond, this process would take about 15 hours.

In practice, it is quite impossible to perform the tests at this speed. An increasing amount of equipment was allocated to allow testing of several cases to continue in parallel, but a new problem then emerged. The tests were comparing a suspect implementation of arithmetic with a "reference implementation", which was a widely used VLSI device. This device had been chosen because of its relatively simple implementation. In view of the problems of validation, however, there seemed to be reason to question whether a reference implementation for floating-point arithmetic exists at all. In fact, a bug was found in this device: Certain operations gave rise to errors caused by "double rounding". Instead of rounding a result directly into its final representation, it was first rounded to an internal representation and then rounded again to the final representation.

In many respects, the occam floating-point package was an ideal candidate for a formal correctness proof. It is not very long, it is intricate, and a great deal depends on its being correct. The idea of constructing a proof arose during a lecture given before the Royal Society by Donald Good [2], who remarked that constructing a verified program in the Gypsy system took "about 5 times longer than the normal (informal) way". Within a short time, Geoff Barrett of the Oxford University Programming Research Group was persuaded to try to construct a proof which, if successful, would demonstrate the use of formal methods in a very important practical application.

One of the immediate problems was that IEEE Standard 754 is expressed in English. The first task, therefore, was to rewrite the standard in a formal notation, and for this purpose Z was used. The package was then derived by standard techniques refining the Z specification into an occam program. This work, which was completed in three months, *overtook the experimental validation.*

4 *Validating Hardware*

While the validation of the software package was proceeding, work started on the design of a transputer incorporating floating-point hardware. Immediately, the problem of verification arose.

A semiconductor manufacturer cannot afford to construct prototypes. They are too expensive and take too long to design and manufacture. For this reason, the industry relies heavily on validating simulations.

Unfortunately, a simulation is very slow— at least a hundred times slower than the real device. In practice, it is normally at least a thousand times slower, because the simulation is executed using technology about four years behind the device it is simulating. The result was that to validate the floating-point design by testing would take more than a year.

In fact, it is normal to use a relatively low-level simulator, which is much slower than an ideal one. Typically, the INMOS simulator operates a million times slower than real time. Although an ideal simulator could be written, it would give rise to the problem of maintaining consistency between several different levels of simulation as the design progresses.

Clearly, it was important to find a way of developing the floating-point hardware formally, possibly starting from the already proven software package. The key to this turned out to be the occam transformation system, which at this stage was still under development at Oxford University.

5 *Occam Transformations*

The algebraic semantics of occam given in [12] consists of a set of laws that define the language constructs. The algebraic semantics has been shown to be consistent with the denotational semantics, thus establishing the validity of these laws. These transformation laws enable a normal form for finite occam programs to be defined.

A transformation law can be used to transform one program into another whose observable behavior is equivalent. Many transformation laws are "obviously true" and are regularly used by programmers. For example, sequential composition of processes is associative:

```
    SEQ              SEQ
     P                SEQ
    SEQ      ≡         P
     Q                Q
     R                R
```

This is the law *SEQ binassoc*. Other transformation laws are more complex and include preconditions for validity but, with a bit of effort, can be seen to be true.

If a sequence of transformations can be found to transform one program into another, then the two programs are known to be equivalent. If, in addition, one of these programs is known to be a correct implementation of a specification, then the correctness of the other program can be inferred.

Using these techniques, it is possible to demonstrate the correctness of implementations by transformation. Doing this by experimental testing takes far too long for problems like floating-point arithmetic.

5.1 *A Transformation Example*

As an example consider the following program fragment:

```
SEQ
    X := A
    Y := Y + X
```

These two assignment statements can be merged into one multiple assignment statement. First the law *AS id* is used to add an identity assignment to each statement.

AS id   x, y := e, y   ≡   x := e

giving the program

```
SEQ
    X,Y := A,Y
    Y,X := Y + X,X
```

Next the law *AS perm* is applied to the second statement

AS perm $< x_i \mid i = 1..n >:=< e_i \mid i = 1..n >$

$$\equiv$$

$< x_{\pi_i} \mid i = 1..n >:=< e_{\pi_i} \mid i = 1..n >$
for any permutation π of $\{1..n\}$

giving

```
SEQ
    X,Y := A,Y
    X,Y := X,Y + X
```

Finally these two statements are merged by the law *SEQ comb*

SEQ comb $SEQ(x := e, x := f) \equiv x := f[e/x]$

giving

X,Y := A,Y + A

5.2 *The Occam Transformation System*

To aid the process of transforming programs, a simple interactive transformation system has been implemented in the language ML [6]. A program can be parsed into this system and then manipulated by the user. All the basic laws in [12] are implemented inside the system, along with some extra ones; the system is extensible and new laws (that have been proven correct) can be coded and added if required. Regularly executed sequences of transformations can be coded as ML functions, giving higher-level transformations. The transformation example shown in the preceding section has been coded as the transformation law *combas*, which itself is used in more powerful transformations. The basic transformations often have only a small localized effect, but when suitably combined they can perform significant transformations which —being constructed from correct component transformations— are known to be correct.

The transformation system's user can select which transformation laws to apply and examine their effects. The use of the transformation system provides the verification of the equivalence between the initial program and the transformed result. If necessary, however, it would be feasible to produce the list of transformations that constitute the proof.

6 *Instruction Development*

The instruction development process consists of specifying the operation of an instruction in the Z specification language [13]. Since Z is a mathematically based language, it enables precise unambiguous statements about operations to be made concisely and —if used in a sympathetic manner— clearly.

Along with the specifications of the instructions there will be a set of specifications of system constants, system state, and other global features of the design. In the case of the IMS T800 floating-point unit, this consists of a formal specification of the IEEE floating-point standard (such as in [1]), a specification of the internal representation of floating-point numbers in registers, a specification of the floating-point unit's state (i.e., the registers and flags), and definitions of various constants. This amounts to a formal description of the overall architecture.

Each instruction specification is refined into a high-level occam implementation. This can involve going via a guarded-command language using pre- and postconditions as in [7]. This high-level implementation is often the sort of implementation that a competent programmer would produce from the specification, but the formal derivation ensures that no mistakes are made.

The occam program is then transformed inside the transformation system into a form equivalent to the microcode assembler source. The steps in this process are motivated by the functions available in the microcode machine. This involves

Refining *IF* conditions into the conditions available on the microcode machine,

Refining the expressions so that they use the ALU and bus operations available on the microcode machine, and

Refining the program's sequential control into a form that simulates the microinstruction control in the microcode machine.

The various stages of simple development used as an example are shown in the next section.

7 An Instruction Development Example

The following example demonstrates the methods that have been found to be useful in the IMS T800 design. This example takes a high-level specification in the Z specification language [13] and refines it in a sequence of steps into a microcoded implementation that will run on a microcode machine similar to the IMS T800 floating-point unit. For brevity, this example makes certain simplifications; notably, it ignores infinities, Not-a-Numbers, and denormalized numbers.

7.1 Preliminary Definitions

Before any instructions are specified and implemented, it is necessary to make a few preliminary definitions. There is a need to specify the format of registers, various constants, and methods for interpreting data. This is a formalization of the top level of architectural description of the device. Only the subset of definitions relevant to this example will be given.

The definition of the real format will contain the specification of the number of bits in the fractional part of a floating-point number and the exponent bias.

> bitsinfrac, bias   : **N**

Now the floating-point register format can be specified.

Floating_Point_Register

> frac, exp   : **N**
>
> sign   : { -1, +1}
>
> ---
>
> $(exp = 0 \wedge frac = 0)$
>
> $\vee$
>
> $(2^{bitsinfrac-1} \leq frac < 2^{bitsinfrac})$

This states that a *Floating_Point_Register* has three fields, two of which, *frac* and *exp*, are positive integers and the third of which, *sign*, is either −1 or +1. The predicate states that both the exponent and fraction are 0 or that *frac* is between $2^{bitsinfrac-1}$ and $2^{bitsinfrac}$; this ensures that the fraction is normalized.

The valuation function on a floating-point register *fv* establishes the link between a *Floating_Point_Register* and the value it "holds".

> *fv*   : Floating_Point_Register → **R**
>
> ---
>
> $\forall x$: *Floating_Point_Register*.
>
> $\quad fv(x) = x.sign \times$
>
> $\qquad (x.frac \times 2^{1-bitsinfrac}) \times 2^{exp-bias}$

Two constants are used to represent the largest and smallest integers in the integer format. Because the IMS T800 uses 32–bit two's complement integers, these constants are specified by

$$
\begin{array}{|l}
\hline
\text{MinInt, MaxInt}\quad : \mathbf{Z} \\
\hline
\textit{MinInt} = -2^{31} \\
\textit{MaxInt} = 2^{31} - 1 \\
\hline
\end{array}
$$

7.2 *The Instruction Specification*

The instruction under consideration here is a component of the real-to-integer conversion instruction sequence. It checks that the value of Areg lies within integer range; if not, then the error flag must be set to indicate a conversion error.

The Z specification of this instruction is very simple:

Floating_Check_Integer_Range

$$
\begin{array}{|l}
\hline
\text{Areg, Areg}'\qquad\qquad : \text{Floating\_Point\_Register} \\
\text{Error\_Flag, Error\_Flag}' \quad : \mathbf{bool} \\
\hline
\textit{fvAreg} \in \mathbf{Z} \\
\textit{Areg}' = \textit{Areg} \\
\textit{fvAreg} \in [\textit{MinInt}, \textit{MaxInt}] \Rightarrow \\
\qquad\qquad \textit{Error\_Flag}' = \textit{Error\_Flag} \\
\textit{fvAreg} \notin [\textit{MinInt}, \textit{MaxInt}] \Rightarrow \textit{Error\_Flag}' = \mathbf{true} \\
\hline
\end{array}
$$

The first predicate is a precondition to this operation. If *fvAreg* is not an integer, then the effect of this operation will be undefined. In this way, the precise conditions for the correct execution of an operation are stated. This instruction is intended for use in a particular sequence of instructions and the previous instruction will have established this precondition.

It is easy to see that this specification satisfies the requirements for the instruction. Once this has been agreed to be correct, the development process will ensure that the final implementation will also satisfy the requirements.

7.3 *Refining to Procedural Form*

A refinement of a specification can consist of either refining a data type or decomposing the procedural form. Since the major data type —reals— has already been refined into its machine represention, using *Floating_Point_Register* and the abstraction function *fv* enables the specification to be decomposed into procedural form. The specification can be implemented easily by

> **if**
>
> $fv(Areg) \in [MinInt, MaxInt] \rightarrow$ **skip**
>
> $[] \ fv(Areg) \notin [MinInt, MaxInt] \rightarrow Error\_Flag :=$ **true**
>
> **fi**

It can be shown, using the pre- and postcondition laws in [7], that this procedure implements the Z specification.

7.4 *Refining to Occam*

The conditionals used in the procedural implementation's **if**...**fi** construct are not available in occam, so they must be refined into equivalent occam expressions.

To do this the lemmas in Figure 1 will be useful. From Lemmas 1 and 2 we obtain

> $\vdash \forall x : Floating\_Point\_Register\,.$
> $\quad x.exp < LargestINTExp \ \Leftrightarrow \ |fv(x)| < |MinInt|$

Part of the invariant of Floating_Point_Register, $MSBit \le x.frac$, is used to eliminate the disjunct where $x.exp = LargestINTExp$.

Now, using Lemma 3 and adding an extra condition, we obtain

> $\vdash \forall x : Floating\_Point\_Register\,.$
> $\quad fv(x) \in \mathbf{Z} \Rightarrow x.exp < LargestINTExp$
> $\qquad \Leftrightarrow |fv(x)| \le MaxInt$

From these we obtain

> $\vdash \forall x : Floating\_Point\_Register\,.$
> $\quad fv(x) \in \mathbf{Z} \Rightarrow fv(x) \in [MinInt, MaxInt]$
> $\qquad \Leftrightarrow (x.exp < LargestINTExp$
> $\qquad\quad \lor fv(x) = MinInt)$

7.5 *High-Level Occam Implementation*

The previous section allows the high-level occam implementation in Figure 2 to be derived.

Using two laws *IF pri* and *IF or-dist*

IF pri $\quad$ $IF(b_1\,P_1, \ldots, b_n\,P_n)$

$\qquad\qquad\equiv IF(b_1^\star\,P_1, \ldots, b_n^\star\,P_n)$

$\qquad\qquad$**where** $b_i^\star = \neg b_1 \wedge \ldots \wedge \neg b_{i-1} \wedge b_i$

IF or-dist $\quad$ $IF(b_1\,P, b_2\,P, \underline{C})$

$\qquad\qquad\equiv IF(b_1 \vee b_2\,P, \underline{C})$

this can be simplified to the program in Figure 3, which is probably the implementation of the specification that a competent programmer would produce— although the "special" case of MinInt is frequently omitted.

Figure 1.   Lemmas about integer range.

Lemma 1 $\quad\vdash \forall x, y : Floating\_Point\_Register.$

$\qquad\qquad\qquad (x.exp < y.exp \vee (x.frac < y.frac \wedge x.exp = y.exp))$

$\qquad\qquad\qquad \Leftrightarrow |fv(x)| < |fv(y)|$

Lemma 2 $\quad\vdash \forall x : Floating\_Point\_Register.$

$\qquad\qquad\qquad fv(x) = MinInt \Leftrightarrow$

$\qquad\qquad\qquad (x.sign = -1 \wedge x.frac = MSBit \wedge x.exp = LargestINTExp)$

Lemma 3 $\quad\vdash MaxInt = -(MinInt + 1)$

where $MSBit = 2^{bitsinfrac-1}$

$\qquad LargestINTExp = 32 + bias$

7.6 *Transformations towards Microcode*

The previous sections have developed an occam program that correctly implements the specification. This program can now be transformed into an equivalent form that corresponds to microcode assembler source. Full details of this transformation will not be given here.

Each step consists of transforming one aspect of the program towards the form used in the microcode machine. Ideally, the preceding occam program would be transformed into the final program. Because the transformation

---

Figure 2.   High-level occam implementation.

```
IF
  ((Areg.Exp < LargestINTExp) OR
      ((Areg.Sign = 1) AND
          (Areg.Exp = LargestINTExp) AND
              (Areg.Frac = MSBit)))
    SKIP
  NOT ((Areg.Exp < LargestINTExp) OR
          ((Areg.Sign = 1) AND
              (Areg.Exp = LargestINTExp) AND
                  (Areg.Frac = MSBit)))
    ErrorFlag := TRUE
```

Figure 3.   Simplified high-level implementation.

```
IF
  (Areg.Exp < LargestINTExp)
    SKIP
  ((Areg.Sign = 1) AND
      (Areg.Exp = LargestINTExp) AND
          (Areg.Frac = MSBit))
    SKIP
  TRUE
    ErrorFlag := TRUE
```

system is still under development, however, most of the laws it contains are "general", i.e., correct in all environments. This does not allow the required transformation to be performed in a forward direction. Instead, at each step a proposed implementation was constructed and then verified by transforming it back into the current "correct" implementation.

Refining the Conditionals The preceding occam program contains a three-way *IF* statement with the conditionals

1. **(Areg.Exp < LargestINTExp)**

2. **(Areg.Sign = 1) AND**
   (Areg.Exp = LargestINTExp) AND
   (Areg.Frac = MSBit)

3. **TRUE**

The structure of the program must be transformed to take account of the conditional signals available on the microcode machine— i.e., that conditionals are available to signal that the result of an ALU operation is less than 0, or that the result of an ALU subtraction is 0, etc.

This program is shown in Figure 4. The various laws for *IF* constructs in [12] enable this to be verified.

Refining the Expressions The previous section has produced conditionals that are available in the microcode machine. The next step is to take account of how the expressions producing these conditionals are evaluated. This stage involves introducing variables to represent the various buses and conditional flags. The conditional flags, which appear as the *IF* conditionals, are evaluated in terms of the results of the ALU operations before the *IF* statement.

This program is shown in Figure 5. The laws for *SEQ*, *VAR*, and assignment in [12] verify this step.

Introducing Sequencing The program now contains expressions and conditionals that can be formed in the microcode machine, but it does not define the microwords. The final step is to mimic the microsequencing in the microcode machine by using a variable as a microprogram counter and a *WHILE* loop containing an *IF* microinstruction selector. Each branch of the *IF* statement contains the "code" for one microinstruction— i.e., it can have one fractional ALU operation and one exponential ALU operation, and it defines the next microinstruction to execute, possibly with one or two conditionals.

The laws for *WHILE* and *IF* allow this program to be "unwound" back into its previous form.

7.7 *Translation to Microcode*

The program resulting from the preceding transformations is shown in Figure 6.

This corresponds almost one-to-one to the source format for the microcode assembler. A pattern-matching program is used to translate the stylized occam of the final program into the source for the microcode assembler, which produces the definition of the microcode ROM.

Figure 4. Implementation with refined conditionals.

```
IF
   (Areg.Sign = 1)
     IF
       ((Areg.Exp - LargestINTExp) < 0)
          SKIP
        NOT ((Areg.Exp - LargestINTExp) < 0)
          IF
            ((Areg.Exp - LargestINTExp) = 0)
              IF
                ((MSBit - Areg.Frac) = 0)
                  SKIP
                NOT ((MSBit - Areg.Frac) = 0)
                  ErrorFlag := TRUE
            NOT ((Areg.Exp - LargestINTExp) = 0)
              ErrorFlag := TRUE
   NOT (Areg.Sign = 1)
     IF
        ((Areg.Exp - LargestINTExp) < 0)
          SKIP
        NOT ((Areg.Exp - LargestINTExp) < 0)
          ErrorFlag := TRUE
```

Figure 5. Implementation with refined expressions.

```
VAR AregNegative, ExpZbus, ExpZbusNeg, ExpZbusEqZ,
    FracZbusEqZ :
VAR FracZbus :
SEQ
  AregNegative := (Areg.Sign = 1)
  ExpZbus :=  (Areg.Exp - LargestINTExp)
  ExpZbusNeg := ExpZbus < 0
  IF
    AregNegative
      IF
        ExpZbusNeg
          SKIP
        NOT ExpZbusNeg
          SEQ
            ExpZbus :=  (Areg.Exp - LargestINTExp)
            FracZbus := (MSBit - Areg.Frac)
            ExpZbusEqZ := ExpZbus = 0
            IF
              ExpZbusEqZ
                SEQ
                  FracZbusEqZ := FracZbus = 0
                  IF
                    FracZbusEqZ
                      SKIP
                    NOT FracZbusEqZ
                      ErrorFlag := TRUE
              NOT ExpZbusEqZ
                ErrorFlag := TRUE
    NOT AregNegative
      IF
        ExpZbusNeg
          SKIP
        NOT ExpZbusNeg
          ErrorFlag := TRUE
```

Figure 6. Low-level occam implementation.

```
VAR NextInst :
VAR AregNegative, ExpZbusNeg, ExpZbusEqZ, FracZbusEqZ :
VAR FracZbus, ExpZbus :
SEQ
  NextInst := FloatingPointCheckIntegerRange
  WHILE NextInst <> NOWHERE
    IF
      NextInst = FloatingPointCheckIntegerRange
        SEQ
          AregNegative := (Areg.Sign = 1)
          ExpZbus := (Areg.Exp - LargestINTExp)
          ExpZbusNeg := ExpZbus < 0
          IF
            AregNegative
              IF
                ExpZbusNeg
                  NextInst := NOWHERE
                NOT ExpZbusNeg
                  NextInst := CheckMinInt
            NOT AregNegative
              IF
                ExpZbusNeg
                  NextInst := NOWHERE
                NOT ExpZbusNeg
                  NextInst := OutofRange
      NextInst = OutofRange
        SEQ
          ErrorFlag := TRUE
          NextInst := NOWHERE
    ... negative case micro instructions
```

7.8 *Microcode Assembler Source*

Finally the microcode can be derived. This is shown in Figure 7.

The formality of this process has ensured that the "program" in the microcode ROM implements the initial specification correctly. In this simple case, which produces only four microwords, it may seem possible to do this informally. Other instructions contain up to 90 microwords, however, and in such cases informal development can easily introduce subtle bugs. The ability to verify implementations using program transformations has proved invaluable.

Figure 7.   Microcode assembler source.

```
FloatingPointCheckIntegerRange:
  ExpConstantFromLargestINTExp
  ExpXbusFromAreg                  ExpYbusFromConstant
  ExpZbusFromXbusMinusYbus
  GOTO Cond1FromAregSign ->
        (Cond0FromExpZbusNeg ->  (NOWHERE, CheckMinInt),
         Cond0FromExpZbusNeg ->  (NOWHERE, OutofRange))

CheckMinInt:
  ExpConstantFromLargestINTExp
  ExpXbusFromAreg                  ExpYbusFromConstant
  ExpZbusFromXbusMinusYbus
  FracXbusFromMSBit                FracYbusFromAreg
  FracZbusFromXbusMinusYbus
  GOTO Cond1FromExpZbusEqZ ->      (CheckMinInt2, OutofRange)

CheckMinInt2:
  GOTO Cond1FromFracZbusEqZ ->     (NOWHERE, OutofRange)

OutofRange:
  SetErrorFlag
  GOTO NOWHERE
```

8 *Formal Models of Concurrency*

Work on the IMS T800 has shown how correct microcode can be derived from a high-level specification. This work has relied, however, only on the sequential aspects of the occam language.

Other aspects of the transputer that could benefit from a formal design approach are the process scheduler and the transputer communication system. As in floating-point arithmetic, intricate algorithms are employed in the interests of efficiency, and correctness is equally important. The communication system, however, is a collection of hardware devices operating concurrently in a concurrent external environment; it is even more difficult than arithmetic to validate experimentally, even if prototypes are available. This is not peculiar to the transputer; all computers have similar input-output systems.

Work has recently started on developing a formal specification of the transputer scheduler and communication system and on refining it into an implementation in hardware and microcode.

9 *A View of Silicon Design*

The work described in this chapter tackles only one part of the verification process: It enables correct designs at the microcode level to be produced from high-level specifications. To produce a fully verified processor design, it will be necessary to apply the same degree of rigor to the design of the microcode machine. This necessitates refining the specifications of microfunctions into hardware description language implementations. The INMOS CAD system already ensures that silicon layout is equivalent to its HDL specification.

Various small designs are currently being examined to experiment with this topic. By defining axioms for the behavior of low-level modules in the HDL module library, tools such as HOL [5] can be used to verify HDL designs. This will enable provably correct VLSI designs to be produced.

A further step will be to fully integrate these tools to enable rapid rechecking of the correctness proof. This is essential because modifications continue to be made throughout the design process.

Future silicon designs will involve a combination of standard microcomputers and specialized designs. An integrated design system must provide tools such as

> A proof system to manipulate Z specifications and to develop occam implementations,
>
> An occam transformation system,
>
> Silicon compiler(s) to compile occam directly into HDL implementations,

A proof system to check designs performed at the HDL level, and

A layout system to generate and check layout from HDL.

Clearly, this involves an integration of programming tools and silicon design tools. It also involves a change in the skills needed by a VLSI design team. The design of the T800 floating-point unit was performed by

one	computer architect	product specification
one	system designer	microcode, logic, datapath
one	"pure" mathematician	formal specification and proof
two	electronic engineers	circuit design and layout
one	programmer	compiler and instruction set tuning
one	"applied" mathematician	scientific function library

Large and complex designs are achieved by combining simple components. The relatively small set of basic modules are designed by electronic engineers to perform logical functions. As the technology advances, the design tools —and design skills— needed are those that enable large designs to be assembled reliably and quickly from the small set of basic modules. Software specialists, system designers, and mathematicians have an increasingly important role to play in this area.

10 *Simulation and Proof in VLSI Design*

It is common practice to make extensive use of simulation in VLSI design. As the number of devices on a VLSI chip increases, the simulation tools must be increased in speed to enable the design verification to be completed in an acceptable time. The purpose of a simulator, however, is to check the *behavior* of the design by examining test cases. As the designs increase in complexity, the number of test cases to be examined in simulation grows much faster than the number of devices used in the design. Consequently, it seems unlikely that simulation tools can keep up with VLSI technology, *even if massive concurrency is employed to accelerate simulation.*

Simulation is needed in VLSI design systems to model electrical properties of silicon devices, but only for simple modules and simple combinations of modules. Simulation is also useful to demonstrate the functional properties of a proposed device, but this can operate at a very high level.

Simulators of datapaths, logic, and microcode cannot tackle current VLSI designs. In contrast, even the existing primitive transformation and proof tools can tackle these aspects of the design. They enable a design to be completely verified much more rapidly than a simulator can provide a partial verification. These tools are therefore the key to future VLSI designs; they must be developed further and made interactive by the use of parallelism.

11 *Conclusion*

Techniques enabling formal design of *all* aspects of a computer are now required urgently, especially in such intricate areas as computer arithmetic and input-output. Most computers are now used in embedded systems where the cost of errors is very high— easily high enough to justify substantial investment in formal design techniques.

Work at INMOS suggests, moreover, that the use of formal techniques is already *cost-effective,* enabling designs to be produced more quickly with fewer designers and with less design hardware than by conventional techniques.

Existing theory is adequate in many areas of practical importance, although further development is needed to provide the theoretical foundations for work involving concurrency and timing.

Computer-aided design systems require substantial further development to allow integration of the various tools. Sufficient information must be included in the design database to allow rapid automatic checking of the correctness proof.

These problems are not unique to the semiconductor industry; anyone designing computers has encountered similar problems of validating complex hardware and microcode designs. It seems strange that the computer industry has made little use of formal design techniques, resulting in bugs in areas such as arithmetic units, interrupt systems, and virtual memory systems. It is to be hoped that the use of formal techniques will give rise to a new generation of computers that are, at last, free of design errors.

References

[1] Barrett, G. "Formal methods applied to a floating point number system". Technical Monograph PRG–58, Oxford University Computing Laboratory, Programming Research Group, 1987.

[2] Good, D. I. "Mechanical proofs about computer programs". *Mathematical Logic and Programming Languages*, C. A. R. Hoare and J. C. Shepherdson, eds., pp. 55–74. Prentice-Hall International, Englewood Cliffs, N.J., 1985.

[3] Gordon, M. "Proving a computer correct". Technical Report 42, University of Cambridge Computer Laboratory, 1983.

[4] Gordon, M. "LCF_LSM". Technical Report 41, University of Cambridge Computer Laboratory, 1983.

[5] Gordon, M. "HOL: A machine-oriented formulation of higher-order logic". Technical Report 68, University of Cambridge Computer Laboratory, 1985.

[6] Gordon, M., Milner, R., and Wadsworth, C. *Edinburgh LCF,* Chapter 2. Lecture Notes in Computer Science, vol. 78. Springer-Verlag, Berlin, 1979.

[7] Gries, D. *The Science of Programming.* Springer-Verlag, New York, 1981.

[8] Hanna, F. K. and Daeche, N. "Specification and verification using higher-order logic". *Proceedings of the 7th International Conference on Computer Hardware Design Languages.* Tokyo, 1985.

[9] Hanna, F. K. and Daeche, N. "The VERITAS theorem prover". Electronics Laboratory, University of Kent at Canterbury, 1984–present.

[10] Homewood, M., May, D., Shepherd, D., and Shepherd, R. "The IMS T800 Transputer. *IEEE Micro 7,* 5 (October 1987).

[11] INMOS, Ltd. *The Occam Programming Manual".* Prentice-Hall International, Hemel Hempstead, U.K., 1984.

[12] Roscoe, A. W. and Hoare, C. A. R. "The laws of occam programming". Technical Monograph PRG–53, Oxford University Computing Laboratory, Programming Research Group, 1986.

[13] Sufrin, B. A., ed. "The Z handbook". Oxford University Computing Laboratory, Programming Research Group, 1986.

Multicomputers

5

Charles L. Seitz
California Institute of Technology

Background

For nearly a decade, my students and I have been studying the architecture, design, programming, and applications of a class of message-passing concurrent computers that have come to be known aptly as multicomputers. Some earlier results of our work with an experimental multicomputer called the Cosmic Cube [27] have been transferred to industry, and can be seen in the architecture, design, and programming methods of the first-generation "hypercube" multicomputers made by Intel Scientific Computers, Symult Systems, and N-CUBE.

Our current efforts are aimed at learning to exploit concurrency between relatively small execution units in message-passing programs [2, 4] and to design machines and programming systems that will support such computations efficiently [3, 10, 30, 31]. Programs that expose concurrency at a finer "granularity" promise to extend the range of multicomputer design possibilities and applications. Decreasing the number of instructions executed between message operations while increasing the degree of concurrency, however, escalates the demands on a multicomputer message system. Streamlining the message handling required a number of new ideas about the physical design and programming of multicomputers. These ideas are being incorporated into a second generation of commercial multicomputers [28], and also into an experimental fine-grain multicomputer system called Mosaic.

The difficulties of exposition that I face in describing the current status of, near-term prospects for, and new ideas about multicomputers are similar to the pitfalls inherent in the entire enterprise of computer architecture. The computer architect is called upon to mediate between the uses or applications of computation and the capabilities of technology. These end points are too diffuse, and the distance between them too great, for definitive solutions. Instead, we may seek an intermediate point in the form of a specific computer architecture or design. Multicomputer architecture is our intermediate point (Section 1). We can then study how to span between technology and the architecture (Sections 2, 3, and 4), and between the architecture and applications (Sections 4, 5, and 6). These studies extend over long periods of time, so that only occasionally do we have the opportunity to adjust our intermediate point (Section 7).

1 *Multicomputer Architecture*

One virtue of multicomputers is their simplicity. An idealized view portrays a multicomputer as an ensemble of programmable computers, called *nodes,* connected by a *message-passing network* (Figure 1).

Each of the N node computers executes programs concurrently, coordinating its activities with the other nodes only by sending and receiving messages. There is no global memory or address space; rather, each node has its own private memory and address space.

A multiprogramming operating system or run-time system in each node allows multiple *processes* to share a single node. Just as the memory and address space of a node are private to that node, the variables of a process are private to that process. Whether they are in the same or different nodes, processes interact only through messages. Of course, all processes are concurrent, whether by virtue of residing in different nodes or by being interleaved in execution within a single node. The close relationship between the expression of a computation in terms of processes and messages and the physical structure on which these computations are executed is evident and deliberate.

Within this structural definition, two different types of commercial multi-computers have appeared. Transputer-based multicomputers implement the primitives of CSP [15] or occam [16]. The statically defined processes are connected by statically defined channels that convey messages with unbuffered, synchronous communication. Although my ideas about the architecture and programming of multicomputers were strongly influenced by CSP —a pioneering creation of C. A. R. Hoare, the scientific director of this institute of the Year of Programming— my students and I made different design choices in developing the Cosmic Cube type of multicomputer. For example, in the Cosmic Cube and its commercial descendants, processes are created dynamically by other processes, messages are directed to processes rather than to channels, and messages are buffered asynchronously in transit. Occam programs can be executed on Cosmic Cube multicomputers by using functions that implement the communication and other primitives of occam in terms of the Cosmic Cube primitives (see Section 5.2); Cosmic Cube programs, however, cannot in general be executed on transputer arrays.

I shall return in Section 1.5 to comparisons between these two types of multicomputers, but first will describe the characteristics of the multicomputer systems that my students and I have developed.

1.1 *Processes*

A process is an *instance* of a program written in a sequential programming notation, such as C, FORTRAN, LISP, or Pascal, that has been extended with a library of functions for creating processes, sending messages, and receiving messages. Most of our research group's programming experiments have

Figure 1.   Block diagram of a multicomputer.

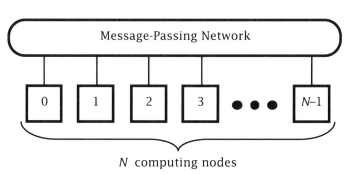

used the C programming language with its library of process-creation and message-handling functions, a combination that we refer to as *Cosmic C* [30]. It is convenient in this opening exposition of multicomputer architecture to introduce the primitive functions of Cosmic C in order to explain those operations supported by the lowest levels of the programming system. Analogous functions exist in the libraries associated with other programming notations used to express process code.

The characteristics of the application suggest to the programmer a way to formulate the computing problem as an explicitly concurrent, multiprocess program. For example, physical computations are often homogeneous, because the same laws govern all parts of the physical system. Also, the set of parts can often be partitioned in a uniform way. A homogeneous problem typically requires only one program. The numerous processes created from this one program might deal with different regions, particles, electrical-circuit nodes, or elements of a discrete-event simulation. A less regular problem might be partitioned according to function, with a separate program for each required function. These programs serve as templates for creating processes as they are required. Such computations typically involve numerous instances of each program, and use many more processes than nodes.

In addition to using the processes in the multicomputer nodes, a computation may employ processes in host computers connected either directly to the multicomputer or indirectly through networks. Host processes typically deal with specialized parts of a computation, such as display generation or other interaction on the user's workstation computer.

A process is bound to a node or host when it is created, and the low-level programming system of a multicomputer does not relocate processes. The premise behind both the multiprocessor architecture and the dataflow model —that it is necessary to bind runnable processes dynamically to processors— is obsolete in the metrics of today's technologies, in which communication is more costly than storage and computing. For example, the processors used in fine-grain multicomputers require only as much silicon area and power as a few kilobytes of storage, whereas the communication associated with a node requires more area than does a processor, and consumes the majority of the power consumed by a node. Thus, it is more effective to use silicon area for providing more processors, even if they are to be used at a low duty factor, than it is to provide the mechanisms for communicating the code and data for a process to an idle processor.

Messages are directed to processes; hence, each process must have a unique *identifier,* or *reference.* Since the binding of a process to a node persists for the life of the process, it is efficient to include the node number —the physical location of a process— as part of its unique identifier. The fixed numbering $(0, 1, \ldots, N-1)$ of the nodes, together with the uniqueness of the process identifier (**pid**) within a node, establishes a globally unique identifier for each node process. Host processes are similarly identified with a node value, HOST, which is outside the range $0, 1, \ldots, N-1$; and a unique **pid** is maintained for each host process by a host run-time system. These identifiers, or IDs, are thus represented in the low-level programming system as an ordered pair, **(node, pid)**, in which the first coordinate represents the distribution of processes across the nodes. Since multicomputers do not have a global memory-address space, IDs are used to provide a global name space.

All that is required to create a node process is a call (from either a node or a host process) to the Cosmic C function:

```
spawn("filename", node, pid, "mode");
```

The file specified by **filename** contains a compiled program that is loaded into the **node** and given the **pid** and **mode** specified in the function arguments. If the file or node does not exist, if the **pid** is already in use, or if any of a number of other error conditions occurs, the function returns a nonzero error code and produces an error message. A variant of the spawn function places the process automatically and returns the ID. The function **ckill(node, pid, "mode")** eliminates a process together with any messages that may be queued for it.

A set of N processes that are spawned from the same program and given the same **pid** in each node, e.g., the set of IDs **(0, p)**, **(1, p)**, ..., **(N-1, p)**, is referred to as a *set of cohorts*. Within the set, each cohort has implicit reference to the other cohorts. Because this process structure is used so frequently in multicomputer programs, the process-creation function supports a broadcast-spawn operation, **spawn("filename", ALL, pid, "mode")**.

1.2 *Messages*

Messages convey arbitrary byte streams that may represent variables, arrays, or structures. A message may be queued at the source node and in transit through the message-passing network until the physical channels required for its transmission become available. Similarly, because a message may arrive at the destination node before the process to which it is directed calls for it, messages are queued at the destination node. A message is accordingly specified as exhibiting an arbitrary delay between the time it is sent and the time it arrives at the destination node. Between pairs of processes, however, message order is preserved. The message system also exhibits fairness in message injection; that is, a process or node will not be blocked indefinitely from injecting a message into the message system.

All that is required for one process to send a message to another process is that the sending process have reference to the destination process. The *process structure* is a snapshot of the set of processes involved in a computation, together with each process's references to other processes. Of course, the process structure may evolve during a computation as a result of processes being created or destroyed, or of references to processes being passed in messages. Figure 2 depicts a process structure as a directed graph in which the vertices (drawn here as open circles) represent processes, and the arcs represent reference. The arcs may be visualized as channels, with messages (small filled dots) enqueued on the channels. In accordance with the properties of the message system, the messages may be visualized as "traveling" at an arbitrary speed; however, one message cannot pass another on a reference arc.

1.3 *Primitive Message Functions*

Process execution and message transport take place concurrently. The blocking behavior of certain of the send and receive functions executed by a process serves to create synchronization events between process execution and message-system activities. A blocking function does not return until the required activities in the message system have been completed.

Figure 2.   Graph representation of a process structure.

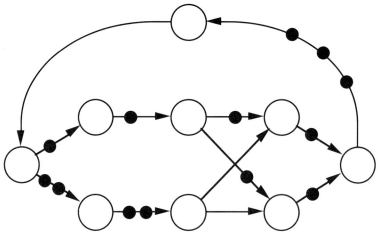

The primitive message functions exchange data through dynamically allocated storage that can be accessed by both the process and the message system. These message functions are distinguished by an "x" prefix. Other message functions may be defined in terms of these primitive functions, as illustrated in Section 5, or for reasons of performance may be implemented on a particular multicomputer by separate system calls.

A message buffer can be allocated by the statement

   p = xmalloc(length);

where **length** is the length in bytes, and **p** is a pointer to the message buffer. A message buffer can be deallocated by

   xfree(p);

Except for the message space on which they operate, these functions are semantically identical to the UNIX **malloc** and **free** functions, which are familiar to C programmers.

The contents of the message buffer pointed to by **p** can be sent as a message to the process **(node, pid)** by

   xsend(p, node, pid);

which also deallocates the message buffer. That is, **xsend(p, ...)** resembles **xfree(p)**, except that it also sends a message. Thus, there is no need for blocking until after the message has been sent, nor is there any need for a mechanism to test whether the message has been sent.

A blocking variant of **xsend** exists as the nonprimitive function **sendb**. The **sendb** function takes an additional length parameter, is not restricted to sending data from a message buffer, and does not deallocate the memory from which the data is sent. Of course, **sendb** can be expressed in terms of **xsend** by allocating a message buffer of the specified length, copying the message data into the message buffer, and calling **xsend**.

The next available message for a process can be received by

   p = xrecvb();

which is semantically similar to **xmalloc**, except that the initial contents and length of the message buffer pointed to by **p** are determined by the contents and length of the message received. A message buffer thus allocated can be freed after the message is used, either with the **xfree(p)** function or by building another message in the message buffer and freeing the message buffer with the **xsend(p, ...)** function. It is common in message-passing programs for a process to receive a message, modify its contents, and then send it on to another process.

The suffix "b" of **xrecvb** denotes that this is a blocking function, which will not return until a message has been received. The nonblocking variant is the primitive function **xrecv**. Just as the `malloc` function in the UNIX environment may return a NULL (in C, a zero or false) pointer if there is no space available, the **xrecv** function may return a NULL pointer if no message is present. It is accordingly possible for a process to do other work while waiting for a message, as in

```
if (p = xrecv()) operate_on_message(p);
else do_other_work();
```

The ability of **xrecv** to indicate the presence or absence of a message takes the place of a receive probe [23]. Although **xrecvb** can be expressed in terms of **xrecv**, for example by

```
char *xrecvb() {
    char *p; while(!(p = xrecv())); return(p);
}
```

the **xrecvb** function is defined as a primitive function in most implementations in order to make process scheduling more efficient.

To complete the list of functions that we shall use in Cosmic C programming examples:

xlength(p) returns the length of the message buffer pointed to by **p**.

mynode() returns the calling process's node number.

mypid() returns the calling process's **pid**.

nnodes() returns the number of nodes, *N*.

1.4 *Scheduling*

It is sufficient in writing and verifying programs to treat all processes as if they execute concurrently. Nevertheless, to understand the *reactive-process* programming discipline, it is useful at this point to indulge in some discussion of process scheduling.

The idea that many processes can share a node provides more than abstractive convenience and generality — it is a technique by which these computations exhibit a degree of insensitivity to message latency. When one process becomes blocked, as occurs when the message required for that process to progress has not yet arrived, the node operating system can "switch context" by saving the state of the blocked process and running another process. Specifically, when process *A* calls **xrecvb** or **xrecv** and the next queued message is for process *B*, the system may save the state of process *A* and start running process *B*. The appearance of **xrecvb** or **xrecv** marks preferred *choice points* for switching execution to another process; it is in this sense that the scheduling is *reactive* or *message-driven*. The simplicity and the consequent small overhead of this reactive form of scheduling make it the clear choice for the lowest level of operating-system scheduling. As long as a process is making progress, why force a context switch?

It is also necessary for the node operating system to interleave process execution in a way that is at least weakly fair, to ensure that the interactions between concurrent processes will be the same whether they are within a node or distributed across different nodes. Reactive scheduling would be sufficient for computations in which all processes execute for short, bounded periods between choice points. For processes that are not so well behaved, however, the operating system enforces fairness between processes by interrupting any process that has run for a predetermined period without executing an **xrecvb** or **xrecv** function. Reactive scheduling is also bypassed in dealing with exceptional events, for example, priority messages for system services such as process spawning, the remote procedure call (RPC) mechanism used by system services, and error-condition handling.

That processes are ordinarily scheduled directly from the node receive queue encourages a shift of viewpoint toward message-passing programs. We have noticed that, as programmers gain experience with multicomputers, their way of reasoning about the collective behavior of entire message-passing programs shifts from a process-centered to a message-centered view. Each message is a token that allows its destination process to run. When the message causes the process to resume execution at the return from an **xrecvb** call, the process performs computations that may change its persistent internal state, create additional processes, send messages, and finally either call **xrecvb** again or exit. The sequential actions represented by the instruction trace between two **xrecvb** calls can be regarded as an atomic action that involves an input, state change, and output. If, in response to a single input, the output includes messages sent to multiple processes, the execution has increased the potential concurrency; if the output includes no messages sent, the execution has decreased the concurrency. A program such as a grid-point computation can be expected to sustain a constant degree of concurrency: One would expect that for *b* boundary points, each *b* executions would result in exactly *b* messages being sent. Similar arguments can be applied to process-creation actions to analyze the way in which a process structure is constructed.

1.5 *Relationship with Other Models*

In place of a summary, it may be helpful for the reader who is familiar with Actors, CSP or occam, or multiprocessors to understand the relationship between multicomputers and these other, closely related models of concurrent or parallel computation.

The Actor model In response to receiving a message, a process can operate on its internal variables, create new processes, and send messages. It can then either prepare to receive another message or exit. In these respects there are no major differences between our framework for multicomputer computations and the Actor model [1]. The few minor differences consistently comprise restrictions not present in the Actor model.

The Actor model may treat processes and messages interchangeably, whereas we treat them as distinct entities. Both processes and messages encapsulate data; their other properties, however, are complementary. Processes are active, stationary, and potentially persistent; messages are inert, mobile, and transitory. One may regard all the processes as executing concurrently, although some may be blocked in synchronization actions with messages. Similarly, one may regard all the messages that exist at a given moment as flowing concurrently, except that, unlike Actor-model messages, they are constrained to maintain message order between pairs of communicating processes. Our experience indicates that the lack of message-order preservation between pairs of communicating processes would introduce needless complications into programs and unnecessary additional nondeterminacy into the operation of the message system.

Perhaps the most significant difference between the Actor model and what we have implemented in such multicomputer programming systems as Cosmic C [30, 33] and Cantor [2, 3, 4] is that we make a distinction between a process and its definition. A definition is simply a program and is referred to by its file name. A definition may serve as a template for creating any number of processes, which are distinct and are referred to by their references or IDs.

CSP and Occam Whereas our framework for multicomputer computations is consistently more restrictive than the Actor model, it is consistently more permissive than CSP [15] or occam [16].

Occam programs employ a static process structure in which the number of processes and their connectivity is known before the program is executed. Our preference is to be able to express computations in which the process structure is built dynamically as part of the computation. The dynamic structure of processes and references obviates the possibility of channels, suggesting instead the approach originally used in CSP of sending messages to processes.

Each occam channel connects exactly two processes, and communication through the channel is synchronous; that is, the number of completed send actions at one end of the channel is identical to the number of completed receive actions at the other end. Instead of this zero-slack form of communication, the Cosmic Cube multicomputers use an unbounded-slack, asynchronous form of communication in which the number of completed receive actions does not exceed the number of completed send actions. Buffering is implicit, and the size of the buffer is bounded by its use. As illustrated in Section 5.2, the implementation of the occam send and receive operations in terms of the Cosmic Cube operations is remarkably simple and efficient.

The asynchronous properties of the Cosmic Cube message system result from our decision to provide arbitrary and variable connectivity of processes. This decision is in contrast to transputer multicomputers, where even separate logical channels between transputers must be implemented with separate physical channels. In order to allow for a variety of routing methods in different implementations, it is essential that routing itself be expressible in a process. An unbounded-slack message that is relayed by process B from processes $A \rightarrow B \rightarrow C$ cannot be distinguished by A or C from a message that is sent directly. Synchronous channels, however, cannot be composed $A \rightarrow B \rightarrow C$ by an occam process B so that the resulting action will be synchronous with respect to A and C. The best one can do is to employ a reply-message protocol so as to simulate a synchronous channel, but this would require different programs for A and C.

Multiprocessors The multicomputer belongs to the same general classification as the shared-memory multiprocessor: Both are multiple-instruction, multiple-data (MIMD) concurrent computers. The informed observer of a decade ago might have expected that the multiprocessor would become the most common form of MIMD parallel computer, as indeed it is for systems with relatively small numbers of processors. For large-N (say, $N \geq 64$) systems, however, multicomputers substantially outnumber multiprocessors. The dominance of message-passing for large-N concurrent and parallel systems —multicomputers, systolic arrays, and the Connection Machine— is due to technical feasibility and cost/performance considerations [26].

We have found that the same concurrent formulations and algorithms can generally be cast equally easily into a shared-variable program for a multiprocessor or a message-passing program for a multicomputer; ideally, one program should serve for either architecture. In fact, message-passing programs written in Cosmic C are routinely run on multiprocessors. The way that this is achieved provides a good illustration of the portability of the primitive functions. The **xmalloc** and **xfree** functions in a multiprocessor implementation allocate and free shared memory. The **xsend(p, node, pid)** function *passes ownership* of the block pointed to by **p** to process **(node, pid)**, and appends the pointer to its task queue. A process obtains a new task by calling the **xrecv** function. Thus, the implementation of these few functions under the multiprocessor's native task system suffices for running Cosmic C programs. Such implementations exist on numerous multiprocessor systems.

The inverse problem of running multiprocessor programs on multicomputers, although more difficult, has been demonstrated repeatedly. The efficiency of this approach depends on having a compiler trace the data dependencies in shared variables, replacing assignments to shared variables with message-passing operations.

2 *Hardware Grain Size*

The idealized computing structure illustrated in Figure 1 leaves open many design choices, such as the following:

1. What is the memory size and performance level of the node computers? Within a fixed budget, is it more advantageous to use 10,000 small nodes, 1000 intermediate-size nodes, or 100 large nodes?

2. What is the form of the message-passing network? It is obviously impossible for large N to connect every pair of computers since this would require $N(N-1)$ physical channels.

3. To what extent can existing or standardized computer components, interfaces, operating systems, compilers, and programming languages be used to build and program multicomputer systems?

Instead of considering these questions in the abstract, I shall describe in this and the following two sections the design decisions that my students and I have made for multicomputer systems that occupy two of the most interesting points in the design space. Although this section begins with a discussion of technology, I have simplified the examination of the first choices we face when designing multicomputers so as to clarify these issues for readers who have little background in physical electronics. The simplification does only slight disservice to the engineering realities.

One of the beautiful characteristics of modern digital technologies is uniformity. The high-complexity silicon CMOS (complementary metal-oxide semiconductor) processes are suitable for both storage and logic, and are used to implement nearly all of the electronic components of personal and work-station computers. Other technologies may be used in specialized circumstances, but their density, performance, and cost can generally be related to those characteristics of the mainstream CMOS technologies.

Suppose that the budget for building a high-performance computer were to be given as the equivalent of $1m^2$ ($= 10^6mm^2$) of silicon in a modern CMOS process having a minimum feature size of $1\mu m$. Because of the exponentially decreasing fabrication yield as a function of the area of an individual microelectronic chip, the $1m^2$ of silicon ideally would be distributed in today's technology across $\approx 1.6 \times 10^4$ chips, with an average area of $\approx 60mm^2$ per chip. Chips of this size balance the cost of the silicon with the cost of packaging. Substantially larger chips exhibit such small yield that the cost is unfavorably dominated by the silicon; substantially smaller chips could be fabricated with nearly perfect yield, but more of the computer's interconnection would have to be accomplished at higher cost using circuit-board or multichip-carrier technologies.

The one figure of merit of this computer that depends nearly linearly on silicon area is the size of the primary random-access memory. Processor performance as a function of silicon area is strikingly sublinear. The tendency of contemporary computer designs to devote the majority of the silicon-area budget to memory may be simply a case of allocating the budget to the place where it makes a difference. If, without stronger justification than engineering experience, we devote 60 percent of the silicon-area budget to the primary memory and 40 percent to the processor(s), our final conclusions would not be very different than if we had partitioned the area 75/25 or 50/50. In CMOS processes that are specialized toward dynamic random-access storage, a silicon area of $0.6m^2$ is sufficient to produce about 10^{10} bits of storage ($\approx 10^4$ $60mm^2$ chips with $\approx 10^6$ bits per chip), or 1Gbyte after allowing for error detection and correction.

Let us now examine three choices of hardware "grain size" in MIMD architectures, corresponding to $N = 4$, $N = 256$, and $N = 16,384$ within the $1m^2$ silicon-area budget. The steps between these points are large; each is a factor of 64. The intermediate choices of N are interesting as well, but for present purposes we wish only to sample these interesting points in the design space.

2.1 *Vector Supercomputers*

Single-processor performance is a weak function of silicon area in the range 0.05–$0.4m^2$. Performance is limited more severely by packaging density and the partitioning of system parts across chips than by the number of logic components. In this regime of diminishing returns of performance for silicon area, the substantially higher throughput of a multiprocessor will generally be preferred over the only slightly faster single-stream performance that would result from devoting all of the silicon-area budget to one processor. The small-N multiprocessor is the sensible compromise that was adopted in the design of such vector supercomputers as the Cray X-MP/416 ($N = 4$) and Y-MP/832 ($N = 8$). Because the size of the processors or nodes of such an MIMD machine is quite large, we refer to it as a *large-grain* system.

While 0.4m^2 of silicon is sufficient for a cache, four to eight processors, and the switch network between the processors and memory, such machines as the Cray X-MP and Y-MP do not implement these system parts with 6000 high-complexity chips, nor within an equivalent budget. Instead, the remarkable Cray Y-MP/832 [7] employs $\approx 10^5$ chips in lower-complexity but higher-speed technologies for the processors, switch network, and 256Mbytes of primary memory, and relegates the 1Gbyte of CMOS memory to the solid-state disk. The equivalent complexity in 1μm CMOS technologies is probably 3–4m^2 of silicon. A multiprocessor with $N = 4$ is slightly more expensive to build than a multicomputer, but is an easier target for automatic translation of sequential programs into programs that can exploit this small number of processors.

The performance of vector supercomputers is advancing relatively slowly. The peak performance in the evolution from the Cray 1S (1 processor × 160Mflops) to the Cray X-MP (4 processors × 210Mflops) to the Cray Y-MP (8 processors × 300Mflops) shows a 13-year gain of not quite 2× due to single-processor performance, but 8× due to parallelism.

2.2 *Medium-Grain Multicomputers*

A homogeneous multicomputer with $N = 256$ and 1m^2 of silicon partitions the 1Gbyte of memory into 4Mbytes per node. The remaining ≈ 1500mm^2 of silicon per node can be devoted to cache memory; one or more processors; read-only memory for initialization, self-test, and bootstrap code; an interface to the message system; and the node's own part of the message-passing network (Figure 3). A node of this size can be packaged as a single circuit board. We refer to multicomputers that resemble this description, such as the Intel iPSC/2 [17] and the Symult Series 2010 [28], as second-generation, *medium-grain* multicomputers.

This hardware grain size is popular because it fits today's commodity-chip and commodity-software technology. Because the node resembles a workstation computer, we can use many of the same components and programming tools. Single-chip processors with floating-point coprocessors, such as the Intel 80386/80387 used in the iPSC/2 nodes or the Motorola 68020/68882 used in the Symult Series 2010 nodes, provide 4–5MIPS integer and ≈0.2Mflops scalar-floating-point performance per node. Although a single-chip processor has a number of technological advantages, the processor in the current second-generation medium-grain multicomputers is equivalent to only about 50mm² of the silicon-area budget, with the result that these nodes are somewhat underpowered. The advent of million-transistor, 150mm², single-chip processors, such as the Intel i860 [20], whose floating-point performance is ≈0.3 that of a Cray X-MP processor, promise to remedy this deficiency. In the meanwhile, floating-point accelerators with a peak performance of ≈20Mflops are used on each node in configurations intended for high-speed scientific computation. The aggregate performance of such a system is ≈1000MIPS and ≈5000 peak Mflops, and the ≈$5M cost is in a ≈10× more favorable relationship to performance than the cost/performance of vector supercomputers.

The disadvantage of this way of distributing the silicon-area budget, if one chooses to regard it as such, is that there is no reasonable hope that such

Figure 3.   Major components and structure of a node.

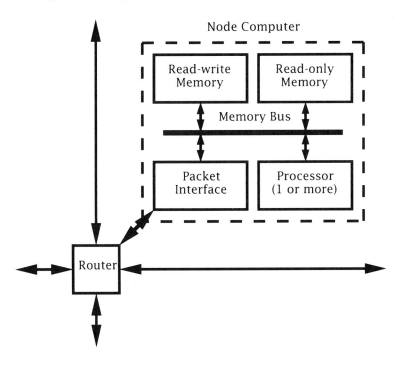

performance can be achieved by the automatic translation of sequential programs for execution on medium-grain multicomputers. Concurrent programs are necessary for exploiting the favorable cost/performance characteristics of these systems. The programming systems that can be accommodated in each 4Mbyte node are largely compatible with those found in workstation computers; thus, existing programming languages and compilers, together with the functional extensions described in Section 1, have proven to be adequate for writing application programs.

Multicomputers that are based on single-circuit-board nodes have evolved rapidly in step with advances in single-chip-processor and -memory technologies. The 1982 Cosmic Cube nodes have 128Kbytes of primary memory and a ≈ 0.15MIPS processor; the 1985 Intel iPSC/1 nodes have 512Kbytes of primary memory and a ≈ 0.6MIPS processor; the 1988 Intel iPSC/2 nodes have 4–8Mbytes of primary memory and a ≈ 5MIPS processor. The predominant evolution has been in node performance, memory size, and hardware support for the message system within a constant physical size of a node, rather than in the number of nodes.

2.3 *Fine-Grain Multicomputers*

A homogeneous multicomputer with $N = 16,384 = 2^{14}$ within our $1m^2$ budget allows just $61mm^2$ per node; thus, a node is a chip. The ability to localize the communication between the parts of a node to the internal wiring of a single chip makes this node size a very interesting point in the space of multicomputer designs. The usual allocation of 60 percent of the silicon area to primary storage would allow 64Kbytes for the node memory, leaving $25mm^2$ for the other parts of the node. Such is the progress in microelectronics that this node resembles a minicomputer of 20 years ago but is $\approx 40\times$ faster and more than $1000\times$ less expensive. There is also a close resemblance between this $61mm^2$ node and the 128Kbyte nodes in the Cosmic Cube. As I reported in 1985 [27], "The Cosmic Cube nodes were designed as a hardware simulation of what we expect to be able to integrate onto one or two chips in about five years."

My students and I have designed such a single-chip node, and are working toward assembling 16,384 of them into an experimental *fine-grain* multicomputer called Mosaic. The memory and the other parts shown in Figure 3 occupy a chip whose area in a $1\mu m$ CMOS process is very close to $61mm^2$. The 16-bit processor executes programs at a ≈ 14MIPS rate and has a number of unusual features to support efficient context switching. The 16,384-node system will achieve an aggregate memory bandwidth of more than 10^{12} bytes/s to support a peak (16-bit) integer-instruction bandwidth of $\approx 200,000$MIPS.

The message-network characteristics are described in Section 3.5.

Highly concurrent application programs developed for medium-grain multicomputers and for the fine-grain-SIMD Connection Machine [14] suggest that computing problems having the size and degree of concurrency that can exploit a 16K-node Mosaic are fairly common. There do not appear to be any insurmountable problems in formulating and writing concurrent programs in which the processes are quite small [2, 4, 10, 33] so as to fit within these small nodes. Unlike the medium-grain multicomputers, however, for which many of the necessary programming tools were adapted from the programming systems for personal computers and workstations, programming systems that directly support fine-grain concurrent programming had to be constructed from scratch.

Cantor [2, 3, 4], a "minimalist" programming notation based on Actor semantics, has allowed us to explore some of the mysteries of writing highly concurrent, fine-grain programs. Measurements of the number of processes, concurrency, and message load produced by the execution of Cantor application programs provided the parameters that guided the Mosaic hardware design. Cantor is a compiler-based system that circumvents much of the run-time checking that is necessary in the medium-grain systems. The Cantor compiler does not detect concurrency; rather, the source Cantor program already expresses the concurrency that may be used in execution. The compiler and run-time system are responsible only for managing the resources of the target computer.

2.4 *Summary*

As we scale the hardware grain size of multicomputers, we find that the same silicon area or cost is able to produce not only more concurrency with increasing N, but also higher aggregate performance, and hence improved cost/performance. Whether or not the fundamental difficulties of programming increase with increasing N and decreasing grain size, the mechanics of programming do become increasingly unconventional. Hence, such programming will be regarded as fundamentally more difficult by those who do not make the distinction.

3 *Message-Passing Networks*

The message-passing network is the backbone of a multicomputer: It spans the entire system, connects to every node, and conveys messages from any node to any other node. The *throughput* of the message system is a measure of the quantity of service that the message system can provide; the *message latency* is a measure of the quality of this service. Throughput and latency interact: When the applied load on the message system exceeds its throughput capacity, the message latency increases because of queueing at the source. In a reactive program, a sufficiently large message latency will deprive processes of messages, thereby regulating the computation's throughput. Thus, the message system limits the performance of programs that require more or better communication performance than the message system can deliver and, accordingly, defines the range of applications of the multicomputer.

The message load and the sensitivity of computing performance to message latency depend not only on the program, but also on the number of nodes over which it is distributed. A computation is insensitive to a message latency that is less than the interval during which messages would wait in the node receive queue. When the same processes are distributed over a larger number of nodes, the message load increases proportionally, and the average node-receive-queue waiting time decreases proportionally. Thus, increasing N places more severe requirements on both the throughput and the message latency. The form of scaling illustrated in the previous section, in which node size decreases as N increases, makes the message system requirements for large-N systems even more forbidding. The expression of a computing problem in terms of smaller processes tends to increase the rate at which processes produce messages because smaller processes are necessarily more highly interdependent. It was, in fact, from studying how to build low-latency message-passing networks for the difficult case of large-N, fine-grain multicomputers that we developed the techniques that also allowed a significant advance in message-passing performance between the first- and second-generation medium-grain multicomputers.

Not only are the requirements more severe as N increases, but the message system itself becomes physically more difficult to build. An arbitrated bus or ethernet could be used as an economical message-passing network for a multicomputer, but only up to a small value of N before its throughput limit would be reached. On the opposite extreme, a complete graph of channels connecting the nodes would entirely eliminate contention, but would use each channel at a low duty factor and be prohibitively expensive for large N. The compromise that has been adopted for multicomputers is to use a regular, direct network over which messages can be routed (Figure 4).

Multicomputer networks have little in common with wide-area networks. The multicomputer is a small, physically protected environment that allows high-bandwidth channels to operate with very small delays and immeasurably low error rates. The network is regular, such as a binary n-cube (hypercube) or mesh, in order to permit simple, fast, algorithmic routing. A direct and bidirectional network allows locality between processes that communicate frequently. The network must also be extensible, or scalable up to some limit, to allow for systems with different numbers of nodes. The design of message-passing networks involves many mutually interdependent design choices and goals. The choices include the network topology and the methods of achieving flow control, routing, deadlock avoidance, and fairness. The goals include high throughput, low latency, reasonable cost, scalability, and reliability. A survey of these issues would be less informative than a chronology of the design decisions that have shaped the evolution of multicomputer networks.

3.1 *Low-Level Flow Control*

The small delay on the physical channels provides an opportunity to regulate the information flow in small units, referred to as flow-control units, or *flits*. The physical channel may be regarded as a queue that conveys a sequence of flits; when contention blocks a channel, the flow is simply *blocked* by the queue discipline [5]. Because the individual flits carry no routing information, they cannot be interleaved on a channel. Instead, a sequence of flits forms a *packet* whose first several flits are a *header* that carries routing

Figure 4. Tessellation of nodes within a regular routing network.

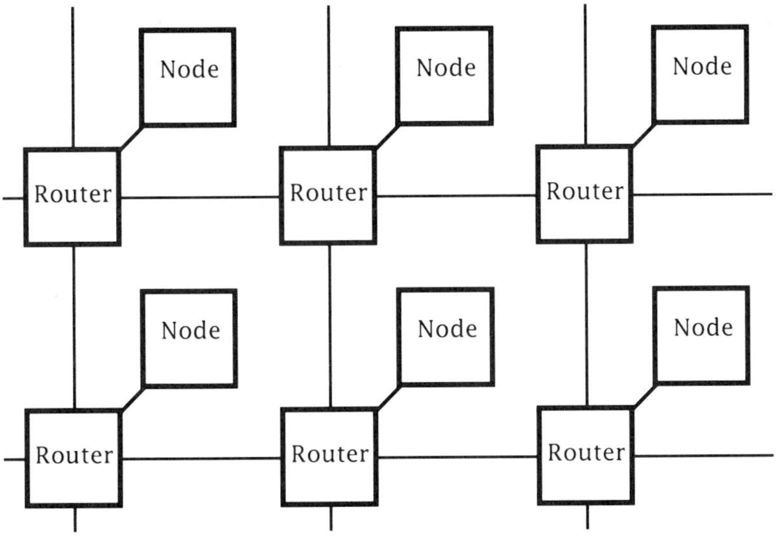

information and whose last flit is tagged as the *tail*. Fair interleaving of packets that require the same channel makes the packet the elementary unit not
only of routing, but also of network fairness. A limit on the maximum length
of a packet increases fairness and simplifies management of the storage in
the source and destination nodes. If a message is longer than the maximum
packet length, it is fragmented into a sequence of packets for transmission
and reassembled into a single message on arrival. This fragmentation and reassembly operation, which assures that a long message will not block a short
message for more than one packet-transmission time, is particularly important in situations in which one user's long messages, such as file accesses,
compete for the same channels as another user's short messages.

This hierarchy of messages, packets, and flits governs the communication
on each channel. Of course, mechanisms below the level of messages are in-
visible to the programmer. Because flow control is provided at the flit level,
the packet-level communication may employ simple and efficient "one-trip"
protocols that require neither replies nor acknowledgment packets. We have
used this hierarchy beginning with the design of the Cosmic Cube message
system and continuing through the Mosaic and the Symult Series 2010. De-
partures from this scheme, such as the use of packets for flow control in the
Intel iPSC/1, have proved to be troublesome.

3.2 *Cosmic Cube Message System*

The choice of the binary n-cube (hypercube) to connect $N = 2^n$ nodes for the
Cosmic Cube was based principally on these considerations:

1. The binary n-cube is scalable in powers of two according to its recursive
   definition: A 0-cube is a single node. A $(i+1)$-cube is constructed from two
   i-cubes by connecting like channels (Figure 5). Each node must have n
   channels, which are numbered $0, 1, \ldots, n-1$. This network is wireable and
   has feasible degree for practical values of N, even though not asymptoti-
   cally.

2. The number of channels that cross the bisection of this graph, and hence
   its throughput for nonlocal messages, scales with N.

3. There is an elegantly simple deadlock-free routing algorithm for binary
   n-cubes: The e-cube algorithm [22] requires that packets traverse the dimensions in order. Deadlock freedom can be demonstrated inductively: A
   packet arriving on channel $n-1$ is necessarily destined for the node, which
   consumes it; hence, channel $n-1$ cannot remain blocked indefinitely. A
   packet arriving on channel $n-2$ is destined either for the node, which

consumes it, or for channel $n - 1$, which will not be blocked indefinitely; hence, channel $n - 2$ cannot remain blocked indefinitely, etc.

4. The binary n-cube is a $\log_2 N$-diameter graph that is an excellent target for embedding other computation graphs. It also accommodates an optimal embedding of processes used by "doubling" algorithms for performing operations on distributed sets in logarithmic time. These common operations include sum, min, max, rank, and parallel prefix (see Section 5.3).

To permit experiments with different routing methods, the Cosmic Cube channels were designed to function under (operating system) program control. The queue-connected channels are 4 bits wide, but the channel-control logic provides an interface for 64-bit logical flits. In the original node operating system, the Cosmic Kernel, routing was performed in conventional store-

---

Figure 5.   Recursive construction of a binary n-cube.

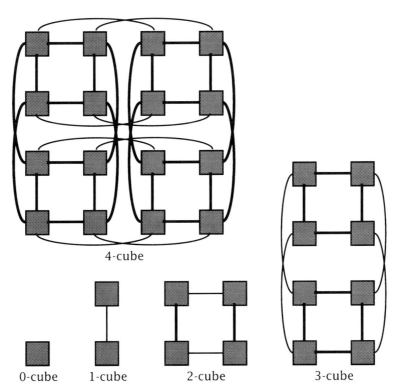

4-cube

0-cube   1-cube   2-cube   3-cube

and-forward fashion; i.e., an entire packet was stored in the node before it was sent to the next channel. We knew even at the time that *cut-through routing* [19], which allows an incoming packet to advance directly to the required outgoing channel as soon as sufficient header is read, would have the same property of being free of deadlock as store-and-forward routing; however, some vague and incorrect concerns about the performance of cut-through routing under heavy network loads inhibited us from using this approach from the outset. The fragmentation of long messages into packets and the pipelining of packets in the routing process allow the routing nodes to convey long messages without introducing excessive latency or requiring buffering of full messages. This store-and-forward packet-cut-through routing on a binary *n*-cube was adopted by all the first-generation commercial multicomputers, which were introduced in 1985. They did not adopt the low-level flow-control discipline, however, apparently because their designers did not appreciate its importance.

3.3 *Cut-Through Routing*

It was an obvious next step to design a VLSI chip to take care of routing within the message-passing network. If cut-through routing could be superimposed on the blocking flow-control discipline, the routing could be accomplished without using storage bandwidth in the routing nodes, and the routing chip associated with each node would not need to buffer entire packets. The other advantage of cut-through routing is the reduced latency of nonlocal packets. For a packet of length L and channels of bandwidth B, the time required to send a packet to a neighboring node is L/B. Store-and-forward routing of this packet over distance D then exhibits a network latency $T_{S\&F} = D(L/B)$, which depends on the *product* of D and L. If the head of a packet can be advanced directly into the next channel, however, taking time T_p to do so, the network latency is only $T_{C-T} = T_p D + L/B$, which depends on a *weighted sum* of D and L.

   In practice on a binary *n*-cube with bit-serial channels, T_p may be $\approx 0.1 \mu s$ and B may be ≈ 5Mbytes/s; hence, a 50-byte message that traverses an average distance of 4 in a binary 8-cube would require only $0.4 \mu s$ for path formation, but $10 \mu s$ to spool the message through the channels. Thus, the network latency of cut-through routing in a lightly loaded binary *n*-cube is essentially independent of message distance.

   How does cut-through routing perform under conditions of heavy network traffic? The analyses and elementary simulations that I did in 1984 and the extensive simulations on the Cosmic Cube that Wen-King Su did in 1985 finally persuaded us that cut-through routing had excellent performance properties.

The characteristic performance of blocking cut-through routing under conditions in which messages are sent to randomly selected nodes in a 16×16 mesh is illustrated in Figure 6 (adapted from [25]).

The throughput and applied load are expressed in units normalized to the network bisection capacity. The throughput increases linearly with the network load up to nearly half the available bandwidth across the bisection of the network, remaining stable at this maximum throughput at any higher load. Of course, the message latency, including the source-queueing time, increases steeply as the network becomes saturated.

In the spring of 1985, I worked with a team of students from my VLSI class to design a hypercube communication chip based on this blocking cut-through routing scheme. The students referred to this scheme as "wormhole routing," perhaps because of a presentation in which I depicted cut-through routing of packets by a flit-segmented worm whose head was leaving the network while its tail was still entering, or perhaps because of the possibility suggested by astrophysicists of "cosmic wormholes" that may allow instant travel between distant points in space. The implementation of the Reactive Kernel node operating system on the Cosmic Cubes incorporated wormhole routing, and a variant of this technique was used for the binary *n*-cube routing on the Intel iPSC/2, introduced in 1987.

Figure 6.   Throughput performance of blocking cut-through routing.

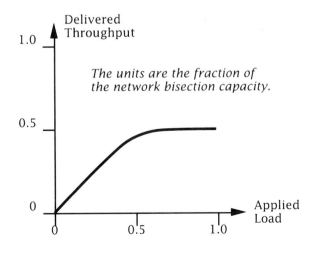

3.4 *Low-Dimension Networks*

The next step in improving message-passing networks was to replace the binary n-cube topology that had served well for the early experiments with two- and three-dimensional mesh networks.

The bisection bandwidth of a network effectively determines the aggregate throughput for nonlocal traffic. Circuit technology places a practical limit on the signaling rate of a single wire, b, currently at about 50Mbits/s. A channel of W wires has a bandwidth $B = Wb$. The bisection bandwidth is related by the constant b to the *wire bisection* of the network. The wire bisection contributes a significant component to the cost of a network; hence, if we hold the wire bisection constant, we are holding the throughput constant and the cost approximately constant. We should then be free to choose whatever graph will minimize the latency.

A d-dimensional (bidirectional) mesh, $N^{\frac{1}{d}} \times N^{\frac{1}{d}} \times \ldots$ (d times), $1 \le d \le \log_2 N$, includes the binary n-cube when $d = \log_2 N = n$. The bisection of this graph is $N^{\frac{d-1}{d}}$ channels. If the bisection bandwidth is normalized to that of a bit-serial binary n-cube, $Nb/2$ (in each direction), the bandwidth allowed on each channel reduces to $B = (b/2)N^{\frac{1}{d}}$. The average distance in the d-dimensional mesh is $\frac{1}{3}d(N^{\frac{1}{d}} - N^{-\frac{1}{d}})$, or approximately $\frac{1}{3}dN^{\frac{1}{d}}$ for $d \ll n$.

Under these constant-throughput conditions, what value of d provides the lowest latency with cut-through routing? From the expression for the latency, $T_{C-T} = T_p D + L/B$, this is a straightforward optimization for a given N, message length L, and T_p. In practice, $T_p \approx 2/b$, or two flit times. Expressed in terms of d, $T_{C-T} = (1/b)(\frac{2}{3}dN^{\frac{1}{d}} + 2LN^{-\frac{1}{d}})$. This function is plotted in Figure 7 with $L = 256$ bits (32-byte packets) and $N = 256$ and 16,384.

The latency is expressed in units of $1/b$, or flit times. A high-dimension network minimizes the first term at the expense of the second; that is, path formation takes much less time than spooling the message through the channels, such as in the previous example for the binary n-cube. A low-dimension network minimizes the second term at the expense of the first. The minimum occurs when the two terms are nearly equal. The surprise is that minimum latency is achieved with a relatively low-dimension, large-diameter graph: a two-dimensional mesh for $N = 256$, and a three-dimensional mesh for $N = 16,384$.

This derivation of the latency optimality of low-dimension meshes is simpler than the analysis [10] of the k-ary n-cube (hypertorus) graph [26] that originally persuaded us to consider low-dimension networks. Furthermore, the mesh, an aperiodic form of the torus, is the network we actually use (see Figure 8).

Although our preference has been for networks that have the same structure when viewed from every point, such as the *k*-ary *n*-cube (the binary *n*-cube included), the mesh has several decisive advantages:

1. *Simpler deadlock-free routing:* The mesh is acyclic in each direction and dimension, so dimension-order routing suffices to assure freedom from deadlock. The torus requires a more complex technique, such as virtual channels [12]. The greater simplicity of the routing scheme translates into a simpler and faster routing chip.

2. *Edge connectivity:* A mesh provides numerous unused channels around its edges; this is a phenomenal I/O bandwidth that can be used for communication with hosts and for secondary storage. The torus has no edge.

3. *Space sharing:* In the usual mode of operation of our binary *n*-cube multi-computers, different users may have programs resident in different sub-cubes. For example, a 6-cube may have one job running in a logical 5-cube

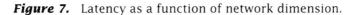

Figure 7. Latency as a function of network dimension.

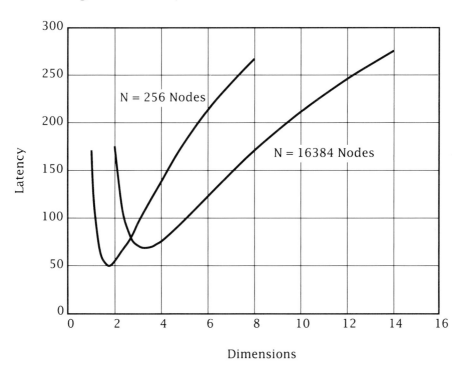

concurrently with two others running in logical 4-cubes. Subcubes of binary n-cubes are still binary n-cubes. There is no corresponding way to cut a torus so that the part assigned to one user is still a torus; a subdivision of a mesh, however, is also a mesh.

4. *Wire length:* The mesh and torus ($n \leq 3$) are networks that can be projected directly into the packaging medium so that all channels are short. In order to make all adjacent nodes in a 2–D or 3–D torus physically close, the structure must be folded, as shown in Figure 8, which complicates the packaging.

5. *Performance:* For equivalent wire bisection and dimension, the bidirectional mesh exhibits somewhat lower latency than does the bidirectional torus.

Queueing theory tells us that it is more effective to share a small number of high-capacity resources than a large number of low-capacity resources. Indeed, our performance simulations of binary n-cubes, torus networks, and meshes show that the low-dimension networks exhibit lower latency, better "hot-spot" characteristics, increased utilization of the bisection, and nearly perfect regulation of the network throughput at maximal levels. Although these studies employed the worst-case condition of nonlocal traffic, the higher channel bandwidth of a low-dimension network also improves the performance for localized messages.

Figure 8.   Comparison of 2–D torus and mesh networks.

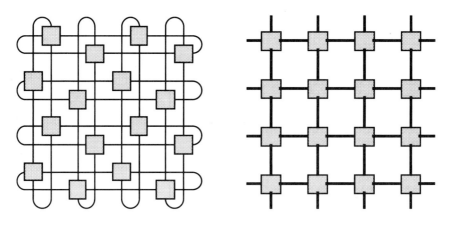

3.5 *Engineering and Technology*

The techniques of flow control, cut-through routing, and network topology that we had in hand by mid-1986 provided an exciting opportunity to achieve improvements of more than 100× in the latency of nonlocal messages and ≈20× in the channel bandwidth over the message networks of the first-generation medium-grain multicomputers. Low-dimension mesh networks also provided the opportunity to match the form of the network to two- and three-dimensional packaging technologies while using *no* long wires.

A joint project between my Caltech research group and Symult Systems, Inc. that resulted in the design of the Symult Series 2010 (S2010) provided the means of incorporating these ideas into a medium-grain multicomputer. My students and I designed a *mesh-routing chip* (MRC) [13] that is used in the routing-mesh backplane of the S2010 (Figure 9).

The MRC is self-timed (see the chapter by Alain J. Martin in this volume),

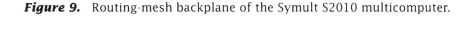

Figure 9.   Routing-mesh backplane of the Symult S2010 multicomputer.

and is fabricated by the MOSIS service in 1.6μm CMOS technology. Its 8-bit-wide channels operate at $T_p \approx$ 80ns and $B \approx$ 25Mbytes/s. (A later version, which is being used in the Intel Touchstone prototypes, operates with $T_p \approx$ 70ns, including a 20-flit internal queue, and $B \approx$ 65Mbytes/s.) A unidirectional channel requires 11 wires: eight data lines, a tail bit, and a request/acknowledge pair for timing and queue flow control. The MRC has five bidirectional channels, one for each compass direction, and one connected to the node computer, for a total of 110 wires plus a reset and multiple power and ground lines. The first two flits of the packet contain Δx and Δy, and the magnitudes of these displacements are decremented as the packet is routed to its destination. The internal organization of the MRC is based on a *routing automata* framework in which the two-dimensional router is composed of two identical one-dimensional routers that are in turn composed of elementary queue, decision, merge, and header-processing automata. The fairness of the merge automaton assures fairness in the arbitration for each channel, including the channel to and from the node computer.

The message system of the S2010, the most recently introduced (in 1988) and advanced of the commercial multicomputers, fully lives up to our expectations [28]. The bandwidth of a channel is nearly the same as the memory bandwidth of a node. Even including fragmentation and reassembly of long messages, the S2010 is able to transfer messages *between* nodes faster than its processor can copy data *within* a single node. In addition, as shown in Figure 9, the mesh construction is dramatically simpler than that of the earlier binary *n*-cube machines. The manufacturing unit is a 16-node 4×4 submesh that can be stacked both horizontally and vertically to construct systems of up to any number of nodes. Because the bisection of the square mesh varies with $\sqrt{N}$, configurations smaller than our 256-node design centerline have a surplus of message bandwidth, whereas larger configurations with communication-intensive programs are capable of saturating the message system unless message traffic is localized.

These same techniques allowed us to design a message system that we expect to be adequate for the 16,384-node Mosaic. It is a 40MHz, synchronous, three-dimensional routing mesh with four-data-bit-wide channels, yielding a channel bandwidth B = 20Mbytes/s and routing time T_p = 50ns. A synchronous network is possible because a clock can be distributed on a mesh such that its skew is controlled between neighbors [32]. Each unidirectional channel requires six wires: four data bits, an escape bit for control information, and a queue flow-control signal in the reverse direction. Thus, the six bidirectional channels required for the three-dimensional mesh use 72 (of 84) package pins on the single-chip Mosaic node.

The bilateral bandwidth of the smaller bisections of this 32×32×16 mesh is

10Gbytes/s. Utilizing half of this bisection, the nodes can generate traffic to random destinations at an average rate of 1.25Mbytes/s, e.g., a 20-byte message every 16μs, or every $\approx$200 instructions. These message rates are consistent with measurements of a diverse sample of fine-grain message-passing programs [2, 10]. The average message distance is 27 channels, yielding a path-formation component of the latency of 1.3μs. The time required to convey the 20-byte message is an additional 1μs. The average 2.3μs latency for this 20-byte message corresponds to $\approx$30 instructions, nearly the same as required by the run-time system to handle the message at the source and destination. Thus, we do not expect computations on the Mosaic to be seriously limited by the latency of the message network.

3.6 *Summary*

The cost of the message-passing network is closely tied to its wire bisection and throughput. Within these constraints, organizational refinements in the way in which the wires are used (cut-through routing), deployed (low-dimension networks), and joined with VLSI technology (routing chips) make it possible to achieve message latencies that are quite tolerable even for multicomputers in the range of 10,000 nodes.

4 *Low-Level Programming Systems*

The first programming system that we developed for the Cosmic Cube was a multiprogramming system that was nearly conventional, except that its processes were distributed across the nodes of the multicomputer. The Cosmic Kernel node operating system interleaved execution within a node by using round-robin scheduling. A type parameter was included with every message as it was sent, and the receive functions specified the type of message to be assigned to a given variable, structure, or array. (This *discretionary* receive operation is discussed in greater detail in Section 5.1.) Programs that processed messages singly could use blocking receive functions; since only one such receive could be pending at a time, the operating system would not run this process until the message was available. Programs that involved complex progress conditions, such as the availability of particular combinations of messages, required nonblocking receive functions that would allow several receive operations to be pending concurrently. This situation is analogous to compound guards in CSP and to trigger mechanisms [21, Chapter 5]. The completion of the pending receive operations could be tested, and a process unable to make progress could call a system function (**flick**) to defer execution to the next process.

Extensive use of this low-level programming system on the Cosmic Cubes and of compatible or similar systems on the first-generation commercial multicomputers did not reveal any serious deficiencies with this conventional way of organizing a distributed multiprogramming system. This programming system was reasonably convenient for scientific and engineering applications, and sufficiently powerful to allow the programmer to express any guard or trigger condition.

4.1 *Reactive-Process Programming*

As our experience with writing message-passing programs grew, we found ourselves organizing these programs more and more often in a reactive-process programming discipline. The efforts of three of my doctoral students were crucial to the evolution of these ideas and to the practical development of this style of programming. William J. Dally used the Concurrent Smalltalk programming notation for his experiments with concurrent data structures [10]; William C. Athas devised the Cantor programming notation for his compilation and application-programming experiments [2]; Wen-King Su developed the Cosmic Environment system to serve as a host run-time system for medium-grain multicomputers and as a portable, generic, message-passing programming system [30, 33]. None of these programming systems uses an explicit receive operation at the lowest levels; instead, a process is run only in response to the arrival of a message.

As was discussed in Sections 1.4 and 1.5, a *reactive process* is normally at rest, executes *for a bounded time* in response to a message, and finally either exits or prepares to receive another message. The way in which the message-dispatching mechanism invokes the process is similar to a procedure call in which a reference to the message is passed to the procedure. Although the procedure that acts as a process must return to the message-dispatching caller within a bounded time, it does not return a value; accordingly, this mechanism is different from a remote procedure call (RPC). The effects of running a process are confined to the process's own state and to any messages or new processes that it may produce. The reactive process can be made part of a programming notation; it can also serve as a structuring discipline for message-passing programs in ordinary programming notations. To avoid introducing another programming notation and to lay bare the underlying mechanisms of reactive-process programming, the following examples are expressed in C (see [33] for an exposition of *Reactive C*).

The structure that represents a process may be as simple as a pair of pointers, one to the entry point of a function and the other to the persistent variables associated with the process:

```
typedef struct {FUNC_PTR entrypoint; DATA_PTR data;}
PROCESS;
```

A process containing a set of *embedded processes* deals with an incoming message by first translating the message-header field specifying the destination process into a pointer to the selected **PROCESS**, and then calling the process entry point as a function. If **msg** is a pointer to a message, the C idiom for performing these actions within the process containing embedded processes is:

```
MESSAGE *msg;
PROCESS *process;
...
/* Translate header.   */
process = lookup_process_from(msg);
/* Dispatch to process.*/
(*process->entrypoint)(process, msg);
...
```

By passing the **process** pointer in the function call, the embedded process can access its data, and can also change its behavior on future invocations by modifying its own entry point. When the function has completed its finite actions and has prepared to receive another message, it simply returns. A process exits by freeing its resources and deleting its own entry in the set of processes before it returns. Of course, an embedded process that is invoked in this way may in turn contain embedded processes. The message, together with the right that it imparts to control execution, may be passed along an acyclic path of embedded processes until it is finally processed.

This program fragment enlists a remarkably simple and efficient mechanism for managing and dispatching messages to embedded processes. Since these processes may coexist in the same address space, using a function call to give control to the embedded process and a function return to return control to the parent is a low-cost context-switch operation. Just as a function returns only if the functions that it calls return, the process that uses this mechanism is reactive only if its embedded processes are reactive. So long as the processes at every level are reactive, it is nearly as easy and efficient to nest processes as functions. Although it seems unlikely that people will express reactive-process application programs in this unadorned syntax, the underlying mechanism has been employed extensively in our system programming.

4.2 *The Reactive Kernel*

The Reactive Kernel (RK), a new node operating system for medium-grain multicomputers, was written in 1987 by Jakov Seizovic as a master's thesis project [31]. RK supports all of the functions described in Section 1 and runs on the Cosmic Cube, Symult Series 2010, and Intel iPSC/2.

RK is itself a reactive-process program, except for the main program, which is the infinite loop:

```
while (1) {       /* Main dispatch loop. */
    /* Get a packet from the recv queue.*/
    p = get_packet(&tag);
    /* Call its destination handler.    */
    dispatch(tag, p);
}
```

The **get_packet** function returns a pointer, **p**, to the next packet in the receive queue, and also a **tag** that is extracted from the header of this packet. The **dispatch** function performs an operation analogous to the translation and dispatch illustrated previously.

The *inner kernel* of RK consists of this dispatch loop and a set of system services, including functions for allocating storage, sending messages, receiving packets, reporting errors, and obtaining information about the multicomputer configuration. The dispatch loop selects a reactive process called a *handler,* which may call these system services. RK consists entirely of the inner kernel and a set of handlers.

As part of the node operating system, handlers run in the same privileged mode as does the inner kernel. When control is turned over to a handler, the reactive property of the handler assures that it will return within a bounded time, and that its actions can be treated as atomic. As usual, these actions may consist of changing the internal state of the handler (possibly including its entry point), sending messages, and creating new handlers. Each packet that is processed by the node thus invokes a specific, bounded action that is determined by the tag. For example, packets that are fragments of messages are dispatched to an *assembly* handler. When the assembly handler receives a packet that completes a message, it calls the **dispatch** function with a pointer to and the tag of the assembled message. Other handlers that deal with system functions include *spawn, error,* and *broadcast.* When RK is initially loaded into a node, it contains the inner kernel and at least the spawn handler, whose purpose is to load additional handlers. If its code is not already resident when a handler is spawned, the code is linked dynamically to the inner kernel when it is loaded; thus, calls from a handler for system services do not involve the cost of a system call, but only the cost of a function call.

A user interface consists of a handler and a library. Specialized user-programming interfaces can be developed for different programming languages and applications. The *Reactive Handler* (RH) and a library provide the user interface described in Section 1. Using the interface specification "reactive" to allocate nodes causes an instance of RH to be loaded into each node assigned to a user. Messages produced by this user's processes are tagged so as to dispatch control to this handler. As a handler, RH is a reactive process, although a rather complex one. In yet another level of recursive application of reactive-process programming, RH manages a set of handlers that perform such services as spawning user processes. In addition, RH must be able to run user processes and to service their system calls.

To run a user process, RH performs a full-scale context switch into a protected user mode. Whereas a handler is described by a pair of pointers, a user process is described by reference to its address-translation map, entry point, data segment, stack pointer, and scheduling state. In contrast to the lack of processor state when a handler returns, a user process must restore and save the processor state each time it is run. As a protection against faulty or long-running user processes, RH sets a timer interrupt to limit the running time of a user process; in this manner, reactive scheduling devolves into time-driven scheduling. Another part of the context switch involves directing the system-call interrupts to the table of RH entry points for these functions. There are three categories of system calls. First, receive functions change the scheduling state of the user process and cause RH to return. Second, the **spawn** and **ckill** functions cause a message to be sent to the node in which the process is to be created or killed, and place the calling process into an RPC-blocked state before RH returns. When the user process is in this state, incoming messages for this process are queued until the RPC-reply message is received. Finally, all other system calls, including send and utility functions, are resolved within the node, allowing execution of the calling process to resume.

The use of this simple, layered structure with its well defined interfaces has paid excellent dividends in the manageability and portability of RK. In addition to modularity by function, the RK code has been organized to make its implementation on different multicomputers highly systematic. For example, the **get_packet** function illustrated earlier is one of the *machine-specific* RK functions; accommodating the hardware interface to the message system requires a different version of the **get_packet** function for each type of multicomputer. By contrast, the **dispatch** function is *generic* to all implementations of RK. "Porting" the inner kernel requires machine-specific functions for node initialization, **get_packet**, message-sending operations, and storage allocation. Except for the function used to run user processes, the handler code is entirely generic. RK was written using the Cosmic Cube for testing and debugging; the first "porting" of RK to the Symult Series 2010 retained 90 percent of its code.

4.3 *The Cosmic Environment*

The Cosmic Environment (CE) [30, 33] consists of a set of dæmon processes, utility programs, and libraries. Except for host-process spawning, CE provides exactly the same message-passing and other functions for UNIX processes that RK provides for node processes. Although message passing is about one hundred times slower in local-area networks than in today's multicomputer networks, CE can be used as a stand-alone system for running message-passing programs on collections of network-connected UNIX hosts. CE can also handle the allocation of, and interfaces to, one or more multicomputers. CE and RK together provide uniform communication between processes, independent of the multicomputer node or network host on which they may be located.

The entire set of processes involved in a single computation is called a *process group.* A process group and a (possibly empty) set of multicomputer nodes are allocated by the user with a utility program, **getcube**, whose arguments specify the options of the process group, such as the user-process interface and the number and model of multicomputer nodes to be allocated. The **getcube** program acquires the specified multicomputer nodes from the *cube daemon*, CE's central allocation process. Multicomputers are normally not time shared, but *space shared.* As shown in the status display in Figure 10, CE may allocate different sets of nodes in the same multicomputer to different users.

The first set of entries in Figure 10 is organized by process group. The first three of these entries show that a 32-node **s2010** multicomputer called **:ginzu** is allocated with 8 nodes free, 20 nodes assigned to the process group **{optic chuck}**, and 4 nodes assigned to the process group **{Zipcode skjellum}**. Space-sharing allows a user to select the number of nodes appropriate to the number of processes and to the load-balancing characteristics of a particular computation, produces predictable run times, and prevents one user's processes from upsetting the load balance of another process group.

The second set of entries in the status display lists the host processes in the process group of the user requesting the display. The **optic** program is the user's host process. In addition, **getcube** creates two processes: a **SERVER** process that prints messages and accesses program files for process spawning, and a **FILE MGR** process that performs file accesses for node processes. If the process group includes a multicomputer, **getcube** will also establish communication with the **CUBEIFC** process that conveys messages to and from the multicomputer.

The internal mechanisms used by CE to perform message passing differ from those used in multicomputers, but the concepts are similar. As a runtime system under UNIX, CE uses Internet sockets for interprocess communication. Because sockets operate between processes on different network-connected hosts in the same way they do in a single host, CE allows the distribution of host processes across a network of UNIX hosts. After the **getcube** program establishes a process group, it goes into the background to provide message queueing and flow control between the host processes. To enter the process group with a specified ID, a UNIX process calls the CE **cosmic_init** function. This function also establishes a socket connection with the process group's **getcube** process. All messages between host processes flow through the **getcube** process, which may be thought of as analogous to a multicomputer's message system. Although CE uses a low-level flow-control protocol to deal with the limited queueing capacity of sockets, the communication between host processes and **getcube** is conceptually the same queue-connected communication that is achieved by the low-level flow control in a multicomputer (see Section 3.1).

Figure 10.   Cosmic Environment status display.

```
CUBE DAEMON version 7.2, up 70 days 1 hour on host ganymede

{                       }  8n s2010      , b:0000 [ psyche  :ginzu ]   4.8d
{  optic chuck     }  20n s2010      , b:000a [ icarus  :ginzu ]  14.0m
{Zipcode skjellum}   4n s2010      , b:0003 [mercury  :ginzu ]  55.7m
{ cantor nanette }  16n ghost cube , b:0000 [   juno nanette]   3.9m
{ cosmos jakov     }  64n s2010      , b:0003 [  pluto :S2010 ]  19.6m
{network nancy     }   4d ipsc2 cube , b:0000 [  metis :iPSC2 ]  17.9s

GROUP {optic chuck}  TYPE reactive   IDLE 0s

    ( -1    0)        optic  46s  46r   0q  [icarus 352   ] 13.9m
    ( -1   -1)       SERVER   0s   0r   0q  [icarus 346   ] 14.0m
    ( -1   -2)     FILE MGR   0s   0r   0q  [icarus 347   ] 14.0m
    (--- ---)       CUBEIFC  49s  54r   0q  [psyche 20122] 14.0m
```

The functions described in Section 1 are implemented in CE as library routines whose organization is similar to the three categories of system calls in the reactive handler of RK. Because any message in the queue from the **getcube** process is for the process, there is no message dispatch. When the blocking-receive routine within a user process is called, it is able to schedule the UNIX process by putting the process into an I/O-wait condition in the absence of a queued message. The send routines place messages into an outgoing queue. The functions for creating node processes send messages to the affected node, and do not return until a reply is received.

In addition to the processes and libraries that allocate multicomputers and support message-passing functions on UNIX hosts, CE includes utility programs for compiling, loading, debugging, and monitoring programs, as well as a "ghost cube" feature for precisely and efficiently simulating multicomputers. Along with its use with commercial medium-grain multicomputers, CE has been distributed from Caltech to 160 research organizations, which run it under numerous different UNIX implementations. Many multicomputer application programs have been developed by using CE alone at sites that do not have regular access to a multicomputer.

4.4 *Cantor*

The Cantor programming notation and system [2, 3, 4] were devised specifically for fine-grain multicomputers such as the Mosaic; Cantor programs can also be run, however, on medium-grain multicomputers, multiprocessors, and sequential computers. A Cantor program consists of a sequence of process definitions followed by the definition of a "main" process. Cantor processes are created from these definitions and are reactive. Each definition is composed of a name, a list of persistent variables, and the program that defines the way in which a process created from this definition responds to a message. Cantor variables are statically typed as symbol, boolean, integer, real, or reference (to a process).

The terms in which Cantor computations can be expressed differ from those of CE/RK in only one important way: The storage that is allocated for the persistent variables of a process is fixed, and a process cannot allocate additional storage dynamically. Process creation is the only avenue to growth in the persistent storage used by a computation. One way to appreciate this restriction is to observe that a Cantor process has strictly bounded time (the reactive property) and space (fixed storage) in which to process a message.

Because so little complexity can be concealed within a Cantor process, the main activities of a computation occur in the interaction between processes. It is therefore realistic to portray the dynamic behavior of a Cantor program through the idealization that process executions require a constant time, or, equivalently, that process executions are synchronized across all of the nodes of a multicomputer. The time unit is called a *sweep*. For example, the graph in Figure 11 (adapted from [2]) portrays the *concurrency index,* the number of processes eligible for execution, as a function of the sweep for a Cantor Gaussian-elimination program for a 64×64 matrix. This program initially created 4096 processes, one for each matrix element, and assigned each process to a unique node. The alternation between the "find-pivot" activity, which exhibits at best $\log n$ concurrency, and the "row-reduction" activity, which is n-wise concurrent for a matrix whose current rank is n, is evident as the rank is reduced.

Sweep simulations can also be carried out when the number of nodes is less than the number of processes by permitting only one message in each node to be processed on each sweep. Similarly, various nonideal characteristics of the message system can be included. Simulations can also keep track of many other characteristics of program execution, such as process count, memory utilization, and message load. The "bursty" character of the concur-

Figure 11.   Concurrency index for a Gaussian-elimination program.

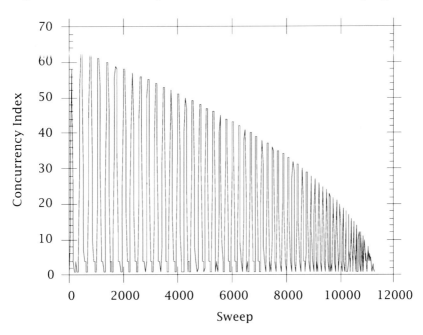

rency in this Gaussian elimination example is not at all unusual. The sweep-simulation window into the dynamics of the execution of a concurrent program has been quite revealing, both to the programmer and to the computer architect, of the dynamic behaviors of these programs. We have used such simulations in studying programs and algorithms, in determining the consequences of different message-system throughput and latency characteristics, and in examining different process-placement strategies.

In an experiment that included the design of the Cantor programming language, a compiler-based implementation of Cantor, the instrumentation described earlier, and the writing by 10 people of approximately one hundred application programs, we again followed the experimental method that we have used in earlier system-building experiments. Studying the relationships between the expression and implementation of concurrent computations under a given computational model apparently requires writing programs and implementing a system that executes them.

The Cantor experiment provided several insights into the implementation of fine-grain message-passing computations. Cantor programs depend heavily on process creation. A Cantor process is created as a side effect of evaluating an expression that consists of the name of a definition followed by a list of the initial values of the persistent variables. The value of this expression is a reference to the new process. Process creation is nearly as fast as message sending. Process placement is determined within the source-node run-time system, which generates a process-creation message that at the destination node becomes the persistent-variable list of the new process. The high frequency of process-creation operations, the encapsulation of the placement decision, and the instrumentation of Cantor programs have made Cantor an excellent vehicle for studying different strategies for automatic process placement.

The Cantor implementation also demonstrated that compiler-based programming systems have an even greater value for reactive-process programming than we might have expected. We did anticipate the advantage of being able to compile a program into code that could execute safely within a single address space, so that context-switching delays would not dominate the execution time of fine-grain programs. In addition, the flow analysis performed by the Cantor compiler eliminates most run-time checking of the types of variables within messages, including those messages used for process creation. The compiler is also able to extract from the text of each definition a measure of the number of messages and processes that may be produced, and to pass this information to the run-time system to guide decisions about process placement. Thus, it was a success of the Cantor experiment that the programming system has the entire responsibility for mapping the program to the target machine: Programs are written with absolutely no reference to machine resources.

This version of Cantor (called Cantor 2.0) also taught us a lesson about the negative consequences of the bounded-time, bounded-space restrictions on Cantor processes in comparison with the processes of the CE/RK programming systems. Although these restrictions greatly simplify the implementation within the limited resources of a fine-grain-multicomputer node, certain Cantor 2.0 programs are needlessly difficult to express [4]. The problem is that reactive-process programming in the absence of message discretion, i.e., the ability to receive messages selectively according to a message property or type, leads to the following difficulty:

Suppose that a process has the task of maintaining an information structure of arbitrary size, such as a queue. The messages directed to this process are tagged to *get* an element from the front of the queue or *put* an element at the rear of the queue. Because the queue process cannot store an arbitrary number of elements, it acts as a master that accepts the *put* and *get* messages while the values are stored in a chain of element processes. Each element process stores a value and a reference to the next element. The master maintains references to the front and rear of the queue, as illustrated in Figure 12.

The master responds to a *put* message by creating a new element process whose variables are initialized to the *put* value and a nil reference, then sending the reference to this new process as a *ref* message to the old rear element. The master deals with a *get* message by sending an *exit* message to the front element. The property of message order being preserved between pairs of

Figure 12.   Process structure for an unbounded queue.

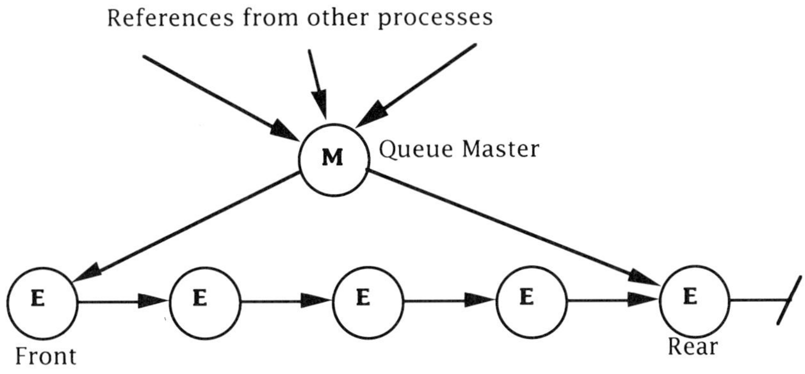

processes assures that the front element will receive the *ref* message, if any, before the *exit* message. The front element responds to the *exit* message by replying with its value and next-element reference before exiting the scene.

What does the master do with *get* messages that are received in the arbitrary period before the reference to the new front element is received? Evidently, it can continue to process *put* messages immediately, but must enqueue *get* messages. Although one cannot require an unbounded queue to implement an unbounded queue, a secondary queue for *get* messages can be implemented by the same scheme, but without recourse to still more queues. This secondary queue is able to process *put* messages immediately, but needs to deal with only one *get* message at once.

This example shows that it is possible to implement message discretion in reactive-process programs by enqueuing messages according to their type. The existence of this bounded-processing-time, bounded-process-space program is not, however, a reason to expect application programmers to complicate their programs with code that implements message discretion. Instead, it is an opportunity for creating a robust, distributed implementation of message discretion within the Cantor run-time system. The scheme illustrated by this example will allow receive queues that are distributed rather than dependent on the limited memory in the destination node. Message discretion will be incorporated into the definition of a future version of Cantor, and its run-time implementation will take advantage of this technique for distributing queues.

4.5 *Conclusions*

Our obsession with machine independence and even a degree of architecture independence in our low-level programming systems has been largely rewarded. The CE/RK system allows the same programs to be run not only on multicomputers made by different manufacturers, but also on multiprocessors and across conventional networks of distributed computers. The Cantor system achieves the additional goal of completely managing the resources of the target system. I like to think that the attention my students and I have given to these mundane aspects of "portable" concurrent programs has been in the same spirit as the architecture-independent programming that Professors Chandy and Misra have advanced with their UNITY notation, reported in this volume and in [9]. Now that high-performance concurrent computers are commercially available, it is no surprise that the use of concurrent computing is limited by programming and applications. The people who are considering investing their time and energy in writing application programs need to be assured that their investments will pay dividends in the long term and are not tied to a particular machine.

Because the implementation of these programming systems has been an interesting challenge, I have not hesitated to expose the critical details for those who encounter similar requirements. The manageability and portability of these programming systems is better attributed to the primitive functions' structure and simplicity, however, than to clever programming.

5 *Programming Techniques*

The nondeterminacy that is inherent in the process and message concurrencies of message-passing programs allows the system executing the computation a choice of alternative execution orders. Within the constraints of the program, these choices are exploited opportunistically but fairly to maintain the throughput at many levels in a multicomputer system. These levels include arbitration for channel use within the message-passing network, distribution of processes across the nodes, and interleaving of execution between processes within a node. At least for the imperative style of message-passing programming illustrated here, the programmer controls the potential nondeterminacy in a computation by constraining the order in which messages are sent and received, as well as the conditions under which program segments within processes are executed.

The primitive functions of sending and receiving messages on a buffered, arbitrary-delay channel provide relatively weak constraints. In contrast to the design philosophy of systems whose primitive operations involve strong forms of synchronization that cannot be relaxed when they are not required, our strategy for multicomputers has been to implement weakly synchronized primitive operations from which stronger and higher-level synchronization operations can be constructed easily and efficiently. This section illustrates several of the most common ways of introducing message-order, execution-order, and synchronization constraints into programs, and at the same time presents introductory programming examples that depict the typical use of message functions.

5.1 *Message Discretion*

From the discussion of message discretion in Cantor, it is evident that some situations require a process to defer one type of message in favor of another. In other situations, it may simply be more convenient for a process to deal with messages of different types in a specific order. In systems that allow processes to allocate storage dynamically, message discretion is easily implemented by defining a set of message functions that maintain separate input queues for each message type. Even though the number of types is typically small, the first **long** integer of a message is reserved as the type field, so as to retain word alignment of the structures that follow. Referring to the typed message via a pointer to the location following the type field hides the type information.

For each of the **x** functions (**xsend**, **xrecvb**, etc.) described in Section 1, a similar **t** (typed) function is defined. This technique of layering customized message functions on top of the **x** functions can be carried to much greater lengths than shown by the **t** functions illustrated here. For example, the standard user-interface library for FORTRAN is a set of routines similar to those shown here; the FORTRAN functions, however, include both the type and the sender ID in the message, and allow the programmer to filter messages directly into FORTRAN arrays by type and/or sender ID.

The **t** functions are so similar to their corresponding **x** functions that several of the "functions" can be defined as C macros (Figure 13). A **ttype** function, analogous to **tlength**, is included to return the hidden message type. The purpose of these cryptic manipulations is to maintain yet hide the type field in a message buffer.

The usage of the **tsend** function is the same as **xsend**, but with the addition of a message type as the last argument. Its implementation is straightforward (Figure 14).

The usage of the **trecvb** and **trecv** functions is the same as the corresponding **x** functions, but with the addition of the message type as the argument. The blocking **trecvb** function (Figure 15) calls functions **get_q(type)** and **put_q(type)** (not shown) that manage the queue. Of course, these routines do not store the actual messages, but only the pointers to them. If the maximum number of queued messages is small, these routines can reasonably be written to keep the pointers in a simple list that is searched by the **get_q** function and appended to by the **put_q** function.

The implementation of the nonblocking **trecv** function (Figure 16) is similar to **trecvb**. It is interesting that **while** could correctly replace the second

---

Figure 13.   C macros for the simpler **t** functions.

```
#define tmalloc(n)   (((long *) xmalloc(n+sizeof(long)))+1)
#define tfree(m)     (xfree(((long *)m)-1))
#define tlength(m)   (xlength(((long *)m)-1)-sizeof(long))
#define ttype(m)     (((long *)m)[-1])
```

if in the **trecv** function. As it is written, the function returns after moving no more than one message from the system's queue to its private queue. This one message is sufficient to assure progress on each call. The **while** version would not return NULL unless its internal **xrecv** call returned NULL, even if it would have to move all the messages queued for this process out of the system's receive queue and into its own private queue. The weak semantic specification of **trecv** (**xrecv**) permits such alternative implementations, which differ only in the progress during one call.

When these standard typed-message routines are included in the user interface, it is immaterial to the programmer whether they appear in a library

---

Figure 14.   Implementation of the **tsend** function.

```
tsend(m, n, p, t)              /* Send buffer m to process    */
    long *m;                   /* (n, p) with type t.         */
    int n, p, t;
{
    *--m = t;                  /* Copy type into hidden long  */
    xsend(m, n, p);            /* word; then send message.    */
}
```

Figure 15.   Implementation of the **trecvb** function.

```
long *trecvb(t)                        /* Blocking receive will not */
    int t;                             /* return until a message of */
{                                      /* type t is received.       */
    long *m;

    if(m = get_q(t)) return(m+1);   /* Check private queue for    */
                                       /* message of type t.        */
    while (1)
    {                                  /* Repeatedly receive msgs,  */
        m = (long*) xrecvb();          /* and return only if the    */
        if(*m == t) return(m+1);       /* type of the message is t. */
        else put_q( m );               /* Else, save the message.   */
    }
}
```

or in the Reactive Handler. It is so easy and efficient to layer customized message functions on top of the **x** functions that the performance advantage of locating such functions in the Reactive Handler is only marginal.

As an example of a situation in which it is convenient but not essential to use the typed-message functions, consider a simple grid-point computation. The process for each grid point repetitively (1) sends messages to each of its neighbors reporting its own state or influence at their common boundary, (2) receives corresponding messages from each of its neighbors, and (3) updates its own state. Generally, messages from different neighbors must be distinguished, but because all messages arrive through a single queue, distinguishing them requires a field within the message.

It may be less obvious that the iteration number must also be distinguished. After a neighbor has received the process's message for iteration i, it may send a message for iteration $i+1$. Although the message-order-preserving property of the message system assures that the iteration-$(i + 1)$ message *from this neighbor* will arrive after its iteration-i message, there is nothing in this scheme that constrains the iteration-$(i + 1)$ message to arrive after the iteration-i messages from other neighbors. Because the number of iteration-$(i + 1)$ messages is bounded, the process could queue them. Instead of complicating the process in this way, however, the programmer may choose to employ message discretion, i.e., to use the typed-message functions to do the necessary queueing. According to the way in which the grid-point process is

---

Figure 16.   Implementation of the **trecv** function.

```
long *trecv(t)                   /* Nonblocking typed receive  */
    int t;                       /* returns a message of type  */
{                                /* t if found; else returns a */
    long *m;                     /* NULL (0) pointer.          */

    if(m = get_q(t)) return(m+1);  /* Return type t msg if one  */
                                   /* is in private msg queue.  */
    if(m = (long*) xrecv())        /* Otherwise check receive   */
    {                              /* queue.  If type matches,  */
        if(*m == t) return(m+1);   /* return the msg; else save */
        else put_q( m );           /* it in private queue.      */
    }
    return(0);                     /* Return 0 if not found.    */
}
```

organized, either the iteration number or the identity of the neighbor could be used as the message type.

5.2 *Synchronous Message Functions*

Even though the send and receive operations create a synchronization between a process and a message, events within two or more processes can be synchronized by using protocols composed of send and receive operations.

The message-passing operations of CSP and occam synchronize the send operation in one process and the receive operation in another process. As described in Section 1.5, this synchronous (zero-slack) communication is defined such that the number of completed send operations at one end of the channel is identical to the number of completed receive operations at the other end. In a physically distributed system, an equivalent but realizable requirement is that there will be some interval during which the control of one process is in the send function while the control of the other process is in the receive function. It is evident that this requirement cannot be satisfied by a single message from process *A* to process *B*, since process *A* would not have any information about when process *B* entered or returned from the receive routine. Instead, it is necessary that each process communicate with the other.

Several formulations of synchronous send–receive pairs are useful in programming the Cosmic Cube multicomputers. One of these, a synchronous version of the typed functions, has exactly the same usage. Although synchronous, these functions do not refer to a channel; instead, the receive operation synchronizes with any send operation of the required type that is directed to the process. Because these message functions are sender-initiated and zero-slack, they are prefixed with **s0_**. The type −1 is reserved for the reply message. In order to convey the ID of the sender, the message buffer contains two extra long integers:

```
#define s0_tmalloc(n)  (((long *) tmalloc(n+2*sizeof(long)))+2)
#define s0_tfree(m)    (tfree(((long *)m)-2))
```

and the functions may be written as shown in Figure 17. As shown in the time–space diagram in Figure 18(a), the internal send and receive operations are completely ordered: (1) sending the message, (2) receiving the message, (3) sending the reply, (4) receiving the reply. The sending process is assured to be in the **s0_send** routine between events (2) and (3) in the **s0_recvb** routine, thus satisfying the synchronization requirement. The receiver-initiated versions of these functions, in which an **r0_tsend(m, type)** function in process **(x,y)** is synchronized with an **r0_trecvb(x, y, type)** function in any other process, are implemented similarly.

An RPC may use the same message protocol as the sender-initiated synchronous message functions. The call is similar to the **s0_tsend** function, except that a value is returned from the contents of the reply message. The remote procedure behaves in the same way as the **s0_trecvb** function, except that a function of the received message provides the reply value.

When the send operation specifies the receiving process *and* the receive operation specifies the sending process, we have the symmetrical form of synchronous communication of CSP and occam. Because all of the communicating-process pairs in a CSP program or channels in an occam program are denoted in the program text, it is possible to assign a message type to each. (It would suffice to assign message types to communicating-process pairs or channels such that all of the types associated with any process would be distinct.) Then, as shown in Figure 19, the implementation of the **csp_** family of typed message functions is remarkably concise and efficient. The time relationships are depicted in the time–space diagram in Figure 18(b). Because

---

Figure 17. Sender-initiated zero-slack message functions.

```
s0_tsend(p, node, pid, type)      /* Sender-initiated 0-slack   */
    long *p;                       /* version of tsend.          */
    int node, pid, type;
{
    p[-2] = mypid();               /* Put the sender ID into the */
    p[-1] = mynode();              /* extra two longs in the msg */
    tsend(p-2, node, pid, type);   /* buffer, and send it.       */
    tfree(trecvb(-1));             /* Wait for the reply msg.    */
}

char *s0_trecvb(type)             /* Sender-initiated 0-slack   */
    int type;                      /* version of trecvb.         */
{
    long *p;

    p = trecvb(type);              /* Receive the message.       */
    tsend(tmalloc(0), (int) p[0],  /* Send the reply.            */
              (int) p[1], -1);     /* Return the pointer to the  */
    return(p+2);                   /* body of the msg buffer.    */
}
```

---

the send operation in each function precedes the completion of the receive

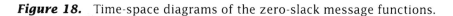

Figure 18. Time-space diagrams of the zero-slack message functions.

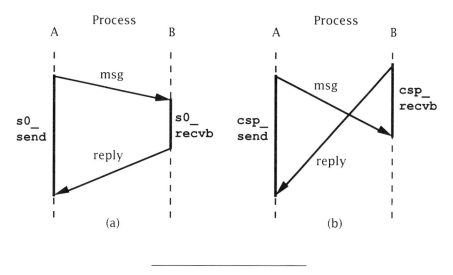

Figure 19. Implementation of the CSP message functions.

```
#define csp_tmalloc(n) tmalloc(n)
#define csp_tfree(m)    tfree(m)

csp_tsend(m, node, pid, type)              /* CSP send function.    */
    char *m;
    int node, pid, type;
{
    tsend(m, node, pid, type);             /* Send the message, and */
    tfree(trecvb(type));                   /* wait for the reply.   */
}

char *csp_trecvb(node, pid, type)          /* CSP receive function. */
    int node, pid, type;
{
    tsend(tmalloc(0), node, pid, type);    /* Send the reply, and   */
    return(trecvb(type));                  /* wait for the message. */
}
```

operation in the other, we are assured that neither routine can return until the other has been called; thus, the interval during which both functions are active satisfies the requirement for synchronous communication. The functions shown here are so simple that they could also be expressed as C macros.

If there is to be a future version of the transputer that will separate the concepts of physical and logical channels and support message routing, the way in which these synchronous message functions are built from arbitrary-slack, typed messages suggests a possible hardware implementation. The efficiency of this protocol also demonstrates, however, that multicomputers employing arbitrary-slack communication have no difficulty in running CSP, occam, or other programs that require zero-slack communication.

5.3 *Barrier Synchronization and Global Operations*

An obvious generalization of synchronous communication between pairs of processes is synchronization across sets of processes. This operation, commonly called *barrier synchronization,* is used in message-passing programs to assure that one phase of a computation has terminated before another, possibly conflicting, phase begins.

Barrier synchronization is most often performed among a set of cohorts (a set of N processes created with the same **pid** and from the same program, as defined in Section 1.1). By using an algorithm based on *doubling,* barrier synchronization can be performed in a time that is proportional to $\log N$. For simplicity, this algorithm is presented under the restriction that N is a power of two. Then, the process structure between the cohorts for the doubling algorithm is a binary n-cube; the cohort in node i communicates with cohorts in nodes $i \oplus 2^d, 0 \leq d < log_2 N,$ where d is the dimension traversed and $\oplus$ is the *bitwise* exclusive-or. In the **cohort_barrier** routine shown in Figure 20, pairs of cohorts exchange messages along successive dimensions. In the same way that the message exchange in the **csp_** routines produces zero-slack synchronization, each message exchange in the **cohort_barrier** routine assures that the dth iteration in process i will not terminate until the dth iteration in the cohort in node $i \oplus 2^d$ is reached. Because the synchronizations occur across *successive* dimensions, the completion of iteration d in node i assures that the set of cohorts in nodes $i \oplus j, 0 \leq j < 2^d,$ have entered the barrier. In other words, each iteration doubles the set of cohorts known to each other to have entered the barrier. Thus, when the $log_2 N$th message is received, all N cohorts will have entered the barrier and the function can return.

The same doubling scheme can combine a barrier synchronization with the computation and distribution of the results of a so-called *global opera-*

tion, such as the sum, min, max, rank, or parallel prefix operation of elements provided by each of the cohorts. These parallel algorithms [18] are usually described for synchronous SIMD or PRAM architectures, but are equally elegant in their MIMD message-passing form. As an illustration, the program fragment shown in Figure 21 computes the maximal element and its origin from a set of elements distributed across N cohorts, where N is a power of two. A practical application of this operation is locating the pivot element in matrix-reduction computations. Given the **cohort_barrier** routine as background, the only subtlety to this program fragment is the complex **if** condition. If only the first clause comparing the maxima were to appear, having equal elements would cause the iterations that are synchronized across a pair of processes to both execute the **else** clause. This case would be harmless for computing the maximal element, but would propagate different decisions as to its origin. The additional condition for equality induces a total ordering of the set of elements.

Whereas the performance advantage of incorporating customized message functions into the Reactive Handler is marginal, barrier synchronization and global operations perform a sufficient number of send and receive operations, log_2N of each, to justify putting them into the Reactive Handler. Because of the high cost of the user-process context switch, send and receive operations at the user-process level can be 10 times slower than they are at the handler

---

Figure 20. Cohort-barrier synchronization based on doubling.

```
void cohort_barrier(b)          /* Barrier synchronization.       */
     int b;                     /* N must be a power of 2.         */
{                               /* b is the largest type used      */
     int D; char *p;            /* in calling program.             */
                                /* D = 2**dimension, so it is      */
     D = 1;                     /* initially 2**0 = 1.             */
     p = tmalloc(0);            /* Allocate working msg buffer.    */

     while (D < nnodes())       /* Exchange msgs logN times.       */
     {
         tsend(p, mynode()^D, mypid(), b + D);
         p = trecvb(b + D);
         D = D * 2;
     }
     tfree(p);                  /* Free working msg buffer.        */
}
```

Figure 21. An example of a global operation.

```
typedef struct { float   max;          /* Each msg contains max */
                 int origin; } msg;    /* and origin elements.  */
float max;                             /* Local max and origin. */
int    origin, D;                      /* D = 2**dimension.     */
msg    *p;
. . .
max = maxelement(my_subset);           /* Initialize maximum and */
origin = mynode();                     /* its origin from this   */
D = 1;                                 /* node, and D=2**0.      */

p = (msg*) tmalloc(sizeof(msg));       /* Get working msg buffer */
p->max    = max;                       /* and initialize its max */
p->origin = origin;                    /* and node elements.     */

while (D < nnodes())                   /* Iterate logN times.    */

    tsend(p, mynode()^D, mypid(), D);  /* Exchange msgs across    */
    p = (msg*) trecvb(D);              /* dimension log(D).       */
    if (max > p->max ||                /* If my max > max in msg */
        (max == p->max &&              /* or they are equal and  */
         origin > p->origin))          /* my origin is larger,   */
    {
        p->max    = max;               /* assign my values to    */
        p->origin = origin;            /* working msg buffer;     */
    }
    else                               /* else                    */
    {
        max    = p->max;               /* assign msg buffer max   */
        origin = p->origin;            /* and node to my vars.    */
    }
    D = D * 2;                          /* Next dimension.         */
}
tfree(p);                              /* Free working buffer.    */
. . .       /* max now contains the maximum element, origin       */
            /* specifies the node from which it originated, and a */
            /* barrier synchronization has been accomplished.      */
```

level. If they were implemented in a handler, barrier synchronization and global operations would require only about twice the time required for user processes to send and receive a single message. We are currently incorporating such operations into a new version of the Reactive Kernel.

5.4 *Conclusions*

Starting with the message functions intrinsic to the architecture, we have shown how to build successive layers of (1) discretionary message functions that receive messages selectively according to the message type, (2) synchronous message functions similar to those used in CSP and occam, and (3) barrier synchronization and global operations. This clean and efficient layering allows the programmer to employ message or synchronization functions whose properties are appropriate for the application.

A data structure distributed across a set of cohorts is a modest extension of the idea of global operations. If the distributed data structure is encapsulated within a separate set of cohorts, a process invokes operations by sending a message to any cohort, but typically to the cohort residing in the same node. The data structure might also be implemented as a set of cohort handlers accessed by system calls, or as a set of embedded processes within cohorts. The concerted actions amongst the cohorts takes care of any internal serialization or locking required between concurrent requests. Thus, a set of cohorts that maintain an instance of a data structure can be regarded as a single entity capable of handling concurrent transactions, much as the postal service is a single entity whose services can be obtained at any post office. While the implementation of distributed data structures, such as ordered sets [10], may be internally intricate, their use is straightforward. It appears that many application programs are simplified by encapsulating the communication and synchronization requirements of a computation within a distributed data structure.

6 *Multicomputer Applications*

The low-level programming systems and techniques described in the two preceding sections support the construction of explicitly concurrent programs whose behavior and performance are closely tied to the operations performed by the underlying multicomputer hardware and system software. Until the invention of higher-level programming systems that offer greater productivity and comparable expressivity, generality, and efficiency, multicomputer application programs will continue to be expressed in terms of processes, messages, and the slightly higher-level operations (synchronization, global operations) and abstractions (distributed data structures) that can be implemented efficiently in terms of processes and messages. Although some people will forever regard this as an approach that is at too low a level of abstraction for constructing application programs, the adventurous programmers who have given it a try have many practical successes to their credit.

Multicomputers have been applied to an interesting range of demanding computations, predominately applications in science and engineering. Although these scientific and engineering computations have diverse purposes, the underlying algorithms and numerical methods often include matrix computations; partial-differential-equation solution by a variety of methods, both direct and iterative; finite-element analysis; finite-difference methods; multigrid methods; distant- or local-field many-body integrators; Monte Carlo particle-in-cell simulations; fast Fourier transforms; and signal-processing, image-processing, computational-geometry, and graphics algorithms. In addition to these specialized or numerical components, scientific and engineering computations may employ general methods for searching, sorting, pattern matching, recursive subdivision, discrete-event simulation, and distributed data structures. These general methods are also found in other application areas, such as combinatorial- or heuristic-search problems, number theory, graph theory, logic simulation, network simulation, computer-aided design, game playing, and databases.

Such computations are not unusual in themselves; this abbreviated list includes many of the common tasks of high-speed sequential computers. It is, nevertheless, remarkable that the application programs developed during the several years since multicomputers became available are so numerous and diverse. One of the most important but least recognized factors in the development of concurrent application programs is that the fundamental concurrent algorithms and numerical methods developed by computer scientists and applied mathematicians before the widespread availability of concurrent computers have proved to be of real value in practice. Many of these algorithms are the concurrent forms of well-known sequential algorithms, such as the FFT, Gaussian elimination, multigrid, and searching and sorting methods. Other algorithms, such as the Chandy-Misra-Bryant distributed discrete-event simulation algorithm [6, 8, 24], are unique to or attractive only for concurrent or distributed computations.

In addition to the programs themselves, the application-programming experience of the past several years has yielded many useful paradigms for the formulation of computing problems for concurrent execution. Although there has been no shortage of proposals for general principles to guide the design of concurrent programs, those I have encountered either have obvious counterexamples or are too vague to be helpful. Hence, following some preliminary discussion of multicomputer-program performance, this section proceeds directly to examples that are meant to illustrate the considerations that influence the design of application programs.

6.1 *Performance Issues*

The design of a message-passing program begins with a plan for distributing the data and operations among a set of processes. Generally, there are many ways to partition a problem. The program designers may be influenced by a pre-existing sequential program for the same task, but should use their understanding of the computing *problem* rather than of the sequential program to develop alternative formulations.

Because performance most often motivates the effort to develop a concurrent application program, alternative formulations are evaluated according to their expected execution time. It has become part of the standard practice in this field, however, that a stronger criterion is ordinarily applied: The program design should not be specific to a given size of machine or problem, but should scale efficiently with N and the problem size. When this objective is carried to an extreme, researchers publish plots of

$$\text{Speedup}(N) = \frac{\text{execution time on 1 node}}{\text{execution time on } N \text{ nodes}}$$

to show how nearly their programs approach the ideal of $\text{Speedup}(N) \approx N$. Speedup should not be a goal in itself, and speedup plots obscure direct comparisons with the best sequential programs by expressing only a measure of improvement relative to a one-node program of unknown characteristics. The execution time is better depicted directly as a function of N by plotting $T(N)$ against N on a *log–log* scale, as shown in Figure 22.

The dashed line represents the ideal of $T(N) \cdot N$ equaling the execution time for the sequential program; the hyperbolas generated by $T \cdot N$ equaling a constant appear as straight lines in a log–log plot. Another advantage of the log–log plot is that it is able to depict performance characteristics over a very wide range of N.

The curve shown in Figure 22, which is typical of a practical application program, exposes clearly the features that are of principal interest to the program designer. An algorithm that allows a computation to be distributed will not necessarily be as efficient, even when run on a single node, as the best sequential algorithm; hence, the intercept at $N = 1$ will generally be somewhat above the execution time for the sequential program. Starting at this intercept, each doubling of the number of nodes nearly halves the execution time in the linear-speedup regime. Finally, the curve reaches or approaches a minimum time as the available concurrency is exhausted or other limiting effects are reached. Of course, programs are complex entities that can exhibit bizarre variations in execution time as a function of N. Generally, however, the gross features of program performance can be estimated from the concurrent formulation and the characteristics of the target multicomputer.

6.2 *Ray-Tracing Example*

The simplest applications of multicomputers involve the execution of numerous tasks that are independent, or nearly so. Examples of such computations include local operations on images, the generation of a statistical sample from a set of independent simulations, the examination of the sensitivity of a transient analysis to a set of slightly differing initial conditions, brute-force decryption trials, and the compilation of independent subprograms of a larger program.

Consider the example of a program that computes a ray-traced image of an intricate crystal chandelier. The chandelier is mathematically described and symmetrical; thus, a single node is able to store its description, including the positions and shapes of the thousands of crystals and dozens of light sources. The image to be computed is 1000×1000 picture elements (pixels).

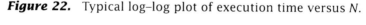

Figure 22.   Typical log–log plot of execution time versus N.

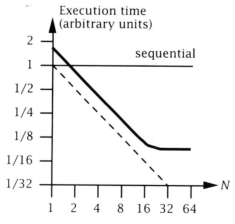

The brightness of a pixel is computed by tracing a ray from the viewpoint. A ray may encounter multiple reflections and refractions, and may split into a reflected ray and a refracted ray at an air-crystal boundary. Each ray must be followed until it terminates on a light source, terminates on the background, or becomes sufficiently attenuated. A ray from the viewpoint could miss the chandelier altogether, in which case its computation would require only 1ms, whereas rays that are split many times may require as much as 1s. The average computing time per ray from the viewpoint is 10ms; thus, the computing time on one node for all 10^6 rays would be 10^4s (almost three hours).

This problem certainly does not lack concurrency; for the purposes of this example, the computation of the 10^6 pixels can be regarded as independent. Ray-splitting could be used to generate additional concurrency, but there is already much more concurrency than there are nodes in today's largest-N multicomputers. Because there is little point in creating duplicates of the ray-tracing process in a single node, it is reasonable to formulate the computation based on N cohorts. The program designer's concerns are to distribute the operations in a way that balances the load and to serialize the operations in a way that controls the storage and communication demands.

The unpredictability in the computing time per ray does not obviate the possibility of a systematic subdivision of the rays to the ray-tracing processes. If the image were divided such that each node had to compute a contiguous patch of pixels, the clustering of detail in images makes it likely that some nodes would have nearly all easy rays, and others nearly all difficult rays. Instead, the image might be divided such that the pixel with coordinate (x, y) would be computed in node $(x + 1000y)$ mod N. This assignment would cause the $10^6/N$ pixels computed in a single node to be sensibly independent. The typical performance of this formulation is easily estimated (Figure 23).

Because of the large variation in ray-tracing times, the averaging effect of computing many rays in each node is able to assure near-perfect load balance and ideal speedup only for $N \leq \approx 3 \times 10^3$, even though the degree of concurrency is 10^6. The worst-case ray-tracing time limits the asymptotic time to 1s and the speedup to 10^4. The details of the transition from the linear-speedup to the asymptotic-minimum-time regimes could be calculated from the distribution of ray-tracing times. In practice, the performance might be limited on a large-N multicomputer not by the ray-tracing computations, but by the volume of message traffic associated with getting pixel-brightness data to a display process.

A more deterministic approach to achieving load balancing might be desired if either the number of pixels to be computed were smaller or the variation in ray-tracing times were larger. Just as the players in certain casino games are all playing concurrently against the dealer rather than against each other, even though they are sitting at the same table, programs involving many independent cases may be organized with a "dealer" process that deals out cases to a set of "player" processes. Unlike the casino dealer, however, the dealer process is not constrained to play the same number of games with each player.

The dealer process is ordinarily a host process that communicates with N player processes in the nodes. Its tasks for this ray-tracing example are to send messages containing sets of rays to the ray-tracing processes, accept the pixel-brightness messages in reply, and display the image as it is constructed. The node processes respond to a message containing a set of rays by computing the pixel brightnesses and sending them back to the dealer. The dealer process cannot be expected to respond instantly with a new set of rays; it is perfectly acceptable, however, for the dealer to employ a protocol in which a *limited* number of additional messages are sent to a player before the results from previous messages have been received. These messages are simply queued by the message system. Although logically correct, it is not acceptable for the dealer to get *arbitrarily* far ahead of the ray-tracing processes: The load balancing will no longer be effective after all of the cases have been dealt. In addition, the node receive queues may overflow.

The characteristic performance of dealer problems shows near-ideal speed-up until the computation becomes limited by the throughput of the dealer. If the throughput of the dealer for this example were limited more by the volume of messages than by the volume of pixels, it would be advantageous to

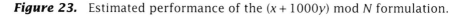

Figure 23. Estimated performance of the $(x + 1000y)$ mod N formulation.

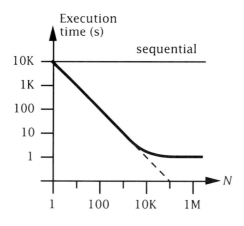

convey a larger set of pixels in each message. The dealer formulation applies also to applications in which the independent cases cannot be predetermined by a few parameters, and is most appropriate for problems in which the node-process computing times are relatively large and exhibit a large variation.

The program and communication structures are elementary for either of these formulations. This first example was meant to illustrate the capabilities and limitations of statistical load balancing, the use of program-adaptive load balancing, and the program designer's concerns with the message-queueing limitations of the nodes. Ray tracing is also an example of a problem in which the available concurrency grows directly with the problem size.

6.3 *Matrix-Multiplication Example*

Many scientific and engineering computations are expressed in terms of matrices, and the multiplication of full matrices is a kernel operation in matrix computations. Matrix multiplication on multicomputers is also a well-worn but useful example of the way in which the data-distribution decision can determine nearly completely how a program is to be written and how well it will perform. The performance is easily predicted from the ratio of computation to communication. These formulation issues did not appear in the ray-tracing example because there was little data or communication.

A multicomputer matrix package will be designed for large matrices. If the matrices were $n{\times}n = 2048{\times}2048$ eight-byte double-precision floating-point quantities, then each matrix would require 32MB of storage. Not only is 32MB more storage than one can expect in a node, there also is no reason to wish to store the matrix in a single node, for it would simply create a bottleneck for the operations to be performed on the matrix. Instead, considerations of program structure and flexibility suggest that the elements of all matrices be distributed in a standard pattern. For example, a 2048×2048 matrix might be stored in a 256-node multicomputer as a 16×16 matrix of processes, each of which maintains in dynamically allocated storage a number of 128×128 submatrices (each submatrix requires 128KB). If the multicomputer is mesh-connected, one might as well place the submatrices so that the logical rows and columns correspond to the physical rows and columns of the message-passing network. It is convenient in any case to number the processes with coordinates (u, v), such that element a_{jk} of matrix A is stored in process $(u, v) = (\lfloor \frac{j}{128} \rfloor, \lfloor \frac{k}{128} \rfloor)$. (Matrix-element subscripts here start with 0.) The submatrix in process (u, v) is referred to as A_{uv}.

The matrix product $C = AB$, where A, B, and C are each composed of submatrices, is simply

$$C_{jk} = \sum_{m=0}^{15} A_{jm}B_{mk}.$$

This expression is the specification for the computation; it remains only to decide how to traverse the range $0 \le j, k, m < 16$, and where to compute each of the C_{jk}. If we make the sensible decision to compute the submatrix C_{jk} in process (j, k), in which it will be stored, the computation will be distributed as uniformly as the submatrices. The computation of the 16 components of the submatrix product, $A_{jm}B_{mk}$, $0 \le m < 16$, requires that the processes (j, m) and (m, k) send copies of their submatrices A_{jm} and B_{mk} to process (j, k). This is effectively a broadcast of A_{jm} in rows and B_{mk} in columns, but to avoid clogging the message system with 16 copies of each submatrix, these message operations can be serialized for $m = 0, 1, \ldots, 15$. In fact, the recipient of one of these submatrices can compute where it will next be required, and pass along a single copy.

Load balancing is not an issue for this highly regular computation. The matrices and operations are distributed uniformly across whatever size multicomputer is used for the computation. Any variation from ideal speedup will be due to the time required to pass the submatrices as messages. This variation is easy to predict from the ratio of computation to communication in the processes. For this example, the process performs 128 $(n/\sqrt{N})$ multiply-add operations for each matrix element that is received. If the sustained multiply-add bandwidth of a medium-grain multicomputer node with a floating-point accelerator is 8M operations/s, the message bandwidth need be only 63K operands/s, or about 0.5MB/s.

The message bandwidth for long messages on a Symult Series 2010, a second-generation medium-grain multicomputer that has a relatively fast message system (see Section 3.5), is $\approx$10MB/s, or 1.25M eight-byte operands/s. If this message bandwidth is compared with 8M operations/s, an S2010 could perform matrix multiplications efficiently with a computation-to-communication ratio of as little as six operations per operand. Such small ratios would be encountered, however, only for such small submatrices, such as 6×6 (288B), that the application would use very little of the storage available in a medium-grain node, and the performance would be limited by message latency. The message latency for the S2010 is $\approx(177 + 0.1L)\mu$s [30], where the message length L is measured in bytes. The 177μs component is due to system-call and context-switching delays rather than to the message network. This software component of the message latency is divided roughly equally between the sending and receiving node, and signficantly limits the available message bandwidth for messages shorter than about 2KB, or 256 eight-byte operands.

Thus, the limit on the performance of matrix multiplication on an S2010 occurs when the submatrices are smaller than about 16×16, and is due to message latency.

The comments at the beginning of Section 3 about the difficult requirements placed on the message systems of fine-grain multicomputers can be verified by this matrix-multiplication example. Although a 16K-node Mosaic will have about the same total storage as a 256-node medium-grain multicomputer, a 2048×2048 matrix would be distributed as 128×128 submatrices, each 16×16. The computation-to-communication ratio for matrix multiplication scales as $n/\sqrt{N}$ from 128 for the 256-node multicomputer to only 16 operations per operand for the 16,384-node multicomputer. In the Mosaic, however, the $\approx(3+0.05L)\mu s$ message latency does not seriously limit the bandwidth for 256-operand (2KB) messages. The Mosaic's 2.5M operand/s message bandwidth would be capable of supporting a node floating-point rate in matrix multiplications of 40M operations/s.

In common with mesh and grid-point computations, in which the volume-to-surface or area-to-perimeter ratios provide a large computation-to-communication ratio, matrix multiplication illustrates how organizing the computation to achieve a large computation-to-communication ratio confines the demands on message bandwidth. In addition, managing message data in large blocks allows the length-dependent component of the message latency to dominate the relatively large software component of the message latency in medium-grain multicomputers. The program design is otherwise straightforward, and is essentially completely determined by the initial decision of how to distribute the data.

6.4 *Discrete-Event-Simulation Example*

Discrete-event simulations compute the behavior of systems composed of elements whose individual behaviors and interactions are modeled in terms of discrete events. In contrast to the simulation of systems described by differential equations that represent the way in which the change in an element's state depends on the states of other elements at that same instant, discrete-event simulation does not involve solving simultaneous equations, but rather tracing from causes to later effects. An element may have multiple inputs and outputs, and is represented by its state and by a program that computes the behavior of this type of element; thus, a simulation element fits easily within the reactive-process framework described in Section 4.1. Ordinarily, the system being simulated is itself distributed and exhibits concurrency. Military engagements, computer networks, and logic circuits are typical subjects of discrete-event simulations. The phenomenon that constitutes an event —a command to move a tank, the transmission of a packet, or the change in state of a signal— depends on the simulation subject, but always involves a discrete action that takes place at a specific time.

Initially, my students and I became interested in distributed discrete-event simulation from our experiences using the first-generation multicomputers to simulate our designs for the message-passing networks of the second-generation machines. Whereas network properties such as freedom from deadlock and injection fairness can be treated mathematically, certain performance characteristics of networks that exhibit contention cannot generally be predicted analytically but can be modeled accurately by simulation. The excellent results of these network simulations encouraged us to look more deeply into distributed discrete-event simulation techniques [34], with the result that simulation has become a "model application" that has significantly influenced the development of reactive-process programming [33].

Sequential discrete-event simulation can employ the efficient technique of maintaining an *event list* that is ordered by the time of scheduled input events. An item in the event list consists of a time and an event. The simulator repeatedly removes the earliest item from the event list and passes this input event to the specified element process. The process computes its new state and inserts any resulting events into the event list. Sequential simulators also generally allow element processes to remove previously scheduled events from the event list. The possibility of nonphysical elements that exhibit negative or zero delays will be excluded from this discussion; hence, any event inserted into the event list will be strictly later than the input event.

The sequential simulation algorithm is not a good starting point for constructing a concurrent simulator. It would be possible to distribute a simulation program by employing a dealer process that maintains the event list; however, if the dealer process were to issue input events concurrently to two or more element processes, the earlier input events might result in output events that would be earlier than events already processed. A formulation that continues to pursue this route of distributing the sequential program leads into perilous territory. A description of the network topology and the minimum input-to-output time of each element would allow the dealer process to compute which simulation processes could safely execute concurrently. The dealer would certainly become the bottleneck in this formulation. Another possibility is to perform computations based on the speculation that the results will be used, and to roll back the simulation computations if the dealer-process speculations are wrong; this formulation, however, makes it difficult to demonstrate progress and to limit the storage utilization.

Fortunately, there is a much more straightforward approach. A fully distributed discrete-event-simulation algorithm was discovered in the late 1970s independently by Randal Bryant [6] at MIT and by Mani Chandy and Jay Misra [8] at the University of Texas at Austin. This Chandy-Misra-Bryant (CMB) algorithm is suitable for either multiprocessors or multicomputers, but is usually described in terms of processes and messages [24]. The essential idea is to convey the event times within the messages, enabling each element process to keep track of its own simulation time. These messages contain a record of the events during an interval of simulation time. The element processes can get as far out of step in their simulation times as their interdependencies allow.

For example, consider the simulation element for a unit-delay logical-AND gate whose inputs and last output message are defined as shown in Figure 24.

The possible response of the simulation process to a message falls into one of three categories:

1. The message may be unable to advance the local simulation time due to other inputs that are defined only up to earlier simulation times. For example, a message may convey the information that input b remains 1 up to $t = 13$, and then switches to 0 at $t = 14$; because input a is defined only up to $t = 10$, however, the state of the output cannot be determined beyond $t = 11$. The events within the message are recorded in the simulation process, but no messages are generated.

2. The message may advance the local simulation time and also allow one or more messages containing output events to be generated. For example, a message that conveys that input a switches to 1 at $t = 11$ (and remains 1 at least until $t = 12$) allows the simulation process to determine that the output becomes 1 at $t = 12$ (and remains 1 at least until $t = 13$).

3. The message may advance the local simulation time, but no output events are produced. For example, a message that conveys that input a remains 0 until it switches to 1 at $t = 15$ allows the simulation process to determine that the output will remain 0 until at least $t = 16$. Although this output

---

Figure 24. Simulation of a unit-delay logical-AND gate.

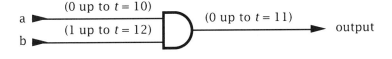

does not include any events (changes in signal state), the simulation process may generate a *null message* to extend the simulation time at its
outputs to a time later than its inputs. It is always possible to extend the
simulation time at the output by the element's own delay from the simulation time of the most lagging input; because the logical-AND function is
nonstrict, however, the output in this case can be determined up to $t = 16$
independent of the state of the b input.

Event-containing messages and null message are operationally similar in distributed simulators. We distinguish between them because sequential simulators do not require null messages, whereas CMB simulators must generally
employ null messages to assure progress. It is evident that having element
simulators maintain a later simulation time at their outputs than at their inputs forms a sufficient condition for progress. If an element-simulation process fails to generate a message when its own simulation time advances, it
may deprive other elements of the ability to act on their inputs. Cyclic dependencies between elements then lead to the possibility of deadlock.

It is practical for certain simulation subjects to employ the eager-message-
sending form of the CMB algorithm. The null-message processing is a small
fraction of the total computing time if the proportion of null messages is
small, or if event-containing messages require sufficiently more computing
time than do null messages that the null-message processing is masked. Many
simulation subjects, however, are much more difficult. For example, although
the simulation of logic circuits may involve very large numbers of elements
and high degrees of concurrency in the simulation subject, the volume of null
messages is typically several times the volume of event-containing messages,
and logic operations are so elementary that the computing time for null and
event-containing messages is nearly the same [34]. The large volume of null
messages is due to the existence of short-delay cycles of low activity, such
as cross-coupled gates used for storage (Figure 25).

Whereas a sequential simulator calls the element-simulation processes for
these gates only when an event occurs on the *set* or *reset* inputs, a CMB simulator is required to invoke the processes for these two gates even in the
absence of events on the *set* or *reset* inputs. The null messages conveyed
between these two gates while they are storing a bit serve only to advance
the simulation time. Of course, it is possible to avoid some null messages
by absorbing these two gates into a single element, but the network will still
generally contain cycles of larger delay.

If the volume of null messages were three times the volume of event-
containing messages, and the average number of concurrent events in the
simulation subject were 2^8, the performance of a CMB logic simulator would

be similar to that shown in Figure 26(a). The overhead of processing null messages appears at $N = 1$ as a factor-of-four increase in the computing time relative to a sequential simulator. The concurrent simulator does not break even with the sequential simulator until $N = 4$. The asymptotic minimum time is determined by the 2^8 event concurrency in the simulation subject; almost all null-message processing represents additional concurrency, so that the speedup extends over a range of 2^{10}. The deviation from ideal speedup as the asymptotic minimum time is approached is, as usual, due to the loss of load balance as the number of element-simulation processes per node is

---

Figure 25. A difficult distributed-simulation subject.

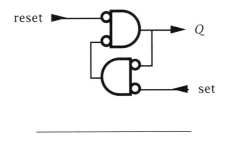

Figure 26. CMB logic-simulator performance.

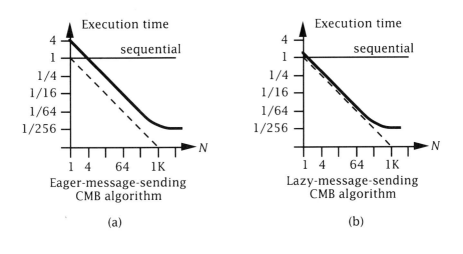

(a)   (b)

reduced, and to sensitivity to message latency under these conditions.

A simulation involving a large null-message-processing overhead might be reasonable on a large-*N,* fine-grain multicomputer; the inefficiency of the eager-message-sending form of the CMB algorithm for small-*N* systems, however, demands that measures be taken to control the volume of null messages. A CMB simulator can employ a *lazy* message-sending strategy in which null messages are combined with subsequent null or event-containing messages to reduce the volume of messages. These simulation processes do not advance the local simulation time at every opportunity; thus, a deadlock may result. Because deadlock will eventually deprive processes of messages, the deadlock can be detected locally by the following use of the nonblocking **xrecv** function within the simulation processes:

```
while (1) {
    if (p = xrecv()) simulate(p);
    else promote_progress();
}
```

A non-NULL pointer returned by **xrecv** is passed to a function that performs the simulation and may either send or enqueue any resulting output messages. A NULL pointer returned by **xrecv** indicates "starvation"— that the processes in this node have exhausted the receive queue. The simulation process must then perform an action that promotes progress, if any is available; for example, it may send one or more queued messages.

This framework permits the simulation processes to employ *any* strategy for reducing message traffic, while still avoiding deadlock. The processes might even withhold all output messages until the onset of starvation; this approach would regulate the message traffic at the minimal levels required to assure progress, but would also reduce the available concurrency. The approach in which the simulation processes withhold null messages in order to combine them with subsequent event-containing messages is generally profitable, because event-containing messages are more likely to promote progress in the destination process. It is also possible to organize the progress-promoting actions in a demand-driven form, in which a starved process sends prompting messages to the source of its lagging inputs. The result of measures such as these is to reduce the null-message overhead to make a CMB simulator more competitive with the sequential simulator, as shown in Figure 26(b).

The program for a CMB simulator will typically consist of a simulation process in each node. The element-simulation processes are embedded in the simulation process using the techniques described in Section 4.1. The simulation process also includes the message-handling routines to implement output-message queueing, and a **promote_progress** routine to implement the actions to be taken when the possibility of a deadlock is detected.

6.5 *Conclusions*

The choice of these three examples was meant to support the idea that multicomputer applications are generally divided into three classes:

1. Easily distributed problems, such as the ray-tracing example, in which the efficiency and scaling of the computation are limited only by the load balance and available concurrency.

2. Problems such as the matrix-multiplication example, in which a near-perfect distribution of the data and computations is possible. The efficiency and scaling of the computation are determined by the relationship between the operation rate and the message latency and bandwidth limitations of the multicomputer.

3. Algorithmically interesting problems, such as discrete-event simulation, in which the distributed computation necessarily involves more operations than its sequential counterpart.

7 *Conclusions and Future Directions*

Multicomputers can be scaled to large numbers of nodes because, unlike multiprocessors, they use different mechanisms for processor-to-memory and interprocess communication. Except for vector and block-move instructions, processor-to-memory communication occurs in units of single words. A memory-access latency of more than about one instruction time forces a processor to become idle while waiting for the memory access to complete; hence, it is a good fit of physical form to logical function to localize this latency-sensitive communication to a single node. Interprocess communication by message passing conveys blocks of data rather than single words. Even for multicomputers with tens of thousands of nodes, it is practical to construct message-passing networks that exhibit an average message latency equal to a few tens of instruction times. The performance of a computation is insensitive to a message latency that is less than the interval during which a message would otherwise have resided in the node receive queue, and this interval can be made larger than the message latency by using sufficiently many processes per node. It is a good fit of function to form that the communication that must span the entire system is tolerant of latency.

The same physical properties that allow multicomputers to be scaled to large numbers of nodes provide for scalability in its broader sense: The same architecture will be able to translate future advances in microelectronic and packaging technologies directly into smaller, faster, lower-power, and less-expensive multicomputers. Today's digital technologies are fundamentally limited by communication [26, 35]; future technologies will exacerbate the communication limitations relative to still higher circuit densities and speeds [29]. The effect of these communication limitations is that even a system as small as a single chip may advantageously be treated as a distributed system. These characteristics of the technology are at odds with the traditional programming models and the sequential-computer and multiprocessor architectures, which persist in treating all data accesses as equivalent (in practice, by making them equally expensive). The architectures that make the best use of the silicon medium are those that respect the communication limits of technology by providing flexible means for programmers or programming systems to map the locality and concurrency in computing problems to distributed memories and processors.

In addition to multicomputers based on advanced circuit and packaging technologies, it is easy to predict near-term variants on the architecture. Fault tolerance and adaptive message routing [25] will be particularly important for fine-grain multicomputers. Processors that are specialized to the context-switching requirements of multicomputers will streamline message handling in the nodes [11]. The physical architecture and programming model allow for multicomputers with multiprocessor nodes. These possibilities are best regarded as variants on the multicomputer, however, rather than as distinct architectures. The essential features of distributed memory, interprocess communication by message passing, and dependence of communication performance on process placement are dictated by technology. Because multicomputers fit digital technologies so well and have proven to be effective for a wide range of applications, I believe that for the immediate future the architecture will persist in much its present form.

Where we must look for conceptual advances is in programming. The programming methods described here might be regarded as early adaptations of distributed-computing techniques and algorithms to a class of distributed systems that employ processes and messages on a finer time scale than is possible for geographically distributed systems. These multicomputer programming systems, only a few years old, necessarily emphasize efficient and portable implementations of low-level functions. The application programs that have been developed using these low-level programming systems have demonstrated the performance and application span of the architecture, but require that the programmer give attention to details that are not directly related to the application. In the CE/RK environment, for example, the distribution of processes to nodes is usually controlled by the programmer, but this detail adds little additional complexity to most programs. The explicit control of process distribution and naming is a necessary feature of a low-level programming system that was planned as a target for higher-level programming systems.

Higher-level and application-specific programming systems for multicomputers are becoming available. It is too early to assess the effectiveness of these systems for applications; what we should expect from higher-level programming systems, however, is not only complete management of the resources of the target computer, but also higher-level abstractions for expressing and composing programs. I look to the work of others for suitable general-purpose concurrent programming notations. In the meanwhile, my students and I hope to continue to contribute to the architecture, designs, low-level programming systems, and applications of multicomputers. Our immediate challenges are the completion of the first prototype of the Mosaic fine-grain multicomputer and the continued refinement of its programming system.

Acknowledgments

This exposition includes and may help to reveal the connections between the research efforts of my present and recent graduate students, William C. Athas (now at the University of Texas at Austin), Nanette J. Boden, William J. Dally (now at MIT), Charles M. Flaig (now at Apple Computer), John Y. Ngai (now at Bellcore), Sven Mattisson (now at the University of Lund, Sweden), Jakov Seizovic, Craig S. Steele, and Wen-King Su. Mistakes and obfuscations are entirely my own responsibility.

The insights, help, and encouragement of my Caltech colleagues, Alain J. Martin and K. Mani Chandy, and of my technical editor, Dian De Sha, are deeply appreciated.

The research described in this paper was sponsored in part by the Defense Advanced Research Projects Agency, DARPA Order Number 6202, and monitored by the Office of Naval Research under contract number N00014–87–K–0745; and in part by grants from Intel Scientific Computers and Symult Systems, Inc.

References

[1] Agha, G. A. *Actors: A Model of Concurrent Computation in Distributed Systems.* MIT Press, Cambridge, Mass., 1986.

[2] Athas, W. C. "Fine-grain concurrent computation". Technical Report 5242:TR:87, Department of Computer Science, California Institute of Technology, 1987.

[3] Athas, W. C. and Seitz, C. L. "Multicomputers: Message-passing concurrent computers". *IEEE Computer 21,* 8 (August 1988), pp. 9–24.

[4] Boden, N. J. "A study of fine-grain programming using Cantor". Technical Report 88–11, Department of Computer Science, California Institute of Technology, 1988.

[5] Browning, S. A. and Seitz, C. L. "Communication in a tree machine". *Proceedings of the Second Caltech Conference on VLSI,* pp. 509–526. Department of Computer Science, California Institute of Technology, 1981.

[6] Bryant, R. E. "Simulation of packet communication architecture computer systems". Technical Report MIT–LCS–TR–188, Massachusetts Institute of Technology, 1977.

[7] The information about Cray supercomputers was derived from 1986–1989 articles in *Cray Channels,* an excellent quarterly publication of Cray Research, Inc., 608 Second Avenue South, Minneapolis, MN 55402.

[8] Chandy, K. M. and Misra, J. "Asynchronous distributed simulation via a sequence of parallel computations". *Communications of the ACM 24,* 4 (April 1981), pp. 198–205.

[9] Chandy, K. M. and Misra, J. *Parallel Program Design: A Foundation.* Addison-Wesley, Reading, Mass., 1988.

[10] Dally, W. J. *A VLSI Architecture for Concurrent Data Structures.* Kluwer Academic Publishers, Norwell, Mass., 1987.

[11] Dally, W. J. "Fine-grain message-passing concurrent computers". *Proceedings of the Third Conference on Hypercube Concurrent Computers and Applications.* ACM Press, New York, 1988.

[12] Dally, W. J. and Seitz, C. L. "Deadlock-free message routing in multiprocessor interconnection networks". *IEEE Transactions on Computers C–36,* 5 (May 1987), pp. 547–553.

[13] Flaig, C. M. "VLSI mesh routing systems". Technical Report 5241:TR:87, Department of Computer Science, California Institute of Technology, 1987.

[14] Hillis, W. D. *The Connection Machine.* MIT Press, Cambridge, Mass., 1985.

[15] Hoare, C. A. R. "Communicating sequential processes". *Communications of the ACM 21,* 8 (August 1978), pp. 666–677.

[16] INMOS, Ltd. *The Occam Programming Manual.* Prentice-Hall International, Hemel Hempstead, U.K., 1985.

[17] Intel Corp. "iPSC/2". Publication order number 280110–001, Intel Scientific Computers, Beaverton, Ore., 1987.

[18] Karp, R. M. and Ramachandran, V. "A survey of parallel algorithms for shared-memory machines". Report [UCB/CSD 88/408], University of California, Berkeley, 1988; to appear *Handbook of Theoretical Computer Science,* North-Holland.

[19] Kermani, P. and Kleinrock, L. "Virtual cut-through: A new computer communication

switching technique". *Computer Networks 3* (1979), pp. 267–286.

[20] Kohn, L. and Fu, S-W. "A 1,000,000-transistor microprocessor". In *Digest of Technical Papers, 1989 IEEE International Solid-State Circuits Conference*. IEEE, New York, 1989.

[21] Miklosko, J. and Kotov, V. E., eds. *Algorithms, Software, and Hardware of Parallel Computers*. Springer-Verlag, Berlin, 1984.

[22] Lang, C. R. Jr. "The extension of object-oriented languages to a homogeneous, concurrent architecture". Technical Report 5014:TR:82, Department of Computer Science, California Institute of Technology, 1982.

[23] Martin, A. J. "The probe: An addition to communication primitives". *Information Processing Letters 20*, 1 (January 1985).

[24] Misra, J. "Distributed discrete-event simulation". *Computing Surveys 18*, 1 (March 1986), pp. 39–65.

[25] Ngai, J. Y. and Seitz, C. L. "A framework for adaptive routing in multicomputer networks". *Proceedings of the 1989 ACM Symposium on Parallel Algorithms and Architectures*. ACM Press, New York, 1989.

[26] Seitz, C. L. "Concurrent VLSI architectures". *IEEE Transactions on Computers C–33*, 12 (December 1984), pp. 1247–1265.

[27] Seitz, C. L. "The cosmic cube". *Communications of the ACM 28*, 1 (January 1985), pp. 22–33.

[28] Seitz, C. L., Athas, W. C., Flaig, C. M., Martin, A. J., Seizovic, J., Steele, C. S., and Su, W.-K. "The architecture and programming of the Ametek Series 2010 multicomputer". *Proceedings of the Third Conference on Hypercube Concurrent Computers and Applications*. ACM Press, New York, 1988.

[29] Seitz, C. L. and Matisoo, J. "Engineering limitations on computer performance". *Physics Today 37*, 5 (May 1984), pp. 38–45.

[30] Seitz, C. L., Seizovic, J., and Su, W.-K. "The C programmer's abbreviated guide to multicomputer programming". Technical Report 88-1, Department of Computer Science, California Institute of Technology, 1988.

[31] Seizovic, J. "The Reactive Kernel". Technical Report 88-10, Department of Computer Science, California Institute of Technology, 1988.

[32] Su, W.-K. "Super Mesh". Technical Report 5125:TR:84, Department of Computer Science, California Institute of Technology, 1984.

[33] Su, W.-K. "Reactive-process programming and distributed discrete-event simulation". Technical Report 89-11, Department of Computer Science, California Institute of Technology, 1989.

[34] Su, W.-K. and Seitz, C. L. "Variants of the Chandy-Misra-Bryant distributed discrete-event simulation algorithm". *Proceedings of the 1989 Eastern Multiconference, Distributed Simulation Conference*. ACM/IEEE, New York, 1989.

[35] Sutherland, I. E. and Mead, C. A. "Microelectronics and computer science". *Scientific American* (September 1977), pp. 210–228.

Specification and Design

of the

X.25 Protocol

A Case Study in CSP

6

He Jifeng
Oxford University

1 Introduction

This paper presents a specification of the X.25 protocol [2], which is well known as the most significant recommendation provided by CCITT for its constituent bodies. The X.25 protocol is intended to define the means by which user terminals connect to a common carrier network. Why, then, do we present a formal specification of it here? Our first goal is pedagogical. The idea of formalizing the specification of a computer-based system has yet to receive widespread acceptance among computing practitioners, largely because very few realistic examples have been investigated. This case study offers us the possibility of showing how to use a mathematical notation to capture important aspects of the behavior of a system that is already more than a toy. Our second goal is to introduce a notation and reasoning method,

based on Communicating Sequential Processes (CSP) [4], which seems to provide a suitable framework for the presentation of large-system specifications.

In this paper we use natural language together with mathematical notation
to specify the behavior of the communication protocol. The specification of
the access procedures of the X.25 protocol will be given in the predicate calculus. In addition, the algebraic properties of the procedures will be explored,
enabling us to develop methods both for gradually transforming a given specification into a program that satisfies that specification and for proving that
a given program has some desired properties. The potential benefits of applying formal, at least mathematically rigorous, methods to software development are currently a topic of much discussion and have been eloquently
expounded elsewhere, for example in [7].

Section 2 provides the mathematical model of the communication proto-
col. It introduces a new bidirectional operator $\leftrightarrow$ which provides the communication between adjacent nodes in the X.25 network. It also explains the
relevant proof methods and algebraic properties of the CSP operators used.
To illustrate the use of the formal method in specification and design of the
X.25 protocol, we investigate some access procedures in Section 3. The final
section contains concluding remarks.

2 *Abstract Model*

Most real-life communication protocols are very complex because they
must perform several distinct functions. The X.25 protocol contains various procedures for data transmission, flow control, and connection management. Nevertheless, data transmission is the purpose of the protocol, and all
the complexities of connection establishment and flow control are just the
means to that end.

Here we make the gross simplification that there is only one transmitting
end and only one receiving end. Consequently, a one-way data transfer protocol can be specified as a process that accepts messages from the transmitting
end and delivers them to the receiving end in the same order as acceptance.
The process must always be ready to input, and it must always be ready to
output as long as there is a message not yet delivered.

The first task is to formalize the preceding specification. We shall do so by
describing a finite sequence *tr* (trace), recording the communications of the
protocol up to any arbitrary monent in time. The elements of the sequence
are either input *in.m* or output *out.m*, where *m* is the value of the message
communicated, and *in* and *out* are the names of the input channel and output

channel, respectively. We borrow the following notations from [4].

  $tr \downarrow c$ is the sequence of messages communicated on channel c, recorded in tr.

  c_r (*cready*), which denotes the status of channel c, takes a value just when the process has completed all internal calculation. This value is true if on stability the process is waiting for a communication on channel c.

  Now a one-way data transfer protocol can be specified:

$$PROTOCOL \; \hat{=} \; (tr \downarrow out \le tr \downarrow in) \land in_r \land (out_r \lor tr \downarrow in = tr \downarrow out)$$

where $s \le t$ means that s begins with a copy of t.

  The first conjunction states that the protocol faithfully copies messages from the *in* channel to the *out* channel. The second conjunction states (unrealistically) that it is always ready to input. The final conjunction states that it is always ready to output, except when no messages are awaiting output.

  In practice, the X.25 protocol is implemented as two processes, a *DTE* (data terminal equipment) and a *DCE* (data circuit terminating equipment), connected by full duplex lines (Figure 1). We therefore here abandon the simplification of one-way communication on just two channels *in* and *out*. In the context of the X.25 protocol, a terminal is any device, connected to the network but not part of it: a source and sink of information that the network is required to pass to another terminal in a reliable and controlled manner. A *DCE* is the other end of a logical wire from the *DTE* towards the network. The *DTE* and *DCE* are in effect "equal partners" in the communication. Both can initiate and terminate a connection, and send data on an established connection (subject to flow control) without waiting to be asked, and neither the *DTE* nor the *DCE* has overall control over the information flow. Furthermore, the sequence of messages passing on the connecting links is totally concealed from the users of the protocol. This kind of connection is modeled in CSP

Figure 1.   *DTE* ↔ *DCE*.

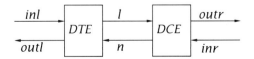

by a double chaining operator $\leftrightarrow$ defined as a generalization of the single chaining operator $\gg$.

A formal definition of $\leftrightarrow$ is given as an operator on the predicates that describe the behavior of its two operands. The result is also a predicate describing the communications of the composite process on channels *inl*, *outl*, *outr*, and *inr* (the internal communications on the connecting channels are concealed).

Let *s* be a trace of *DTE*, let *t* be a trace of *DCE*, and let *tr* be a trace of *DTE* $\leftrightarrow$ *DCE*. Then the sequence of messages $tr \downarrow inl$ input by *DTE* $\leftrightarrow$ *DCE* from the channel *inl* is the same as the input $s \downarrow inl$ of *DTE* from the channel *inl*. Similarly, we can conclude

$$
\begin{aligned}
tr \downarrow outl &= s \downarrow outl \\
tr \downarrow inr &= t \downarrow inr \\
tr \downarrow outr &= t \downarrow outr
\end{aligned}
$$

Because the internal communication along the channels *l* and *n* is synchronized, this yields

$$
\begin{aligned}
s \downarrow l &= t \downarrow l \\
s \downarrow n &= t \downarrow n
\end{aligned}
$$

Note that if a communication can take place on the connecting channels, it does so immediately without consideration of the external environment. Consequently, *DTE* $\leftrightarrow$ *DCE* can communicate on the channels *inl*, *inr*, *outl*, and *outr* only when neither the channel *l* nor the channel *n* is ready for internal chat, i.e.,

$$
\neg(l_{r1} \wedge l_{r2}) \wedge \neg(n_{r1} \wedge n_{r2})
$$

where l_{r1} and n_{r1} stand for the channel status of the channels *l* and *n* of *DTE*, and l_{r2} and n_{r2} are the channel status of *DCE*. For further discussion of stability, see [5].

Let $DTE[s/tr, l_{r1}/l_r, n_{r1}/n_r]$ and $DCE[t/tr, l_{r2}/l_r, n_{r2}/n_r]$ stand for the specifications of *DTE* and *DCE* in which every occurrence of *tr* has been replaced by *s* and *t*, respectively, with similar substitutions for the ready variables. The double chaining operator $\leftrightarrow$ can then be defined as follows:

$$DTE \leftrightarrow DCE \;\; \hat{=}$$

$$\exists s, t, l_{r1}, l_{r2}, n_{r1}, n_{r2}.(DTE[s/tr, l_{r1}/l_r, n_{r1}/n_r] \wedge$$

$$DCE[t/tr, l_{r2}/l_r, n_{r2}/n_r] \wedge$$

$$tr \downarrow inl = s \downarrow inl \wedge tr \downarrow outl = s \downarrow outl \wedge$$

$$tr \downarrow inr = t \downarrow inr \wedge tr \downarrow outr = t \downarrow outr \wedge$$

$$s \downarrow l = t \downarrow l \wedge s \downarrow n = t \downarrow n \wedge$$

$$\neg(l_{r1} \wedge l_{r2}) \wedge \neg(n_{r1} \wedge n_{r2}))$$

This definition is slightly simplified. Although weaker in some respects than the trace definition, it is valid provided that there is no risk of an unbounded sequence of consecutive communications on the connecting channels. This precondition is unlikely to be much of a practical handicap since almost all processes encountered in practice will satisfy this constraint.

Now we turn to some properties of $\leftrightarrow$, beginning with the following one.

The double chaining operator $\leftrightarrow$ is associative:

$$(P \leftrightarrow Q) \leftrightarrow R \;\; = \;\; P \leftrightarrow (Q \leftrightarrow R) \tag{L1}$$

Operator $\leftrightarrow$ distributes through the nondeterministic choice operator $\sqcap$, i.e.,

$$P \leftrightarrow (Q \sqcap R) \;\; = \;\; (P \leftrightarrow Q) \sqcap (P \leftrightarrow R) \tag{L2}$$

$$(P \sqcap Q) \leftrightarrow R \;\; = \;\; (P \leftrightarrow R) \sqcap (Q \leftrightarrow R)$$

The following law shows how input and output can be implemented in $P \leftrightarrow Q$; they enable process description to be expanded to a normal form by a sort of symbolic execution. Here we introduce boolean guards [6] to reduce the number of laws needed and the size of the calculations that use them. A boolean guarded command is simply defined in terms of the predicate P describing the command to be guarded:

$$b\&P \;\; \hat{=} \;\; (b \Rightarrow P) \wedge (\neg b \Rightarrow STOP)$$

where b is a boolean expression.

Since $((\textbf{false} \;\rightarrow P1) [\!] \; P2) = P2$, the following forms describing P and Q are the most general possible. They can be matched to simpler forms by setting

b_i or c_j to **false**. Let

$$P = (\ b_1 \& inl?x \to P_1(x) \tag{L3}$$
$$[]\ b_2 \& outl!u \to P_2$$
$$[]\ b_3 \& n?y \to P_3(y)$$
$$[]\ b_4 \& l!e \to P_4)$$

and

$$Q = (\ c_1 \& l?x \to Q_1(x)$$
$$[]\ c_2 \& n!f \to Q_2$$
$$[]\ c_3 \& inr?y \to Q_3(y)$$
$$[]\ c_4 \& outr!v \to Q_4)$$

Then

$$P \leftrightarrow Q = ((b_3 \wedge c_2) \vee (b_4 \wedge c_1)) \Rightarrow (T [] U) \sqcap U) \wedge$$
$$(\neg((b_3 \wedge c_2) \vee (b_4 \wedge c_1)) \Rightarrow T)$$

where

$$T = (\ b_1 \& inl?x \to (P_1(x) \leftrightarrow Q)$$
$$[]\ b_2 \& outl!u \to (P_2 \leftrightarrow Q)$$
$$[]\ c_3 \& inr?y \to (P \leftrightarrow Q_3(y))$$
$$[]\ c_4 \& outr!v \to (P \leftrightarrow Q_4))$$

and

$$U = ((b_3 \wedge c_2 \wedge b_4 \wedge c_1) \Rightarrow ((P_3(f) \leftrightarrow Q_2) \sqcap (P_4 \leftrightarrow Q_1(e)))) \wedge$$
$$((b_3 \wedge c_2) \wedge \neg(b_4 \wedge c_1) \Rightarrow (P_3(f) \leftrightarrow Q_2)) \wedge$$
$$((b_4 \wedge c_1) \wedge \neg(b_3 \wedge c_2) \Rightarrow (P_4 \leftrightarrow Q_1(e))) \wedge$$
$$(\neg(b_4 \wedge c_1) \wedge \neg(b_3 \wedge c_2) \Rightarrow STOP)$$

The first two lines in the definition of T describe the case in which the external communication on the channel *inl* or *outl* by P takes place first; in the final two lines, the external input or output by Q takes place first. The definition of U identifies the case in which the internal communication takes place first, so that either the value of e is transmitted from P to Q or the value of f is sent by Q to P, but the communication is concealed. In all cases, the process or processes that engage in the communication make the appropriate progress, and they continue to be chained by ↔.

We end this section by quoting and explaining algebraic properties of the CSP operators in use. For details, we refer the reader to [4].

The prefix operator → distributes through nondeterministic choice ⊓, which is expressed

$$x : B \rightarrow (P(x) \sqcap Q(x)) = (x : B \rightarrow P(x)) \sqcap (x : B \rightarrow Q(x)) \tag{L4}$$

The process *SKIP* is the unit of the sequential composition operator **;** :

$$SKIP \mathbin{;} P = P \mathbin{;} SKIP = P \tag{L5}$$

Another property of sequential composition, which will be used later, is

$$(x : B \rightarrow P(x)) \mathbin{;} Q = x : B \rightarrow (P(x) \mathbin{;} Q) \tag{L6}$$

The interleaving operator ||| is used to join processes to operate concurrently without directly interacting or synchronizing with each other. In this case, each action of the system is an action of exactly one of the processes. If one of the processes cannot engage in the action, then it must have been the other one, but if both processes could have engaged in the same action, the choice between them is nondeterministic. Note that the operator ||| in this paper, which requires the synchronization on the termination event √, is slightly different from the original one defined in [4].

When a process P is more deterministic than Q, then it can serve as a perfectly valid implementation of Q. This is expressed by the inequality

$$Q \sqsubseteq P$$

A general method of proving equality and inequality in CSP is to appeal to the unique-fixed-point theorem. It states that a set of equations in X of the form

$$X = F(X)$$

has a unique solution provided that all occurrences of X on the right-hand side are guarded, i.e., preceded by some external communications. Suppose we want to prove that P is better than Q; this proof may be accomplished by showing that

$$Q \sqsubseteq F(Q)$$

and

$$F(P) \sqsubseteq P$$

3 *Access Procedures*

As we remarked in Section 2, data transmission, connection management, and information-flow control are the main functions of a communication protocol. In this section we investigate three typical access procedures in the X.25 protocol, using a mixture of predicate and CSP notations. The first is the link-setup procedure, which is used to establish a connection. The second is the procedure that receives a "receive not ready" (*RNR*) frame, which is for information-flow control. The final one is the procedure that receives an information (*I*) command. The behavior of each procedure will be characterized by giving, for each of the sequences of communications in which it may engage, a collection of predicates relating the observations that can be made before and after that sequence of communications. As a complementary part of the predicate description, a set of algebraic properties will be explored, providing a basis from which to construct a valid implementation.

3.1 *Link Setup*

The *DTE* initiates link setup by transmitting a *setup* command to the *DCE* and starting its timer in order to determine when too much time has been spent waiting for a reply. Upon receipt of a *yes* response from the *DCE*, the *DTE* considers that the link is set up and enters the information-transfer phase. Upon receipt of a *no* response from the *DCE* as a refusal to set up the link, the *DTE* considers that the connection has not been made.

The *DTE*, having sent the *setup* command, ignores and discards any command except a *setup* or *disc* (disconnection) command, or a *yes* or *no* response received from the *DCE*. The receipt of a *setup* or *disc* command from the *DCE* results in a collision state that is specified in [3]. If no reply is received after the *DTE* sends the *setup* command, its timer runs out. The *DTE* resends the *setup* and restarts its timer. If *N* attempts to set up a link fail (i.e., the timer runs out *N* times), appropriate higher-level recovery action is initiated.

As described previously, the *DTE* waits for the link-setup reply after it sends *setup* to the *DCE*. This leads to the following definition:

$$LI\acute{N}K\_SETUP \; \hat{=} \; l!setup \rightarrow (t!start \rightarrow WAIT\_REPLY)$$

where *t* is the name of the channel connecting the *DTE* with its timer, and

$$WAIT\_REPLY \; \hat{=} \; RECEIVE\_REPLY \lor NO\_REPLY$$

which identifies two possible cases: Either the *DTE* eventually receives a response from the *DCE*, or there is no reply from the *DCE* at all.

To proceed further, we introduce a predicate T_OUT_k to specify the case in which the timer runs out k times before the *DTE* receives the response. We then observe that the relationship between *RECEIVE_REPLY* and T_OUT_k is precisely

$$RECEIVE\_REPLY \; \hat{=} \; \bigvee_{k=0}^{N-1} (T\_OUT_k \, ; ACC\_REPLY)$$

where *ACC_REPLY* specifies the behavior of the *DTE* upon receipt of a response from the *DCE*.

T_OUT_k is formally specified by a predicate

$$
\begin{aligned}
T\_OUT_k \quad \hat{=} \quad & \#tr \upharpoonright \{t.out\} \le k \wedge \\
& \#tr \upharpoonright \{t.out\} = k \Rightarrow last(tr) \in \{`\surd', `t.out'\} \wedge \\
& last(tr) \ne `\surd' \Rightarrow (l_r \vee n_r \vee t_r) \wedge \\
& tr \upharpoonright \{n.yes, n.no, n.setup, n.disc\} = <> \; \wedge \\
& \#tr \upharpoonright \{l.setup\} \le^1 \#tr \upharpoonright \{t.out\} \wedge \\
& \#tr \upharpoonright \{t.start\} \le^1 \#tr \upharpoonright \{t.out\}
\end{aligned}
$$

where

$\#s$ is the length of s,

t.out is the timeout signal,

$tr \upharpoonright A$ is the trace restricted to communications in the set A,

$\surd$ stands for a specific event indicating termination,

$last(tr)$ is the final element in tr when it is nonempty,

$<>$ denotes the empty sequence, and

$i \le^1 j$ is an abbreviation of $(i \le j) \wedge (j \le i + 1)$.

The first two lines in the definition of T_OUT_k state that T_OUT_k terminates once the timer runs out k times. The third line states that T_OUT_k is always ready for communication before it terminates. The fourth line simply says there is no response from the *DCE* during that period. The final two lines refer to the fact that the *DTE* retransmits the *setup* command to the *DCE* and restarts its timer whenever it runs out.

The preceding properties of T_OUT_k can be captured by the following algebraic laws:

$$T\_OUT_0 \sqsubseteq SKIP \tag{P0}$$

$$T\_OUT_k \sqsubseteq n?x : \{yes, no, setup, disc\}^- \rightarrow T\_OUT_k \tag{P1}$$

$$T\_OUT_{k+1} \sqsubseteq (t?out \rightarrow (l!setup \rightarrow t!start \rightarrow T\_OUT_k)) \tag{P2}$$

where B^- denotes the complement of B.

Finally we define

$$NO\_REPLY \; \hat{=} \; T\_OUT_N \; ; RECOVERY$$

where *RECOVERY* is the higher-level recovery process that the *DTE* calls after it fails to establish a connection.

Here we omit the details about the definitions of *RECOVERY* and *ACC_REPLY*. The interested reader can find them in [3].

Having defined *WAIT_REPLY*, we next seek a proper implementation. Let $F = \{F_k\}$ be a family of expressions defined by

$$F_N(X) \; \hat{=} \; RECOVERY$$

$$F_K(X) \; \hat{=} \; (ACC\_REPLY$$

$$[\!] \; n?x : \{yes, no, setup, disc\}^- \rightarrow X_k$$

$$[\!] \; t?out \rightarrow l!setup \rightarrow t!start \rightarrow X_{k+1}) \qquad 0 \le k \le N-1$$

The following theorem states that the first component X_0 of the least fixed point of the indexed equations

$$X_k = F_k(X)$$

is a valid implementation of *WAIT_REPLY*.

Theorem 1

$$WAIT\_REPLY \sqsubseteq (\mu X.F(X))_0$$

Proof   First, we define $S = \{S_k\}$ as follows:

$$S_N \; \hat{=} \; RECOVERY$$

$$S_k \; \hat{=} \; \bigvee_{i=0}^{N-k-1} (T\_OUT_i \; ; ACC\_REPLY) \vee T\_OUT_{N-k} \; ; RECOVERY, \quad 0 \le k \le N-1$$

In particular, we have

$$S_0 = WAIT\_REPLY$$

Then we have, for $0 \le k \le N - 1$,

$$S_k \;\equiv\; \bigvee_{i=1}^{N-k-1} (T\_OUT_i \;;\; ACC\_REPLY) \vee T\_OUT_{N-k} \;;\; RECOVERY \vee$$

$$\bigvee_{i=0}^{N-k-1} (T\_OUT_i \;;\; ACC\_REPLY) \vee T\_OUT_{N-k} \;;\; RECOVERY \vee$$

$$T\_OUT_0 \;;\; ACC\_REPLY \hspace{4cm} \text{def of } S_k$$

$$\sqsubseteq\; \bigvee_{i=1}^{N-k-1} (t?out \rightarrow l!setup \rightarrow t!start \rightarrow T\_OUT_{i-1}) \;;\; ACC\_REPLY \vee$$

$$(t?out \rightarrow l!setup \rightarrow t!start \rightarrow T\_OUT_{N-k-1}) \;;\; RECOVERY \vee$$

$$\bigvee_{i=0}^{N-k-1} (n?x : \{yes, no, setup, disc\}^- \rightarrow T\_OUT_i) \;;\; ACC\_REPLY \vee$$

$$(n?x : \{yes, no, setup, disc\}^- \rightarrow T\_OUT_{N-k}) \;;\; RECOVERY \vee$$

$$ACC\_REPLY \hspace{5cm} \text{L5, P0–P2}$$

$$=\; (\; t?out \rightarrow l!setup \rightarrow t!start \rightarrow S_{k+1}$$

$$[]\; n?x : \{yes, no, setup, disc\}^- \rightarrow S_k$$

$$[]\; ACC\_REPLY) \hspace{4cm} \text{L4, L6, and def of } S$$

$$=\; F_k(S) \hspace{6cm} \text{def of } F_k$$

and, for $k = N$,

$$S_N = RECOVERY = F_N(S)$$

which leads to the conclusion by appeal to the unique-fixed-point theorem presented in Section 2. $\square$

The reader should note that the preceding proof is based only on the algebraic properties of T_OUT_k and the unique-fixed-point theorem, without involving the predicate definition of T_OUT_k. This encourages us to generalize Theorem 1 in the following way:

Suppose that R is a specification, defined by

$$R \;\hat{=}\; \bigvee_{k=0}^{N-1} (T_k(P, Q) \;;\; S) \vee T_N(P, Q) \;;\; W$$

where S, T, P, and Q are guarded and satisfy the following conditions:

$$T_0(P, Q) \sqsubseteq T \tag{C0}$$

$$T_k(P, Q) \sqsubseteq Q \text{ ; } T_k(P, Q) \tag{C1}$$

$$T_{k+1}(P, Q) \sqsubseteq P \text{ ; } T_k(P, Q) \tag{C2}$$

Define

$$G_N(X) \; \hat{=} \; W$$

$$G_k(X) \; \hat{=} \; (P \text{ ; } X_{k+1} [\!] \; Q \text{ ; } X_k [\!] \; T \text{ ; } S) \qquad\qquad 0 \le k \le N - 1$$

Then we can show the following theorem.

Theorem 2

$$R \sqsubseteq (\mu X.G(X))_0$$

The proof of Theorem 2 is virtually identical to that of Theorem 1. We omit the details, but the reader should have no trouble supplying them.

3.2 *Receiving an RNR Command*

The "receive not ready" (*RNR*) command is used by the *DCE* to indicate a busy condition, i.e., a temporary inability to accept an additional incoming information (*I*) command. Upon receipt of an *RNR* frame, the *DTE* transmits a supervisory (*S*) command with the poll (*P*) bit set to 1, and starts its timer, in order to determine whether there is any change in the receive status of the *DCE*. The *DCE* should respond to the poll (*P*) bit set to 1 with a supervisory (*S*) response ("receive ready" (*RR*), "receive not ready" (*RNR*), or "reject" (*REJ*)) with the final (*F*) bit set to 1.

Upon receipt of the *DCE* response, the *DTE* acts as follows:

0. If the response is "receive ready" (*RR*) or "reject" (*REJ*), the busy condition is cleared, and the *DTE* may then resume transmitting information (*I*) commands.

1. If the response is "receive not ready" (*RNR*), the busy condition still exists, and the *DTE* repeats the inquiry of the *DCE* receive status.

If the timer runs out before a status response is received, the inquiry process is repeated. If *N* attempts to get a busy-condition-clearance response fail, the *DTE* either initiates a link-resetting procedure or sends a "no" response to ask the *DCE* to initiate a link set-up procedure as described in Section 3.1.

The preceding description can be expressed formally by

$$RECEIVE\_RNR \quad \hat{=} \quad (l!S.command[P = 1] \rightarrow t!start \rightarrow WAIT\_RESPONSE)$$

where $S.command[P = 1]$ stands for a supervisory command with the poll
(P) bit set to 1, and $WAIT\_RESPONSE$ can be defined in the same way as
$WAIT\_REPLY$ in the previous section:

$$WAIT\_RESPONSE \quad \hat{=} \quad \bigvee_{k=0}^{N-1} (RUN\_OUT_k \; ; CLEARANCE) \vee RUN\_OUT_N \; ; FAILURE$$

where RUN_OUT_k is used to describe the case in which the timer runs out k
times before a busy-condition clearance indication is received.

$CLEARANCE$ specifies the behavior of the DTE upon the receipt of an RR or
REJ response:

$$CLEARANCE \quad \hat{=} \quad n?x : \{RR, REJ\} \rightarrow SEND\_I.COMMAND$$

where $SEND\_I.COMMAND$ denotes the send-I-command procedure.

$FAILURE$ identifies the case in which N attempts to get a busy-condition
clearance indication fail:

$$FAILURE \quad \hat{=} \quad LINK\_RESET \sqcap (l!no \rightarrow DISC\_PHASE)$$

where $LINK\_RESET$ and $DISC\_PHASE$ denote the link-resetting procedure and
the disconnected-phase procedure, respectively, and $\sqcap$ is used to reflect the
fact that the DTE behaves either like $LINK\_RESET$ or like $(l!no \rightarrow DISC\_PHASE)$
and that the choice between them is made by the DTE arbitrarily.

We now turn to the definition of RUN_OUT_k. Rather than working out their
predicate definitions, we prefer to explore their properties instead. From the
informal description given earlier, the following properties for RUN_OUT_k
seem intuitively evident:

$$RUN\_OUT_0 \sqsubseteq SKIP$$

$$RUN\_OUT_k \sqsubseteq (n?x : \{RR, REJ\}^- \rightarrow PROC(x) \; ; RUN\_OUT_k)$$

$$RUN\_OUT_{k+1} \sqsubseteq (t?out \rightarrow l!S.command[P = 1] \rightarrow t!start \rightarrow RUN\_OUT_k)$$

where the procedure $PROC(x)$ is used to accept and process the received frame
x.

When we compare these properties with $C0$–$C2$ in Theorem 2, it turns out
that the design of the receive-RNR procedure is straightforward; all that re-

mains is to select the proper P, Q, S, T, and W. Here we choose

$$Q \quad \hat{=} \quad n?x : \{RR, REJ\}^- \rightarrow PROC(x)$$

$$P \quad \hat{=} \quad (t?out \rightarrow l!S.command[P = 1] \rightarrow t!start \rightarrow SKIP)$$

$$S \quad \hat{=} \quad CLEARANCE$$

$$W \quad \hat{=} \quad FAILURE$$

$$T \quad \hat{=} \quad SKIP$$

After simplification, we obtain

$$G_N(X) \quad = \quad W = LINK\_RESET \sqcap (l!no \rightarrow DISC\_PHASE)$$

$$G_k(X) \quad = \quad (P \,;\, X_{k+1} \parallel Q \,;\, X_k \parallel T \,;\, S)$$

$$= \quad (t?out \rightarrow l!S.command[P = 1] \rightarrow t!start \rightarrow X_{k+1}$$

$$\parallel n?x \rightarrow \quad (x \in \{RR, REJ\} \Rightarrow SEND\_I.COMMAND) \wedge$$

$$(x \notin \{RR, REJ\} \Rightarrow PROC(x) \,;\, X_k)$$

$$)$$

and conclude that

$$WAIT\_RESPONSE \sqsubseteq (\mu X.G(X))_0$$

as desired.

3.3 *Receiving an I Command*

When the *DTE* is not busy and receives a valid *I* command whose sequential number $N(S)$ is equal to the *DTE* receive state variable $V(R)$, the *DCE* accepts the information field of the *I* command, increments by one its receive state variable $V(R)$, and acts as follows:

0. If the *DTE* is still not busy:

   (a) If an *I* command is available for transmission by the *DTE*, it may send it to the *DCE* and acknowledge the received *I* command by setting the receive sequence number $N(R)$ in the control field of the transmitted *I* command to the value of the receive state variable $V(R)$. Alternatively, the *DTE* may acknowledge the received *I* command by transmitting an *RR* frame with the $N(R)$ equal to the value of the *DTE* receive state variable $V(R)$.

(b) If no *I* command is available for transmission by the *DTE*, it transmits an *RR* frame with $N(R)$ equal to the value of the *DTE* receive state variable $V(R)$.

1. If the *DTE* is now busy, it transmits an *RNR* frame with $N(R)$ equal to the value of the *DTE* receive state variable $V(R)$.

When the *DTE* is busy, it may ignore the information field in any received *I* command, and returns an *RNR* response with the final *(F)* bit set to 1 if the received *I* command has its poll *(P)* bit set to 1. The *DTE* accepts the acknowledgment contained in the $N(R)$ field and the poll *(P)* bit information of the received *I* command.

When the *DTE* receives a valid *I* command whose send sequence number $N(S)$ is not correct —i.e., not equal to the current *DTE* receive state variable $V(R)$— it discards the information field of the *I* command and transmits an *REJ* frame with the $N(R)$ set to one higher than the $N(S)$ of the last correctly received *I* command. The *DTE* accepts the acknowledgment contained in the $N(R)$ field and the poll *(P)* bit information of the received *I* command.

When the *DTE* receives an invalid *I* command, the command is discarded.

The preceding description can be formalized by

$RECEIVING\_I(x)$ $\hat{=}$

$(valid(x) \wedge \neg busy \wedge x.N(S) = V(R)_0 \Rightarrow$

$(V(R) = V(R)_0 + 1 \;|||\; ACC\_INF(x) \;|||\; ACC\_ACKN(x) \;|||\; ACC\_POLL(x))$;

$RESPONSE) \wedge$

$(valid(x) \wedge busy \wedge x.N(S) = V(R)_0 \Rightarrow$

$((ACC\_INF(x) \sqcap SKIP) \;|||\; ACC\_ACKN(x) \;|||\; ACC\_POLL(x))$;

$(l!RNR[F = \mathbf{if}\ x.Pbit = 1\ \mathbf{then}\ 1\ \mathbf{else}\ 0] \rightarrow SKIP)) \wedge$

$(valid(x) \wedge x.N(S) \neq V(R) \Rightarrow$

$(ACC\_ACKN(x) \;|||\; ACC\_POLL(x))$;

$(l!REJ[N(R) = 1 + lastreceived.N(S)] \rightarrow SKIP)) \wedge$

$(\neg valid(x) \Rightarrow SKIP)$

where

$valid(x)$ is true when the received command *x* is valid,

busy is a boolean variable used to indicate the *DTE* is busy,

$x.N(s)$ is the sequence number $N(s)$ of the I command x,

$V(R)_0$ is the value of the *DTE* receive state variable $V(R)$ before it receives
an I command,

ACC_INF refers to the accept-information procedure,

ACC_ACKN is the accept-acknowledgement procedure,

ACC_POLL is the accept-poll-bit procedure,

RESPONSE is used to specify the reaction of the *DTE* after it receives a correct I command,

lastreceived.N(S) stands for the send sequence number $N(S)$ of the last correctly received I command,

$RNR[F = e]$ denotes the *RNR* frame with the final bit F set to the value of e,
and

$REJ[N(R) = e]$ stands for the *REJ* frame with the receive sequence number
$N(R)$ set to the value of e.

The order in which the *DTE* processes the data and acknowledgment information contained in the received I command is irrelevant. This irrelevance
can be expressed simply by the *CSP* parallel composition of the individual re-
quirements. Here, we use ||| to combine the independent procedures *ACC_INF*,
ACC_ACKN, and *ACC_POLL*.

The nondeterministic choice between *ACC_INF* and *SKIP* in the preceding
definition is used to reflect the fact that the *DTE* may accept the information
contained in the received I command even when it is busy.

In this section we investigate only *RESPONSE*, leaving the other procedures
for the reader. The case analysis in (0) and (1) produces the following definition:

RESPONSE $\hat{=}$

$(\neg busy \wedge availability\_of\_I.command\_for\_transmission \Rightarrow$

$\quad (SEND\_I\_COMMAND \sqcap (l!RR[N(R) = V(R)] \rightarrow SKIP))) \wedge$

$(\neg busy \wedge \neg availability\_of\_I.command\_for\_transmission \Rightarrow$

$\quad (l!RR[N(R) = V(R)] \rightarrow SKIP)) \wedge$

$(busy \Rightarrow (l!RNR[N(R) = V(R)] \rightarrow SKIP))$

where the boolean variable *availability_of_I.command_for_transmission* is true when the *DTE* has an *I* command available for transmission, and *SEND_I.COMMAND* is the procedure for sending *I* commands.

4 *Conclusion*

This paper presents a case study in specification using CSP. We view a specification as having a two-fold purpose: Firstly, it gives a formal system description which provides a basis from which to construct a design, as shown in Section 3. Secondly, it presents a set of system properties, permitting a specification to be validated against an informal statement of requirements.

Within a mathematical framework, we have given a description that is comprehensive enough to describe the essential aspects of the system's behavior but sufficiently abstract not to burden the reader with the kind of detail that appears in the source text. In particular, this framework has allowed us to avoid describing the representation of data and to refrain from presenting details of algorithms. The standard approach to specifying protocols is to provide an abstract algorithm for each of the nodes in the network. In contrast, the mathematical model presented in Section 2 gives us a formal definition of the overall system architecture of the communication protocol. Moreover, it allows us to mix predicate notation with CSP notation in the specification. Specifications of the access procedures are given in the predicate calculus, which is convenient for this purpose because programs can be considered as predicates, and their derivation from specifications can be mathematically verified, as shown in Section 3. So as not to obscure the underlying simplicity of the concepts involved, we avoid being too formal. The reader can consult [1] and [8] to learn more about the mathematical theory of CSP.

As examples, we have chosen three access procedures to illustrate how to apply the theory of Communicating Sequential Process in the specification of communication protocols. The reader can find the formal definitions of all other link-access procedures across the *DTE/DCE* interface, the packet-level *DTE/DCE* interface, and procedures for virtual-circuit service in [3].

By formalizing the essence of the information processed by the access procedures, we have illustrated the two principal techniques used in system specification, namely, representational abstraction and procedural abstraction. By representational abstraction we mean the statement of all essential characteristics of the information structures involved in describing an access procedure, without defining the storage structures used in their representation. By procedural abstraction we mean the statement of the state changes and input-output relationships involved in a procedure, without defining the computational structures used to achieve them. Several possibilities are thereby left open to system designers.

The enterprise of constructing a formal description of a communication protocol is not motivated solely, however, by considerations of self-expression; it is equally motivated by the desire to prove things about properties of the protocol, and to derive and verify implementation. The value of this kind of specification is that it defines the system in question formally, enabling its properties to be determined by reasoning, rather than by performing experiments which could be difficult and costly. The CSP formalism enables us to derive algorithms from the properties of the access procedure being described. Consequently, those procedures of the X.25 protocol that enjoy the same kind of algebraic properties can be tackled in a similar way. This greatly simplifies our design work.

It is often the case that the process of abstraction used to construct a specification results in structures that are more general than those actually required for the system being considered. It is part of our approach to identify and describe such general structures, as illustrated by Theorem 2 in Section 3.1.

This case study highlights aspects of the X.25 protocol that are incompletely or ambiguously described in the original CCITT document. Furthermore, a subtle error involving the liveness property of the system is found.

Another feature of our approach is that the specifications can be transformed into occam programs [6] using laws of occam [9]. Such methods have been advocated and successfully applied in the area of sequential programming.

Acknowledgment

The use of CSP to specify the behavior of protocols was first explained to us by Tony Hoare and Carroll Morgan. The financial support of the U.K. Science and Engineering Research Council is gratefully appreciated.

References

[1] Brookes, S. D., Hoare, C. A. R., and Roscoe, A. W. "A theory of communicating sequential processes". *Journal of the ACM 31* (1984), pp. 560–599.

[2] CCITT Eighth Plenary Assembly. Red Book Volume VIII—Fascicle VIII.3: Recommendation X.20–X.32. International Telecommunication Union, Geneva, 1985.

[3] He Jifeng. "Specification of The X.25 Protocol". Internal paper, Programming Research Group, Oxford University Computing Laboratory, 1987.

[4] Hoare, C. A. R. *Communicating Sequential Processes.* Prentice-Hall International, Englewood Cliffs, N.J., 1985.

[5] Hoare, C. A. R. and Roscoe, A. W. "Programs as executable predicates". *Proceedings of the International Conference on Fifth Generation Computer Systems,* 1984.

[6] INMOS, Ltd. "Occam Programming Manual". Prentice-Hall International, Hemel Hempstead, U.K., 1984.

[7] Jones, C. B. *Systematic Software Development Using VDM.* Prentice-Hall International, Hemel Hempstead, U.K., 1986.

[8] Olderog, E. R. and Hoare, C. A. R. "Specification-oriented semantics for communicating processes". *Acta Informatica 23* (1986), pp. 9–66.

[9] Roscoe, A. W. and Hoare, C. A. R. "The laws of occam programming." PRG–Monograph 53, Oxford University Computing Laboratory, 1985.

Specifying Security Properties

7

J. L. Jacob
Oxford University

Abstract

A model based on possible observations of a system is proposed for measuring the information available to one of its users about the other users of the system. This provides a measure of the degree of security enforced by a system. It also provides a means to specify desired degrees of security of systems that do not yet exist.

1 *Introduction*

This paper describes how to measure the degree of security of a system and how to specify what security properties a system is to have. It does *not* describe how to achieve the desired security properties once they have been specified; readers interested in this aspect should consult a text such as [2].

Suppose we have a community of *users*, communicating with each other only through their effect on some shared resource, or *system*. The system is responsible for enforcing any desired limits on the knowledge one user may have of another. A *security property* of the system is a particular limit on this information. The *security* of a system is the aggregate of the security properties it posseses.

A classic definition of a security model is that of Bell and La Padula [1]. Their model is a *state-based* one. They consider an abstract machine with active *subjects* and passive *objects* as its users. The state of the machine contains a data structure that says which subjects are currently using which objects, and how. For each desirable security property new components are added to the state, and the property is then expressed as the set of permitted values of the extended state. An operation on the machine is correct if it preserves the invariant that describes secure states. Bell and La Padula give several basic operations which are correct in this sense. Finally, they show how to prove that an implementation is secure: The implementer must find a morphism from the implementation to the model.

Our approach is very different. It is entirely unconcerned about the internal structure of a system. Instead we focus on its observed behavior. In particular, we ask what a user can infer about the past interactions of the system with the other users, given the entire history of the interactions between the user and the system up to some point in time; this represents the most information the individual user has about the actual behavior of the system. We will also suppose that each user knows exactly all the potential behaviors of the system; this is the most information about the properties of the system a user can have. From these two pieces of information it is possible for an individual user to calculate all the system behaviors consistent with its local interaction. Both of these pieces of information are maximal; they give the greatest amount of information to which a user might have access. Thus our theory is strong, and errs, if at all, on the safe side.

Rather than build our model from scratch, we base it on Communicating Sequential Processes (CSP) [4]. Here we have a theory which discusses *processes* in terms of their observable characteristics. For the investigation of security properties, there are only two observations we consider. The first is the interface, or *alphabet*, which is a set of possible interactions, or *events*, of the process with its environment. The second observation is the set of *traces* of the process; each trace is a sequence of events, drawn from the alphabet, representing some possible sequence of interactions between the process and its environment. For an arbitrary process P we denote its alphabet by αP and its traces by τP. In this paper we will not consider other observations often made of processes, such as failures and divergences. These observations are associated with liveness, which is not important for security. If a user can detect deadlock we can add an event to the system whose occurrence represents this detection.

In the next section we show how our approach is phrased in terms of CSP. Then we show how to define in our style most of the external security properties discussed in [1].

2 *The Formal System*

2.1 *Observations*

We model systems, and where necessary their users, as CSP processes. A user can observe the system through some window, which is a subset of the system's alphabet. The possible observations that a user which views the system S through the subalphabet B can make are those members of B^* that can be extended by events from $(\alpha S - B)$ to be a member of τS. We call this the *projection of S onto B*. To define this formally, we first define the projection of t onto B.

Definition 1   For any trace t and any set B, the projection of t onto B, written $t \upharpoonright B$, is defined:

$$\langle\rangle \upharpoonright B \quad \hat{=} \quad \langle\rangle$$

$$(\langle e\rangle \hat{} \, t) \upharpoonright B \quad \hat{=} \quad \begin{cases} \langle e\rangle \hat{} \, (t \upharpoonright B) & \text{if } e \in B \\ t \upharpoonright B & \text{otherwise} \end{cases}$$

Definition 2   For any system S, and any $B \subseteq S$, the projection of S onto B, written $S@B$, is

$$S@B \;\hat{=}\; \{t \upharpoonright B \mid t \in \tau S\}$$

We do not intend the operator $@B$ to have the same effect as the hiding operator $\backslash B$: $S@B$ is merely a set of traces, and not a process. Where hiding introduces new traces whenever the process diverges, projection does not.

Some obvious properties of @ are the subject of our first two lemmas.

Lemma 1

For any system S and $B \subseteq \alpha S$, $S@B$ is prefixed-closed and nonempty.

Proof   The proof follows directly from τS being prefixed-closed and nonempty, and from $\upharpoonright B$ being distributive. $\square$

Lemma 2

For any system S

$$S@\alpha S \;=\; \tau S \tag{1}$$

$$S@\{\} \;=\; \{\langle\rangle\} \tag{2}$$

We finish this subsection with four (very) simple examples. We will refer to them later; the reader may delay considering them until then.

Example 1   Let $A = \{a, b\}$ and S be defined by

$$S \;\hat{=}\; a \longrightarrow b \longrightarrow STOP$$

This describes a system, S, which engages first in the event a, then in b, and then halts. We calculate:

$$\tau S \;=\; \{\langle\rangle, \langle a\rangle, \langle a, b\rangle\}$$
$$S@\{a\} \;=\; \{\langle\rangle, \langle a\rangle\}$$
$$S@\{b\} \;=\; \{\langle\rangle, \langle b\rangle\}$$

Example 2   With the same alphabet, we define R by

$$R \;\hat{=}\; (a \longrightarrow b \longrightarrow STOP)[](b \longrightarrow STOP)$$

This system engages in exactly one occurrence of b and one or no occurrences of a; if a occurs it must be before b. We have

$$\tau R \;=\; \{\langle\rangle, \langle a\rangle, \langle b\rangle, \langle a, b\rangle\}$$
$$R@\{a\} \;=\; \{\langle\rangle, \langle a\rangle\}$$
$$R@\{b\} \;=\; \{\langle\rangle, \langle b\rangle\}$$

Notice that the projections of R at $\{a\}$ and $\{b\}$ are the same as for S of Example 1, even though its traces are different.

Example 3   Again, with the same alphabet, define

$$Q \;\hat{=}\; \mu X \cdot ((a \longrightarrow X)[](b \longrightarrow STOP))$$

Q allows any number of a's and one b, after which it terminates. Again, we calculate:

$$\tau Q \;=\; \{a\}^{*} \cup \{t\hat{\ }\langle b\rangle \mid t \in \{a\}^{*}\}$$
$$Q@\{a\} \;=\; \{a\}^{*}$$
$$Q@\{b\} \;=\; \{\langle\rangle, \langle b\rangle\}$$

Example 4   Finally, with alphabet $\{a, b\}$, we define

$$P \mathrel{\hat{=}} (a \longrightarrow STOP) \,[\!]\, (b \longrightarrow STOP)$$

P engages in either one a or one b, but not both, before terminating. We have

$$\begin{aligned} \tau P &= \{\langle\rangle, \langle a\rangle, \langle b\rangle\} \\ P@\{a\} &= \{\langle\rangle, \langle a\rangle\} \\ P@\{b\} &= \{\langle\rangle, \langle b\rangle\} \end{aligned}$$

2.2 *Inferences*

Now we can ask what a user can infer about the past behavior of the other users sharing the system, S say. As explained before, we assume a worst-case position, that each user "knows" completely the full set τS of possible behaviors of the system. Then for each local observation the user can make through its window, B say, it can calculate *all* the possible traces that S could have engaged in that give rise to that particular observation. There is no information from within the system for deciding which of these traces actually occurred, but one of them must have. The machinery to define this formally is simple.

Definition 3   For an arbitrary system, S, the inferences of S, written infer S, is the function defined by:

$$\text{infer}\,S\,B\,\ell \mathrel{\hat{=}} \{t : \tau S \mid t \restriction B = \ell\} \qquad \text{if } B \subseteq \alpha S \wedge \ell \in S@B$$

We may read "infer $S\,B\,\ell$" as "the possible past behaviors of the system S that can be inferred by a user who observes ℓ through the window B".

The functions (infer $S\,B$) and $@B$ are almost inverses, in the following sense:

Lemma 3

For any system S, any set of events $B \subseteq \alpha S$, and any trace $\ell \in S@B$:

$$(\text{infer}\,S\,B\,\ell)@B = \{\ell\}$$

Proof   (infer $S\,B\,\ell) \neq \{\}$ as $\ell \in S@B$, so:

$$\begin{aligned} (\text{infer}\,S\,B\,\ell)@B &= \{t : \tau S \mid t \restriction B = \ell\}@B \\ &= \{t \restriction B \mid t \in \tau S \wedge t \restriction B = \ell\} \\ &= \{\ell\} \end{aligned}$$

$\square$

As with projection, we have the two identities given in the following lemma.

Lemma 4

For any system S and $\ell \in \tau S$

$$\text{infer } S(\alpha S)\ell \;\; = \;\; \{\ell\} \tag{1}$$

$$\text{infer } S\{\}() \;\; = \;\; \tau S \tag{2}$$

The first equation states that if a system is observed fully (the window $= \alpha S$), then it is possible to deduce exactly what has happened. The second states that if we cannot observe a system at all (the window $= \{\}$), then anything could have happened, limited only by the system's capabilities. Lemma 4.2 also shows that traces and inference functions are equivalent: Definition 3 shows how to calculate infer S from τS, while this lemma shows one way to calculate τS from infer S.

Another useful property of inference functions is:

Lemma 5

For any system S, and $B \subseteq \alpha S$:

$$() \in \text{infer } S B ()$$

Proof   The proof follows from $() \restriction B = ()$ and $() \in \tau S$. $\square$

This states that if we have observed nothing, it is always possible that no user has engaged in any interactions with the system; we cannot be sure that anything has happened until we have evidence.

We now illustrate this function with the systems of Examples 1–4.

Example 5   The inferences that can be made of S (Example 1), through $\{a\}$ and $\{b\}$, are:

$$\begin{aligned}
\text{infer } S\{a\}() &\;=\; \{()\} \\
\text{infer } S\{a\}\langle a\rangle &\;=\; \{\langle a\rangle, \langle a, b\rangle\} \\
\text{infer } S\{b\}() &\;=\; \{(), \langle a\rangle\} \\
\text{infer } S\{b\}\langle b\rangle &\;=\; \{\langle a, b\rangle\}
\end{aligned}$$

A user viewing S through $\{a\}$ cannot tell when, or whether, b occurs.

Example 6   For R of Example 2 we have:

$$\text{infer } R\{a\}() \;=\; \{(), \langle b\rangle\}$$

$$\text{infer} \, R \, \{a\} \langle a \rangle \;\; = \;\; \{\langle a \rangle, \langle a, b \rangle\}$$
$$\text{infer} \, R \, \{b\} \langle \rangle \;\; = \;\; \{\langle \rangle, \langle a \rangle\}$$
$$\text{infer} \, R \, \{b\} \langle b \rangle \;\; = \;\; \{\langle b \rangle, \langle a, b \rangle\}$$

Note that while the projections of R are the same as S at $\{a\}$ and $\{b\}$, the set of inferences at each point are at least as large (Example 5). A user viewing R through $\{b\}$ cannot tell whether a has occurred, which is not the case for S.

Example 7   For Q of Example 3 we have:

$$\text{infer} \, Q \{a\} \ell \;\; = \;\; \{\ell, \ell \,\hat{}\, \langle b \rangle\} \qquad \text{for each } \ell \in \{a\}^*$$
$$\text{infer} \, Q \{b\} \langle \rangle \;\; = \;\; \{a\}^*$$
$$\text{infer} \, Q \{b\} \langle b \rangle \;\; = \;\; \{t \,\hat{}\, \langle b \rangle \mid t \in \{a\}^*\}$$

The sets of inferences are at least as big as those for R given in Example 6. A user viewing Q through $\{b\}$ cannot tell how many a's have occurred; all it knows is that no more occur after it has seen one b.

Example 8   Finally, for P of Example 4, we calculate:

$$\text{infer} \, P \{a\} \langle \rangle \;\; = \;\; P @ \{b\}$$
$$\text{infer} \, P \{a\} \langle a \rangle \;\; = \;\; \{\langle a \rangle\}$$
$$\text{infer} \, P \{b\} \langle \rangle \;\; = \;\; P @ \{a\}$$
$$\text{infer} \, P \{b\} \langle b \rangle \;\; = \;\; \{\langle b \rangle\}$$

2.3 *The Security Ordering*

In a comment following Lemma 4, we remarked that inference functions are equivalent to traces. Why then should we introduce such a description of a system? The function $\text{infer} \, S \, B$ tells us what a user viewing the system through B can infer about the rest of the system in a more direct manner than the traces. This function is also the basis for the definition of an ordering on systems. Sets of traces give rise to a natural *safety ordering* in [4]: a system S is at least as safe as a system R, written $S \sqsupseteq R$, if $\tau R \supseteq \tau S$. We now develop a similarly natural *security ordering*.

Consider Examples 5 and 6. We have

$$\text{infer} \, S \{a\} \langle \rangle = \{\langle \rangle\} \subset \{\langle \rangle, \langle b \rangle\} = \text{infer} \, R \{a\} \langle \rangle$$

A user viewing R through $\{a\}$ is less sure of the behavior of the system having observed the trace $\langle \rangle$ than is a similar user observing S. In the latter case the behavior of the system is known exactly, but in the former there are two possibilities. In this sense we say that R is more secure than S through $\{a\}$ at observation $\langle\rangle$. Generally, we say:

Definition 4 R is at least as secure as S through B at observation ℓ, written $R \succeq_{B,\ell} S$, if:

$$\ell \in S@B \cap R@B \;\wedge\; \mathrm{infer}\,S\,B\,\ell \subseteq \mathrm{infer}\,R\,B\,\ell$$

Similarly we say R is at least as secure as S through B, written $R \succeq_B S$, if it is at least as secure at every observation of R:

$$\forall\, \ell : R@B \;\cdot\; R \succeq_{B,\ell} S$$

Note that $R \succeq_B S$ implies $R@B \subseteq S@B$. That is, if R is at least as secure as S through B, then the observations that can be made of R through B are no more than the observations that can be made of S through B.

   We will usually want to say that one system is more secure than another for all of its users. This order is the last one we define, and is the one in which we are most interested.

Definition 5   Let $\mathcal{A}$ be a set of subsets of alphabet A. We say that R is at least as secure as S through $\mathcal{A}$, written $R \succeq^{\mathcal{A}} S$, if it is at least as secure through every member of A:

$$\forall\, B : \mathcal{A} \;\cdot\; R \succeq_B S$$

Often the set of subsets will be a disjoint partition of the alphabet, with each subset being identified with a different user's interface to the system. We use the symbol $\asymp$, with the appropriate subscripts and superscripts, if both $\succeq$ and $\preceq$ hold. Similarly, we use $\succ$ if $\succeq$ holds, but not $\asymp$.

   Before investigating some of the properties of $\succeq$, we give an example of its use:

Example 9   From Examples 5–8, and with respect to the disjoint partition $\mathcal{A} = \{\{a\}, \{b\}\}$ of $\{a, b\}$, we see:

$$Q \succ^{\mathcal{A}} R \succ^{\mathcal{A}} S$$

and

$$
\begin{aligned}
R \quad &\succ^{\mathcal{A}} \quad P \\
S \quad &\prec_{\{a\},\langle\rangle} \quad P \\
S \quad &\succ_{\{a\},\langle a\rangle} \quad P \\
S \quad &\asymp_{\{b\},\langle\rangle} \quad P
\end{aligned}
$$

S and P are incomparable at $(\{b\}, \langle b \rangle)$, through both $\{a\}$ and $\{b\}$, and over $\{\{a\}, \{b\}\}$.

We have the two simple identities stated in Lemma 6.

Lemma 6

For any systems S and R with alphabet A:

$$S \succeq_{\{\}} R \iff \tau S \supseteq \tau R \qquad\qquad (1)$$

$$S \succeq_A R \iff \tau S \subseteq \tau R \qquad\qquad (2)$$

There is no simple relation between $\sqsupseteq$ and $\succeq$. Both $S@B$ and $\operatorname{infer} SB\ell$ as functions of S are antimonotone with respect to $\sqsupseteq$, that is:

$$S \sqsupseteq R \implies (R@B \supseteq S@B) \wedge (\operatorname{infer} RB\ell \supseteq \operatorname{infer} SB\ell)$$

While $S@B$ as a function of S is antimonotone with respect to the security order $\succeq_B$, $\operatorname{infer} SB\ell$ is *monotone* with respect to $\succeq_{B,\ell}$:

$$S \succeq_B R \implies R@B \supseteq S@B$$
$$\wedge \quad S \succeq_{B,\ell} R \implies (\operatorname{infer} RB\ell) \subseteq (\operatorname{infer} SB\ell)$$

The next two examples illustrate this point.

Example 10   Let $A \mathrel{\hat{=}} \{a, b\}$, then

$$STOP_A \sqsupseteq (a \longrightarrow STOP_A)$$

We also have, however,

$$(a \longrightarrow STOP_A) \succ_{\{b\}} STOP_A$$

and

$$STOP_A \succ_{\{a\}} (a \longrightarrow STOP_A)$$

The former follows as

$$STOP_A @\{b\} = (a \longrightarrow STOP_A)@\{b\} = \{\langle\rangle\}$$

and

$$(\operatorname{infer} a \longrightarrow STOP_A \{b\} \langle\rangle) \supset (\operatorname{infer} STOP_A \{b\} \langle\rangle)$$

The latter follows as

$$(a \longrightarrow STOP_A)@\{a\} \supset STOP_A @\{a\} = \{\langle\rangle\}$$

and

$$(\text{infer } a \longrightarrow STOP_A \{a\} \langle\rangle) = (\text{infer } STOP_A \{a\} \langle\rangle)$$

Example 11   For the systems S and R of Examples 1 and 2, we have $S \sqsupseteq R$. Only because $S@\{a\} = R@\{a\}$ and $S@\{b\} = R@\{b\}$ do we also have $R \succ^{\{\{a\},\{b\}\}} S$.

In fact, $\succ^{\mathcal{A}}$ has neither a top nor a bottom, in general. In the case with $\mathcal{A} = \{\{a\}, \{b\}\}$, $STOP_{\{a,b\}}$ is incomparable with any other process. $STOP_{\{a,b\}}$ provides the smallest set of observations for both windows $\{a\}$ and $\{b\}$ (i.e., $\{\langle\rangle\}$), but an observer knows exactly which behavior of the system has been followed (i.e., $\langle\rangle$).

3 *Defining Security Properties*

In the last section we showed how inference functions can measure the degree of security in a system. In this section we show to use these functions to define desired external security properties of a system and other useful concepts. As examples only, we take the external properties and concepts discussed by Bell and La Padula [1]. (Note that these do *not* include the ss-property and the *-property, which certain types of implementation must satisfy to enforce the external properties.) There is no sense in which the definitions given here are intended to be a recommendation for *the* definition of security. Our view is quite the reverse. In any given situation the desired degree of security must be specified afresh, perhaps in terms of the concepts defined here, perhaps in terms of other concepts, perhaps directly in terms of an inference function, or in some combination of these.

We use the same names as in [1] for the subsection headings; we have, however, renamed the properties themselves.

3.1 *Mandatory Security*

We paraphrase Bell and La Padula's definition of mandatory security [1] as preventing a low-security user from discovering anything about the behavior of a high-security user. This is achieved by imposing security classifications ("high", "low", etc.) on the users, together with a partial order on the classifications. They call this property *mandatory* because neither the partial order nor the classifications are under the control of the users: Both are imposed from outside. In our formulation we work directly with users' interfaces to the system and define a preorder[1] over them.

A pre-order, which we will write $\rightarrow$, is defined on a disjoint partition $\mathcal{A}$ of an alphabet A. $B \rightarrow C$ holds exactly when the user viewing the system through B is not prohibited from knowing something about the behavior of the user viewing the system through C; if $B \nrightarrow C$ then the system must not allow anything about the behavior at C to be deduced by observations through B.

Example 12   Let F be the interface to a file and B be the interface to a user. If $B \rightarrow F$ then the user is not prohibited from deducing some facts about the history of the file. The user is not guaranteed to be able to find out *all* about the file; for example, the user may be able to find out only the size of the file, and not its contents. If $B \nrightarrow F$ the user is prohibited from deducing anything about the file: neither its size, nor its contents, nor its date of last access, etc.

A user with window B may have knowledge of all users below it in the preorder. This effectively provides a larger window into the system for this user, which we write $[B]$. It is defined by

$$[B] \,\hat{=}\, \bigcup\{C \mid B \rightarrow C\}$$

Now we can define what it means for a system to satisfy the requirements captured by $\rightarrow$.

Definition 6   A system S restricts information flow with respect to $(\mathcal{A}, \rightarrow)$ if

$$\forall B : \mathcal{A}, \ell : S@B \;\cdot\; [B]^* \cap (\text{infer}\, S\, B\, \ell) \neq \{\}$$

This condition asserts that, whatever observation is made through any $B \in \mathcal{A}$, it is possible that the system has not engaged in any events outside $[B]$. That is, although the user viewing the system through B may know to which behaviors the higher users are restricted, it cannot know how much of those behaviors have occurred. Because nothing may have occurred and each behavior starts from nothing, there is no information in ℓ to distinguish them. There is a relationship between this definition and that of *noninterference* [3]; we discuss this in [5].

---

1. A preorder is a transitive and reflexive relation; if it is also antisymmetric it is a partial order. A preorder over a set divides the set into equivalence classes, each of which represents a security classification; it also generates a natural partial order on the equivalence classes, which is that used in [1].

Example 13   From Example 5 we see that the system S of Example 1 restricts information flow with respect to the disjoint partition $\{\{a\}, \{b\}\}$ and to the preorder defined as the transitive, reflexive closure of $\{\{b\} \mapsto \{a\}\}$.

We now show that increasing the security of a system that restricts information flow preserves the restriction.

Lemma 7

Let S and R be systems with alphabet A, such that

(H1) S restricts information flow with respect to $(\mathcal{A}, \rightarrow)$.

(H2) $R \succeq^{\mathcal{A}} S$.

Then

(R) R restricts information flow with respect to $(\mathcal{A}, \rightarrow)$.

Proof   Let (H3) $B \in \mathcal{A}$ and $\ell \in R@B$; then

(1)	$\ell \in S@B$	(H2), (H3), (D5)
(2)	$[B]^* \cap (\text{infer} \, S \, B \, \ell) \neq \{\}$	(H1), (1), (D6)
(3)	$[B]^* \cap (\text{infer} \, R \, B \, \ell) \neq \{\}$	(H2), (H3), (2), (D5)
(R)		(H3), (3), (D6)

□

Example 14   From Lemma 7, Example 9, and Example 13 we see that R of Example 2 restricts information flow, with respect to the disjoint partition $\{\{a\}, \{b\}\}$ and preorder defined as the reflexive closure of $\{\{b\} \mapsto \{a\}\}$. Of course, we could have deduced this directly from Example 6.

A special case of restriction of information flow is complete isolation.

Definition 7   Let id be the identity relation (and so a preorder). We say that a system *enforces isolation with respect to* $\mathcal{A}$ if it enforces restriction of information flow with respect to $(\mathcal{A}, \text{id})$.

Example 15   The system

$$(\mu X : \{a\} \cdot a \longrightarrow X) \parallel \parallel (\mu X : \{b\} \cdot b \longrightarrow X)$$

enforces isolation with respect to $\{\{a\}, \{b\}\}$.

3.2 *Trusted Users*

The requirement on a system that it must restrict information flow with respect to some partition and preorder can be relaxed in the presence of *trusted* users.[2] A trusted user is one whose good behaviour the system need not enforce. There may be observations through the trusted user's interface that reveal facts about the system behavior. We can trust a user with interface B, if it has been proved never to attempt to engage in any of these observations. That is, it never engages in observations $\ell \in B^*$ such that

$$[B]^* \cap (\text{infer } S B \ell) = \{\}$$

This is a sufficient condition to trust a low-classified user; in the absence of any constraints on the behavior of the higher-classified users, it is also necessary.

We may also trust a low user if no higher user ever engages in a detectable behavior. Suppose the higher users are represented by (the CSP process) H. Then we need to prove that $S \parallel H$ restricts flow of information, with respect to $(\mathcal{A}, \rightarrow)$. This condition and the previous one can be combined in the obvious way: A low user can be trusted if it never tries to observe one of the detectable behaviors of the higher users. That is, we can trust the user with interface B if it never engages in a trace $\ell \in B^*$ such that

$$[B]^* \cap (\text{infer } (S \parallel H) B \ell) = \{\}$$

Example 16   Let $A \,\hat{=}\, \{a1, a2, b\}$ and $\mathcal{A} \,\hat{=}\, \{\{a1, a2\}, \{b\}\}$. Then the system

$$S \,\hat{=}\, (b \longrightarrow a1 \longrightarrow STOP) [\!] (a2 \longrightarrow b \longrightarrow STOP)$$

does not restrict of information flow with respect to set of windows and preorder $(\mathcal{A}, \rightarrow)$, where $\{a1, a2\} \not\rightarrow \{b\}$, as

$$(\text{infer } S \{a1, a2\} \langle a1 \rangle) = \{\langle b, a1 \rangle\}$$

and

$$\langle b, a1 \rangle \notin [\{a1, a2\}]^*$$

It is easy to see that $\langle a1 \rangle$ is the only insecure trace. Thus for a user U (with interface $\{a1, a2\}$) to be trusted we must prove $\langle a1 \rangle \notin \tau U$. An example of such a user is:

$$a2 \longrightarrow STOP_{\{a1, a2\}}$$

---

2. [1] uses the term *trusted subjects*.

Suppose we have a system S that is intended to restrict information flow with respect to $(\mathcal{A}, \rightarrow)$, but that there is some window B and observation ℓ through B for which

$$[B]^* \cap \text{infer } S\,B\,\ell \neq \{\}$$

A good way of closing this hole is to find a user U with interface B that can be trusted completely, and to replace S by $S\|U$. This system does not allow a user with interface B to engage in any traces that violate the security constraint. U should be chosen to be as general as is practical. The most general U is the deterministic process with traces

$$\{\ell : S@B \mid [B]^* \cap (\text{infer } S\,B\,\ell) \neq \{\}\}$$

We leave it to the interested reader to check that this set is nonempty and prefix-closed.

Example 17   With the system S and safe user U of Example 16, we can calculate a secure system, S':

$$
\begin{aligned}
S' \;&=\; S \parallel U \\
&=\; (b \longrightarrow STOP_A) [\![(a2 \longrightarrow b \longrightarrow STOP_A)
\end{aligned}
$$

Of course, S' may not possess all the desirable properties that S does.

3.3 *Integrity*

The next property we specify is *integrity*. It is a dual to the restriction of information flow discussed earlier. Whereas we were concerned to say that the future behavior of a low-classified user cannot be influenced by the past behavior of a high-classified user, we now want to say that the past behavior of a low-classified user cannot influence the future behavior of a high-classified user. This is almost like restriction of "downward" information flow, but now we are concerned with preventing "upward" flow. The same mathematical structure will do.

Example 18   Let F be the interface to a high-integrity file and B be the interface to a low-integrity process. Then we ensure the integrity of the file by restricting information flow with respect to a preorder $\rightarrow$ that satisfies $F \nrightarrow B$.

When we discuss integrity it is perhaps more intuitive to talk about restriction of *instruction* flow, rather than *information* flow. There is no difference in the mathematics, however, because we are not attaching directions or meanings to events.

3.4 *Communication Paths*

This section discusses a topic that lies beyond the scope of the model of Bell and La Padula [1] and of ours: the detection of *covert channels* between users. To quote [1]:

> By [the problem of covert channels] is meant the indirect disclosure of sensitive information, as opposed to the direct disclosure of information .... Indirect disclosure can be effected by transmitting data piecemeal using observable system characteristics as the code medium.

A covert channel is a suitable coding of system characteristics.

In [1], covert channels are divided into two classes: synchronous and nonsynchronous. For synchronous channels it is asserted:

> Possibly the most difficult medium to rule out as a communication path is real time: intervals of real time, delimited by *prearranged* observable events,... can be used to transmit information in bit strings.

The model of [1] does not help in showing the absence of such channels. Our formulation does not help either, because traces abstract away from the time between events. If we moved from the model of CSP in [4] to the model of *timed* CSP in [7], then there is hope that an analagous theory based on *timed traces* could be developed. This is not done here.

Bell and La Padula offer little solace to those concerned with nonsynchronous channels:

> Indirect communication using nonsynchronous [covert channels] remains a very complicated problem.[1]

The problem lies more in the proof that a particular system has the desirable property than in specifying the property. The covert channel may involve subtle combinations of shared data, system variables and the like. Proof of correctness involves "close and careful consideration of every possible action [of the] system" [1]. The specification is easy in our formulation, but the proof is just as hard.[3] As an example we will give a specification for (a paraphrase of) one of the examples Bell and La Padula use in [1] to illustrate this problem.

Example 19   A system has internal state given by an array of n Boolean variables. Interface B contains events to set and unset the variables: $i.set$ and $i.unset$ for each $i < n$. Interface C contains events to read the value of the variables: $i.val.T$ and $i.val.F$ for each $i < n$. The desired security is specified by

---

3. The proof may be eased by the many techniques being developed for the specification, verification, and refinement of CSP processes. See, for example, [8].

demanding that the system restrict the flow of information with respect to a preorder, $\rightarrow$, for which $C \not\rightarrow B$.

When this specification is completed, it may not be possible to find a system that satisfies it together with other demands that may be made in the full specification. For example, it might be required that the system always correctly and immediately obey requests to reveal or change its state.

4 *Discussion*

We have presented a way of assessing the inferences one user of a system can make about the others and have shown how to use them to pose the question of one system being more secure than another (but not how to answer this question with ease). Additionally, we have shown how to use inferences to state precisely certain standard properties related to security. The definitions are not too hard to work with, and, not being tied to a particular model of computation, are directly applicable to all systems, not just those built around a single von Neumann machine.

The specifications we have used as illustrations have the property that they allow either all or no information to pass between two users. This is a very restrictive criterion. Consider a simple system that fills in tax forms for customers. The security property that no customer can discover anything about another's financial affairs can be specified using restriction of information flow. Now consider a clerk whose job is to prepare bills for the use of the service. The system must provide enough information to allow the clerk to determine how many times each customer has consulted it without allowing the clerk to deduce anything about a customer's financial affairs. With restriction of information flow, we can only insist that the clerk is able to discover either nothing or anything, but we cannot insist that he or she can discover only a limited amount of information (e.g., the number of times that each customer has used the service). One answer to this problem uses a generalization of inference functions. This idea is pursued in [5] and [6].

5 *Acknowledgements*

Helpful comments have been made by M. L. Arcus, L. P. Fertig, He Jifeng, C. A. R. Hoare, C. Hughes, and J. C. P. Woodcock. All the errors and infelicities are, of course, mine.

I would also like to acknowledge financial support from International Computers Limited during the course of this work, for which I am truly grateful.

References

[1] Bell, D. E. and La Padula, L. J. "Secure computer system: Unified exposition and Multics". Report ESD–TR–75–306, The MITRE Corporation, March 1976.

[2] Denning, D. E. R. *Cryptography and Data Security*. Addison-Wesley, Reading, Mass., 1982.

[3] Goguen, J. A. and Meseguer, J. "Security policies and security models". In *Proceedings of the 1982 Symposium on Security and Privacy* (Oakland, Calif., April). IEEE Computer Society, New York, 1982.

[4] Hoare, C. A. R. *Communicating Sequential Processes*. Prentice-Hall International, Englewood Cliffs, N.J., 1985.

[5] Jacob, J. L. "On shared systems". Doctoral dissertation, University of Oxford, 1987.

[6] Jacob, J. L. "Security specifications". In *Proceedings of the 1988 Symposium on Security and Privacy* (Oakland, Calif., April). IEEE Computer Society, New York, 1988.

[7] Reed, G. M. and Roscoe, A. W. "A timed model for communicating sequential processes". In *Automata, Languages and Programming: Proceedings of the 13th International Colloquium*, L. Kott, ed. Lecture Notes in Computer Science, vol. 226. Springer-Verlag, Berlin, 1986.

[8] Woodcock, J. C. P. and Hoare, C. A. R. "The problem with lifts...". Internal working paper, Programming Research Group, Oxford University Computing Laboratory, 1987.

Transaction-Processing Primitives and CSP[1]

8

J. C. P. Woodcock
Oxford University Computing Laboratory

Programming Research Group

Abstract

Several primitives for describing requirements in transaction-processing systems are developed using the notations of Communicating Sequential Processes (CSP). The approach taken is to capture each requirement separately, in the simplest possible context; the specification is then the conjunction of all these requirements. Each requirement is expressed as a predicate over traces of the observable events in the system, and also implemented as a simple communicating process; the implementation of the entire system is then merely the parallel composition of these processes. The laws of CSP are then used to transform the system to achieve the required degree of concurrency. This work is intended as a case study in the use of CSP.

1. This chapter was originally published in *IBM Journal of Research and Development 31*, 5 (September 1987), pp. 535–545. Copyright © 1987 by International Business Machines Corporation; reprinted with permission.

---

1 *Introduction*

We describe several primitives for transaction-processing systems using Communicating Sequential Processes [8, 9]: the rather trivial case in which there is just a single process in the system (Section 2); multiple processes with a simple locking protocol to achieve mutual exclusion (Section 3.1); the same but with queuing for busy resources (Section 3.2); and finally, discarding the locking of resources and instead taking the rather optimistic view that conflicts probably won't occur anyway (Section 4). The study of these systems was inspired by the formal description and development of the lock manager in a major transaction-processing system.

As we consider each system's requirements, we capture them as individual predicates on the history of the system. The specifications that we give are of the *safety* properties of the system; implicitly we expect an implementation that is as live as possible. In the style that we are exploring in this paper, the specifications often describe the *firing condition* for an event: If an event occurs, then some predicate must hold on the history of events up to that moment. Given our implicit requirement about liveness, we could have said that given that a firing condition holds, an event must not be refused.

The specification of each system is simply the conjunction of its requirements. This is indeed a powerful and natural way to capture the formal specification of a system. Less familiar perhaps is the approach to implementation in CSP process algebra. As the specification proceeds, we implement each requirement as a simple communicating process. Keeping both predicate and process as small as possible reduces the task of proving the implementation correct. In CSP, parallel combination of processes corresponds to conjunction of their specifications; thus the implementation of the system is just the parallel composition of the processes implementing each requirement.

The result of the development process that we are describing is an implementation consisting of a highly distributed collection of synchronizing and communicating processes. The laws of CSP are then used to transform the implementation. We could, if we wished, transform it into a form that is readily translated into occam [10] and run it on a collection of transputers, or transform it into an efficient, low-level systems program. Both of these transformations have been performed on the lock manager part of the system.

Section 5 contains an example of a formal proof of the correctness of an implementation of part of a transaction-processing primitive.

For the benefit of readers unfamiliar with CSP, the appendixes contain a summary of the notation used in this paper.

2 *A Single-Process System*

We make a gross simplification —for the moment— that there is only one process in the system that accesses the data by reading and writing values. Let **C** be the set (type) of messages communicated between process and system.

In this system, if **a** and **b** are drawn from the set of values **C**, then the event **read.a** corresponds to the process reading the value **a**, while **write.b** corresponds to the process writing the value **b**. Let

$$\mathbf{R} \; \hat{=} \; \{\mathbf{read.c} \mid \mathbf{c} \in \mathbf{C}\}$$

$$\mathbf{W} \; \hat{=} \; \{\mathbf{write.c} \mid \mathbf{c} \in \mathbf{C}\}$$

It is not difficult to see that if there is just a single process, the data behaves as we would expect a programming variable would: If the process reads its contents, then it discovers the most recently written value. We can specify this: We want a process **VAR** with alphabet

$$\alpha\mathbf{VAR} \; \hat{=} \; \mathbf{R} \cup \mathbf{W}$$

and any trace **tr** of **VAR** must satisfy the following predicate:[2]

$$\mathbf{VARSPEC} \; \hat{=} \; (\forall \mathbf{c} \in \mathbf{C} \cdot \overline{\mathbf{tr}}_0 = \mathbf{read.c} \; \Rightarrow \; \mathbf{tr} \restriction \mathbf{W}_0 = \mathbf{write.c})$$

That is, if the last thing that happened in the system is that the process read a particular value **c**, then the most recently written value is also **c**. For this predicate to make sense, there must be at least one **write** before the first **read**. This specification is really describing the firing conditions for events in **R**. The events in **W** are left unconstrained.

An implementation is well-known (see [9, p. 137]):

$$\mathbf{VAR} \quad \hat{=} \; (\mathbf{write?x} \longrightarrow \mathbf{VAR_x})$$

$$\mathbf{VAR_x} \; \hat{=} \; (\mathbf{read!x} \longrightarrow \mathbf{VAR_x}$$
$$\qquad\quad \mid \mathbf{write?y} \longrightarrow \mathbf{VAR_y})$$

The process **VAR** is initially willing to participate only in a **write** event; having done so, it proceeds as **VAR_x**. In this behavior, **VAR** is rather like a nice sort of uninitialized variable: It doesn't permit a **read** before the first **write**. **VAR_x**, on the other hand, behaves like a variable currently holding the value **x**. If the process tries to **read** the variable, it finds that it has the value **x**;

---

2. An even more concise specification follows from using the CSP convention of using the name of a channel to denote the sequence of messages passed on that channel:

$$\forall c \in C \cdot \overline{tr}_0 = read.c \Rightarrow \overline{write}_0 = c$$

this does not change the value (the variable continues to behave like **VAR$_x$**). The process can, however, write a new value —say **y**— replacing the old one (the variable now behaves like **VAR$_y$**).

Note that we could have produced an implementation that avoids the use of a state variable, but it would have appeared rather more complicated.

We have adopted the convention that the specification for a process **P** is called **PSPEC**. In this paper we have included only a few proofs; we did this for reasons of space, rather than difficulty. In Section 5 we present a formal proof that a process satisfies its specification. This proof together with several others taken from this paper have been checked with a mechanical proof assistant. In a development of this kind, it is usual to do proofs in a routine manner: Write down the predicate on traces and refusals; write down the behavior in the process algebra; write down the proof of satisfaction. Developing all three together *does* offer valuable insights. The ability to use a machine to do much of the routine work seems to be an important factor in the feasibility of proving large systems correct.

3 *Multiple-Process Systems*

3.1 *A Simple Locking Protocol*

We now remove the restriction to a single process and specify a multiple tasking system. Let **T** be the set of task names; we shall use task names drawn from **T** to label events. For example, **t.lock** will mean participation in the event **lock** by task **t**. We use the notation **t:P** for the process **P** named by **t**; **t:P** engages in the event **t.a** whenever process **P** would have engaged in the event **a**. Furthermore, we use the notation **t.SPEC** for the specification of process **t:P**, if process **P** satisfies the specification **SPEC**. Further descriptions may be found in the appendixes.

The protocol we wish to describe involves tasks *locking* the data structure before accessing it. We add two new events to the interface: **lock** and **unlock**. Define

$$\text{LOCKED} \ \hat{=} \ (tr{\downarrow}lock - tr{\downarrow}unlock = 1)$$

$$\overline{\text{LOCKED}} \ \hat{=} \ (tr{\downarrow}lock - tr{\downarrow}unlock = 0)$$

LOCKED holds for the trace **tr**—which is free in the definition—just when there is one more **lock** in **tr** than **unlock**. Similarly, **UNLOCKED** holds just when there is an equal number of **lock** and **unlock** events in **tr**. A task may have either locked or not locked the data structure:

$$\alpha\textbf{LOCK} \quad \;\;\hat{=}\; \{\texttt{lock}, \texttt{unlock}\}$$

$$\textbf{LOCKSPEC} \;\hat{=}\; (\textbf{LOCKED} \vee \overline{\textbf{LOCKED}})$$

This is implemented by a process which simply alternates between **lock** and **unlock** events:

$$\textbf{LOCK} \;\hat{=}\; \mu X \cdot (\texttt{lock} \longrightarrow \texttt{unlock} \longrightarrow X)$$

The definition of the process **LOCK** is recursive: It is the process **X** that first engages in the event **lock**, followed by **unlock**, and then behaves like the process **X**.

Each task is guaranteed to access only information that it has previously locked. If a task **read**s a value from the data structure, the data structure must be locked:

$$\alpha\textbf{READ} \quad \;\;\hat{=}\; R \cup \alpha\textbf{LOCK}$$

$$\textbf{READSPEC} \;\hat{=}\; (\overline{\texttt{tr}_0} \in R \Rightarrow \textbf{LOCKED})$$

Similarly, if a task **write**s a value from the data structure, the data structure must be locked:

$$\alpha\textbf{WRITE} \quad \;\;\hat{=}\; W \cup \alpha\textbf{LOCK}$$

$$\textbf{WRITESPEC} \;\hat{=}\; (\overline{\texttt{tr}_0} \in W \Rightarrow \textbf{LOCKED})$$

These two requirements can be implemented by separate, but similar, processes: **READ** and **WRITE**. Instead, we offer their combination: the single process that permits reading and writing only after a **lock**, but before the next **unlock**. Let

$$\alpha\textbf{READWRITE} \;\hat{=}\; \alpha\textbf{READ} \cup \alpha\textbf{WRITE}$$

$$= \alpha\textbf{VAR} \cup \alpha\textbf{LOCK}$$

$$\textbf{READWRITE} \quad \hat{=}\; \mu X \cdot (lock \longrightarrow \mu Y \cdot (\textbf{x} : \alpha\textbf{VAR} \longrightarrow Y$$
$$| \,\texttt{unlock} \longrightarrow X))$$

Notice that, because of the way we have chosen to implement **READWRITE**, with alternating **lock**s and **unlock**s, it also satisfies **LOCKSPEC**. Thus, when we put **LOCK** and **READWRITE** in parallel, we do not constrain the behavior of **READWRITE** at all. Formally,

$$(\textbf{LOCK} \parallel \textbf{READWRITE}) = \textbf{READWRITE}$$

Each task must behave in the way that we have specified, and be guaranteed to follow the locking protocol:

$$\textbf{USESPEC} \;\hat{=}\; (\forall t \in T \cdot t.\textbf{LOCKSPEC} \wedge t.\textbf{READSPEC} \wedge t.\textbf{WRITESPEC})$$

USESPEC is satisfied by

$$\textbf{USE} \;\hat{=}\; \underset{t \in T}{\|} t : \textbf{READWRITE}$$

Since conjunction in the specification corresponds to concurrency in the implementation, the universal quantification in **USESPEC** becomes parallel composition over a set in the process **USE**.

Each task relies on having *exclusive* access to locked information. Thus, when a task **t** acquires a lock, no other task can already have it:

$$\forall t, u \in T \cdot t.\textbf{LOCKED} \wedge u.\textbf{LOCKED} \;\Rightarrow\; t = u$$

MUTEXSPEC is implemented by a process that guarantees that a new lock cannot be acquired between a **lock/unlock** pair:

$$\textbf{MUTEX} = \mu X \cdot (\underset{t \in T}{\Box}\, t.\textbf{lock} \longrightarrow t.\textbf{unlock} \longrightarrow X)$$

We can now combine **MUTEX** with what we already have:

$$
\begin{aligned}
\textbf{USE} \parallel \textbf{MUTEX} \;=\; & \underset{t \in T}{\|}\, \mu X \cdot (t.\textbf{lock} \longrightarrow \mu Y \cdot \;\; (x : \alpha(t : \textbf{VAR}) \longrightarrow Y \\
& \hspace{6.5cm} | t.\textbf{unlock} \longrightarrow X)) \\[2mm]
& \parallel \mu X \cdot (\underset{t \in T}{\Box}\, t.\textbf{lock} \longrightarrow t.\textbf{unlock} \longrightarrow X) \\[2mm]
=\; & \mu X \cdot (\underset{t \in T}{\Box}\, t.\textbf{lock} \longrightarrow \mu Y \cdot (x : \alpha(t : \textbf{VAR}) \longrightarrow Y \\
& \hspace{6.5cm} | t.\textbf{unlock} \longrightarrow X))
\end{aligned}
$$

So far, we have only described the interference that may be caused and that can be tolerated in the system. Now we must say how information changes or persists in the system. In fact, our multiple-process system behaves not unlike a *single-process* system: Anyone reading the contents of a data structure discovers the most recently written value. Define a function that removes *any* task name from an event:

$$\textbf{tstrip} \;\hat{=}\; \underset{t \in T}{\bigcup} \textbf{strip}_t$$

The function **strip$_t$** is the one that removes the particular label **t** from an event [8] (see also Appendix A). The function **tstrip**, then, removes *any* label **t** from an event. Now, if we consider just the sequence of **read**s and **write**s and ignore which tasks initiated them, our structure behaves just like a variable. Since we don't care who initiates **read** or **write** events, we can use our forgetful function **tstrip** to disregard who does what:

$$\textbf{MVARSPEC} \ \hat{=} \ \textbf{VARSPEC}[(\textbf{tstrip}^* \ \textbf{tr}) \upharpoonright \alpha \textbf{VAR} \, / \, \textbf{tr}]$$

The expression **tstrip*** **tr** denotes the trace formed by applying **tstrip** to each element of **tr**. **VARSPEC** is a predicate on the free variable **tr**, and is in terms of the events in α**VAR**; therefore the definition of **MVARSPEC**, which substitutes an expression for **tr**, ensures that the expression mentions only events from α**VAR**.

Of course, we already know how to implement a variable, and we can reuse this implementation, with a suitable relabeling of event names. Since we are unconcerned with the identity of tasks, the inverse image under **tstrip** of **VAR** will give us a promiscuous version of **VAR**: It doesn't care who **read**s its values, nor who **write**s new ones:

$$\textbf{MVAR} \ \hat{=} \ \textbf{tstrip}^{-1} \ \textbf{VAR}$$

Expanding, we obtain

$$\textbf{MVAR} = (\underset{t \, \in \, T}{\big[\!\big]} \textbf{t.write?x} \longrightarrow \textbf{MVAR}_\textbf{x})$$

where

$$\textbf{MVAR}_\textbf{x} \ \hat{=} \ (\underset{t \, \in \, T}{\big[\!\big]} \textbf{t.read!x} \longrightarrow \textbf{MVAR}_\textbf{x}$$
$$|\underset{t \, \in \, T}{\big[\!\big]} \textbf{t.write?y} \longrightarrow \textbf{MVAR}_\textbf{y})$$

We have now completed our specification of a many-process system. We have specified that tasks may **lock** the data structure and that they may **read** and **write** only while they have the lock; we have specified that while a task has the lock it has exclusive access; and we have specified that the shared data behaves like a variable. Our multiple-process system must satisfy all three requirements:

$$\textbf{MUSPEC} \ \hat{=} \ (\textbf{USESPEC} \wedge \textbf{MUTEXSPEC} \wedge \textbf{MVARSPEC})$$

Our system is implemented by

$$\textbf{MU} \ \hat{=} \ (\textbf{USE} \parallel \textbf{MUTEX} \parallel \textbf{MVAR})$$

We already have a simplified version of **USE** $\parallel$ **MUTEX**. Substituting this and our definition of **MVAR** into the definition of **MU**, we obtain

$$
\textbf{MU} = \mu X \cdot \left(\bigsqcap_{t \in T} \textbf{t.lock} \longrightarrow \mu Y \cdot \quad (x : \alpha(t : \textbf{VAR}) \longrightarrow Y
$$
$$
| \textbf{t.unlock} \longrightarrow X))
$$
$$
\| \left(\bigsqcap_{t \in T} \textbf{t.write?x} \longrightarrow \textbf{MVAR}_x\right)
$$

where

$$
\textbf{MVAR}_x \; \mathrel{\hat{=}} \; \left(\bigsqcap_{t \in T} \textbf{t.read!x} \longrightarrow \textbf{MVAR}_x \right.
$$
$$
\left| \bigsqcap_{t \in T} \textbf{t.write?y} \longrightarrow \textbf{MVAR}_y\right)
$$

We can simplify this equation and eliminate the remaining concurrency symbol, obtaining

$$
\textbf{MU} = \left(\bigsqcap_{t \in T} \textbf{t.lock} \longrightarrow \quad (\textbf{t.unlock} \longrightarrow \textbf{MU}\right.
$$
$$
| \textbf{t.write?x} \longrightarrow \textbf{MU}_{t,x}))
$$

where

$$
\textbf{MU}_x \; \mathrel{\hat{=}} \; \left(\bigsqcap_{t \in T} \textbf{t.lock} \longrightarrow \textbf{MU}_{t,x}\right)
$$

$$
\textbf{MU}_{t,x} \; \mathrel{\hat{=}} \; (\textbf{t.unlock} \longrightarrow \textbf{MU}_x
$$
$$
| \textbf{t.read!x} \longrightarrow \textbf{MU}_{t,x}
$$
$$
| \textbf{t.write?y} \longrightarrow \textbf{MU}_{t,y})
$$

Thus **MU** is a process that allows an external choice as to which task gains the lock; only *that* task may **read** or **write** values to the data structure, until that same task yields the lock. The process also ensures that a value is written to the data structure before a value can be read.

3.2 *Queuing for Busy Resources*

The system described in the last section suffers from the dangers of infinite overtaking: An unlucky task wanting a lock may *always* be unsuccessful and be continually preempted by faster tasks. We shall try to solve this by serving requests for locks in order. We introduce a new event: **request**. Let

$$\textbf{REQ1} \ \hat{=} \ (\textbf{tr}{\downarrow}\textbf{request} - \textbf{tr}{\downarrow}\textbf{lock} = 1)$$

$$\overline{\textbf{REQ1}} \ \hat{=} \ (\textbf{tr}{\downarrow}\textbf{request} - \textbf{tr}{\downarrow}\textbf{lock} = 0)$$

$$\textbf{REQ2} \ \hat{=} \ (\textbf{tr}{\downarrow}\textbf{request} - \textbf{tr}{\downarrow}\textbf{unlock} = 1)$$

$$\overline{\textbf{REQ2}} \ \hat{=} \ (\textbf{tr}{\downarrow}\textbf{request} - \textbf{tr}{\downarrow}\textbf{unlock} = 0)$$

Each task has at most one outstanding request:

$$\alpha\textbf{REQUEST1} \qquad \hat{=} \ \{\textbf{request, lock}\}$$

$$\textbf{REQUEST1SPEC} \ \hat{=} \ (\textbf{REQ1} \lor \overline{\textbf{REQ1}})$$

$$\alpha\textbf{REQUEST2} \qquad \hat{=} \ \{\textbf{request, unlock}\}$$

$$\textbf{REQUEST2SPEC} \ \hat{=} \ (\textbf{REQ2} \lor \overline{\textbf{REQ2}})$$

These specifications should by now be quite familiar; they have the implementations

$$\textbf{REQUEST1} \ \hat{=} \ \mu X \cdot (\textbf{request} \longrightarrow \textbf{lock} \longrightarrow X)$$

$$\textbf{REQUEST2} \ \hat{=} \ \mu X \cdot (\textbf{request} \longrightarrow \textbf{unlock} \longrightarrow X)$$

We need to say how these **request**s get serviced. Define, for each task **t** and event **e**, a projection function that tells us which task initiated an event:

$$\textbf{task t.e} = \textbf{t}$$

Also define the sets of all **t.lock** events and **t.request** events, for all possible **t**:

$$\textbf{Tlock} \ \hat{=} \ \textbf{tstrip}^{-1} \ \textbf{lock}$$

$$\textbf{Treq} \ \hat{=} \ \textbf{tstrip}^{-1} \ \textbf{request}$$

Our requirement is that a task obtaining a lock must be the next one deserving it; that is, the longest-outstanding request should be served next:

$$\textbf{QSPEC} \ \hat{=} \ \textbf{task}^*(\textbf{tr} \restriction \textbf{Tlock}) \leq \textbf{task}^*(\textbf{tr} \restriction \textbf{Treq})$$

The expression **tr** $\restriction$ **Tlock** denotes the sequence of **t.lock** events in the trace **tr**, and **task*** (**tr** $\restriction$ **Tlock**) is just the sequence of the names of those tasks that gained the lock. Similarly, **task*** (**trTreq**) is just the sequence of the names of those tasks that issued requests for the lock. **QSPEC** says that the sequence of names of tasks gaining the lock is a *prefix* of the sequence of names of tasks requesting the lock. It is reminiscent of the specification of a buffer: What comes out is a *prefix* of what goes in. This suggests an implementation similar to that of a buffer:

$$Q \quad\; \mathrel{\hat{=}}\; Q_{\langle\rangle}$$

$$Q_{\langle\rangle} \quad\; \mathrel{\hat{=}}\; (\mathop{\square}_{r\,\in\,T} r.\texttt{request} \;\longrightarrow\; Q_{\langle r\rangle})$$

$$Q_{\langle t\rangle\,\hat{}\,s} \quad\; \mathrel{\hat{=}}\; (t.\texttt{lock} \;\longrightarrow\; Q_s$$

$$|\; \mathop{\square}_{r\,\in\,T} r.\texttt{request} \;\longrightarrow\; Q_{\langle t\rangle\,\hat{}\,s\,\hat{}\,\langle r\rangle})$$

Initially, the queue of requests is empty, and the process is willing to accept only a request. When there is at least one request, the task at the front of the queue may obtain the lock, or further requests may be added to the *end* of the queue. This is where the queuing discipline is encoded.

A "fair" multiple-process system behaves like our earlier multiple-process system, allows at most one outstanding request per task, and has the queuing discipline that we have described:

$$\textbf{FAIRMUSPEC} \;\mathrel{\hat{=}}\; (\; \textbf{MUSPEC} \wedge \textbf{QSPEC} \wedge$$

$$\forall t \in T \cdot t.\textbf{REQUEST1SPEC} \wedge t.\textbf{REQUEST2SPEC})$$

$$\textbf{FAIRMU} \;\mathrel{\hat{=}}\; (\textbf{MU} \,\|\, \textbf{Q} \,\|\, \mathop{\big|\big|\big|}_{t\,\in\,T} (t : \textbf{REQUEST1} \,\|\, t : \textbf{REQUEST2}))$$

Of course, in this section we have only been fooling ourselves: We have pushed the problem back from getting the lock to requesting one. As before, a fast task might get into the queue, acquire the lock, release it, and get into the queue again before a slower one gets its act together. Thus it is slightly misleading —in fact downright lying— to call this solution "fair". As pointed out in [9], the correct solution to this problem is probably to regard it as insoluble: If any task is particularly determined on having so much access to a data structure, then something —this task or another requiring access— will inevitably be disappointed. In CSP, we cannot distinguish between a task that takes an infinite amount of time to require access to a particular data structure, and one that does require access but is being discriminated against by our transaction-processing system. It seems that in our Kafkaesque world, paranoia is indistinguishable from genuine persecution. In practical terms, however, we have merely decided to delegate to the implementer the responsibility of ensuring that any desired event that is possible takes place within an acceptable period of time. Hence we ask that the implementation ensure that requests are serviced even-handedly. Fortunately, an implementation may find it a lot easier to be fair to requests than to locks, since the likelihood of a queue for requests may well be negligible. Of course, deadlock and unacceptable delay remain an unaddressed problem.

4 *An Optimistic Approach*

The previous section dealt with a system that allows multiple processes to gain mutually exclusive access to shared data by *locking*. That system can handle contention for resources by allocating them on a first-come, first-served basis. In this section we consider a different strategy: Each task rather optimistically assumes that there will be no interference from other tasks, and so may go blithely about its transaction. There must always, however, be a day of reckoning: Upon completion of a transaction, the system examines whether, with hindsight, the case for optimism was justified or not. If indeed there has been no interference, then the transaction is committed; if interference was possible, then the offending transaction is deemed not to have occurred. Clearly, the suitability of this approach depends on the character of the individual application.

We introduce some new events: **start**, **comnull**, **comread**, **comwrite**, and **fail**. We shall have a different structure for our transactions from before. A transaction has a start point, and it can be finalized in one of four ways: It can be the null transaction; it can be a read-only transaction; it can also have written to the data structure; or it can fail in some way. Which of the options are available to a transaction at any time will depend on what events the transaction comprises and on the interference that the transaction might cause or might have to tolerate.

Our specification starts in a familiar way. Let

$$\textbf{Commit} \; \hat{=} \; \{\textbf{comnull, comread, comwrite}\}$$

$$\textbf{Final} \; \hat{=} \; \textbf{Commit} \cup \{\textbf{fail}\}$$

and define

$$\textbf{ST} \; \hat{=} \; (\textbf{tr} \!\downarrow\! \textbf{start} - \textbf{tr} \!\restriction\! \textbf{Final} = 1)$$

$$\overline{\textbf{ST}} \; \hat{=} \; (\textbf{tr} \!\downarrow\! \textbf{start} - \textbf{tr} \!\restriction\! \textbf{Final} = 0)$$

We shall require that transactions have unique names; a transaction will be started only *once*:

$$\alpha\textbf{UNIQUE} \qquad \hat{=} \; \{\textbf{start}\}$$

$$\textbf{UNIQUESPEC} \; \hat{=} \; (\textbf{tr} \!\downarrow\! \textbf{start} \leq 1)$$

$$\textbf{UNIQUE} \qquad \hat{=} \; (\textit{start} \longrightarrow \textit{STOP})$$

Transactions start and then are finalized either by being committed or by failing:

$$\alpha\textbf{TRANS} \quad \hat{=} \quad \{\textbf{start}\} \cup \textbf{Final}$$

$$\textbf{TRANSSPEC} \; \hat{=} \; (\textbf{ST} \lor \overline{\textbf{ST}})$$

This specification is rather like **LOCKSPEC**; not surprisingly, its implementation is similar to that of **LOCK**:

$$\textbf{TRANS} \; \hat{=} \; \mu X \cdot (\textbf{start} \longrightarrow x : \textbf{Final} \longrightarrow X)$$

Reading and writing may be done only within transactions:

$$\alpha\textbf{RWTRANS} \quad \hat{=} \quad \alpha\textbf{TRANS} \cup \alpha\textbf{VAR}$$

$$\textbf{RWTRANSSPEC} \; \hat{=} \; (\overline{\textbf{tr}_0} \in \alpha\textbf{VAR} \Rightarrow \textbf{ST})$$

This specification is again familiar: It is similar to both **READSPEC** and **WRITESPEC**. Its implementation is correspondingly straightforward:

$$\textbf{RWTRANS} \; \hat{=} \; \mu X \cdot (\textbf{start} \longrightarrow \mu Y \cdot (x : \alpha\textbf{VAR} \longrightarrow Y$$
$$|x : \textbf{Final} \longrightarrow X))$$

A transaction must satisfy all three requirements: It can be started only once; it can end only by being committed or by failing; and reading and writing can be carried out only during transactions:

$$\textbf{TRANSACTSPEC} \; \hat{=} \; (\textbf{UNIQUESPEC} \land \textbf{TRANSSPEC} \land \textbf{RWTRANSSPEC})$$

This is implemented as

$$\textbf{TRANSACT} \; \hat{=} \; (\textbf{UNIQUE} \parallel \textbf{TRANS} \parallel \textbf{RWTRANS})$$

Simplifying, we obtain

$$\textbf{TRANSACT} \; = \; (\textbf{start} \longrightarrow \mu X \cdot (x : \alpha\textbf{VAR} \longrightarrow X$$
$$|x : \textbf{Final} \longrightarrow \textbf{STOP}))$$

This shows quite clearly that a transaction can occur only once, that it either is committed or fails, and that reading and writing are permitted only during the transaction.

The three commit events for a particular transaction **t** are each labeled by **t** taken from **T**, which we now regard as the set of *transaction names*:

$$\textbf{Commit}_t \; \hat{=} \; \textbf{strip}_t^{-1} \, \textbf{Commit}$$

Let **committed s** denote the set of names of *successfully completed* transactions in some trace **s**:

$$\textbf{committed s} \; \hat{=} \; \{t \in T \mid s \restriction \textbf{Commit}_t \neq \langle\rangle\}$$

Of interest at the start of each transaction is the most recently committed value— if it exists. The sequence of **write** events made by successfully committed transactions in a trace **s** is

$$\textbf{succwr s} \; \hat{=} \; s \restriction \{\textbf{t.write.c} \mid t \in \textbf{committed s} \wedge c \in C\}$$

If this isn't empty, then **lastwr s** is its last element, where

$$\textbf{lastwr s} \; \hat{=} \; \overline{\textbf{succwr s}}_0$$

The view that each transaction has of the shared data structure consists simply of the **lastwr**itten value —if it exists— followed by the **read**s and **write**s of the transaction itself. From each of these viewpoints the data structure appears as though it were a variable, possibly with an initial value. If we have

$$\textbf{W}_t \; \hat{=} \; \textbf{strip}_t^{-1} \, \textbf{W}$$

then the requirement is

$$\textbf{OVARSPEC} \; \hat{=} \; \forall t \in T, c \in C \cdot \overline{\textbf{tr}}_0 = \textbf{t.read.c} \; \Rightarrow$$

$$(\textbf{tr} \restriction \textbf{W}_t = \langle\rangle \wedge \exists u \in T \cdot \underline{\textbf{lastwr tr}} = \textbf{u.write.c}) \vee$$

$$(\textbf{tr} \restriction \textbf{W}_t \neq \langle\rangle \wedge \textbf{tr} \restriction \textbf{W}_{t\,0} = \textbf{t.write.c})$$

This should be reminiscent of the specification of a variable, but with a few extra bits and pieces. If a transaction **t** **read**s the value **c** from the data structure, then one of two cases must hold:

> Transaction **t** has not previously written a value, in which case **c** is equal to the last successfully committed written value.

> Transaction **t** has written a value, in which case the last value was also **c**.

This is implemented by a process that maintains a state containing the last successfully committed value and the last written value for each transaction:

$$\textbf{OVAR} \;\; \hat{=} \;\; \textbf{OVAR}(\bot, \{\})$$

$$\textbf{OVAR}(\textbf{v}, \textbf{f}) \;\; \hat{=} \;\; (\underset{\textbf{t} \in \textbf{T}}{\big|\big|}\, \textbf{t.start} \longrightarrow \textbf{OVAR}(\textbf{v}, \textbf{f} \oplus \{\textbf{t} \mapsto \textbf{v}\})$$

$$|\underset{\textbf{t} \in \textbf{T} \mid (\textbf{f}\, \textbf{t}) \neq \bot}{\big|\big|}\, \textbf{t.read}!(\textbf{f}\, \textbf{t}) \longrightarrow \textbf{OVAR}(\textbf{v}, \textbf{f})$$

$$|\underset{\textbf{t} \in \textbf{T}}{\big|\big|}\, \textbf{t.write}?\textbf{x} \longrightarrow \textbf{OVAR}(\textbf{v}, \textbf{f} \oplus \{\textbf{t} \mapsto \textbf{x}\})$$

$$|\underset{\textbf{t} \in \textbf{T}}{\big|\big|}\, \textbf{x} : \textbf{Commit}_\textbf{t} \longrightarrow \textbf{OVAR}((\textbf{f}\, \textbf{t}), \textbf{f})))$$

This *optimistic variable* **OVAR** initially behaves like **OVAR**$(\bot, \{\})$, for some distinguished value $\bot$. The second definition describes the behavior of **OVAR** (**v**, **f**) for some value of the shared data structure $\textbf{v} \in \textbf{C}$, and some function $\textbf{f} : \textbf{T} \longrightarrow \textbf{C}$. When a transaction **t** starts, the function **f** is updated with the maplet $\{\textbf{t} \mapsto \textbf{v}\}$. Values may be read or written by transaction **t**; these are operations on **t**'s copy of the data structure in the mapping **f**. Variable **OVAR**, however, never engages in the event **t.read** $\bot$, for any **t**. Finally, when transaction **t** is successfully committed, the shared value of the data structure is updated with the final value computed by **t**.

We can make the intuitive link between **OVAR** and **VAR** precise by being more explicit about the "view" that each transaction has of the shared data structure. If

$$\textbf{initial}_\textbf{t} \;\; \hat{=} \;\; \begin{cases} \textbf{lastwr (tr \underline{before} t.start)} & \text{if } \textbf{succwr tr} \neq \langle\rangle \\ & \text{and } \textbf{tr} \upharpoonright \textbf{W}_\textbf{t} = \langle\rangle \\[6pt] \langle\rangle & \text{otherwise} \end{cases}$$

$$\textbf{view}_\textbf{t} \;\; \hat{=} \;\; \textbf{initial}^\frown(\textbf{tr} \upharpoonright \alpha(\textbf{t} : \textbf{VAR}))$$

then we can prove that

$$\textbf{OVARSPEC} \Rightarrow \forall \textbf{t} \in \textbf{T} \cdot \textbf{VARSPEC}[\textbf{tstrip}^* \,\textbf{view}_\textbf{t}/\textbf{tr}]$$

That is, each view of the shared data structure reveals it to be just like a variable— no interference, no nasty surprises.

Now consider the various commit events. Event **comnull** corresponds to finalizing the null transaction; hence, if a transaction says that it made no access to a data structure, then this must be the case:

$$\alpha\textbf{NULL} \;\; \hat{=} \;\; \{\textbf{comnull}\} \cup \alpha\textbf{VAR}$$

$$\textbf{NULLSPEC} \;\; \hat{=} \;\; (\overline{\textbf{tr}_0} = \textbf{comnull} \Rightarrow \textbf{tr} \upharpoonright \alpha\textbf{VAR} = \langle\rangle)$$

Reading or writing *disables* the `comnull` event:

$$\text{NULL} \ \hat{=} \ \mu X \cdot \ (\text{comnull} \longrightarrow X$$
$$|\mathbf{x} : \alpha \text{VAR} \longrightarrow \text{STOP}_{\{\text{comnull}\}} \ \| \ \text{RUN}_{\alpha}\text{VAR})$$

A transaction finalized with a `comread` event must have read something:

$$\alpha \text{CR1} \quad \hat{=} \ \{\text{comread}\} \cup R$$
$$\text{CR1SPEC} \ \hat{=} \ (\overline{\mathbf{tr}}_0 = \text{comread} \ \Rightarrow \ \mathbf{tr} \upharpoonright R \neq \langle\rangle)$$

but not written anything:

$$\alpha \text{CR2} \quad \hat{=} \ \{\text{comread}\} \cup W$$
$$\text{CR2SPEC} \ \hat{=} \ (\overline{\mathbf{tr}}_0 = \text{comread} \ \Rightarrow \ \mathbf{tr} \upharpoonright W = \langle\rangle)$$

Therefore reading *enables* the `comread` event:

$$\text{CR1} \ \hat{=} \ (\mathbf{x} : R \longrightarrow \text{RUN}_{\{\text{comread}\} \cup R})$$

and writing *disables* it:

$$\text{CR2} \ \hat{=} \ \mu X \cdot \ (\text{comread} \longrightarrow X$$
$$|\mathbf{x} : W \longrightarrow \text{STOP}_{\{\text{comread}\}} \ \| \ \text{RUN}_W)$$

Putting these two together, we get

$$(\text{CR1} \ \| \ \text{CR2}) \ = \ (\mathbf{x} : R \longrightarrow \mu X \cdot \ (\mathbf{x} : R \longrightarrow X$$
$$|\text{comread} \longrightarrow X$$
$$|\mathbf{x} : W \longrightarrow \text{RUN}_{\alpha}\text{VAR})$$
$$|\mathbf{x} : W \longrightarrow \text{RUN}_{\alpha}\text{VAR})$$

If a transaction says that it has written to the data structure, then it must not be lying:

$$\alpha \text{CW1} \quad \hat{=} \ \{\text{comwrite}\} \cup W$$
$$\text{CW1SPEC} \ \hat{=} \ (\overline{\mathbf{tr}}_0 = \text{comwrite} \ \Rightarrow \ \mathbf{tr} \upharpoonright W \neq \langle\rangle)$$

Writing *enables* the `comwrite` event:

$$\text{CW1} \ \hat{=} \ (\mathbf{x} : W \longrightarrow \text{RUN}_{\{\text{comwrite}\} \cup W})$$

Adding this to (**CR1** ∥ **CR2**), we obtain

$$(\textbf{CR1} \parallel \textbf{CR2} \parallel \textbf{CW1}) \;=\; (\textbf{x}: R \longrightarrow \mu X \cdot \; (\textbf{x}: R \longrightarrow X$$
$$|\textbf{comread} \longrightarrow X$$
$$|\textbf{x}: W \longrightarrow \text{RUN}_{\{\textbf{comwrite}\}\cup\alpha\textbf{VAR}})$$
$$|\textbf{x}: W \longrightarrow \text{RUN}_{\{\textbf{comwrite}\}\cup\alpha\textbf{VAR}})$$

If we now add to this the process **NULL**, we get a description of how processes can be finalized:

$$\textbf{FINAL} \;\hat{=}\; (\textbf{NULL} \parallel \textbf{CR1} \parallel \textbf{CR2} \parallel \textbf{CW1})$$
$$= \mu X \cdot \; (\textbf{comnull} \longrightarrow X$$
$$|\textbf{x}: R \longrightarrow \mu Y \cdot \; (\textbf{x}: R \longrightarrow Y$$
$$|\textbf{comread} \longrightarrow Y$$
$$|\textbf{x}: W \longrightarrow \text{RUN}_{\{\textbf{comwrite}\}\cup\alpha\textbf{VAR}})$$
$$|\textbf{x}: W \longrightarrow \text{RUN}_{\{\textbf{comwrite}\}\cup\alpha\textbf{VAR}})$$

A transaction **t** cannot be finalized with a **t.comread** or **t.comwrite** event if there has been an update of the data structure during **t**'s lifetime. The simplest way of ensuring this is to say that no other transaction can have been finalized with a **comwrite** since **t** started. No interference has been caused to **t** by **u** if

$$\alpha\textbf{NOINT}_{t,u} \quad \hat{=} \; \{\textbf{t.start}, \textbf{t.comread}, \textbf{t.comwrite}, \textbf{u.comwrite}\}$$
$$\textbf{NOINT}_{t,u}\textbf{SPEC} \;\hat{=}\; (\overline{\textbf{tr}}_0 \in \{\textbf{t.comread}, \textbf{t.comwrite}\} \;\Rightarrow$$
$$\overline{\textbf{tr}}\,'_0 = \textbf{t.start})$$

The implementation of this requirement must ensure that **u.comwrite** *disables* **t.comread** and **t.comwrite** events:

$$\textbf{NOINT}_{t,u} \;\hat{=}$$
$$\mu X \cdot \; (\textbf{t.start} \longrightarrow$$
$$(\textbf{x}: \{\textbf{t.comread}, \textbf{t.comwrite}\} \longrightarrow \textbf{u.comwrite} \longrightarrow \text{STOP}$$
$$|\textbf{u.comwrite} \longrightarrow \text{STOP})$$
$$|\textbf{u.comwrite} \longrightarrow \textbf{t.start} \longrightarrow$$
$$\textbf{x}: \{\textbf{t.comread}, \textbf{t.comwrite}\} \longrightarrow \text{STOP})$$

Our description of the optimistic transaction-processing primitives is now complete. The full specification is

$$\textbf{OPTSPEC} \;\hat{=}\; (\textbf{OVARSPEC} \wedge$$

$$\forall t \in \textbf{T} \;\cdot\; t.\textbf{TRANSACTSPEC} \wedge t.\textbf{FINALSPEC} \wedge$$

$$\forall u \in \textbf{T} \cdot u \neq t \;\Rightarrow\; \textbf{NOINT}_{t,u}\textbf{SPEC})$$

That is, the shared data behaves like an optimistic variable; reading and writing can be done only within transactions, which have unique names; transactions must be finalized in the manner described; and the success of a transaction depends on the interference that has been caused or can be tolerated. The implementation puts together the components we have developed:

$$\textbf{OPT} \;\hat{=}\; \textbf{OVAR} \;\|\; \underset{t \,\in\, \textbf{T}}{\|} (t : \textbf{TRANSACT} \| t : \textbf{FINAL} \;\|\; \underset{u \,\in\, \textbf{T}\setminus\{t\}}{\|} \textbf{NOINT}_{t,u})$$

The generally accepted correctness criterion for maintaining the consistency of a database is called *serializability* [13]. A sequence of atomic reads and writes is called *serializable* essentially if its overall effect is as though the processes took turns, in some order, each executing its entire transaction indivisibly. The reader may be wondering how the optimistic transaction processing we have described relates to this notion of serializability.

Define, for each trace **s**, the function $\textbf{f}_\textbf{s}$ that, when applied to transaction **t**, returns the sequence of **read**s and **write**s performed by **t** in **s**:

$$\textbf{f}_\textbf{s}\, t \;\hat{=}\; s \upharpoonright \alpha(t : \textbf{VAR})$$

Clearly, $\textbf{f}_\textbf{s}\, t$ is **t**'s entire transaction in **s**. Now define the function **success** that, when applied to a trace **s**, returns the sequence of names of successfully committed transactions:

$$\textbf{success}\; s \;\hat{=}\; \textbf{trans}^* (s \upharpoonright \bigcup_{t \,\in\, \textbf{T}} \textbf{Commit}_t)$$

where **trans** merely projects the transaction name from an event:

$$\textbf{trans}\; t.e \;=\; t$$

Given a trace **tr** of **OPT**, we can find the sequence of entire transactions in the order of their successful commitment, as follows:

$$\textbf{serial}\; tr \;\hat{=}\; \frown/(\textbf{f}_{\textbf{tr}}^* (\textbf{success}\; tr))$$

If **tr** is a trace of our optimistic transaction-processing system, then **tr** and **serial tr** have the same effect. The proof of this fact follows from each transaction's view of the shared data and the freedom from interference enjoyed by each successfully committed transaction.

5 *Proofs*

Lest the reader think that we have forgotten to do our proofs, we present a short one in this section. We have started work on machine assistance for CSP proofs [4] using B, a program devised by Jean-Raymond Abrial [1]; the following proof was developed with this system. Only a few of the proofs of the systems in this paper have been carried out in such a formal and detailed manner as the proof in this section. Most exist as paper-and-pencil exercises, carried as far as the author felt was necessary; they could all be formalized like this one.

Consider the following pair of predicates on traces:

$$\textbf{in}\, t \;=\; (t{\downarrow}1 = t{\downarrow}r + 1) \qquad\qquad (bracket1.4)$$

$$\textbf{out}\, t \;=\; (t{\downarrow}1 = t{\downarrow}r) \qquad\qquad (bracket1.5)$$

These two predicates should look familiar; they form part of a theory of *bracketed actions* that we have constructed using B. Now consider the following process:

$$\alpha \textbf{b} \;=\; \{1, r\} \qquad\qquad (bracket1.1)$$

$$\textbf{b} \;=\; \mu \textbf{X} \cdot (1 \longrightarrow r \longrightarrow \textbf{X}) \qquad\qquad (bracket1.2)$$

This process, which alternates between its two events, should also be familiar. It is a theorem that **b** satisfies

$$\textbf{bspec}\, t \;=\; \textbf{in} \vee \textbf{out} \qquad\qquad (bracket1.3)$$

that is,

$$\textbf{b sat bspec}\, tr \qquad\qquad (bracket1.10)$$

The theory *bracket1* contains lemmas that are useful in the proof, such as that **b** is guarded in **X**; there are also some simple theorems about **bspec** and **out**:

$$\textbf{guarded}((1 \longrightarrow r \longrightarrow \textbf{X}), \textbf{X}) \qquad\qquad (bracket1.8)$$

$$\textbf{bspec}\, \langle \rangle \qquad\qquad (bracket1.3)$$

$$\textbf{out}\, \langle \rangle \qquad\qquad (bracket1.5)$$

$$tr \leq \langle 1, r \rangle \Rightarrow \textbf{bspec}\, tr \qquad\qquad (bracket1.6)$$

$$\langle 1, r \rangle \leq tr \wedge \textbf{bspec}\, tr\,'' \Rightarrow \textbf{bspec}\, tr \qquad\qquad (bracket1.7)$$

Another theory, *trace*, contains the theory of traces, while another, *satis*, contains the theory of processes satisfying their specifications, as set out in [9]. We refer to these rules in the proof.

First we prove the basis for our induction. The natural-deduction-style proof is presented in a forward direction.

> STOP **sat bspec tr**

Proof

1	STOP **sat** $tr = \langle\rangle$	*satis.5*
2	$0 = 0$	*EQL*
3	$0 = \langle\rangle \downarrow r$	2 *trace2.9*
4	$\langle\rangle \downarrow 1 = \langle\rangle \downarrow r$	3 *trace2.9*
5	**out** $\langle\rangle$	4 *bracket1.5*
6	**in** $\langle\rangle \vee$ **out** $\langle\rangle$	5 *logic.2*
7	**bspec**$\langle\rangle$	6 *bracket1.3*
8	**bspec tr**	7 *HYP.1*
9	$tr = \langle\rangle \Rightarrow$ **bspec tr**	8 *DED*
10	STOP **sat bspec tr**	1 9 *satis.2*

$\Box$

We make this lemma part of the theory, calling it *bracket1.9*. The rest of the proof follows easily:

> b **sat bspec tr**

1	**guarded**$((1 \longrightarrow r \longrightarrow X), X)$	*bracket1.8*
2	STOP **sat bspec tr**	*bracket1.9*
3	$tr \leq \langle 1, r \rangle \Rightarrow$ **bspec tr**	*bracket1.6*
4	$\langle 1, r \rangle \leq tr \wedge$ **bspec tr** $''\Rightarrow$ **bspec tr**	*bracket1.7*
5	**X sat bspec tr**	*HYP.1*
6	$(1 \longrightarrow r \longrightarrow X)$ **sat bspec tr**	3 4 5 *satis.9*
7	**X sat bspec tr** $\Rightarrow (1 \longrightarrow r \longrightarrow X)$ **sat bspec tr**	6 *DED*
8	$\forall X \cdot$ **X sat bspec tr** $\Rightarrow (1 \longrightarrow r \longrightarrow X)$ **sat bspec tr**	7 *GEN*
9	$\mu X \cdot (1 \longrightarrow r \longrightarrow X)$ **sat bspec tr**	1 2 8 *satis.10*
10	b **sat bspec tr**	9 *bracket1.2*

$\Box$

Many of the proofs of satisfaction can be automated in this way: The proof is first constructed by hand and then checked by machine. Since many of the processes and their specifications are very similar, there have been many opportunities to structure and reuse proofs. It seems much more difficult, however, to use a proof assistant such as B to perform process transformations, since there is a rapid expansion in the number of terms in an expression. It seems that a special-purpose tool, such as the occam transformation system [6], is required to conduct such transformations.

6 *Discussion*

This paper describes part of a very successful but fairly primitive kind of system with which we are familiar. We have not described *robust* interfaces: The systems can suffer certain deadlocks if processes do not obey the protocol required to use the shared data. There are, however, well-known techniques that cooperative processes can employ to get around these problems, and we do not pursue the matter further (but see, for example, [3] or [14]). In the real-life system we have been studying, locks are actually organized hierarchically.

The optimistic transaction-processing system should be able to avoid these tiresome outcomes: Transactions need not wait upon other transactions to finish before they can start. Of course, processes should be warned that the possibility of deadlock has been traded for the possibility of starvation.

The work discussed in this paper has started to show that CSP is a practical tool that can be used in industry. Just like other formal methods that have been introduced into industry, such as Z [7, 15] or VDM [12], however, education is essential before any degree of fluency in using CSP is achieved, or even before a paper such as this can be understood. The use of CSP allows a designer the opportunity to specify systems concisely. For example, the optimistic transaction-processing system has a very short and simple specification even though it is much more sophisticated than the other systems considered, as borne out by its design and implementation.

The style adopted in this paper seems quite successful: Specify each requirement separately, in the simplest context that seems appropriate; implement each requirement as a simple process; form the specification from the conjunction of requirements and the implementation from the parallel combination of the processes. The development of two complementary descriptions —a predicate and a piece of process algebra— helped us to understand what we were describing much better than a single description would have done. Our confidence was bolstered by performing the usually simple proof that the process was indeed an implementation of the specification, that is, that the two descriptions were of the same thing.

Many of the specifications and implementations in the systems presented in this paper are really the same predicates and processes in different guises. Although we could have obtained an economy of expression by the widespread use of relabeling functions, this approach often leads to rather obscure descriptions. The reader's first reaction is often to try to do all the substitutions in his or her head, to see what the definition really means. Hence we have limited such relabeling to situations where it is easy to see what is going on. For example, in promoting a property of a process to being a property of a labeled process, for any label in some set, relabeling is a powerful technique which actually makes it easier to understand the system. Drawing a rather tenuous link between disparate system properties, on the other hand, seems to obscure the issues. The insight about the connection is more valuable as a way of reducing the burden of proof than as a way of making the description more comprehensible. We still get the economy of an easy implementation and its proof, the strategy being merely to exhibit a relabeling scheme to establish the connection with an existing satisfaction proof.

The style of writing the predicate as a firing condition for an event was also helpful. Instead of writing rather complicated predicates —with plenty of existential quantifiers— that we *thought* captured a requirement, we wrote several smaller predicates describing firing conditions that matched our intuition for the problem.

It would be fairly straightforward to translate the CSP implementations of the systems that we have described into occam [10]. This would be a good idea because occam has direct language support for many of the concepts of CSP; it was designed with this in mind. Occam is also a simple language with a relatively simple semantics; a proof of the translation would not be too difficult. For many reasons, however, occam is not *yet* everyone's first choice for the implementation of concurrent systems. Companies have in-house standards, supporting some languages and not others, and they have concerns about compatibility and about running systems on a large variety of different computers.

In this paper we have omitted most of the proofs that we conducted in the develoment of each system. We have found three sorts of proof: proofs of theorems about predicates over traces; proofs that processes satisfy their specifications; and proofs of equivalence between processes, i.e., process transformations. None of the proofs we have carried out seem particularly difficult; the proofs are often long and tedious, however, and we have made many a slip. Now that we understand how the proofs can be done, we would like to check each one with mechanical assistance; we propose to conduct some research in this area. *Appropriate* mechanical assistance will have a large impact on the acceptance of a notation such as CSP in industry; we must get it right.

7 *Acknowledgments*

This work has been carried out under a contract with IBM United Kingdom Laboratories, Hursley Park, Winchester, to which we are most grateful for continuing support and interest. The problem of describing these kinds of transaction-processing systems in the notations of CSP was suggested by Peter Lupton, who also made some very helpful comments on an earlier draft of this paper, as did Geoff Barrett, Jeremy Jacob, and Steve King. The inclusion of a potentially more difficult system, using an optimistic strategy, was suggested by a description of the Amœba file service written in Z [5]. Paul Gardiner provided many important insights into this and other problems. Some elegant solutions to problems in transaction-processing —developed independently and entirely in CSP process algebra, without trace specifications— can be found in [2]. Another approach using functional programming to produce some rather surprising results is being explored by John Hughes at Glasgow University and Phil Trinder at Oxford. Jim Davies has formalized many of the proofs in this paper using B [4]. Although his work is only just beginning, it shows great potential. Anonymous referees gave some extremely useful comments on an earlier draft of the paper. Finally, thanks —as usual— to Jock McDoowi.

Appendix A

This glossary of symbols is taken from [9]. Here, however, we include substitution for free variables in predicates. Also, we do not require relabeling functions to be injections, but find the definition given in [8] to be more convenient.

A.1 *Definitions*

Notation	*Meaning*	*Example*
$\widehat{=}$	is equal to by definition	$R \widehat{=} \{\mathbf{read}.c \mid c \in C\}$

A.2 *Predicates*

Notation	*Meaning*	*Example*
$=$	equals	$x = x$
$\neq$	is distinct from	$x \neq x + 1$
$P \wedge Q$	P and Q	$x \leq x + 1 \wedge x \neq x + 1$

$P \vee Q$	**P** or **Q**	$x \leq y \vee y \leq x$
$\neg P$	not **P**	$\neg 3 > 5$
$P \Rightarrow Q$	**P** implies **Q**	$x < y \Rightarrow x \leq y$
$P \equiv Q$	**P** if and only if **Q**	$x < y \equiv y > x$
$\exists x \in A \cdot P$	there exists an **x** in set **A** such that **P**	
$\forall x \in A \cdot P$	for all **x** in set **A**, **P**	
$P[a/b]$	**P** with **a** substituted for **b**	$(x < 9)[3/x] \equiv (3 < 9)$

A.3 *Sets*

Notation	Meaning	Example
$\in$	is a member of	$2 \in \{1, 2, 3\}$
$\notin$	is not a member of	$4 \notin \{1, 2, 3\}$
$\{a\}$	the singleton set containing **a**	$\{\textbf{start}\}$
$\{a, b, c\}$	the set with members **a**, **b**, and **c**	$\{\textbf{request}, \textbf{lock}, \textbf{unlock}\}$
$\{x \mid P\ x\}$	the set of all **x** such that **P x**	$\{\textbf{read}.c \mid c \in C\}$
$A \cup B$	**A** union **B**	$tt\{1\} \cup \{2, 3\} = \{1, 2, 3\}$
$A \setminus B$	**A** minus **B**	$\{1, 2, 3\} \setminus \{2\} = \{1, 3\}$
$\bigcup_{i \in I} S_i$	the union of a family of sets	

A.4 *Functions*

Notation	Meaning	Example
$f\ x$	function application, **f** of **x**	$\textbf{succ}\ tr$
$strip_l$	the function that removes the label **l**	
		$strip_t\ t.lock = lock$
$strip_l^{-1}$	the function that adds the label **l**	$strip_t^{-1} req = t.req$
$f^{-1}\ S$	the inverse image under **f** of **S**	$strip_t^{-1}\ R =$
		$\{t.read.c \mid c \in C\}$
$a \mapsto 1$	**a** maps to 1	$f \mathrel{\hat{=}} \{a \mapsto 1, b \mapsto 2\}$
$f \oplus g$	function override	$f \oplus \{a \mapsto 3\}$

A.5 *Traces*

Notation	*Meaning*	*Example*
$\langle\rangle$	the empty trace	
$\langle a\rangle$	the trace containing only **a**	$\langle$t.commit$\rangle$
^	one trace followed by another	$\langle$t$\rangle$^s
^/	distributed catenation	$^\wedge/\langle\langle a\rangle, \langle b, c\rangle\rangle = \langle a, b, c\rangle$
s $\restriction$ A	s restricted to **A**	tr $\restriction$ W
s $\leq$ t	s is a prefix of t	$\langle a, b\rangle \leq \langle a, b, c\rangle$
s **in** t	s is in t	$\langle b, c\rangle$ **in** $\langle a, b, c, d\rangle$
s↓a	the number of **a**s in s	$\langle a, a, b, a, c\rangle = 3$
s_0	the head of s	$\langle a, b, c\rangle_0 = a$
s $'$	the tail of s	$\langle a, b, c\rangle\,' = \langle b, c\rangle$
$\overline{s}$	the reverse of s	$\overline{\langle a, b, c\rangle} = \langle c, b, a\rangle$
$\overline{s}_0$	the last element of s	$\overline{\langle a, b, c\rangle}_0 = c$
$\overline{s}\,'_0$	the penultimate element of s	$\overline{\langle a, b, c\rangle}\,'_0 = b$
f* s	**f** applied to every element of s	$f^* \langle a, b, c\rangle = \langle f\,a, f\,b, f\,c\rangle$

A.6 *Events*

Notation	*Meaning*	*Example*
l.a	participation in event **a** by process named l	t.lock
c.v	communication of value **v** on channel **c**	readb
l.c.v	communication of value **v** on channel l.c	t.readb

A.7 *Processes*

Notation	*Meaning*
αP	the alphabet of process **P**
(a $\longrightarrow$ P)	a then **P**
(a $\longrightarrow$ P $\mid$ b $\longrightarrow$ Q)	a then **P** choice b then **Q**
(x : A $\longrightarrow$ P x)	choose **x** from **A** then **P** **x**
μX $\cdot$ F X	the process **X** that satisfies **X** = **F** **X**
P $\parallel$ Q	**P** in parallel with **Q**

1 : P	P with name 1
P $\square$ Q	P choice Q
b!e	on channel b output the value of e
b?x	from channel b input to x
f^{-1} P	the inverse image under f of the process P
tr	an arbitrary trace of the specified process
ref	an arbitrary refusal of the specified process
P sat S	process P satisfies specification S

Appendix B

The notations used in this paper are all drawn from [8, 9], with the following exceptions, which either are derived or are notational conveniences.

Given a sequence of events **s** containing an event **e**, then

s before e

is the largest prefix of **s** not containing **e**. That is,

$\neg(\langle e \rangle$ **in** (**s before** e))

and

(**s before** e)$^\wedge\langle e \rangle \leq$ s$^\wedge\langle e \rangle$

Given a predicate on traces **PSPEC**,

1.PSPEC

denotes a new predicate that may be satisfied by a process named by **1**.

1.PSPEC $\; \hat{=} \;$ **PSPEC**[strip$^*_1$tr / tr]

In CSP we have the proof rule (taken from [9, p. 91])

if P **sat** PSPEC

then f^{-1} P **sat** PSPEC[f^* tr / tr]

We can therefore derive the following proof rule:

if P **sat** PSPEC

then 1 : P **sat** 1.PSPEC

since

$$1 : P \ \hat{=} \ \mathbf{strip}_1^{-1} \, P$$

Also, since

if P **sat** S

and Q **sat** T

then $(P \parallel Q)$ **sat** $(S[\mathbf{tr} \upharpoonright \alpha P \, / \, \mathbf{tr}] \wedge T[\mathbf{tr} \upharpoonright \alpha Q \, / \, \mathbf{tr}])$

we can derive

if P **sat** PSPEC

then $\underset{1 \,\in\, L}{\parallel} \ 1 : P$ **sat** $\forall 1 \in L \cdot 1.\text{PSPEC}$

References

[1] Abrial, J.-R. *The B User Manual.* First Draft, Oxford University Computing Laboratory, Programming Research Group, November 1986.

[2] Arcus, M. and Jacob, J. "Flagship synchronisation problems in CSP". Industrial Software Engineering Unit, Report Number 1, Oxford University Computing Laboratory, Programming Research Group, 1986.

[3] Ben-Ari, M. *Principles of Concurrent Programming.* Prentice-Hall International, Hemel Hempstead, U.K., 1982.

[4] Davies, J. "Assisted proofs for communicating sequential processes". Master's thesis, Oxford University Computing Laboratory, Programming Research Group, September 1987.

[5] Gleeson, T. "The Amœba file service". Distributed Computing Software Project, Oxford University Computing Laboratory, Programming Research Group, September 1986.

[6] Goldsmith, M. "Occam transformation at Oxford". Oxford University Computing Laboratory, Programming Research Group, August 1987.

[7] Hayes, I., ed. *Specification Case Studies*, Prentice-Hall International, Hemel Hempstead, U.K., 1987.

[8] Hoare, C. A. R. "Notes on communicating sequential processes". Technical Monograph PRG–33, Oxford University Computing Laboratory, Programming Research Group, August 1983.

[9] Hoare, C. A. R. *Communicating Sequential Processes.* Prentice-Hall International, Hemel Hempstead, U.K., 1985.

[10] INMOS Ltd. *Occam Programming Manual*. Prentice-Hall International, Hemel Hempstead, U.K., 1984.

[11] Jackson, M. A. *System Development*. Prentice-Hall International, Hemel Hempstead, U.K., 1983.

[12] Jones, C. B. *Systematic Software Development Using VDM*. Prentice-Hall International, Hemel Hempstead, U.K., 1986.

[13] Papadimitriou, C. H. "The serializability of concurrent database updates". *Journal of the ACM 26*, 4 (1979), pp. 631–653.

[14] Raynal, M. *Algorithms for Mutual Exclusion*. Translated by D. Beeson. North Oxford Academic, London,1986.

[15] Sufrin, B. A., ed. "Notes for a Z handbook". Oxford University Computing Laboratory, Programming Research Group, March 1986.

Algebraic Specifications and Proofs for Communicating Sequential Processes

9

C. A. R. Hoare
Oxford University

Abstract

A restricted notation is suggested for the description of communicating sequential processes (CSP). The notation is defined by algebraic equations, permitting proof of further equations that describe relevant properties of the operators. Equations are also used to specify and define the behavior of particular processes and to prove that they meet their specifications.

The examples cover a range of simple one-way communication devices between a single sender and a single receiver. A simple theory is used at first; this is extended when its inadequacies become too obvious.

1 *Communication*

We describe a process in terms of the sequence of communications in which it engages. The simplest but least useful description is one that describes all processes whatsoever. It is the predicate "true", abbreviated to

$$\mathsf{T} \hspace{10cm} \text{(true)}$$

If P describes a process and e is an expression, then

$$!e \rightarrow P \hspace{8cm} \text{(output } e \text{ then } P\text{)}$$

describes a process that first outputs the value of e and then behaves as described by P. If Px describes a process whose behavior may depend on the value of the message x, then

$$(?x \rightarrow Px) \hspace{7cm} \text{(input } x \text{ then } P \text{ of } x\text{)}$$

describes a process that first inputs a message m and then behaves as described by Pm. In this formula, the variable x is a bound variable; hence the following axiom.

Axiom

$$(?x \rightarrow Px) \;=\; (?y \rightarrow Py) \hspace{5cm} \text{(bound var)}$$

(Each axiom is given a name in brackets against the right-hand margin.)

Our first example,

$$?x \rightarrow (!x \rightarrow \mathsf{T})$$

describes any process whose first action is an input and whose second action is an output of the same message that it has just input. Nothing is said of subsequent behavior, so this formula describes many different processes. Some of these are also described (at greater length and in greater detail) by the next example, which copies at least two messages:

$$?x \rightarrow !x \rightarrow (?y \rightarrow !y \rightarrow \mathsf{T})$$

Here, unnecessary brackets have been omitted. For input, however, brackets have been retained to indicate the scope of the bound variable.

Recursion can be used to describe the behavior of processes into the unbounded future. For example, a process that repeatedly inputs and then outputs the same message is defined by the following recursive definition.

Definition

$$COPY \stackrel{\triangle}{=} (?x \rightarrow !x \rightarrow COPY)$$

The meaning of any formula in mathematics is unchanged when one replaces a defined term by the right-hand side of its definition. Therefore:

Theorem

$$COPY \; = \; (?x \rightarrow !x \rightarrow (?x \rightarrow !x \rightarrow COPY))$$

This substitution can be carried out again and again, revealing as much as desired of the behavior of the process:

$$COPY \; = \; ?x \rightarrow !x \rightarrow ?x \rightarrow !x \rightarrow ?x \rightarrow \ldots$$

To ensure sucess in definition by recursion, the right-hand side of a recursive definition must be *guarded*, in the sense that every recursive occurrence of the process name must be preceded by at least one input or output. Under this condition, the defining equation for the process has only one solution. This fact is formalized as the law of unique fixed points:

Axiom

$$P = F(P) \; \wedge \; F(Q) = Q \; \Rightarrow \; P = Q \hspace{4cm} \text{(ufp)}$$

provided F is guarded.

For example, consider the process C, defined recursively:

Definition

$$C \; \stackrel{\triangle}{=} \; (?x \rightarrow !x \rightarrow (?y \rightarrow !y \rightarrow C))$$

By substituting and changing the bound variable in the definition of *COPY*, we know the following:

Theorem

$$COPY \; = \; (?x \rightarrow !x \rightarrow (?y \rightarrow !y \rightarrow COPY))$$

Thus *COPY* and C are both solutions of the same guarded recursive equation. There is only one solution, however, so these apparently different solutions are identical.

Theorem

$$COPY \; = \; C \hspace{7cm} \text{ufp}$$

(The justification for each theorem is given by writing the name of the axiom used on the right-hand margin.)

Examples

1. A process *CPAIR* faithfully copies messages from input to output but batches them into pairs before delivery:

$$CPAIR \stackrel{\wedge}{=} (?x \to (?y \to !x \to !y \to CPAIR))$$

2. A process *REVPR* copies pairs of messages from input to output but reverses the order of delivery within each pair:

$$REVPR \stackrel{\wedge}{=} (?x \to (?y \to !y \to !x \to REVPR))$$

3. A process *SINK* loses every message:

$$SINK \stackrel{\wedge}{=} (?x \to SINK)$$

Exercises

Using only notations introduced earlier, describe the following:

1. A process *LOSEHALF* copies the first of each pair of messages and loses the second.

2. A process *K0* never inputs, and outputs only messages with value 0.

2 *Disjunction*

If *P* and *Q* are process descriptions, then their disjunction

$$P \vee Q \qquad\qquad\qquad\qquad (P \text{ or } Q)$$

describes all processes described by either *P* or *Q*. This disjunction satisfies the familiar algebraic laws of propositional logic:

Axioms

$$P \vee P = P \qquad\qquad\qquad\qquad (\vee \text{ idempotent})$$

$$P \vee Q = Q \vee P \qquad\qquad\qquad\qquad (\vee \text{ symmetric})$$

$$P \vee (Q \vee R) = (P \vee Q) \vee R \qquad\qquad\qquad\qquad (\vee \text{ associative})$$

An operator that gives T when either of its operands is T is called *strict*. An operator that distributes both leftward and rightward through disjunction is called *disjunctive*. For example, disjunction is both strict and disjunctive:

Axiom

$$P \vee T = T \qquad\qquad\qquad (\vee \text{ strict})$$

Theorem

$$P \vee (Q1 \vee Q2) = (P \vee Q1) \vee (P \vee Q2) \qquad\qquad (\vee \text{ disjunctive})$$

A process that first communicates and is then described by $Q1$ or $Q2$ could also be described as a process that either communicates and then behaves like $Q1$, or performs the same communication and then behaves like $Q2$. This fact is clearly and briefly expressed as a pair of algebraic axioms:

Axioms

$$!e \rightarrow (Q1 \vee Q2) = (!e \rightarrow Q1) \vee (!e \rightarrow Q2) \qquad (! \text{ disjunctive})$$

$$?x \rightarrow (Q1 \vee Q2x) = (?x \rightarrow Q1x) \vee (?x \rightarrow Q2x) \qquad (? \text{ disjunctive})$$

Disjunction is useful for describing possible transient faults in message-passing systems.

Examples

1. A communication device that may sometimes duplicate a message:

$$DUP \;\hat{=}\; (?x \rightarrow !x \rightarrow (DUP \vee (!x \rightarrow DUP)))$$

2. A device that may sometimes lose a message:

$$LOSS \;\hat{=}\; (?x \rightarrow ((!x \rightarrow LOSS) \vee LOSS))$$

3. A device that may sometimes interchange the order of delivery of a pair of consecutive messages:

$$SWOP2 \;\hat{=}\; (?x \rightarrow ((!x \rightarrow SWOP2) \vee (?y \rightarrow !y \rightarrow !x \rightarrow SWOP2)))$$

Exercises

1. Rewrite the preceding processes so that they deliver at least one message correctly after an error.

2. Prove that disjunction is disjunctive.

A description P is as precise as Q (or more so) if everything described by P is also described by Q (but not necessarily vice versa). In this case, we write

$P \leq Q$ or $Q \geq P$

This concept can be defined in terms of disjunction:

Definition $P \leq Q$ means $(P \vee Q) = Q$.

From the definition, it is easy to prove that $\leq$ is an upper semilattice, in the sense that it obeys the following laws:

Theorems

$P \leq P$ ($\leq$ reflexive)

$P \leq Q \wedge Q \leq P \;\Rightarrow\; P = Q$ ($\leq$ antisymmetric)

$P \leq Q \wedge Q \leq R \;\Rightarrow\; P \leq R$ ($\leq$ transitive)

$P \leq T$ ($\leq$ top T)

$(P \vee Q) \leq R \;\Leftrightarrow\; P \leq R \wedge Q \leq R$ ($\leq$ lub $\vee$)

$P \leq P \vee Q$ (a fortiori)

A function F is defined to be monotonic if it preserves the ordering of its operands. In symbols:

Definition F is monotonic if and only if

$$F(P) \leq F(Q) \quad \text{whenever} \quad P \leq Q,$$

$$F(P1, P2) \leq F(Q1, Q2) \quad \text{whenever} \quad P1 \leq Q1 \text{ and } P2 \leq Q2,$$

and so on for functions of more than two arguments.

It is easy to prove the following:

Theorem
All disjunctive functions are monotonic.

Theorem
All combinations of monotonic functions are monotonic.

A function in mathematics represents the engineering concept of an assembly, with a slot into which different components (arguments) may be plugged.

A nonmonotonic function would be an assembly with the peculiarity that its behavior becomes more predictable and controllable when you plug in a less predictable and controllable component. Such assemblies are fortunately rare in engineering: If they existed, they would be very difficult to work with. For this reason (and others that will be discussed later) all the functions we introduce and use for describing processes will be monotonic.

The introduction of the precision ordering ≤ permits a simple and useful extension of the unique-fixed-point law.

Axiom

$$P \leq F(P) \;\wedge\; F(Q) \leq Q \;\Rightarrow\; P \leq Q \qquad\qquad \text{(ufp)}$$

provided F is guarded.

We use this axiom to prove that the behavior described by *COPY* is also described by *LOSS*: Since *LOSS* does not actually specify that messages *must* be lost, it could in fact describe a process that copies faithfully all the time.

Theorem

$$COPY \leq LOSS$$

Proof

		$!x \rightarrow LOSS \leq (!x \rightarrow LOSS) \vee LOSS$	a fortiori
(1)	∴	$(?x \rightarrow (!x \rightarrow LOSS)) \leq (?x \rightarrow ((!x \rightarrow LOSS) \vee LOSS))$	? monotonic
(2)	∴	$(?x \rightarrow !x \rightarrow LOSS) \leq LOSS$	def *LOSS*
(3)	but	$COPY \leq COPY$	≤ refl
(4)	∴	$COPY \leq (?x \rightarrow !x \rightarrow COPY)$	def *COPY*
	∴	$COPY \leq LOSS$	ufp (4) (2)

A similar proof may be given for

$$SINK \leq LOSS$$

and from (≤ lub ∨) we conclude that

$$COPY \vee SINK \leq LOSS \qquad\qquad\qquad \square$$

Exercises

Prove the following:

1. $COPY \leq DUP$

2. *COPY* ∨ *REVPR* ≤ *SWOP*2   (Hint: use ≤ lub ∨)

Note that a process described by (*COPY* ∨ *SINK*) may either copy messages or lose them, but after the first cycle it remains forever consistent. If the second action is an output, all subsequent messages are also copied; otherwise they all are lost. *LOSS* describes not only these processes but also ones that behave differently on successive cycles. It is therefore a vaguer description than (*COPY* ∨ *SINK*).

3 *Foundations*

I have introduced and given some examples of a notation for describing the behavior of communicating processes. The concept of a process can be defined more formally by a set of axioms similar to those formulated by Peano [**?**] for natural numbers.

Definition   Let **P** stand for the set of all processes. Then

1. T ∈ **P**

2. (!*e* → *P'*) ∈ **P** ≡ (*P'* ∈ **P** and *e* is a message)

3. (?*x* → *Px*) ∈ **P** ≡ (*Px* ∈ **P** for all messages *x*)

4. (*P*1 ∨ *P*2) ∈ **P** ≡ (*P*1 ∈ **P** and *P*2 ∈ **P**)

5. Every process takes one of the four forms

$$\text{T,} \quad (!e \to P), \quad (?x \to Px), \quad (P1 \vee P2)$$

6. Every set of guarded recursive equations defines the corresponding processes uniquely.

If we were interested only in finite processes, the last two axioms would be combined into the more familiar axiom, "Everything that is a process can be proved so by application of the first four axioms." The reason for the new formalization of the last axiom is that we wish to include infinite processes.

In the theory of natural numbers, primitive recursion is used to define functions by showing how they apply to the two permitted forms of numbers (i.e., zero and the successor of some number). Functions on processes can be similarly defined by considering all four forms that a process may take. For example, let us define a *minus* function on processes. The process (−*P*) is defined as a process that behaves like *P*, except that whenever *P* would output an integer message *x*, (−*P*) outputs (−*x*) instead.

Definition   The definition of minus deals with the four cases.

1. If we don't know anything about a process, then we don't know anything about its minus:

$$-(T) = T$$

2. If a process behaves like P or Q, its negation behaves like the minus of P or the minus of Q:

$$-(P \vee Q) = (-P) \vee (-Q) \qquad\qquad\qquad\qquad (- \text{ disj})$$

3. If a process begins with output of e, its minus begins with output of minus e, and its subsequent behavior is also changed:

$$-(!e \rightarrow P) = !(-e) \rightarrow (-P) \qquad\qquad\qquad\qquad (- \text{ dist !})$$

4. If a process begins with input, its minus begins with the same input, but its subsequent behavior is changed:

$$-(?x \rightarrow Px) = (?x \rightarrow -(Px)) \qquad\qquad\qquad\qquad (- \text{ dist ?})$$

The definition of minus takes the form of algebraic equations that show how the function distributes through the operators used to construct a process. The intention is that any call of the function can be eliminated from any finite expression describing a process by pushing it inwards until it reaches the occurrences of T and (by 1, preceding) disappears. Moreover, it permits the behavior of an infinite or recursively defined process to be explored as deeply as desired, deep enough at least to apply the theorem of unique fixed points.

Examples

1. $-(?x \rightarrow !x \rightarrow ?y \rightarrow !y \rightarrow T)$

$= (?x \rightarrow !(-x) \rightarrow ?y \rightarrow !(-y) \rightarrow T)$

2. $-COPY$

$= (?x \rightarrow !(-x) \rightarrow (-COPY))$

$= NEG$ ufp

where $NEG \triangleq (?x \rightarrow !(-x) \rightarrow NEG)$

In the theory of natural numbers, the properties of functions defined by primitive recursion can be proved by mathematical induction. The corresponding technique for functions defined on other recursively defined domains is known as *structural* induction. Structural induction deals with all the possible structures of the induction variable, appealing to the hypothesis that all components of the structure satisfy the theorem. Here is the proof of an obvious theorem that when you minus a process twice you get back the original process.

Theorem

$$-(-P) = P$$

Proof   By induction on the structure of P.

Case 0: $P = \mathsf{T}$

$$- (-\mathsf{T}) \;=\; (-\mathsf{T}) \;=\; \mathsf{T} \qquad\qquad\qquad\qquad -\text{strict}^2$$

(The superscript 2 indicates that the law *strict* has been used twice.)

Case 1: $P = (P1 \vee P2)$

$$
\begin{aligned}
- (-(P1 \vee P2)) \;&=\; -((-P1) \vee (-P2)) && \text{def} - \\
&=\; (-(-P1)) \vee (-(-P2)) && \text{def} - \\
&=\; P1 \vee P2 && \text{by the induction hypothesis}
\end{aligned}
$$

Case 2: $P = {!}e \to P'$

$$
\begin{aligned}
- (-P)) \;&=\; -({!}(-e) \to (-P')) && \text{def} - \\
&=\; {!}(-(-e)) \to -(-(P')) && \text{def} - \\
&=\; {!}e \to P' && \text{induction hyp.}
\end{aligned}
$$

Case 3: $P = (?x \to Px)$

The proof is easier than Case 2.   □

Processes differ from natural numbers in that each natural number is finite, whereas a process may be infinite. As a result, we must restrict the kinds of predicates to which structural induction is applied. They must be simple universally quantified equations, or finite disjunctions and conjunctions of such equations. Negation and infinite existential quantification are prohibited. It is this restriction that protects us from proving propositions that are true only of finite processes.

Another important restriction is necessary in the definition of functions by structural recursion. The need for this restriction is revealed in the following example. Let f be a function that selects the first alternative of each disjunction. Then

$f(\text{T}) = \text{T}$

$f(P \vee Q) = P$, etc.

From the second clause we get

$f(Q \vee P) = Q$

But by symmetry of disjunction

$(P \vee Q) = (Q \vee P)$

$\therefore \quad P = f(P \vee Q) = f(Q \vee P) = Q$ for *all* P and Q

We have proved that all processes are equal to each other. Clearly we need to forbid definition of such disastrous functions as f. Fortunately, if the function f is defined as strict and disjunctive (which is often most reasonable anyway), the only further restriction is that the right-hand sides of the definitions $f(!e \rightarrow P')$ and $f(?x \rightarrow Px)$ should be disjunctive. If the right-hand sides of these equations are also guarded in $f(P)$ and $f(Px)$, respectively, then there is only one function that satisfies the recursive definition.

Exercises

1. Define a function $\sim P$ that negates each number before *input* by P.

2. Prove that $(\sim -COPY) = COPY$.

4 *Interleaving*

Let P and Q be processes. Let us connect their two input channnels into a single input channel in such a way that each message input on the single channel is input either by P or by Q, but that for any particular input we do not know which. Similarly, let us combine their output channels so that each output message comes either from P or from Q, we know not which. As a result, all we know is that the sequence of communications performed by the pair of processes is an arbitrary interleaving of two communication sequences of each of the processes individually. The result of such a connection is called the *interleaving* of P and Q; its behavior is denoted

$(P \,|||\, Q)$

It is represented pictorially in Figure 1.

This informal description of the connection of two processes can be formalized in a definition by a simultaneous recursion on the structure of both operands.

Definition   In principle there are 16 cases, which fortunately can be classified under three headings:

1. If nothing is known about one of the operands of the interleaving, then nothing is known about the behavior of their combination. This means that the interleaving operator is strict in each of its arguments:

$$T \mid\mid\mid Q = T = P \mid\mid\mid T \qquad\qquad (\mid\mid\mid \text{strict})$$

2. If it is not known whether one of the operands will behave like $P1$ or like $P2$, then both possibilities are preserved in their combination. This means that the interleaving operator is disjunctive:

$$(P1 \lor P2) \mid\mid\mid Q = (P1 \mid\mid\mid Q) \lor (P2 \mid\mid\mid Q)$$

and

$$P \mid\mid\mid (Q1 \lor Q2) = (P \mid\mid\mid Q1) \lor (P \mid\mid\mid Q2)$$

Figure 1. $P \mid\mid\mid Q.$

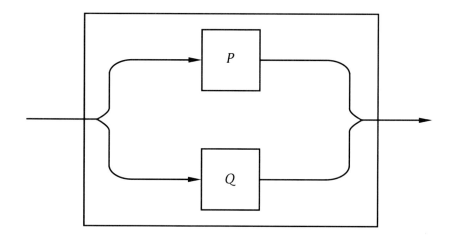

---

3. The two classes just described cover all cases in which either operand is T or a disjunction. In all remaining cases, therefore, both operands begin with a communication. In these cases, the first communication of the interleaving is the first communication either of the left operand or of the right operand. Whichever it is, the other operand does nothing, and its future behavior remains unchanged. This description applies equally, whether the communication is input or output, either of which will be represented by the letters c and d. Let us define

$$P \mathrel{\hat{=}} c \to P' \text{ and } Q \mathrel{\hat{=}} d \to Q'$$

Then

$$(P \,|||\, Q) = (c \to (P' \,|||\, Q)) \vee (d \to (P \,|||\, Q')) \qquad \text{(||| dist. →)}$$

This clause shows how interleaving distributes through the arrow.

Example   Let

$$K0 \mathrel{\hat{=}} !0 \to K0 \text{ and } K1 \mathrel{\hat{=}} !1 \to K1$$

That is, $K0$ only outputs zeros and $K1$ only outputs ones. Then

$$
\begin{aligned}
K0 \,|||\, K1 \;=\;& (!0 \to K0) \,|||\, (!1 \to K1) & \text{by def. } K0, K1 \\
=\;& (!0 \to (K0 \,|||\, (!1 \to K1))) & \text{||| dist} \\
& \vee\, (!1 \to ((!0 \to K0) \,|||\, K1)) & \text{||| dist} \\
=\;& (!0 \to (K0 \,|||\, K1)) \vee (!1 \to (K0 \,|||\, K1)) & \text{by def. } K0, K1 \\
=\;& K01 & \text{by ufp}
\end{aligned}
$$

where

$$K01 \mathrel{\hat{=}} (!0 \to K01) \vee (!1 \to K01)$$

$K01$ outputs an arbitrary interleaving of zeros and ones.

Exercise   Prove that $SINK \,|||\, SINK = SINK$.

An important property of the $|||$ operator is that it is symmetric. The proof follows the structure of the definition of the operator.

Theorem

$$(P \,|||\, Q) = (Q \,|||\, P) \qquad \text{(||| symm)}$$

Proof   by simultaneous induction on P and Q.

Case 1: One of the operands is T.

$$\text{T} \,|||\, Q \;=\; \text{T} \;=\; Q \,|||\, \text{T} \qquad\qquad\qquad ||| \text{ strict}$$

Case 2: One of the operands is a disjunction.

$$
\begin{aligned}
(P1 \vee P2) \,|||\, Q \;&=\; (P1 \,|||\, Q) \vee (P2 \,|||\, Q) && ||| \text{ disj} \\
&=\; (Q \,|||\, P1) \vee (Q \,|||\, P2) && \text{ind. hyp.} \\
&=\; Q \,|||\, (P1 \vee P2) && ||| \text{ disj}
\end{aligned}
$$

Case 3: Both operands begin with communication.

$$P = c \to P' \text{ and } Q = d \to Q'$$

$$
\begin{aligned}
P \,|||\, Q \;&=\; (c \to P') \,|||\, (d \to Q') \\
&=\; (c \to (P' \,|||\, Q)) \vee (d \to (P \,|||\, Q')) && ||| \text{ dist} \to \\
&=\; (c \to (Q \,|||\, P')) \vee (d \to (Q' \,|||\, P)) && \text{ind. hyp.} \\
&=\; (d \to (Q' \,|||\, P)) \vee (c \to (Q \,|||\, P')) && \vee \text{ symm} \\
&=\; Q \,|||\, P && ||| \text{ dist} \to
\end{aligned}
$$

□

Other theorems that may be similarly proved are as follows:

1. If one operand of $|||$ begins with a communication, then that communication may happen first, but perhaps does not:

$$(c \to P) \,|||\, Q \;\le\; c \to (P \,|||\, Q) \qquad\qquad (||| \text{ det})$$

2. When P is interleaved with Q, we do not rule out the possibility that all communications turn out to be with P, and Q is always unfairly neglected:

$$P \,|||\, Q \;\ge\; P \qquad\qquad\qquad\qquad\qquad (||| \text{ unfair})$$

This law may be written $P \vee (P \,|||\, Q) = P$.

3. When three processes are interleaved, it does not matter in which order they are connected:

$$(P \,|||\, Q) \,|||\, R \;=\; P \,|||\, (Q \,|||\, R) \qquad\qquad (||| \text{ assoc})$$

5 *Communication Services*

A simple unswitched communication service is a process that inputs messages posted in one location and delivers them at another. The most general
definition of such a service is that it cannot deliver more copies of any message than have been previously posted.

A specific example of such a service is the *COPY* process, which alternates
acceptance and delivery of messages. In general, a service can accept many
more messages than have been delivered, holding the balance in a buffer,
which often has some limit on its size. The *COPY* process has a maximum
buffer size of just one, whereas *CPAIR* can buffer two messages. Some services (including the letter service of the British post office) may reorder messages before delivery. For example, *REVPR* and *SWOP*2can reorder adjacent
messages. Some communication services are allowed to lose messages like
LOSS, or even like *SINK*, which avoids delivering unposted messages by the
lazy expedient of not delivering any messages at all.

Suppose that *P* and *Q* are communication services, both connecting the
same sender to the same receiver, but perhaps by different routes across the
mountains that separate them. A message service of increased capacity is
provided by their interleaving $P \| Q$. Each message posted may be carried by
either route, and we neither know nor care which service carries a particular
message. Messages sent on one route may overtake messages held in the
buffer of the other route. The maximum buffer capacity of the combined
service is the sum of the maxima of the individual routes.

The simplest example of a two-route service is the interleaving of two
simple copying processes:

$$
\begin{aligned}
C \| C &= (?x \rightarrow !x \rightarrow C) \| (?x \rightarrow !x \rightarrow C) & \text{def. } COPY \\
&= ?x \rightarrow ((!x \rightarrow C) \| C) \vee (?x \rightarrow (C \| (!x \rightarrow C))) & \\
&= ?x \rightarrow (C \| (!x \rightarrow C)) & \| \text{-symm} \\
&\geq ?x \rightarrow ?y \rightarrow ((!y \rightarrow C) \| (!x \rightarrow C)) & \| \text{-det} \\
&\geq ?x \rightarrow ?y \rightarrow !x \rightarrow !y \rightarrow (C \| C) & \| \text{-det}^2
\end{aligned}
$$

and
$$
C \| C \geq ?x \rightarrow ?y \rightarrow !y \rightarrow !x \rightarrow (C \| C) \qquad \| \text{-det}^2
$$

The last two lines of this calculation are in a form that permits application
of the unique-fixed-point theorem to prove the inequations.

$$(C \| C) \geq CPAIR$$
$$(C \| C) \geq REVPR$$

from which we conclude that

$$(C \mathbin{|||} C) \ge COPY \lor CPAIR \lor REVPR \qquad\qquad (\le \text{lub} \lor)$$

Exercise   Prove $(C \mathbin{|||} C) \ge SWOP2$.

A two-route communication service can be extended to an n-route system, thereby further increasing the buffering capacity. The definition uses normal mathematical induction on the number of routes:

$$C_1 \quad = \quad C$$

$$C_{n+1} \quad = \quad C_n \mathbin{|||} C$$

$$\quad = \quad \underbrace{C \mathbin{|||} C \mathbin{|||} \cdots \mathbin{|||} C}_{1+n \text{ times}}$$

We now prove the existence of a reordering communication service (known as a *BAG*) with unbounded buffering capacity. The addition of another buffer to such a bag should not make any difference, i.e.,

$$BAG = BAG \mathbin{|||} C$$

This equation itself cannot be used as a recursive definition because its right-hand side is unguarded, and there are many solutions, including $BAG = \mathsf{T}$! This problem is solved by using instead the guarded definition

$$BAG \triangleq (?x \to (BAG \mathbin{|||} (!x \to C)))$$

The essential property of an unbounded bag can now be proved as a theorem.

Theorem

$$BAG \mathbin{|||} C = BAG$$

Proof

$$
\begin{aligned}
LHS \quad = \quad & (?x \to ((BAG \mathbin{|||} (!x \to C)) \mathbin{|||} C) && \left\{ \begin{array}{l} \text{def } BAG \\ \text{def } C \\ \mathbin{|||} \text{ dist } \to \end{array} \right. \\
& \quad \lor (?x \to (BAG \mathbin{|||} (!x \to C))) \\[2mm]
= \quad & (?x \to ((BAG \mathbin{|||} C) \mathbin{|||} (!x \to C))) && \left\{ \begin{array}{l} \mathbin{|||} \text{ symm} \\ \mathbin{|||} \text{ assoc} \end{array} \right. \\
& \quad \lor (?x \to (BAG \mathbin{|||} (!x \to C))) \\[2mm]
= \quad & ?x \to ((BAG \lor (BAG \mathbin{|||} C)) \mathbin{|||} (!x \to C)) && \to \mathbin{|||} \text{ disj} \\[2mm]
= \quad & ?x \to ((BAG \mathbin{|||} C) \mathbin{|||} (!x \to C)) && \mathbin{|||} \text{ unfair} \\[2mm]
= \quad & BAG && \text{ufp}
\end{aligned}
$$

Theorem

$$BAG \parallel\!\parallel BAG = BAG$$

Proof   The proof is left as an exercise.

Since we can prove that $SINK \geq BAG$, we know that one of the possible behaviors of an unbounded bag is to lose all messages. It cannot be relied upon, however, even to do that! For some purposes, therefore, the $SINK$ is actually *better* than a bag— for example, if it connects a traitor in your own camp to the tent of the enemy general. Furthermore, there is no purpose for which a BAG is reliably better than $SINK$.

This result indicates a deficiency in the expressive power of the notation we are using to specify buffered communication services. A solution will be given in Section 8.

Exercise   Define an interrupt operator $^\wedge$ by recursion (on its first argument only). A process $P^\wedge Q$ (i.e., P interrupted by Q) behaves initially like P; but at any time (including at the start) P may stop, and Q start instead. Prove that this operator is strict and disjunctive in both its arguments, and also associative. Show also that

$$P \vee Q \leq P^\wedge Q \leq P \parallel\!\parallel Q$$

$$BAG^\wedge BAG = BAG$$

6 *Chaining*

Let P and Q be processes. Let us connect the output channel of P directly to the input channel of Q in such a way that a message passes on the shared channel whenever P outputs it and Q inputs it simultaneously. These communications are private to the pair of processes that engage in them, and cannot be observed from their external environment. All messages input by the pair are in fact input by P, and all output in fact comes from Q, but since both processes are enclosed together in a black box, we cannot observe this fact after the connection has been made. The result of such a connection is called the *chain* of P and Q, and is denoted

$$P \gg Q$$

It is represented pictorially in Figure 2.

The informal description of chaining can be formalized in a definition by simultaneous recursion on the structure of both operands.

Definition

1. As usual, chaining is both strict and disjunctive.

2. If the first action of the left operand is output and the first action of the right operand is input, then both these actions occur immediately, simultaneously, and imperceptibly. In the subsequent behavior of the right operand, the input variable will take the value of the message communicated:

$$(!e \rightarrow P) \gg (?x \rightarrow Qx) = (P \gg (Qe))$$

Note that the right-hand side of this definition is not guarded. This causes some problems, which will be described later.

3. If the first action of both operands is output, the output by the left operand is delayed until the right operand is ready to input it. Hence the output by the right operand is the only possible initial action of the chain:

$$(!e \rightarrow P) \gg (!f \rightarrow Q) = !f \rightarrow ((!e \rightarrow P) \gg Q)$$

4. If the first action of both operands is input, similar reasoning applies; the first action of the chain is the input by the left operand:

$$(?x \rightarrow Px) \gg (?y \rightarrow Qy) = (?x \rightarrow (Px \gg (?y \rightarrow Qy)))$$

Figure 2. $P \gg Q$.

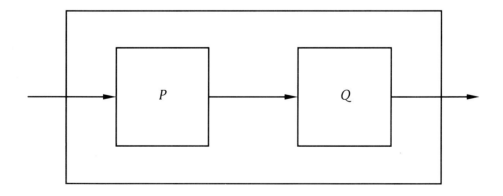

5. If the first action of the left operand is input and the first action of the right operand is output, then either action may occur first, and the subsequent behavior is defined accordingly:

$$(?x \rightarrow Px) \gg (!f \rightarrow Q) \quad = \quad (?x \rightarrow (Px \gg (!f \rightarrow Q)))$$

$$\vee \, (!f \rightarrow ((?x \rightarrow Px) \gg Q))$$

From this definition, it is possible to prove that chaining enjoys properties similar to those of |||.

Theorem

$$(?x \rightarrow P) \gg Q \quad \geq \quad ?x \rightarrow (P \gg Q) \qquad\qquad \gg\text{--det}$$

$$P \gg (!f \rightarrow Q) \quad \geq \quad !f \rightarrow (P \gg Q) \qquad\qquad \gg\text{--det}$$

$$P \gg (Q \gg R) \quad = \quad (P \gg Q) \gg R \qquad\qquad \gg\text{ assoc}$$

A telegraph service is defined as a communication service with the additional useful property that it delivers messages in the same order that they are posted, though possibly after some delay. A specific example of such a service is the *COPY* process. Another example is the process *CPAIR*, which buffers up to two messages before delivery. Another less useful example is the process *SINK*, which obeys the specification in its characteristically lazy way.

Suppose now that we have two telegraph services, one of which passes messages from the sender to an intermediate point in the mountains between the sender and receiver, and the other of which connects the intermediate point with the receiver. To complete the connection between the sender and the receiver, all that is needed is to chain together these two services. The simplest example is the chain consisting of two copying services:

$$\begin{aligned}
C \gg C \quad &= \quad (?x \rightarrow ((!x \rightarrow C) \gg (?y \rightarrow !y \rightarrow C))) \\
&= \quad (?x \rightarrow (C \gg (!x \rightarrow C))) \\
&= \quad (?x \rightarrow [(!x \rightarrow (C \gg C)) \vee (?z \rightarrow ((!z \rightarrow C) \gg (!x \rightarrow C)))])
\end{aligned} \right\} \text{def} \gg$$

So

$$C \gg C \quad \geq \quad (?x \rightarrow !x \rightarrow (C \gg C)) \qquad\qquad \rightarrow\text{-dist, a fortiori}$$

and

$$\begin{aligned}
C \gg C \quad &\geq \quad (?x \rightarrow ?z \rightarrow ((!z \rightarrow C) \gg (!x \rightarrow C))) \qquad &\rightarrow\text{-dist, a fortiori} \\
&= \quad (?x \rightarrow ?z \rightarrow !x \rightarrow ((!z \rightarrow C) \gg C)) \qquad &\text{def} \gg \\
&\geq \quad (?x \rightarrow ?z \rightarrow !x \rightarrow !z \rightarrow (C \gg C)) \qquad &\text{exercise}
\end{aligned}$$

Therefore

$$C \gg C \;\geq\; COPY \vee CPAIR$$

A telegraph service with greater buffering capacity can be constructed by adding yet more copying processes to the chain. A buffer of size n is defined by induction, like a bag of size n, but with chaining rather than interleaving:

$$BUF_1 \;=\; C$$
$$BUF_{n+1} \;=\; BUF_n \gg C$$

An unbounded buffer is defined like an unbounded bag:

$$BUF \;=\; (?x \rightarrow (BUF \gg (\,!x \rightarrow C)))$$

It is not valid to assume from its appearance that the right-hand side of this equation is guarded; nevertheless, we will make this assumption without proof.

It is now easy to prove that chaining another buffer (bounded or unbounded) at either end of an unbounded buffer makes no difference.

Theorem

$$
\begin{aligned}
BUF \;&=\; BUF \gg C \\
&=\; C \gg BUF \\
&=\; BUF \gg BUF
\end{aligned}
$$

Clearly, to behave like a buffer is one of the possibilities for a bag.

Theorem

$$BUF \leq BAG$$

Furthermore, chaining or interleaving buffers or bags to a bag makes no difference. These facts are summarized in the following series of equations:

Theorem

$$BAG \quad = \quad BUF \gg BAG$$

$$= \quad BAG \gg BUF$$

$$= \quad BAG \gg BAG$$

$$= \quad BUF \,|||\, BAG$$

$$= \quad BUF \vee BAG$$

$$= \quad BAG \,|||\, BAG$$

Thus any combination of bags and buffers (including at least one bag) will be a bag; for example,

$$(BAG \gg ((BUF \vee BAG) \,|||\, BUF)) \,|||\, (BAG \gg BUF) \; = \; BAG$$

The left-hand side of this inequality describes the structure of a simple unswitched store-and-forward message-passing system consisting of a number of nodes connected in series or in parallel. If each node acts as a mail service, we have proved that the whole network also does so. A theorem of this kind explains the success of message services like the *ARPANET*. The significance of this particular version of the theorem is much diminished by the fact that a *SINK* meets the same specification.

7 *Divergence*

The time has come to describe some of the problems arising from the fact that one of the clauses in the definition of the chaining operator is unguarded. Consider the process

$$K0 \gg SINK \quad = \quad (!0 \to K0) \gg (?x \to SINK) \qquad \text{def. } K0,\ SINK$$

$$= \quad K0 \gg SINK \qquad\qquad\qquad\qquad \text{def} \gg$$

$$= \quad (!0 \to K0) \gg (?x \to SINK) \qquad \text{def. } K0,\ SINK$$

$$= \quad \dots$$

It is clearly impossible for either man or machine ever to discover the first action of this process. Such an ill-defined process is said to *diverge*. We may believe that it will never perform any action at all, but we cannot prove this, or even describe this behavior in our restricted notations. The only description we can validly give is the vacuous description T.

Consider now the result of chaining this divergent process to $K0$:

$$(K0 \gg SINK) \gg K0$$

Since there is no way of discovering the first action of the left operand of the chain, it is not possible to use any of the distribution laws for chaining to calculate the first action of this triple chain. We may believe that the first action can only be (or even must be) the output of a zero by the rightmost process, but the axioms do not permit a proof of this, or of any other nontrivial fact about the chain.

The same phenomenon of divergence arises if we permit unguarded expressions on the right hand side of a recursive definition. Consider, for example,

$$DIV \; \hat{=} \; DIV \vee (\,!0 \to DIV)$$

$$= \; (DIV \vee (\,!0 \to DIV)) \vee (\,!0 \to (DIV \vee (\,!0 \to DIV)))$$

$$= \; DIV \vee (\,!0 \to DIV) \vee (\,!0 \to (\,!0 \to DIV)) \vee \dots$$

Again, it is not possible to discover by substitution (any number of times) what the possible initial actions of this process might be. We do not know whether the first action of *DIV* will or will not be output, or indeed whether it diverges without performing any action at all. Because it is unguarded, the recursive equation that was supposed to define *DIV* has many solutions, including $K0$, $SINK|||K$, $K0|||K1$, and even T, which is the vaguest of all process descriptions.

If this is regarded as a problem, one widely accepted solution is to identify all processes that may diverge with the process T. This extreme measure can be justified on both practical and theoretical grounds.

A potentially divergent process is of no practical use to man or machine, so its occurrence in a specification can only be a mistake. Its occurrence in a program submitted for execution on a computer is an even worse mistake. There is no point in making subtle distinctions between different kinds of mistakes; it is much simpler to lump them all together and call them T.

The theoretical justification comes from the simplest and most widely accepted theory of recursion, proposed by Dana Scott [3], to which we give a very simple introduction. A *finite* process is one that can be described by a single expression without using recursion, so the expression's ultimate components can only be T. An infinite process is determined by the set of all finite processes (called approximations) that are equal to it or less precise than it. The set of approximations that determines a recursively defined process,

$$R = F(R)$$

is generated by iterating or unfolding the function of *F*:

$$R = \bigcup_{n \geq 0} \{X \mid X \text{ is finite and } X \geq F^n(\mathrm{T})\}$$

where

$$F^0(X) \quad = X$$

$$F^{n+1}(X) = F(F^n(X))$$

For example, the approximations of $K0$ are

$$\{T, (!0 \rightarrow T), (!0 \rightarrow !0 \rightarrow T), \ldots\}$$

and those of *SINK* are

$$\{T, (?x \rightarrow T), (?x \rightarrow ?x \rightarrow T), \ldots\}$$

In the case of a guarded recursion, each successive approximation reveals more and more of the process's initial behavior. For an unguarded recursion like *DIV*, however, *all* the approximations are equal to T; hence *DIV* also is equal to T, which is the most general and least precise of all solutions of its defining equation.

The finite approximations of a process described by an introduced operator like interleaving are obtained by applying the operator to the approximations of its operands. For example, a typical approximation of

$$K0 \gg SINK$$

involves n outputs by $K0$ and m inputs by *SINK*:

$$(!0 \rightarrow !0 \rightarrow \ldots \rightarrow T) \gg (?x \rightarrow ?x \rightarrow \ldots T)$$

By the laws that define chaining, all such approximations are equal to T, and so is the chain itself.

8 *Choice*

Suppose I have the opportunity of using a process P described by the disjunction

$$P = P1 \vee P2$$

where $P1 = !e \rightarrow P1$ and $P2 = (?x \rightarrow P2x)$. The process P may start with either output or input, and I cannot predict or control which the first action will be. If I want the process to input it may actually output; and if I want it to output, it may input. In the first case, I would have preferred to use a process described by the stronger specification $P1$; in the second case, I would have preferred one satisfying the stronger specification $P2$. Their disjunction P is adequate only in cases in which I really don't care which the first action is, and in which I would be equally satisfied with *P*1 or *P*2. So *P*1 is always as good as *P*, and sometimes better.

Thus we can interpret the ordering

$$P1 \leq P$$

to mean that a process with specification *P*1 is (in general) more predictable than *P*, more controllable, and more useful in all circumstances than a process of which the strongest thing we know is that it may behave like *P*1 or like *P*2.

This reasoning shows that alternative behaviors are never a desirable possibility in a delivered product. The value of disjunction lies in the specification: It abstracts from detail and allows alternative implementations. As a *specification*, therefore, (*P*1 ∨ *P*2) can actually be *better* than *P*1, provided that it is easier or cheaper to implement.

Now I want to specify a new kind of process whose first action is either input or output. However, I also specify that *I myself* wish to choose between these alternatives *after* the process has been made and delivered to me. Thus the process must initially be *ready* to input (if that's what I eventually choose), and it must be initially ready to output (if that's what I choose instead). It is not permitted for the implementer to make this choice before delivery. To express this new requirement, a new operator ▯ is introduced into our notation:

$$(\,!e \rightarrow P)\ ▯\ (?x \rightarrow Qx)$$

describes a process that initially offers a choice of input or output. Only one of these actions will actually occur. If the first action is input, the subsequent behavior of the process will be described by *P*; if the first action is input of a message value *m*, the subsequent behavior will be (*Qm*).

The meaning of the new operator is made more precise by the following axioms.

1. Like most other operators, ▯ is strict and disjunctive.

2. A choice between input and output is the same as a choice between output and input:

$$(\,!e \rightarrow P)\ ▯\ (?x \rightarrow Px)\ =\ (?x \rightarrow Px)\ ▯\ (\,!e \rightarrow P)$$

This law is not guarded, and gives no way to eliminate the ▯ operator, even from finite processes.

3. A choice between input and input is impossible for me to make. Both alternatives remain possible, however, so the effect of ▯ is the same as that of disjunction:

$$(?x \rightarrow Px)\ ▯\ (?y \rightarrow Qy)\ =\ (?x \rightarrow Px) \vee (?y \rightarrow Qy)$$

4. Choice between outputs is also impossible. I am not allowed to look at the message about to be delivered before making my choice:

$$(!e \rightarrow P) \parallel (!f \rightarrow Q) \ = \ (!e \rightarrow P) \vee (!f \rightarrow Q)$$

5. Finally, a process that offers a choice can never be worse than one that may make that choice arbitrarily:

$$P \parallel Q \ \leq \ P \vee Q$$

This axiom may seem strange; it could be replaced (if you prefer) by postulating idempotence of $\parallel$, which is more obvious, and from which this axiom can be proved.

These laws are adequate for proof of the most obvious properties of choice.

Theorem

The operator $\parallel$ is idempotent, symmetric, and associative. Furthermore, $\vee$ distributes through $\parallel$.

The introduction of a new primitive operator to describe a new feature of the behavior of processes now requires that all previous definitions of operators be extended to deal with this new case; all theorems should also be re-examined. Instead, however, we will give definitions of two completely new operators $\widehat{\gg}$ and $\widehat{\parallel\parallel}$, which are very similar to $\gg$ and $\parallel\parallel$ except that whenever there are alternative actions, the user is offered a choice between them. Both operators are strict and disjunctive.

Axiom   Let

$$P \ = \ (c1 \rightarrow P1) \parallel (c2 \rightarrow P2)$$
$$Q \ = \ (d1 \rightarrow Q1) \parallel (d2 \rightarrow Q2)$$

Then

$$\begin{aligned} P \ \widehat{\parallel\parallel} \ Q \ &= \ (c1 \rightarrow (P1 \ \widehat{\parallel\parallel} \ Q)) \parallel (c2 \rightarrow (P2 \ \widehat{\parallel\parallel} \ Q) \\ &\quad \parallel (d1 \rightarrow (P \ \widehat{\parallel\parallel} \ Q1)) \parallel (d2 \rightarrow (P \ \widehat{\parallel\parallel} \ Q2)) \end{aligned}$$

The relevant equation when P or Q does not initially offer choice can be deduced from this by idempotence of $\parallel$.

The distribution law for $\widehat{\gg}$ is more complicated. Let

$$P \ = \ (?x \rightarrow P1x) \parallel (!e \rightarrow P2)$$
$$Q \ = \ (?y \rightarrow Q1y) \parallel (!f \rightarrow Q2)$$

Then we define

$$P \overset{\gg}{\gg} Q = (R \,[\!]\, S) \vee R$$

where

$$R = P2 \overset{\gg}{\gg} (Q1e)$$

$$S = (?x \to (P1x \overset{\gg}{\gg} Q)) \,[\!]\, (!f \to (P \overset{\gg}{\gg} Q2))$$

The process R describes what happens when the internal concealed communication occurs first; this may happen autonomously and outside the control or knowledge of the user. The process S describes what happens if the user engages in a communication before the internal communication has occurred. The asymmetric combination of R and S by $[\!]$ and $\vee$ is necessary: $(R \,[\!]\, S)$ offers the user too much choice, and $(R \vee S)$ too little, while $(R \,[\!]\, S \vee R)$ is a compromise which can be efficiently implemented.

Using these improved operators, we can define improved versions of the bounded and unbounded buffers and bags:

$$\hat{B}_1 \quad \hat{=} \quad \hat{C}_1 \hat{=} C$$

$$\hat{B}_{n+1} \quad \hat{=} \quad \hat{B}_n \,\widehat{|\!|\!|}\, C$$

$$\hat{C}_{n+1} \quad \hat{=} \quad \hat{C}_n \overset{\gg}{\gg} C$$

$$\widehat{BAG} \quad \hat{=} \quad (?x \to (\widehat{BAG} \,\widehat{|\!|\!|}\, (!x \to C)))$$

$$\widehat{BUF} \quad \hat{=} \quad (?x \to (\widehat{BUF} \overset{\gg}{\gg} (!x \to C)))$$

For these processes, one can no longer prove such undesirable properties as

$$\hat{B}_n \leq \hat{B}_{n+1} \leq \widehat{BAG}$$

$$\hat{C}_n \leq \hat{C}_{n+1} \leq \widehat{BUF}$$

$$SINK \leq \widehat{BAG}$$

$$SINK \leq \widehat{BUF}$$

However, they satisfy many of the more desirable algebraic equations.

It is useful also to define buffers and bags in a way that allows *any* finite buffer size, either with a limit n or without one:

$$BB_1 \quad \hat{=} \quad BC_1 = C$$

$$BB_{n+1} \quad \hat{=} \quad \hat{B}_{n+1} \vee BB_n$$

$$BC_{n+1} \quad \hat{=} \quad \hat{C}_{n+1} \vee BC_n$$

$$BBAG \quad \hat{=} \quad (?x \to ((!x \to C) \vee (BBAG \,\widehat{|\!|\!|}\, (!x \to C))))$$

$$BBUF \quad \hat{=} \quad (?x \to ((!x \to C) \vee (BBUF \overset{\gg}{\gg} (!x \to C))))$$

It would be interesting to see whether these processes can be composed into arbitrary serial and parallel networks, in the same way as the mail services defined in Section 6.

9 *Acknowledgments*

The technical substance of this paper is due primarily to A. W. Roscoe [2] and He Jifeng. The idea of defining the concept of a process by its algebra is due to Robin Milner [1], and the application of algebra to the specification and proof of properties of protocols has been developed in a series of papers by the ACP group at CWI, Amsterdam.

References

[1] Milner, Robin. *Communication and Concurrency.* Prentice-Hall International, Hemel Hempstead, U.K., 1989.

[2] Roscoe, A. W. and Hoare, C. A. R. "The laws of occam programming". Technical Monograph PRG–53, Programming Research Group, Oxford University Computing Laboratory, 1986.

[3] Scott, D. S. "Outline of a mathematical theory of computation". *Proceedings of the Fourth Annual Princeton Conference on Information Science and Systems*, pp. 169–176, 1970.

Design and Proof
of a
Mail Service

10

C. A. R. Hoare
He Jifeng
Oxford University

Abstract

*T*he design of a complicated system may proceed through many stages in its progress from specification to implementation. The correctness of the implementation should be established by subjecting each design decision to careful proof. This recommendation is illustrated here by the first stage in the specification and design of a simplified mail service. The fundamental theorem is that such a service can be implemented by a store-and-forward message-passing network, including both serial and concurrent links. The definitions and proof methods are those of a simplified trace model of Communicating Sequential Processes (CSP) [1].

1 *Definition of a Mail Service*

A mail service is a communication mechanism that accepts messages and delivers them later, though possibly in an order different from that of acceptance. If there are several messages posted but not yet delivered, it is nondeterministic which of them will be delivered next. In this paper we make the gross simplifications that there is only one sender and only one recipient and that the buffering capacity of the mail service is unlimited.

The first task is to formalize the specification just described. This will be done by describing a typical finite sequence *tr*, recording the communications of the service up to an arbitrary moment in time. The elements of the sequence are either inputs ?*m* or outputs !*m*, where *m* is the value of the message communicated. We use the following notations:

  $bag(s)$ is the *bag* (multiset) of messages in *s*.

  $s{\downarrow}?$ is the sequence of messages whose input is recorded in *s*.

  $s{\downarrow}!$ is the sequence of output messages in *s*.

For example, if

   $s = \langle ?3, ?4, !4, ?3, !3 \rangle$

then

   $s{\downarrow}! = \langle 4, 3 \rangle$

and

   $bag(s{\downarrow}?) = \{3, 3, 4\}$

Now, the specification of the mail service states that it outputs only messages it has previously received, or, more formally, we define

   $MAIL \ \hat{=} \ bag(tr{\downarrow}!) \subseteq bag(tr{\downarrow}?)$

where $\subseteq$ denotes inclusion of bags.

2 *Composition in Series*

Suppose now that we wish to implement a mail service by two connected processes *P* and *Q*, each of which perhaps traverses only part of the total distance between the sender and the receiver. To achieve this, the channel on which *P* outputs messages is connected to the channel on which *Q* inputs them (Figure 1). A message passes on the connecting channel only when *P* outputs it at the same instant as Q inputs it. This event, however, is totally concealed from the users of the service, who communicate only with the input channel of P and the output channel of Q. This kind of connection in series is modeled in CSP by the chaining operator $\gg$.

A more formal specification of $P \gg Q$ is given in terms of the specifications of its operands P and Q. Let s be a trace of P, let t be a trace of Q, and let tr be a trace of $(P \gg Q)$. Then the sequence of messages $tr\!\downarrow$? input by $(P \gg Q)$ is the same as the input of $(s\!\downarrow?)P$, and similarly $tr\!\downarrow!$ is always equal to the output of $(t\!\downarrow!)Q$. Furthermore, because the internal communication is synchronized, the outputs of $(s\!\downarrow!)P$ are at all times the same as the inputs of $(t\!\downarrow!)Q$. Let P_s^{tr} and Q_t^{tr} stand for the specifications P and Q in which every occurence of tr has been replaced by s and t, respectively. For simplicity, the chaining operator is specified by an implication rather than an equivalence— that is all we shall need in a proof of design correctness.

$$P \gg Q \implies \exists s, t . P_s^{tr} \wedge Q_t^{tr} \wedge tr\!\downarrow? = s\!\downarrow? \wedge tr\!\downarrow! = t\!\downarrow! \wedge s\!\downarrow! = t\!\downarrow?$$

(*Technical Note:* This implication is valid provided that there is no risk of an unbounded sequence of consecutive communications on the connecting channel. In the example of a *MAIL* service, this is guaranteed by the fact that the number of outputs never exceeds the number of inputs.)

We now return to the design of the mail service, in which the next question is: What should be the specifications of the components P and Q, to ensure that their composition in series $(P \gg Q)$ will meet the original specification *MAIL*? With a modest flash of insight, we guess that P and Q should also be mail services. This insight needs to be checked by proving that the design

Figure 1. $P \gg Q$.

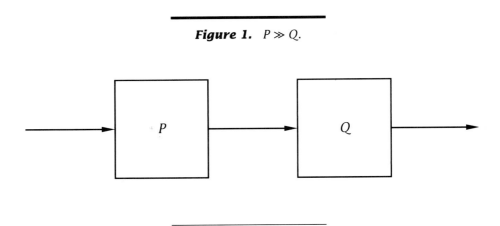

satisfies the original specification, i.e., that

$$(MAIL \gg MAIL) \Longrightarrow MAIL$$

The proof is given in Figure 2.

3 *Composition in Parallel*

Suppose now that we wish to implement a mail service by a pair of independent concurrent processes P and Q, each of which links the sender with the receiver, but by different routes. The processes are composed (Figure 3) in such a way that any message posted may be transmitted by either P or Q, the choice being made (nondeterministically) by the service and not by the sender. Similarly, the recipient of the message cannot choose whether the received message comes via P or via Q; that will depend on which of them has a waiting message, and if both have, the choice is nondeterministic. This kind of parallelism is modeled in CSP by the interleaving operator $|||$.

We must now give a more formal specification of $P \,|||\, Q$ in terms of the specifications of its operands P and Q. Any trace of $(P \,|||\, Q)$ is an interleaving of some trace of s of P and some trace of Q. More formally,

$$(P \,|||\, Q) \Longrightarrow \exists s, t \,.\, tr \in int(s, t) \wedge P_s^{tr} \wedge Q_t^{tr}$$

To proceed with the design of the mail service, we need to decide what specification of P and Q will ensure that their composition $(P \,|||\, Q)$ will meet the original specification *MAIL*. More formally, we must find predicates P and

---

Figure 2. $MAIL \gg MAIL \Longrightarrow MAIL.$

$MAIL \gg MAIL$

{expanding the definitions}

$\Longrightarrow \exists s, t \,.\, tr{\downarrow}? = s{\downarrow}? \wedge tr{\downarrow}! = t{\downarrow}! \wedge s{\downarrow}! = t{\downarrow}?$

$\qquad\qquad \wedge\, bag(s{\downarrow}!) \subseteq bag(s{\downarrow}?) \wedge bag(t{\downarrow}!) \subseteq bag(t{\downarrow}?)$

{by substitution of identities}

$\Longrightarrow \exists s, t \,.\, bag(s{\downarrow}!) \subseteq bag(tr{\downarrow}?) \wedge bag(tr{\downarrow}!) \subseteq bag(s{\downarrow}!)$

{by transitivity of $\subseteq$}

$\Longrightarrow bag(tr{\downarrow}!) \subseteq bag(tr{\downarrow}?)$

Q such that

$P \,|||\, Q \implies MAIL$

Again, the obvious suggestion is that P and Q should themselves be mail services; the correctness of this idea can be assured by proving

$(MAIL \,|||\, MAIL) \implies MAIL$

An outline of the proof is given in Figure 4.

4 *The Components*

The previous two sections have shown that a mail service can be constructed from a pair of smaller mail services by composition either in series or in parallel. Each of these mail services can again be split (in series or in parallel) into two yet smaller services; the result will still be a mail service. For example,

$[(((MAIL \,|||\, MAIL \,|||\, MAIL) \gg MAIL) \,|||\, (MAIL \gg MAIL)] \implies MAIL$

The proof of this depends only on the monotonicity of the operators $|||$ and $\gg$ with respect to logical implication; for example,

$P1 \,|||\, Q \implies P2 \,|||\, Q$ whenever $P1 \implies P2.$

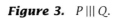

Figure 3. $P \,|||\, Q.$

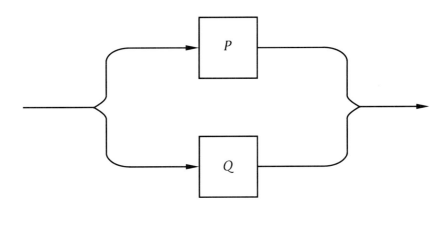

We are left only with the task of designing and implementing the ultimate link components of this serial-parallel network.

A telegraph service is like a mail service in that it delivers only messages that have previously been posted, but with the additional guarantee of delivery in the same order as posting. More formally, let $s \leq t$ mean that t begins with a copy of s. Then the telegraph service can be specified:

$$TEL \triangleq (tr{\downarrow}! \leq tr{\downarrow}?)$$

From this definition, it can be shown that serial composition of telegraph services is also a telegraph service. The simple proof is left as an exercise.

To show that a telegraph service is an implementation of a mail service, it is necessary only to prove

$$TEL \implies MAIL$$

which is an immediate consequence of the fact that

$$s \leq t \implies bag(s) \subseteq bag(t)$$

Because of monotonicity, we can immediately conclude (for example) that

$$[((TEL \,|||\, TEL) \gg TEL) \,|||\, (TEL \gg TEL)] \implies MAIL$$

—a fact which (when you think about it) may appear less than immediately obvious.

Figure 4.   *MAIL* ||| *MAIL* ⟹ *MAIL*.

$MAIL \,|||\, MAIL$

{by expanding the definitions}

$\implies \exists s, t . \; tr \in int(s, t) \wedge bag(s{\downarrow}!) \subseteq bag(s{\downarrow}?) \wedge bag(t{\downarrow}!) \subseteq bag(t{\downarrow}?)$

{adding the inequalities}

$\implies \exists s, t . \; tr \in int(s, t) \wedge bag(s{\downarrow}!) + bag(t{\downarrow}!) \subseteq bag(s{\downarrow}?) + bag(t{\downarrow}?)$

{$tr{\downarrow}! \in int(s{\downarrow}!, t{\downarrow}!)$ and $tr{\downarrow}! \in int(s{\downarrow}?, t{\downarrow}?)$; and the bag of an interleaving is the sum of the bags of the interleaved sequences}

$\implies bag(tr{\downarrow}!) \subseteq bag(tr{\downarrow}?)$

---

5 *Discussion*

This paper illustrates the fundamental principles of software engineering that a system should be properly specified before implementation, that the design should be broken down into parts, and that the correctness of this decomposition should be proved before more detailed coding starts.

We have used the definitions and proof methods of the theory of Communication Sequential Processes [1], simplified and specialized for the task at hand. More complicated methods are required to prove identities such as

$$MAIL \;=\; MAIL \,|||\, MAIL \;=\; MAIL \gg MAIL$$
$$=\; MAIL \,|||\, TEL \;=\; MAIL \gg TEL$$
$$=\; TEL \gg MAIL$$

In order to strengthen implication to equivalence, it is necessary to be more precise about the exact set of traces of the process being specified. Consider, for example, the trace

$$s = \langle ?3, !3, !7, ?7, ?12 \rangle$$
$$s{\downarrow} = \langle 3, 7 \rangle \quad s{\downarrow}? = \langle 3, 7, 12 \rangle$$

This trace satisfies the specification both of *MAIL* and of *TEL*. In fact, however, such a trace is impossible because it would require that after the first three communications the trace must have been

$$\langle ?3, !3, !7 \rangle$$

and this subtrace does *not* satisfy the specification. (Indeed, it would be possible only for clairvoyant service, which could foresee that the next input is going to be ?7.)

Hence we need to strengthen the specification, excluding all traces having any initial subsequence that fails to satisfy the specification. For example, *MAIL* and *TEL* should be strengthened respectively to

$$\forall s. s \leq tr \implies bag(s{\downarrow}!) \subseteq bag(s{\downarrow}?)$$

and

$$\forall s. s \leq tr \implies s{\downarrow}! \leq s{\downarrow}?$$

In order to simplify this kind of strengthening of specifications, we define a modal operator

$$\Box P \;\triangleq\; (\forall s. s \leq tr \Longleftarrow P_s^{tr})$$

It is easy to show that $\Box\Box P = \Box P$ and $\Box P \Rightarrow P$. A specification P is said to be *prefix-closed* if it is true of the empty trace, and

$$P = \Box P$$

The definition of the interleaving operator can be strengthened from an inequality to an equation provided that its operands are prefix-closed:

$$(\Box P) \,|||\, (\Box Q) \;\; = \;\; \exists s, t \,.\, tr \in int(s, t) \wedge (\Box P)_s^{tr} \wedge (\Box Q)_t^{tr}$$

The result of such an interleaving is also prefix-closed. The definition of the chaining operator $\gg$ can be similarly strengthened.

Another simplification in the formal apparatus of this paper is that we have specified only the safety properties of the services, ignoring liveness. For example, the empty trace $\langle\rangle$ satisfies both predicates *MAIL* and *TEL*; hence the process STOP (which immediately deadlocks and has $\langle\rangle$ as its only trace) will satisfy both our specifications. An even more subtle danger is that the implementation will meet the specification but refuse to output until at least three messages are waiting for output, or refuse to input whenever an output reduces the number of waiting messages to an exact nonzero multiple of 13.

In order to exclude such bizarre behavior, we need to be able to describe it. The easiest known way of doing this is to introduce two new variables which (like *tr*) have conventional meanings:

inr (inready) is false when the process is in a stable state, but *not* waiting
  for input.

outr (outready) is false when the process is in a stable state, but *not* waiting
  for output.

To specify that a process never deadlocks, one of these conditions must always be true:

inr ∨ *outr*

To rule out bizarre behavior in an unbounded communication service, we specify that it must always be ready to input and that it must always be ready to output as long as there is a waiting message. So our specification of *MAIL* and *TEL* must be strengthened by the addition of

$$LIVE \;\triangleq\; inr \wedge (outr \vee \#tr\!\downarrow! = \#tr\!\downarrow?)$$

(For technical reasons, the readiness variables must never be directly or indirectly negated in a specification.) For a bounded communication service, the liveness condition for input should be weakened to

$$inr \lor \#tr{\downarrow}! < \#tr{\downarrow}? - n)$$

This allows (but does not compel) refusal of further input when the buffer reaches a certain size. (To compel refusal, add the clause $(tr{\downarrow}? \leq tr{\downarrow}! + M).$) The definition of $\gg$ also needs to be changed to deal with readiness. For further details, see [1].

The removal of the simplifications in the mathematical apparatus makes it possible to prove theorems that are more powerful and more useful. It still remains, however, to remove the gross oversimplification in our model of a communication network. In practice, such a network must serve many senders and many receivers; for this purpose, each node of the network will have additional input and output channels to serve its local users. This will require significant changes in the specifications of the service, the nodes, and the operations by which the nodes are connected. To deal with the additional complexity will require the use of yet more powerful mathematical laws, many of which remain to be discovered.

This paper suggests that in principle it would be possible to prove the correctness of the design of a complete network protocol before embarking on the implementation of the individual nodes. Whether such a project is worthwhile is another question.

Reference

[1] Hoare, C. A. R. *Communicating Sequential Processes.* Prentice-Hall International, Hemel Hempstead, U.K., 1985.

Proofs of Distributed Algorithms

An Exercise

11

K. Mani Chandy
California Institute of Technology

Jayadev Misra
University of Texas at Austin

1 Introduction

It is generally assumed that formal proofs of programs are considerably longer and more tedious than their informal counterparts. Informal proofs employ a form of common-sense reasoning whereby "obvious" facts are often omitted and the steps in the proof rely upon the intuition of the reader. Typically informal proofs are operational; arguments consist of the properties of program executions as they unfold over time.

Our goal in this paper is to suggest, by means of an example, that formal proofs can be made as concise as the informal ones. This argument rests upon two observations: (1) Informal proofs tend to be long and difficult (in addition to being error-prone) when there are many interleaved execution sequences to consider, as is the case in multiprocess programs, and (2) formal proofs can be made concise by employing a logic that is appropriate for the problem domain and whose operators possess a number of useful properties that can be exploited in proofs.

In recent years, we have developed a programming and proof theory called UNITY [3]. Our experience in using the UNITY proof theory on a wide range of problems has led us to believe that formal proofs need not be outrageously long or tedious. In this paper, we apply the UNITY proof theory to a problem in distributed computing: termination detection. We specify the problem and develop a correctness proof of a solution without relying upon the operational aspects of program execution. Use of our logic allows us to eliminate arguments about a program's execution sequences. We believe strongly that formal proofs cannot be made concise as long as they mimic the arguments in the informal proofs.

Most of this paper is about UNITY theory and the specification of message-communicating processes; only Sections 4 and 6 contain the proof of the termination-detection algorithm. The paper is self-contained; no familiarity with UNITY or termination detection is assumed.

1.1 *Termination Detection*

Here we give a brief informal overview of the termination-detection problem and its proposed solution.

We are given a finite set of processes that communicate by messages. A process sends a message to another process by depositing it in a channel that is directed from the former to the latter; the message is received after an arbitrary, but finite, delay and is then removed from the channel. A process is either *idle* or *nonidle*. An idle process remains idle until it receives a message, and an idle process does not send messages. A nonidle process may become idle autonomously. The system of processes is said to be *terminated* when all processes are idle and all channels are empty, because all processes will remain idle and all channels will remain empty from then on. The problem of termination detection is for some process to ascertain that the system has terminated; in order to do so, processes carry out some additional termination-detection computation along with their basic computation.

The following algorithm can be employed to detect termination. From time to time, each process records its state (idle or nonidle), the number of messages it has received along each of its incoming channels, and the number of messages it has sent along each of its outgoing channels. Different processes may record these values at different times. Clearly, the recorded values become obsolete if a process sends or receives a message or changes its state. Remarkably, though, the system is terminated if the recorded state of each process is idle and if for each channel the recorded number of messages sent is equal to the recorded number of messages received. Therefore the synchronous computation required to detect termination can be replaced by asynchronous recordings and computations.

As a trivial optimization, note that processes need not do any recording as long as they are nonidle —because the recorded state of a process will then be nonidle and hence the termination condition would not be met— and therefore only the number of messages sent and received along incident channels need be recorded by a process when it is idle. The nondeterminism inherent in this solution —there is no restriction on *when* a process records— makes it possible to develop a number of different algorithms from the one just sketched by specifying the order of recording. We shall outline two algorithms that are obtained by restricting the order of recordings.

The detection algorithm may employ a single token. Computation involving the token is separate from the given underlying computation; thus, idle processes in the underlying computation may send and receive the token. The token visits the processes in some fixed order, carrying all the recorded information (the recorded states of all processes and the recorded number of messages sent and received for each channel). A process does the recording sometime after it receives the token; it then updates the recorded information in the token appropriately and sends the token to the next process. Termination is detected by the token (or by the process holding the token or by a prespecified "detector" process) if the recorded information shows each process to be idle and each channel to be empty. Note that the introduction of the token is merely an artifact for restricting the order in which the recordings are made. Correctness of this solution follows from the correctness (yet to be shown) of the original nondeterministic solution.

Another strategy is to introduce a special process, *detector*, that sends messages to all other processes asking them to record and send it the recorded information. The detector can declare termination based on the information it receives from the processes. The order in which the detector queries the processes is irrelevant for correctness.

Now we sketch an informal proof of correctness of the proposed solution. This proof relies on the reader's intuition about how a message-communicating system operates. The proof has the flavor of a typical informal proof of a distributed algorithm; it is not necessary to read this proof for understanding the main ideas —formal proofs in UNITY— of this paper.

Let the recorded state of each process be idle and the recorded number of messages sent and received be equal for each channel. We show that the system is then terminated. Assume the contrary. Then there is a process, i, that became nonidle after it last recorded its state. Process i can become nonidle only by receiving a message, say message m from process j. Consider the following events and the times at which the events occur:

Time	Event
α :	process i last records its state (idle) and the message counts
β :	process i becomes nonidle (upon receiving message m)
γ :	process j sends message m
δ :	process j records its state (idle) and the message counts

Without loss in generality, let i be the first process to become nonidle after its last recording. We have $\alpha < \beta$; also, $\gamma < \beta$ because message m is sent at γ and received at β. Furthermore, $\gamma < \delta$. This is because (1) $\gamma \neq \delta$, since process j is idle at δ and nonidle at γ, and (2) if $\delta < \gamma$, then process j becomes nonidle at γ (or earlier) after its last recording (at δ); hence it becomes nonidle before β ($\gamma < \beta$), thus contradicting our choice of process i.

The diagram in Figure 1 depicts the relationships among α, β, γ, and δ schematically: An arrow is drawn from one time instant to another if the former precedes the latter.

Let

f = the number of messages sent by j to i as recorded by j (at time δ)

g = the number of messages received by i from j as recorded by i (at time α)

Since message m was received at β, and $\beta > \alpha$, this message is not included in the count g. Since f is recorded at δ and $\gamma < \delta$, message m is included in the count f. Therefore, $f \neq g$. This contradicts our assumption that the recorded numbers of messages sent and received for every channel are equal.

A number of implicit assumptions have crept into the informal proof. Presumably no process can perform a recording at the same time that it sends

---

Figure 1.   Relationships among certain instants in the recording algorithm.

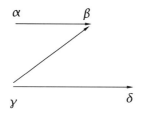

or receives a message. Similarly, it is assumed that no process can receive a message unless it has been sent earlier, i.e., sending and receiving of one message cannot be simultaneous. Furthermore, the last part of the proof assumes that messages are received in the order sent. The arguments dealing with time —events happening before or after some point in time— reflect the way we understand the program execution to unfold over time. One reason for constructing a formal proof is to make all assumptions explicit. Another is to replace arguments about unfolding computations —a temporal entity— by arguments about the program text —a nontemporal entity.

The formal proof that we propose in this paper is completely different in character. We do not argue about the program execution. Our arguments are based on programs' specifications and texts, not on their effects when executed on computers. We prove that the following is invariant for any set of processes X. If

1. All processes in X have been recorded idle,

2. For all internal channels of X (i.e., those directed between processes in X), equal number of sends and receives have been recorded, and

3. For all incoming channels to X (from processes outside X), the recorded number of receives equals the actual number of receives,

then

1. All processes in X are idle,

2. For all internal channels of X, the number of receives and sends are equal, and

3. For all outgoing channels from X (to processes outside X), the recorded number of sends equals the actual number of sends.

Letting X be the set of all processes in the preceding invariant —condition (3) in the antecedent of the invariant is then vacuously *true*— proves the desired theorem.

The problem of termination detection, and a solution for it, first appeared in [5]. The algorithm just sketched was invented by Chandy [1] and, independently, by Helary et al. [6]. A description of Chandy's algorithm appears in [11]. Proofs appear in [2, 9, 7]. Nondeterminism, first postulated by Dijkstra [4], is at the core of UNITY programming. UNITY logic is deeply influenced by temporal logic [10, 15].

2 *A Brief Introduction to UNITY*

In this section, we describe those aspects of UNITY that are essential for understanding this paper; for a full description see [3, Chapters 2, 3, and 7 in particular]. First we give a brief overview of the operational behavior of UNITY programs. We do not describe the syntax of UNITY programs in this paper; Section 3.4 gives a program whose syntax is explained with reference to that program alone.

2.1 *Operational Descriptions of UNITY Programs*

A UNITY program has a set of variables; initial values of (some of) these variables may be specified in the program. The body of the program consists of a finite set of multiple-assignment statements. A program execution starts in a state where the initial values of the variables are as specified. In each step of the execution, a statement from the program body is selected for execution. Statements are selected arbitrarily, with the restriction that in an infinite execution (i.e., an execution with an infinite number of steps), each statement is executed infinitely often.

Notions of process, channel, and message communication are not part of the UNITY theory. A UNITY program's variables and statements may be partitioned in various ways for execution on multiple processors. Such a partitioning does not affect the correctness of the program. Therefore we deal with correctness issues by ignoring the question of implementation of the program as a set of communicating processes at the outset.

2.2 *The Logical Operator unless*

Notational Convention   Throughout this paper p, q, r denote arbitrary predicates that may name program variables, bound variables, and free variables (free variables are those that are neither program variables nor bound variables), and F and G denote arbitrary UNITY programs. All formulae are (implicitly) quantified universally over all free variables appearing in them.

Safety properties are expressed by a logical operator, *unless*, which is defined as follows. For any program F,

$$\frac{\langle \forall\, t \,:\, t \text{ is a statement in } F \,::\, \{p \wedge \neg q\}\ t\ \{p \vee q\}\rangle}{p\ unless\ q\ \text{ in } F}$$

This inference rule should be read as follows: *p unless q* in F can be inferred provided that for every statement t in F, if $p \wedge \neg q$ holds prior to the execution of *t*, then $p \vee q$ holds upon completion of the execution of *t*. (We assume that execution of every statement always terminates.)

Note   The form of quantification shown in the foregoing definition appears several times in the paper. The notation $\{p\}\ s\ \{q\}$ is from [8].

From *p unless q* in *F* we can deduce that if *p* holds at any point during an execution of *F*, it continues to hold at least as long as *q* does not hold. To see this suppose that *p* holds at some point during an execution. If *q* holds then the foregoing claim is valid. If *q* does not hold, i.e., $p \wedge \neg q$ holds, then execution of any statement establishes $p \vee q$ in the next step. If $\neg q$ holds in the next step, then $p \wedge \neg q$ holds and the same argument can be repeated; if *q* holds then the claim is seen to be valid.

We define two more concepts using *unless*. In the following, "initially *p* in *F*" means that *p* follows from the initial conditions of program *F*.

> *p* stable in *F*   ≡   *p unless false* in *F*
>
> *p* invariant in *F* ≡   (initially *p* in *F*) $\wedge$ (*p* stable in *F*)

From the definition, *p* stable in *F* means that for all statements *t* in *F*,

> $\{p\}\ t\ \{p\}$

Thus, once *p* is *true* it remains *true*. An invariant is initially *true* and remains *true* throughout any execution of the program.

Notational Convention   The program name is omitted from a property if it is clear from the context.

2.3 *Derived Rules About unless*

For formal proofs in this paper, we do not rely on the intuitive meaning of *unless*; instead we use the following derived rules, proofs of which may be found in [3, Section 3.6.1]; also see [13].

1. Consequence weakening

$$\frac{p \ unless \ q \ , \ q \Rightarrow r}{p \ unless \ r}$$

2. Conjunction and disjunction

$$\frac{p \ unless \ q \ , \ p' \ unless \ q'}{\begin{array}{l} p \wedge p' \ unless \ (p \wedge q') \vee (p' \wedge q) \vee (q \wedge q') \qquad \{\text{conjunction}\}, \\ p \vee p' \ unless \ (\neg p \wedge q') \vee (\neg p' \wedge q) \vee (q \wedge q') \quad \{\text{disjunction}\} \end{array}}$$

Simpler forms of conjunction and disjunction are often useful; these are obtained from the above rule by weakening the consequence to $q \vee q'$ in both cases:

3. Simple conjunction and simple disjunction

$$\frac{p \ unless \ q \ , \ p' \ unless \ q'}{}$$

$p \wedge p' \ unless \ q \vee q'$ {simple conjunction}

$p \vee p' \ unless \ q \vee q'$ {simple disjunction}

The following rules generalize the conjunction and disjunction rules to an arbitrary —perhaps infinite— number of *unless*es; for a proof, see [12]. In the following, m is quantified over some arbitrary set.

4. General conjunction

$$\frac{\langle \forall \ m \ :: \ p.m \ unless \ q.m \rangle}{\langle \forall \ m \ :: \ p.m \rangle \ unless \langle \forall \ m \ :: \ p.m \vee q.m \rangle \ \wedge \ \langle \exists \ m \ :: \ q.m \rangle}$$

5. General disjunction

$$\frac{\langle \forall \ m \ :: \ p.m \ unless \ q.m \rangle}{\langle \exists \ m \ :: \ p.m \rangle \ unless \langle \forall \ m \ :: \ \neg p.m \vee q.m \rangle \ \wedge \ \langle \exists \ m \ :: \ q.m \rangle}$$

The following rule is a corollary of general disjunction:

6. Free-variable elimination

$$\frac{p \ \wedge \ x = k \ \ unless \ \ q}{p \ \ unless \ \ q}$$

where x is a set of program variables and k is free.

Axiom   (Substitution Axiom)

The substitution axiom allows us to replace any invariant by *true*, and vice versa, in any predicate occurring in a property. Thus, given that I is invariant, we may conclude from

$p \ \wedge \ I \ unless \ q$

that

$p \ unless \ q$

2.4 *Program Composition by union*

As in other programming theories, it is often convenient to view or design a UNITY program as a composition of several program components. In this paper, we consider a particularly simple kind of program composition: *union*. The union of programs F and G, denoted by F [] G, is obtained by combining the appropriate portions of F and G. In particular, the variables of F [] G are the ones in F or G; a variable is initialized to a value as prescribed in F or in G (we assume that if the initial value of a variable is prescribed in both F and G then these initial values are identical); and the set of statements in the body of F [] G is the union of the corresponding sets of F and G.

The union operation is often referred to as "parallel composition". This is the primary structuring mechanism for building networks of processes that communicate by messages or shared variables; see [3] for details.

We describe one part of the union theorem that is fundamental for the study of the union operation; for the proof of this theorem, see [3, Section 7.2.1] and [13].

Union Theorem   (Safety)

$$p \ \textit{unless} \ q \ \text{ in } F \,[]\, G \ = \ (p \ \textit{unless} \ q \text{ in } F) \ \wedge \ (p \ \textit{unless} \ q \text{ in } G)$$

Corollary 1

$$p \text{ is stable in } F \,[]\, G \ = \ (p \text{ is stable in } F) \ \wedge \ (p \text{ is stable in } G)$$

Corollary 2

$$\frac{p \text{ is stable in } F, \ p \text{ is invariant in } G}{p \text{ is invariant in } F \,[]\, G}$$

A particularly useful observation about the stability of a predicate p is that p is stable in F if p mentions no variable that can be changed in F.

Note   For a composite program, the substitution axiom can be applied only with an invariant of the composite program. Thus it is illegal to: (1) deduce p *unless* q in F using the substitution axiom with an invariant of F, and (2) deduce p *unless* q in G using the substitution axiom with an invariant of G and then deduce p *unless* q in F [] G applying the union theorem. Such a deduction is valid provided the substitution axiom is applied in each case with an invariant of F [] G.

3 *Problem Description*

Let program D denote the programs for the given set of message-communicating processes. Properties of D are described in Section 3.2; some notations are introduced in Section 3.1 to facilitate this description. We view the problem of termination detection as designing a recording program R such that in the composite program $D \, [] \, R$ some predicate p holds only if D is terminated; in our case, program R contains statements to record the states of each process and the number of messages it sends/receives along the channels incident on it, and predicate p states that the recorded states of all processes are idle and that all channels are empty. Note that R only reads but does not write into the variables of D.

3.1 *Notation*

We use symbols i, j for processes and W, X, Y for sets of processes. The set of all processes (assumed finite and nonempty) is denoted by Z. The symbol $\overline{X}$ denotes the complement of X, i.e., the set of processes not in X. Let $q.i$ be *true* iff process i is idle; $q.X$ is the conjunction of $q.i$, for all i in X. Symbol c is used to denote a channel; $r.c$ and $s.c$ are the number of messages received along c and sent along c, respectively. The set of channels directed from processes in X to processes in Y will be denoted by XY. In particular, XZ is the set of all outgoing channels from the processes in X (including those directed between the processes in X) and ZX is the set of all incoming channels to the processes in X (including those directed between the processes in X). Hence the set of outgoing channels of process i is denoted by iZ and the incoming ones by Zi; assume that no channel is directed from a process to itself, i.e., ii is empty for all i.

A particularly useful notational abbreviation for a predicate over a set of channels is $p.XY$, where p is of the form $(s = r)$, $(s \geq r)$ or $(s > r)$. These are defined as follows:

$$(s = r).XY \;\equiv\; \langle \forall c \,:\, c \text{ in } XY \,::\, s.c = r.c \rangle$$

$$(s \geq r).XY \;\equiv\; \langle \forall c \,:\, c \text{ in } XY \,::\, s.c \geq r.c \rangle$$

$$(s > r).XY \;\equiv\; (s \geq r).XY \,\wedge\, \neg(s = r).XY$$

Observe that for $p.XY$ of the first or the second form,

$$p.XY \qquad\qquad = \quad true \text{ if } X \text{ or } Y \text{ is empty}$$

$$p.(X \cup X')(Y \cup Y') \;=\; p.XY \,\wedge\, p.XY' \,\wedge\, p.X'Y \,\wedge\, p.YY'$$

In particular,

$$p.XZ \;=\; p.XX \land p.X\overline{X}$$
$$p.ZX \;=\; p.XX \land p.\overline{X}X$$

For *p.XY* of the third form,

$$p.XY \;=\; \textit{false} \quad \text{if } X \text{ or } Y \text{ is empty}$$
$$p.XZ \;\Rightarrow\; p.XX \lor p.X\overline{X}$$
$$p.ZX \;\Rightarrow\; p.XX \lor p.\overline{X}X$$

Throughout this paper *L.XY* denotes a free variable (of type, set of integers) that has one integer corresponding to each channel in *XY*.

3.2 *Specification of Program D*

Program *D* has the following properties. The number of messages sent along any channel is at least the number received, and both of these are nonnegative (D1). The number of messages received along a channel is nondecreasing, as is the number of messages sent (D2). An idle process remains idle as long as it does not receive a message (D3) (it may stay idle after receiving a message). An idle process does not send messages (D4).

We reiterate that the notions of process, channel, message, etc. are outside the UNITY theory. Thus, program *D* manipulates the variables $q.i$, $r.c$, $s.c$, for all i and c, without assigning them meanings. The restrictions that we put on *D* for manipulations of these variables reflect the nature of a message-communicating system; this was described informally earlier, and is described formally next.

In (D1–D4) the properties are of program *D*. The symbols m and n denote arbitrary integer constants.

Property D1

$s.c \geq r.c \geq 0$ invariant

Property D2

$r.c \geq m$ stable

$s.c \geq n$ stable

Property D3

$q.i \wedge (r = L).Zi \; unless \; (r > L).Zi$

Property D4

$q.i \wedge (s = L).iZ \; unless \; \neg q.i \wedge (s = L).iZ$

The reader may understand D3 and D4 better by writing them out in terms of pre- and postconditions, using the definition of *unless*. For instance, D4 says that for any statement t in D,

$$\{q.i \wedge (s = L).iZ\} \; t \; \{(s = L).iZ\}$$

That is, execution of a statement never causes an idle process to send a message.

Observation   The variables $q.i$, $r.c$, $s.c$ are *local* to program D, i.e., they cannot be modified in any other program G. Therefore, using the union theorem and its corollaries, properties (D1–D4) are also properties of $D \, [] \, G$, for any G.

Note   We have not specified that the channels be first-in-first-out, nor that every message be delivered eventually. These are not required for the correctness of the proposed termination-detection algorithm. Also, several processes may receive and/or send messages in one step; from D4, however, a process may not receive a message, become nonidle, and send a message, all in one step. This restriction prevents cyclical dependence among sends and receives as in the following scenario. Idle processes A, B receive, become nonidle, and send messages, all in one step, where the message m sent by A is received by B, causing it to send m' to A, which caused A to send m in the first place.

3.3 *Some Derived Properties of Program D*

In this section we derive some properties of program D, from D1–D4. The first property, D5, says roughly that for any set of processes X: If all processes in X are idle and for all internal channels of X (i.e., those between processes in X) the number of sends and receives are equal, then they remain so and no message is sent by any process in X until a message is received by a process in X from outside X. Formally,

Property D5

$$q.X \land (r = L).ZX \land (s = L).XZ \quad unless$$
$$(r > L).\overline{X}X \land (s = L).X\overline{X} \text{ in } D$$

The result is proved by taking the conjunction of D3,D4 and then applying the general conjunction rule over all i in X. In the following proof, justifications for proof steps are enclosed within braces.

Proof   Applying conjunction to D3 and D4,

$$q.i \land (r = L).Zi \land (s = L).iZ \quad unless \quad (r > L).Zi \land (s = L).iZ$$

Applying conjunction over all i in X,

$$\text{lhs} \equiv \langle \forall i : i \in X :: q.i \land (r = L).Zi \land (s = L).iZ \rangle$$
$$\equiv q.X \land (r = L).ZX \land (s = L).XZ$$

The right-hand side has two conjuncts. The first one is

$$\equiv \langle \forall i : i \in X :: [q.i \land (r = L).Zi \land (s = L).iZ] \lor$$
$$[(r > L).Zi \land (s = L).iZ] \rangle$$
$$\Rightarrow (r \geq L).ZX \land (s = L).XZ$$

and the second one is

$$\equiv \langle \exists i : i \in X :: (r > L).Zi \land (s = L).iZ \rangle$$
$$\Rightarrow \langle \exists i : i \in X :: (r > L).Zi \rangle$$

Hence

$$\text{rhs} \Rightarrow (r \geq L).ZX \land (s = L).XZ \land \langle \exists i : i \in X :: (r > L).Zi \rangle$$
$$\Rightarrow (r > L).ZX \land (s = L).XZ$$
$$\Rightarrow \{ (r > L).ZX \Rightarrow (r > L).XX \lor (r > L).\overline{X}X$$
$$(s = L).XZ \Rightarrow (s = L).XX \Rightarrow \neg(r > L).XX$$

(applying the substitution axiom; see the observation in Section 3.2)

$$(s = L).XZ \Rightarrow (s = L).X\overline{X} \}$$
$$(r > L).\overline{X}X \land (s = L).X\overline{X} \quad \square$$

Note   The left-hand side of D5 implies that the number of sends and receives are equal for all internal channels of X.

Note   The operational argument for proving D5 is to assume that all processes in X are idle, that sends and receives are equal for all internal channels of X, and that no message will be received by any process in X from outside X, and then to show that all processes in X remain idle and that no message will be sent by any process in X. The typical proof assumes the contrary — that some process in X becomes nonidle— and derives a contradiction by noting that this process must have received a message from some process in X (because it is assumed that processes outside X do not send messages) which must be nonidle when it sends the message, and that therefore there is no first process in X that becomes nonidle. This temporal reasoning is completely avoided in our formalism.

Termination   Define predicate T as follows.

$$T \equiv q.Z \wedge (s = r).ZZ$$

Program D is said to be *terminated* if T holds, i.e., all processes are idle and for each channel the number of message sends and receives are equal. It is not obvious that T is stable or that message transmissions cease once T holds. (Stability of T does not guarantee that message transmissions cease once T holds; both $s.c$ and $r.c$ may change simultaneously, for some c, while preserving $s.c = r.c$ and hence preserving T.)

Property D6

$T \wedge (s = L).ZZ$ stable in D

Proof   Replace X by Z in D5. Note that the term $(r > L).\bar{Z}Z$ in the right-hand side of D5 is *false* because $\bar{Z}$ is empty.   □

Property D7

T stable in D

Proof   Eliminating free variable $L.ZZ$ in D6.   □

Summary of Properties of D

D1. $s.c \geq r.c \geq 0$ invariant

D2. $r.c \geq m$ stable,
$s.c \geq n$ stable

D3. $q.i \land (r = L).Zi$ *unless* $(r > L).Zi$

D4. $q.i \land (s = L).iZ$ *unless* $\neg q.i \land (s = L).iZ$

Derived Properties

D5. $q.X \land (r = L).ZX \land (s = L).XZ$ *unless* $(r > L).\overline{XX} \land (s = L).\overline{XX}$

D6. $T \land (s = L).ZZ$ stable

D7. T stable

3.4 *The Recording Program, R*

Program R, given in Figure 2, is used to record the values of variables of D.
We introduce local variables of R —$vq.i$, $vr.c$, and $vs.c$— in which the values of
variables $q.i$, $r.c$, and $s.c$ are recorded, respectively, for all i and c. Initially the
recorded values are $vq.i = false$, $vr.c = 0$, and $vs.c = 0$, for all i and c. For each
process i there is a statement in the program body —i.e., in the program's

---

Figure 2.   Program R.

Program R

    initially

        $\langle [\!] \ i \ :: \ vq.i = false \rangle$

        $[\!] \ \langle [\!] \ c \ :: \ vs.c, vr.c = 0, 0 \rangle$

    assign

        $\langle [\!] \ i \ ::$

            $vq.i \ := \ q.i$

            $\| \langle \| \ c \ : \ c \in Zi \ :: \ vr.c \ := \ r.c \rangle$

            $\| \langle \| \ c \ : \ c \in iZ \ :: \ vs.c \ := \ s.c \rangle$

        $\rangle$

    end $\{R\}$

---

assign-section— to assign simultaneously

1. $q.i$ to $vq.i$,
2. $r.c$ to $vr.c$, for all channels c incoming to i, and
3. $s.c$ to $vs.c$, for all channels c outgoing from i.

We give a very brief and incomplete description of UNITY syntax in order to explain program R. The symbol [] is used to separate statements in the assign-section and equations in the initially-section; the symbol || is used to separate the components of a single assignment. Angled brackets, ⟨ and ⟩, denote quantification. Interpret

initially ⟨[] i :: $vq.i = false$⟩

to mean that for each i (where $i \in Z$), equation $vq.i = false$ holds initially in the program. Similarly, the quantified statement in the assign-section is to be interpreted as: For each i there is a single statement in the program; this single statement (for any i) consists of three components which must be executed simultaneously:

1. $vq.i := q.i$,
2. ⟨|| c : $c \in Zi$ :: $vr.c := r.c$⟩, and
3. ⟨|| c : $c \in iZ$ :: $vs.c := s.c$⟩.

The component ⟨|| c : $c \in Zi$ :: $vr.c := r.c$⟩ is to be interpreted as: For all c, where c is in Zi, perform the assignment $vr.c := r.c$ simultaneously, and similarly for the last component.

3.5 *The Termination-Detection Theorem*

We have previously defined program D to be terminated if $q.Z \wedge (s = r).ZZ$ holds. The termination-detection theorem says that D is terminated if the preceding condition, with q, s, r replaced by vq, vs, vr, holds.

Termination Detection Theorem

$vq.Z \wedge (vs = vr).ZZ \Rightarrow q.Z \wedge (s = r).ZZ$ is invariant in D [] R

4 *Proof of the Termination-Detection Theorem*

4.1 *Informal Outline of the Proof*

Consider some point during the execution of program D [] R when, for some i, $vq.i \wedge (vr = r).Zi$ holds. From $vq.i$, we can claim that $q.i$ was *true* (process

i was idle) when the last recording was made for process i. From $(vr = r).Zi$, we can claim that process i has received no message since the last recording. Therefore,

1. Process i is still idle, i.e., $q.i$ is *true*.

2. Process i has sent no message since the last recording, i.e., $(vs = s).iZ$ holds.

That is, we claim that

$$vq.i \;\wedge\; (vr = r).Zi \;\Rightarrow\; q.i \;\wedge\; (vs = s).iZ \quad \text{invariant} \quad \text{in } D \;[\!]\; R$$

We consider a generalization of the preceding property with i replaced by an arbitrary set X. How do we define the idleness of a set of processes X? That all processes in X are idle and all internal channels of X are empty. Thus $q.i$ is generalized to $q.X \wedge (s = r).XX$. The appropriate generalization of $vq.i$ is $vq.X \wedge (vs = vr).XX$. Hence we postulate, for all X:

Property DR1

$$vq.X \;\wedge\; (vs = vr).XX \;\wedge\; (vr = r).\overline{XX} \;\Rightarrow$$
$$q.X \;\wedge\; (s = r).XX \;\wedge\; (vs = s).X\overline{X}$$
invariant in $D \;[\!]\; R$

The termination-detection theorem follows from DR1 by setting X to Z (since $\overline{Z}$ is the empty set, $(vr = r).\overline{Z}Z = true$).

In the remaining parts of Section 4, we prove DR1. Using Corollary 2 of the union theorem (Section 3.4), we undertake to show that the proposition in DR1 is stable in D and invariant in R:

Property DR2

$\langle \forall\, X \;::$
$\quad vq.X \;\wedge\; (vs = vr).XX \;\wedge\; (vr = r).\overline{XX} \;\Rightarrow$
$\quad\quad q.X \;\wedge\; (s = r).XX \;\wedge\; (vs = s).X\overline{X}$
$\rangle$
stable in D

Property DR3

$\langle \forall\, X \;::$
$\quad vq.X \;\wedge\; (vs = vr).XX \;\wedge\; (vr = r).\overline{XX} \;\Rightarrow$
$\quad\quad q.X \;\wedge\; (s = r).XX \;\wedge\; (vs = s).X\overline{X}$
$\rangle$
invariant in R

Proofs of DR2 and DR3 are given in Sections 4.2 and 4.3, respectively. Property DR4, given next, is used in the proofs of DR2 and DR3. We leave the (rather trivial) proof of DR4 to the reader; for the proof, use Corollary 2 of the union theorem and assume that initially $s.c \geq vs.c$ and $r.c \geq vr.c$ in $D \, [\!] \, R$.

Property DR4

$s.c \geq vs.c \geq 0$ invariant in $D \, [\!] \, R$

$r.c \geq vr.c \geq 0$ invariant in $D \, [\!] \, R$

4.2 *Proof of DR2*

The proof of DR2 uses D2 (see Section 3.2), D5 (see Section 3.3), DR4 (section 4.1), properties of *unless* (see Section 2.3), and the fact that vq, vs, and vr are constants in D. In the following proof all properties are of Program D. From D5,

$q.X \;\wedge\; (r = L).ZX \wedge\; (s = L).XZ \;\; unless \;\; (r > L).\overline{XX} \;\wedge\; (s = L).X\overline{X}$

Rewrite the left-hand side using

$(r = L).ZX \;\equiv\; (r = L).XX \;\wedge\; (r = L).\overline{XX}$

$(s = L).XZ \;\equiv\; (s = L).XX \;\wedge\; (s = L).X\overline{X}$

Weaken the right-hand side to $(r > L).\overline{XX}$.

$q.X \;\wedge\; (s = r).XX \;\wedge\; (r = L).XX \;\wedge\; (r = L).\overline{XX} \;\wedge\; (s = L).X\overline{X}$

$unless \;\; (r > L).\overline{XX}$

Eliminate free variables $L.XX$ and hence the term $(r = L).XX$ from the left-hand side.

$q.X \;\wedge\; (s = r).XX \;\wedge\; (r = L).\overline{XX} \;\wedge\; (s = L).X\overline{X} \;\; unless \;\; (r > L).\overline{XX}$

From D2, $(r > L).\overline{XX}$ stable. Applying disjunction with the preceding,

$(r > L).\overline{XX} \;\vee\; [q.X \;\wedge\; (s = r).XX \;\wedge\; (r = L).\overline{XX} \;\wedge\; (s = L).X\overline{X}]$ stable

Replace $L.\overline{XX}$ by $vr.\overline{XX}$ and $L.X\overline{X}$ by $vs.X\overline{X}$, respectively. The latter lists are constants in D and hence this instantiation is permissible.

$(r > vr).\overline{XX} \;\vee\; [q.X \;\wedge\; (s = r).XX \;\wedge\; (r = vr).\overline{XX} \;\wedge\; (s = vs).X\overline{X}]$ stable

Since vq, vs, vr are constants in D, $\neg[vq.X \wedge (vs = vr).XX]$ is stable. Taking simple disjunction with the preceding and rewriting the expression,

$$[vq.X \wedge (vs = vr).XX \wedge \neg(r > vr).\overline{XX}] \Rightarrow$$

$$[q.X \wedge (s = r).XX \wedge (r = vr).\overline{XX} \wedge (s = vs).X\overline{X}] \text{ stable}$$

From DR4 (Section 4.1), $(r \geq vr).\overline{XX}$. Hence, $\neg(r > vr).\overline{XX} \equiv (r = vr).\overline{XX}$. Using the substitution axiom, replace this term in the antecedent. Also, the term $(r = vr).\overline{XX}$ can be dropped from the consequent of the implication:

$$[vq.X \wedge (vs = vr).XX \wedge (r = vr).\overline{XX}] \Rightarrow$$

$$[q.X \wedge (s = r).XX \wedge (s = vs).X\overline{X}] \text{ stable} \qquad \qquad \square$$

4.3 *Proof of DR3*

DR3 is of the form

$$\langle \forall\ Y\ ::\ vp.Y \Rightarrow p.Y \rangle \text{ invariant in } R$$

where

$$vp.Y \equiv vq.Y \wedge (vs = vr).YY \wedge (vr = r).\overline{Y}Y$$

and

$$p.Y \equiv q.Y \wedge (s = r).YY \wedge (vs = s).Y\overline{Y}$$

All properties in the rest of this subsection are of Program R. The proof of DR3 follows directly by using the "assignment axiom" because all statements in R are assignments. For completeness, we give this proof in some detail; the proof is easy, however, and the reader is encouraged to construct it.

From the initial condition of R, each $vq.Y$ is false, and hence so is $vp.Y$. Thus $\langle \forall\ Y\ ::\ vp.Y \Rightarrow p.Y \rangle$ holds initially. Next, we prove the stability of $\langle \forall\ Y\ ::\ vp.Y \Rightarrow p.Y \rangle$. Consider any statement, $t.j$, that records for process j. We have to show that

$$\{\langle \forall\ Y\ ::\ vp.Y \Rightarrow p.Y \rangle\}\ t.j\ \{\langle \forall\ Y\ ::\ vp.Y \Rightarrow p.Y \rangle\}$$

We prove the postcondition for an arbitrary set of processes X. We apply the *assignment axiom* to compute a precondition from $vp.X \Rightarrow p.X$ by replacing in it all occurrences of $vq.j$ by $q.j$, $vr.c$ by $r.c$ for all c incoming to j and $vs.c$ by $s.c$ for all c outgoing from j.

If $j \notin X$, then the precondition as just computed is $vp.X \Rightarrow p.X$ and hence the proof is trivial. Therefore, consider the case where $j \in X$. Let $W = X - \{j\}$. We have, before execution of t_j (where $A \equiv vp.W$ and $B \equiv p.W$),

$$A \Rightarrow B$$

where

$$A \;\equiv\; vq.W \;\wedge\; (vs = vr).WW \;\wedge\; (vr = r).\overline{W}W$$

$$B \;\equiv\; q.W \;\wedge\; (s = r).WW \;\wedge\; (vs = s).W\overline{W}$$

The precondition computed from $vp.X \Rightarrow p.X$ by applying the assignment axiom is

$$U \;\Rightarrow\; V$$

where

$$U \equiv [vq.W \;\wedge\; q.j] \;\wedge\; [(vs = vr).WW \;\wedge\; (s = vr).jW \;\wedge\; (vs = r).Wj]$$
$$\wedge\; [(vr = r).\overline{X}W \;\wedge\; (r = r).\overline{X}j]$$

$$V \equiv q.X \;\wedge\; (s = r).XX \;\wedge\; [(vs = s).W\overline{X} \;\wedge\; (s = s).j\overline{X}]$$

We will show that

$$(A \;\Rightarrow\; B) \;\Rightarrow\; (U \;\Rightarrow\; V)$$

i.e., that

$$[U \;\wedge\; (A \;\Rightarrow\; B)] \;\Rightarrow\; V$$

We prove this in two steps:

1. $U \;\Rightarrow\; A$ (Lemma 2), and

2. $U \wedge B \;\Rightarrow\; V$ (Lemma 3).

Lemma 1

$$U \;\Rightarrow\; (s = r = vr).jW$$

Read $(s = r = vr).jw$ as $(s = r).jw \;\wedge\; (r = vr).jw$.

Proof

$(s \geq r \geq vr).jW$	from D1 and the substitution axiom used with DR4
$(s = vr).jW$	from U
$(s = r = vr).jW$	from the two previous steps ☐

Lemma 2

$$U \;\Rightarrow\; A$$

Proof   All conjuncts in A follow trivially from U except $(vr = r).\overline{W}W$. This follows from

$(vr = r).\overline{X}W$	from U
$(vr = r).jW$	from U using Lemma 1
$(vr = r).(\overline{X} \cup \{j\})W$	from the two previous steps
$(vr = r).\overline{W}W$	$\overline{W} = \overline{X} \cup \{j\}$ □

Lemma 3

$$U \wedge B \; \Rightarrow \; V$$

Proof   We prove each conjunct of V in a separate sublemma.

Sublemma 1 $q.X$

$q.W$	from B
$q.j$	from U
$q.X$	from the two previous steps because $X = W \cup \{j\}$

Sublemma 2 $(s = r).XX$

$(vs = s).W\overline{W}$	from B
$(vs = s).Wj$	from the preceding step because $j \in \overline{W}$
$(vs = r).Wj$	from U
$(s = r).Wj$	from the two previous steps
$(s = r).WW$	from B
$(s = r).jW$	from U using Lemma 1
$(s = r).XX$	from the three previous steps because $X = W \cup \{j\}$

Sublemma 3 $(vs = s).W\overline{X}$

$(vs = s).W\overline{W}$	from B
$(vs = s).W\overline{X}$	from the preceding step because $\overline{X} \subseteq \overline{W}$ □

5 *UNITY Logic: Progress*

Two logical operators, *ensures* and *leads-to* (also written as ↦), defined on pairs of predicates, are used to prove progress properties of UNITY programs. Briefly, *p ensures q* says that *p* remains *true* as long as *q* is not *true* (i.e., *p unless q*) and that there is a statement in the program whose execution establishes *q*, starting in any state that satisfies $p \wedge \neg q$. The operator *leads-to* is the transitive, disjunctive closure of *ensures*: $p \mapsto q$ means that if *p* holds at any point during the program execution, then *q* holds eventually.

In most cases we are interested in establishing *leads-to* properties. The reason we introduce *ensures* is twofold:

1. The only way to establish *leads-to* is by using a set of *ensures* properties (*ensures* serves as the basis of induction for defining *leads-to*).

2. It is possible to formulate a union theorem, akin to the union theorem of Section 2.4, for *ensures*, but there is no analogous theorem for *leads-to*.

5.1 *The Logical Operator ensures*

For a program *F*, we define the operator *ensures* by the following inference rule:

$$\frac{p \ unless \ q \ \text{in} \ F \ \wedge \ \langle \exists \ t \ : \ t \ \text{is a statement in} \ F \ :: \ \{p \ \wedge \ \neg q\} \ t \ \{q\}\rangle}{p \ ensures \ q \ \text{in} \ F}$$

From the hypothesis of the inference rule, it follows that once *p* becomes *true*, it remains *true* as long as *q* is not *true* —from *p unless q*— and that there is a statement *t* in *F* whose execution with precondition $p \wedge \neg q$ establishes *q*. From our fairness assumption, the statement *t* is executed sometime after *p* becomes *true* and hence, once *p* is *true*, *q* is established eventually. The following theorem is analogous to the union theorem of Section 2.4:

Union Theorem   (Progress)

$$p \ ensures \ q \ \text{in} \ F \ [] \ G = \quad (p \ unless \ q \ \text{in} \ F \ \wedge \ p \ ensures \ q \ \text{in} \ G) \ \vee$$

$$(p \ ensures \ q \ \text{in} \ F \ \wedge \ p \ unless \ q \ \text{in} \ G)$$

Corollary 3

$$\frac{p \ \text{is stable in} \ F \ , \ p \ ensures \ q \ \text{in} \ G}{p \ ensures \ q \ \text{in} \ F \ [] \ G}$$

5.2 *The Logical Operator leads-to*

For a program F, p *leads-to* q, typically written as $p \mapsto q$, is defined as the strongest relation satisfying the following (i.e., $p \mapsto q$ can be deduced only by applying the following rules). The program name, F, is omitted in the following discussion.

1. $\dfrac{p\ ensures\ q}{p \mapsto q}$

2. (Transitivity) $\dfrac{p \mapsto q\ ,\ q \mapsto r}{p \mapsto r}$

3. (Disjunction)   Let $p.m$ be a predicate with a free variable m that ranges over any arbitrary set W and does not occur free in q.

$$\frac{\langle \forall\ m\ ::\ p.m \mapsto q \rangle}{\langle \exists\ m\ ::\ p.m \rangle \mapsto q}$$

We state two results in connection with *leads-to* that are used in this paper:

1. (Implication Theorem) $\dfrac{p \Rightarrow q}{p \mapsto q}$

2. (Completion Theorem; special case)   In the following, m is quantified over any finite set:

$$\frac{\begin{array}{c} \langle \forall\ m\ ::\ p.m \mapsto q.m \rangle, \\[4pt] \langle \forall\ m\ ::\ q.m\ \text{stable} \rangle \end{array}}{\langle \forall\ m\ ::\ p.m \rangle \mapsto \langle \forall\ m\ ::\ q.m \rangle}$$

6 *Progress of the Termination-Detection Algorithm*

We showed in Section 4 that

$$vq.Z \wedge (vs = vr).ZZ \;\Rightarrow\; T \;\;\text{in}\; D \;[\!]\; R$$

where T, as defined in Section 3.3, is $q.Z \wedge (s = r).ZZ$. Thus it is safe to report termination if the left side of the preceding implication holds. We now show

Property DR5

$$T \;\mapsto\; vq.Z \wedge (vs = vr).ZZ \;\;\text{in}\; D \;[\!]\; R$$

That is, $vq.Z \wedge (vs = vr).ZZ$ becomes *true* within a finite time of termination.

We begin with a preliminary result. Define $u.i$ as follows:

$$u.i \;\equiv\; (vq.i = q.i) \wedge (vr = r).Zi \wedge (vs = s).iZ$$

Property D8

$T \wedge u.i$ stable in D

Proof   All properties in the following proof refer to D. Let $Y = Z - \{i\}$.

$T \wedge (s = L).ZZ$ stable

    from D6 (Section 3.3)

$T \wedge (s = L).Zi \wedge (s = L).iZ \wedge (s = L).YY$ stable

    from the preceding: $Z = Y \cup \{i\}$

$T \wedge (s = L).Zi \wedge (s = L).iZ$ stable

    eliminating free variable $L.YY$

$vq.i$ stable

    $vq.i$ is constant in D

$T \wedge vq.i \wedge (s = L).Zi \wedge (s = L).iZ$ stable

    simple conjunction of the previous two

$T \wedge (vq.i = q.i) \wedge (r = L).Zi \wedge (s = L).iZ$ stable

    $T \wedge vq.i \ \equiv \ T \wedge (vq.i = q.i) \ ; \ T \wedge (s = L).Zi \ \equiv T \wedge (r = L).Zi$

$T \wedge (vq.i = q.i) \wedge (r = vr).Zi \wedge (s = vs).iZ$ stable

    replacing $L.Zi, L.iZ$ by $vr.Zi, vs.iZ$, which are constants in D □

Now we can present the proof of Property DR5.

Proof

T *ensures* $T \wedge u.i$ in R

    from the text of R

T *ensures* $T \wedge u.i$ in $D [\!] R$

    applying Corollary 3 on D7 (T stable in D) and the preceding

$T \ \mapsto \ T \wedge u.i$ in $D [\!] R$

    applying the definition of *leads-to* to the preceding   (1)

T stable in R

    all variables in T are constants in R

$u.i$ stable in R

    from the text of R

$T \wedge u.i$ stable in R

simple conjunction on the preceding two

$T \wedge u.i$ stable in $D \; [\!] \; R$

applying Corollary 1 on D8 ($T \wedge u.i$ stable in D) and the preceding

$T \;\mapsto\; \langle \forall i \;::\; T \wedge u.i \rangle$

completion theorem on (1) and the preceding

$\langle \forall i \;::\; T \wedge u.i \rangle \;\equiv\; T \wedge \langle \forall i \;::\; u.i \rangle$

predicate calculus

$T \wedge \langle \forall i \;::\; u.i \rangle \;\Rightarrow\; vq.Z \wedge (vs = vr).ZZ$

from the definitions of T and $u.i$

$T \;\mapsto\; vq.Z \wedge (vs = vr).ZZ$

using transitivity and implication on the previous three   □

7 Discussion

7.1 Why Bother with Formal Specifications?

It may be argued that since we could construct an informal proof of the correctness of the termination-detection algorithm —see Section 1— without
defining the properties of D precisely, formal specifications are merely "icing
on the cake". This argument is often valid because formal specifications are
rarely used in a constructive manner to derive other properties of programs
or to aid in program designs. There seems to be little reason for formalism,
except to avoid ambiguity, if the goal is merely to reach agreement among a
group of designers.

Once we start using the specification for deductions and program designs,
however, informal specifications doom us to commonsense reasoning, a costly
and error-prone procedure. Formal specifications force us to state (1) not too
much, because then we cannot manipulate them as effectively and the specification will not apply to a broad range of systems, and (2) not too little,
because then we cannot deduce the properties we want to hold. Thus, while
properties D1 and D2 of program D —that the number of receives along a
channel never exceeds the number of sends, and that numbers of sends and
receives along a channel never decrease— would be taken for granted in informal discussion, in a formal specification we are forced to write them out.
Most informal proofs would assume D5, D6, and D7 as properties of program
D; we believe that it is interesting in its own right to prove these from the
simpler properties D1–D4.

7.2 *Proof Length*

It should be clear by now that our formal proof consists of a relatively small number of steps; most of the proof consists of explaining the notation and relating the proof to its informal counterpart. The short informal proof given in Section 1 suffers from many deficiencies; among them are uncertainties about what can be assumed regarding message communication systems (e.g., can a message be sent and received simultaneously, is FIFO order on channels required?) and about what the precise steps of the recording algorithm are. The great virtue of informal reasoning (besides being easily accessible and hence more democratic) is that reasoning is carried out with a description whose level is far higher than is available in traditional programming languages; thus, we can talk informally about "search the list from left to right" as a single program step. In UNITY we have attempted to combine this flavor of high-level description with the precision of a formal language.

7.3 *Proof Structure*

Some features of the UNITY-style proof are worth noting. First, we associate properties with *programs*, not with program points. Proofs of program properties are therefore carried out in the style of formal proofs in mathematics, outside the program text. The number of references to the program text in a proof is quite small: In the current proof, there is one reference to the text of R in Section 4.3 (application of the assignment axiom) and two references in the proof of DR5, in Section 6.

Second, associating properties with programs makes it simpler to construct "compositional" proofs whereby properties of a composite program, say $F \; [] \; G$, are deduced from the properties of its components, F and G. This feature is particularly attractive because it allows us to work with specifications in the absence of code; see, for instance, the way in which the specification of D (in the absence of the code of D) was used in the current proof. This is in contrast to proofs by noninterference, as advocated in [14], where proofs are intimately tied to program codes.

Third, the success of a formal system relies crucially on a rich body of derived rules that can be exploited effectively in practice. We have stated a few derived rules about our logical operators —*unless, ensures, leads-to*— in this paper, and we have applied these effectively in the proof.

Fourth, as we have said earlier, the UNITY theory does not include "process" as a basic construct. This is a deliberate decision. One outcome of this decision is that we are able to study composition of programs as a concept orthogonal to the composition of processes. For instance, we viewed the overall program as the union of two programs, D and R, and we partitioned the proof obligation suitably between these two programs. Program D represents the basic computations of *all* processes; program R represents the recording actions of *all* processes. Clearly, $D \, [] \, R$ can be implemented on a set of communicating processes, but it is considerably more difficult to partition the proof obligation among these processes, or to construct the proof in a manner independent of the schedule for recording states and message counts.

Acknowledgments

We are grateful to the Austin Tuesday Afternoon Club, under the guidance of Edsger W. Dijkstra, for initiating discussions about the proof of this problem; to Ernie Cohen, Wim Hesselink, and Devendra Kumar for showing us alternative proofs; to Wim Feijen for many constructive criticisms during the development of this proof; and to the participants in the workshop on "Concurrency in Hardware and Software" (directed by Alain J. Martin), La Jolla, California, February 22–26, 1988, for comments on this proof. We are indebted to Alan Fekete, Jürg Gutknecht, Bengt Jonsson, and Martin Rem for their comments on the first draft; particular thanks are due to Nissim Francez, C. A. R. Hoare and J. R. Rao for their insightful comments.

The work by K. Mani Chandy reported here is partially supported by Office of Naval Research Contracts N00014–86–K–0763. Jayadev Misra's contribution is based in part upon work supported by the Texas Advanced Research Program under Grant No. 003658–065, by support from the Office of Naval Research, Grant No. N00014–90–J–1640, and by a fellowship from the John Simon Guggenheim Foundation.

References

[1] Chandy, K. M. Unpublished notes, 1983.

[2] Chandy, K. M. "A theorem on termination of distributed systems". TR–87–09, Department of Computer Sciences, University of Texas at Austin, March 1987.

[3] Chandy, K. M. and Misra, J. *Parallel Program Design: A Foundation*. Addison-Wesley, Reading, Mass., 1988.

[4] Dijkstra, E. W. *A Discipline of Programming*. Prentice-Hall, Englewood Cliffs, N.J., 1976.

[5] Francez, N. *Fairness*. Springer-Verlag, New York, 1986.

[6] Helary, M., Jard, C., Plouzeau, N., and Raynal, M. "Detection of stable properties in distributed applications". *Proceedings of the Sixth Annual ACM Symposium on Principles of Distributed Computing*, pp. 125–136. ACM, New York, 1987.

[7] Hesselink, W. H. H. "Chandy's theorem on termination detection". Wim H. Hesselink, WHH4, Austin, Texas, Jan. 21, 1987.

[8] Hoare, C. A. R. "An axiomatic basis for computer programming". *Communications of the ACM 12* (1969), pp. 576–580.

[9] Kumar, D. "Efficient algorithms for distributed simulation and related problems". Doctoral dissertation, University of Texas at Austin, 1987.

[10] Manna, Z. and Pnueli, A. *The Temporal Logic of Reactive Systems.* Springer-Verlag, Berlin (to appear).

[11] Misra, J. "Distributed discrete event simulation". *Computing Surveys 18,* 1 (March 1986), pp. 39–66. (In particular, see the last paragraph of page 62 and the first paragraph of page 63.)

[12] Misra, J. "General conjunction and disjunction of *unless*". Notes on UNITY 01–88, University of Texas at Austin, 1988.

[13] Misra, J. "Soundness of the substitution axiom". Notes on UNITY 14–90, University of Texas at Austin, 1990.

[14] Owicki, S. and Gries, D. "An axiomatic proof technique for parallel programs I". *Acta Informatica 6,* 1 (1976), pp. 319–340.

[15] Owicki, S. and Lamport, L. "Proving liveness properties of concurrent programs". *ACM Transactions on Programming Languages and Systems 4,* 3 (July 1982), pp. 455–495.

The Authors

K. MANI CHANDY received his B.Tech. from the Indian Institute of Technology, Madras, his M.S. from the Polytechnic University of New York, and his Ph.D. from M.I.T., all in Electrical Engineering. He has worked at Honeywell and IBM, and has been a professor and chairman at The University of Texas at Austin. He is now a professor at the California Institute of Technology. He was given the Michelson Award for his contributions to computer performance modeling in 1985. He was a Sherman Fairchild Scholar at Caltech in 1987. Address: California Institute of Technology, Computer Science Department 256–80, Pasadena, CA 91125.

C. A. R. HOARE has been Professor of Computation at Oxford University since 1977. Since 1981 he has established the first three degree programs in Computing Science at Oxford. During the academic year 1986/87 he occupied the Admiral B. R. Inman Centennial Chair in Computing Theory at The University of Texas at Austin. Address: Oxford University Computing Laboratory, 11 Keble Road, Oxford OX1 3QK, U.K.

JEREMY L. JACOB received his D.Phil. in Computation from Oxford University in 1988. He is currently a Research Assistant at the Programming Research Group, on the project called "Formal Methods for Computer Security". He has contributed to two IEEE Symposia on Security & Privacy, and to the Workshop on the Foundations of Computer Security, and has worked on formal methods in areas other than security. Address: Oxford University Computing Laboratory, 11 Keble Road, Oxford OX1 3QK, U.K.

JIFENG HE is currently working at Oxford University Computing Laboratory, and is Professor of Computer Science at East China Normal University, Shanghai. His major research interests include programming language semantics, software engineering, and distributed computing. Address: Oxford University Computing Laboratory, 11 Keble Road, Oxford OX1 3QK, U.K.

ALAIN J. MARTIN graduated from the Institut National Polytechnique de Grenoble in 1969. He is currently a professor of computer science at the California Institute of Technology. His research interests include concurrent and distributed programming and its application to the design of VLSI circuits. Address: California Institute of Technology, Computer Science Department 256–80, Pasadena, CA 91125.

DAVID MAY graduated from Cambridge University in 1972 with a degree in Computer Science. He then worked at Warwick University on artificial intelligence and robotics. In 1979, he joined Inmos to design VLSI components for concurrent systems. He was responsible for the design of the occam language and the architecture of the Inmos transputer. In 1989 he was appointed Visiting Professor of Engineering Design at Oxford University and in 1990 he received an honorary DSc from Southampton University for his contributions to the development of parallel computing. He is currently working at Inmos on the architecture of a new product range for introduction in 1994. Address: Inmos Limited, 1000 Aztec West, Almondsbury, Bristol BS12 4SQ, U.K.

JAYADEV MISRA is a Professor of Computer Sciences at The University of Texas at Austin. He received a Ph. D. from The Johns Hopkins University. He was a visiting professor at Stanford University in 1983–84. Dr. Misra co-authored the book *Parallel Program Design: A Foundation* with Prof. K. Mani Chandy. He was a 1988 John Simon Guggenheim Fellow. Dr. Misra is an editor of the *Journal of the ACM* and *Formal Aspects of Computing*. Address: Department of Computer Sciences, Taylor Hall 2.124, The University of Texas at Austin, Austin, TX 78712–1188.

CHARLES L. SEITZ earned B.S., M.S., and Ph.D. degrees from M.I.T. Before joining the Computer Science faculty at Caltech in 1977, he worked as a computer designer for the Evans & Sutherland Computer Corporation from 1969 to 1971, as an Assistant Professor of Computer Science at the University of Utah from 1970 to 1972, and as a consultant to Burroughs Corporation from 1971 to 1978. He is currently a Professor of Computer Science at Caltech, where his research and teaching activities are in the areas of VLSI architecture and design, concurrent computation, and self-timed systems. Address: California Institute of Technology, Computer Science Department 256–80, Pasadena, CA 91125.

J. C. P. WOODCOCK received his doctorate from the University of Liverpool in 1980 for work in computation, and subsequently researched the industrial application of formal methods at GEC Research Laboratories. He then founded a degree in software engineering while lecturing on formal software development at the University of Surrey. He is at present at Oxford University, where he is Atlas Research Fellow at Pembroke College and a member of the Programming Research Group. His main interests are formal specification and development of industrial scale software, machine-assisted proof, concurrency, Z, VDM, CSP, and CCS. Address: Oxford University Computing Laboratory, 11 Keble Road, Oxford OX1 3QK, U.K.

The Year of Programming on Videotape

———

*A*ll six of the Programming Institutes were recorded on videotape, and edited versions of these tapes have been prepared by MPA Productions, Inc., under the auspices of the Computer Sciences Department of The University of Texas at Austin. They are available for purchase in various combinations from individual lectures to the complete set. Tapes can be provided in all formats and standards; for most sessions, photocopies of the speakers' overhead-projector transparencies are also available.

For a complete listing of the tapes, including prices, please write to

Year of Programming (Tapes)
3103 Bee Caves Road, Suite 235
Austin, TX 78746
U.S.A

or call (512) 328–9800.